AF454126

Conquer Quants

OrangeBooks Publication

1st Floor, Rajhans Arcade, Mall Road, Kohka, Bhilai, Chhattisgarh - 490020

Website:**www.orangebooks.in**

First Edition, 2024

ISBN: 978-93-5621-474-3

CONQUER QUANTS

A PROFOUND KNOWLEDGE ON QUANTITATIVE APTITUDE

KARTHIGA J

OrangeBooks Publication

www.orangebooks.in

CONTENTS

NUMBER SYSTEM

Various types of numbers:

1. Natural Numbers:

All the positive numbers 1, 2, 3, etc. that are used in counting are called Natural numbers.

Types of Natural Numbers based on divisibility:

- **Prime Numbers:** A natural number larger than unity is a prime number, if it does not have other divisors except for itself and unity.

  Examples for Prime numbers are 2, 3, 5, 7, 11, 13, 17, 19, etc.

  <u>Note</u>: Unity, i.e., 1 is neither a prime nor a composite number.

- **Composite Numbers:** Any number other than 1, which is not a prime number, is called a composite number. Examples for composite numbers are 4, 6, 8, 9, 10, 14, 15, etc.

2. Whole Numbers:

All counting numbers and 0, form the set of whole numbers.
Eg: 0, 1, 2, 3…, etc. are whole numbers.

3. Integers:

All counting numbers, Zero and negative of counting numbers, form the set of integers.
Eg: -3, -2, -1, 0, 1, 2, 3, etc are all integers.

4. Rational Numbers

A number which can be expressed in the form p/q, where p and q are integers and q $\neq$ 0, is called a rational number.
Eg: 2 can be written as 2/1, therefore 2 is a rational number.

5. Irrational Numbers

Numbers which are not rational but can be represented by points on the number line called irrational numbers.
Eg: $\sqrt{2}, \sqrt{3}, \sqrt{5}$

6. Even and Odd Numbers

Numbers divisible by 2 are called even numbers whereas numbers that are not divisible by 2 are called odd numbers.
For example, 2, 4, 6, etc are even numbers and 3, 5, 7, etc are odd numbers.

Factorization Method for LCM and HCF

- <u>**LCM:**</u> Here we can write all the given numbers in their prime factorization format.

Eg: Consider LCM of 21,36,48

$21 = 3 \times 7$;

$36 = 3^2 \times 2^2$;

$48 = 2^4 \times 3$

Now take all primes number the given numbers and write their maximum powers.

LCM of 21, 36, 48 = $2^4 \times 3^2 \times 7 = 1008$

- <u>HCF:</u> The product of common factors is taken

  Eg: Consider HCF of 8, 12

  $8 = 2^3$;

  $12 = 2^2 \times 3$

  HCF of 8 and 12 = $2^2 = 4$

For two numbers,

HCF $\times$ LCM = Product of the two numbers

$$\text{HCF of fractions} = \frac{\text{HCF of Numerator}}{\text{LCM of Denominator}}$$

$$\text{LCM of fractions} = \frac{\text{LCM of Numerator}}{\text{HCF of Denominator}}$$

Tests of divisibility of numbers:

If a number is divisible by

- 2: If its unit digit of any of 0, 2, 4, 6, 8

- 3: When the sum of its digits is divisible by 3

- 4: If its last two digits is divisible by 4

- 5: When its unit digit is 0 or 5

- 6: When the number satisfies the divisibility rule for both 2 & 3.

- 8: If the number formed by hundred's, ten's and unit's digit of the given number is divisible by 8.

- 9: When the sum of its digits is divisible by 9.

- 10: When its unit digit is 0.

- 11: If the difference between the sum of its digits at odd places and the sum of its digits at even places is either 0 or a number divisible by 11.

Important algebraic formulae:

- $(a + b)^2 = a^2 + 2ab + b^2$
- $(a - b)^2 = a^2 - 2ab + b^2$
- $(a + b)^2 + (a - b)^2 = 2(a^2 + b^2)$
- $(a + b)^2 - (a - b)^2 = 4ab$
- $a^2 - b^2 = (a + b)(a - b)$
- $(a + b + c)^2 = a^2 + b^2 + c^2 + 2ab + 2bc + 2ca$
- $(a + b)^3 = a^3 + b^3 + 3ab(a + b)$
- $(a - b)^3 = a^3 + b^3 - 3ab(a - b)$

Laws of indices:

- $a^m \times a^n = a^{m+n}$
- $(a^m)^n = a^{mn}$
- $a^m \div a^n = a^{m-n}$
- $a^0 = 1$
- $a^{-1} = \frac{1}{a}$; $a^{-m} = \frac{1}{a^m}$
- $a^{\frac{1}{2}} = \sqrt{a}$; $a^{\frac{1}{q}} = \sqrt[q]{a}$
- $a^{\frac{p}{q}} = (a^{\frac{1}{q}})^p = (\sqrt[q]{a})^p$

Some basic formulas (Using Binomial theorem):

- $(a + b)^0 = 1$
- $(a + b)^1 = a + b$
- $(a + b)^2 = a^2 + 2ab + b^2$
- $(a + b)^3 = a^3 + 3a^2b + 3ab^2 + b^3$

EXERCISE

1. Find the product of first 5 prime numbers.
   A) 2315   B) 2310
   C) 2305   D) 2320
   E) None of these

2. Which of the following numbers is exactly divisible by first double-digit prime number?
   A) 376195   B) 256197
   C) 391754   D) 458913
   E) None of these

3. The total number of prime factors in the expression, $2^8 \times 4^6 \times 6^2 \times 10^5$ is
   A) 34   B) 32
   C) 31   D) 33
   E) None of these

4. Four prime numbers are taken. The product of first three prime numbers written in ascending order is 1001. The product of last three is 2431. Find the difference between the first and last number.
   A) 13   B) 8
   C) 11   D) 10
   E) None of these

5. Find missing digit such that the number 476_78 is divisible by 11.
   A) 1   B) 2
   C) 4   D) 5
   E) None of these

6. The smallest number to be added to 2806 to make it exactly divisible by 45 is
   A) 29   B) 39
   C) 25   D) 32
   E) None of these

7. The divisor is 3 times the quotient and 9 times the remainder. If quotient is 33, the dividend is
   A) 3376   B) 3272
   C) 3284   D) 3278
   E) None of these

8. The product of two positive numbers is 1280 and their quotient is $\frac{16}{5}$. Find the difference of two numbers.
   A) 48   B) 42
   C) 44   D) 54
   E) None of these

9. How many numbers up to, 1295 are divisible by 3 and 5 together?
   A) 89   B) 87
   C) 84   D) 85
   E) None of these

10. A number to be multiplied by $^4/_3$, was multiplied by $^3/_4$ mistakenly. The result was 14 less than the correct answer. Find the number.
    A) 24   B) 42
    C) 28   D) 16
    E) None of these

11. Find the HCF & LCM of 60,90
    A) (60,180)   B) (30,180)
    C) (60,90)   D) (45,120)
    E) None of these

12. Find the HCF of
    $2^3 \times 3^2 \times 5^4 \times 7$; $2^2 \times 3^4 \times 5^2 \times 7^2$ and $2^3 \times 5^2 \times 3$.
    A) 120   B) 150
    C) 600   D) 300
    E) None of these

13. Find the LCM of 0.12, 2.4 ,0.6
    A) 4.8   B) 1.2

C) 2.4   D) 6
E) None of these

14. The least number, which when divided by 10, 15, 20 and 30 leaves a remainder of 5 in each case, is

A) 45   B) 65
C) 95   D) 35
E) None of these

15. If six bells commence tolling together and ring at intervals 4, 6, 8, 10, 12, 24 seconds, how many times do they ring together in 10 minutes?

A) 6   B) 8
C) 4   D) 12
E) None of these

16. Sixteen times a positive integer is less than its square by 192. Find the integer.

A) 24   B) 20
C) -8   D) Both A & C
E) None of these

17. The HCF of two nos. is 15 and LCM of two nos. is 180. If one number is 60, then find the other number.

(A) 40   (B) 48
(C) 50   (D) 45
(E) None of these

18. Find the LCM of 0.08, 0.24, 0.48, 0.32.

(A) 0.64   (B) 0.96
(C) 0.92   (D) 0.8
(E) None of these

19. The digits in unit's place of the product
21 × 22 × 23 × 24 × ... ... × 29

(A) 1   (B) 2
(C) 3   (D) 5
(E) None of these

20. The sum of two nos. is 85 and their difference is 9. The product of the two nos. is

(A) 1678   (B) 1876
(C) 1768   (D) 1786
(E) None of these

21. Average of four nos. arranged in ascending order is 26. Sum of smallest and largest no is 55. If difference between other two nos. is one, then square of the third no. is

(A) 529   (B) 576
(C) 676   (D) 625
(E) None of these

22. Three nos. a, b, c, are given. Product of a and c is 700. Sum of a & b is 60. If b is twice of a, then find 120% of (a +b + c).

(A) 110   (B) 114
(C) 112   (D) 116
(E) None of these

23. When a 2-digit number is reversed, the no. so formed is 63 more than the original no. If the sum of the digits of the no. is 11, find the value of twice the original number.

(A) 52   (B) 56
(C) 58   (D) 60
(E) None of these

24. Five runners start a race from a point on the circular track. They took 200sec, 250sec, 300sec, 500sec and 600sec respectively to complete one round. After how much time will they all meet at the beginning point again?

(A) 40 min   (B) 60 min
(C) 45 min   (D) 50 min
(E) None of these

25. If the numerator is increased by 5 and denominator is doubled, then resulting fraction equals to the original fraction. If we add 4 to the numerator of the fraction & increase denominator by 50% then numerator & denominator become equal. What will be half of that original fraction?

(A) $^{10}/_5$ (B) $^5/_{12}$

(C) $^5/_6$ (D) $10/_6$

(E) None of these

SOLUTIONS:

1. (B) First 5 prime numbers are 2, 3, 5, 7, 11
   Product = $2 \times 3 \times 5 \times 7 \times 11$ = 2310

2. (C) First double-digit prime number is 11.
   $391754 = (3+1+5) \sim (9+7+4) = 9 \sim 20 = 11$.

3. (A) $2^8 \times 4^6 \times 6^2 \times 10^5$
   $= 2^8 \times (2 \times 2)^6 \times (2 \times 3)^2 \times (2 \times 5)^5$
   $= 2^{27} \times 3^2 \times 5^5$
   No. of prime factors = 27+2+5 = 34

4. (D) Let the nos. be a, b, c and d
   $a\,b\,c = 1001$
   $b\,c\,d = 2431$
   $\dfrac{abc}{bcd} = \dfrac{1001}{2431} = \dfrac{7}{17}$
   $\dfrac{a}{d} = \dfrac{7}{17}$ $\therefore a \sim d = 10$

5. (B) 476_78
   $4 + 6 + 7 = 17$
   $7 + ? + 8 = 15 + ?$
   The possible no. is 2.

6. (A) $2806 = 62\dfrac{16}{45}$
   45 - 16 = 29
   29 must be added in order to make it divisible by 45.

7. (D) Divisor = $3 \times 33 = 99$
   Remainder = $\dfrac{99}{11} = 9$
   Dividend = (Divisor × Quotient) + Remainder
   $= 99 \times 33 + 11 = 3267 + 11 = 3278$

8. (C) Let numbers be x and y.
   $xy = 1280$
   $\dfrac{x}{y} = \dfrac{16}{5}$
   $xy \times \dfrac{x}{y} = 1280 \times \dfrac{16}{5}$
   $x^2 = 256 \times 16$
   $x = 16 \times 4 = 64;$
   $\dfrac{x}{y} = \dfrac{16}{5};$ $\dfrac{64}{y} = \dfrac{16}{5}$
   $y = \dfrac{64 \times 5}{16} = 20;$
   $x = 64,\ y = 20$
   $x \sim y = 44$

9. (E) LCM of 3 and 5 is 15.
   $1295 = (15 \times 86) + 5$
   So, 86 number are divisible by both 3 and 5.

10. (A) $x \times \dfrac{4}{3} - x \times \dfrac{3}{4} = 14$
    $x \left(\dfrac{16-9}{12}\right) = 14$
    $x \left(\dfrac{7}{12}\right) = 14;$ $x = \dfrac{12 \times 14}{7};$
    $x = 24$

11. (B) $60 = 2 \times 2 \times 3 \times 5;$
    $90 = 2 \times 3 \times 3 \times 5$
    LCM $= 2^2 \times 3^2 \times 5 = 4 \times 9 \times 5$
    $= 180$
    HCF $= 2 \times 3 \times 5 = 30$

12. (D) Common factors are $2^2, 3, 5^2$
    HCF $= 2^2 \times 3 \times 5^2 = 300$

13. (C) Suffix equal number of zeros to each no. such that each no. can be written as a whole no.

$0.12, 2.4, 0.6 \rightarrow 12, 240, 60$

LCM $= 240$

Then neglect the added zeros

$\therefore$ LCM $= 2.4$

14. (B) LCM of 10, 15, 20, 30 $= 60$

Thus number $= 60 + 5 = 65$

In this case, 5 is remainder.

15. (A) LCM of 4, 6, 8, 10, 12, 24 $= 120$

Bells will ring together after an interval of each 120 seconds $= 2$ minutes

No. of times that the bell will ring in 10 minutes $= \dfrac{10}{2} + 1 = 5 + 1 = 6$ times.

16. (D) Let the integer be x.

Acc. to the qn.,

$16x = x^2 - 192$

$x^2 - 16x - 192 = 0$

$x^2 - 24x + 8x - 192 = 0$

$x(x - 24) + 8(x - 24) = 0$

$(x + 8)(x - 24) = 0$

$x = 24, -8$

17. (D) Product of two nos. $=$ LCM of two nos. $\times$ HCF of two nos.

$60 \times x = 15 \times 180$

$x = \dfrac{2700}{60}$

$x = 45$

18. (B) LCM of 0.08, 0.24, 0.48, 0.32

$= \dfrac{\text{LCM of } 8,24,48,32}{100} = \dfrac{96}{100} = 0.96$

19. (E) The digit in the unit place will be same as the unit digit of the product of 1 to 9 which is 0.

20. (D) Let the nos. be a and b.

$a + b = 85$

$a - b = 9; \quad 2a = 94; \quad a = 47$

$b = a - 9 = 38$

Product $= 47 \times 38 = 1786$

21. (D) Let the 4 nos. be a, b, c, d.

$a + b + c + d = 4 \times 26 = 104$

$a + d = 55$

$b + c = 104 - 55 = 49$

Given $c - b = 1 \quad 2c = 50 \quad c = 25$

Square of third no. is 625.

22. (B) Given: $ac = 700$

$a + b = 60$

$b = 2a, \; 3a = 60$

$a = 20, \; b = 40$

$c = \dfrac{700}{a} = \dfrac{700}{20} = 35$

Required value $= \dfrac{120}{100}(20 + 40 + 35) = \dfrac{120 \times 95}{100} = 114$

23. (C) Let the original no. be $10a + b$

After reversing, the no. is $10b + a$

Acc. to the qn.,

$10b + a = 10a + b + 63$

$9b - 9a = 63$

$b - a = 7$

$a + b = 11$

$b = 9, \; a = 2$

Original no. $= 29$

Twice the no. $= 58$

24. (D) Required time $=$ LCM of 200, 250, 300, 500, 600 $= 3000$ seconds

$= 50$ minutes

25. (B) Let numerator & denominator of a fraction be x and y respectively.

$\dfrac{x+5}{2y} = \dfrac{x}{y}$

$\dfrac{x+5}{2} = x$

$x + 5 = 2x$

$x = 5$

& $x + 4 = 1.5\, y$

$1.5y = 9$

$y = 6$

The original fraction $= \dfrac{5}{6}$

Half of the fraction $= \dfrac{5}{6} \times \dfrac{1}{2} = \dfrac{5}{12}$

PRACTICE QUESTIONS:

1. A prime number, in the range of 10 to 100, remains unchanged when its digits are reversed. Find the cube of the number.

   (A) 4913   (B) 1331
   (C) 2197   (D) 1728
   (E) None of these

2. How many numbers up to largest four-digit number are divisible by 30?

   (A) 444   (B) 666
   (C) 333   (D) 999
   (E) None of these

3. The smallest number to be added to 1252, so that 23 divides the sum exactly, is

   (A) 13   (B) 12
   (C) 14   (D) 10
   (E) None of these

4. Four consecutive even nos. is given. The sum of first two and last no. is 116. Find the product of first and last no.

   (A) 1516   (B) 1532
   (C) 1512   (D) 1520
   (E) None of these

5. A four-digit number formed by repeating a 2-digit number is always exactly divisible by

   (A) 111   (B) 121
   (C) 99   (D) 101
   (E) None of these

6. The sum of three consecutive natural numbers each divisible by 3 is 99 what is the smallest among them?

   (A) 30   (B) 27
   (C) 33   (D) 36
   (E) None of these

7. The sum of first 40 numbers from 1 to 40 is divisible by

   (A) 21   (B) 40
   (C) 39   (D) 41
   (E) None of these

8. A student was asked to find the value of $5/7^{\text{th}}$ of the sum of money. She divides the sum by 5/7 instead of multiplying. So, she exceeds the actual answer by 576. Find the initial sum of money.

   (A) Rs 800   (B) Rs 840
   (C) Rs 820   (D) Rs 760
   (E) None of these

9. Each friend, while going out for dinner spent 5 times as many rupees as the total number of members and they spent Rs 845 in total. How many members were there?

   (A) 13   (B) 11
   (C) 15   (D) 9
   (E) None of these

10. If 5/7 of a land is worth Rs 70,000, find the value of 3/8 of it.

    (A) Rs 37,000   (B) Rs 36,250
    (C) Rs 36,750   (D) Rs 35,560
    (E) None of these

11. Find the LCM of $2^2 \times 3 \times 5, 3^2 \times 5, 5 \times 7$

    (A) 1260   (B) 1280
    (C) 1240   (D) 1250
    (E) None of these

12. The HCF and LCM of two nos. are 5 and 200 respectively. If one of the two numbers is 25. Find the other no.

(A) 45 (B) 40
(C) 50 (D) 30
(E) None of these

13. If the students of a class can be grouped exactly into 4 or 6 or 8, then the minimum number of students in the class must be.

(A) 20 (B) 12
(C) 24 (D) 28
(E) None of these

14. Chocolates were distributed equally among children of a class. The no. of chocolates each child got was $1/8^{th}$ of the no. of children. Had the no. of children been half, each child would have got 16 chocolates. How many chocolates were distributed in all?

(A) 512 (B) 256
(C) 384 (D) 640
(E) None of these

15. When digits of the two nos. are reversed, number obtained is 2 less than thrice the original number. Also, the unit digit is 4 times the tens digit in original number. Find the sum of the digits of the number.

(A) 9 (B) 12
(C) 8 (D) 10
(E) None of these

16. There are 150 questions in an exam. A student gets 2 marks for every correct answer and -0.5 for every wrong answer. If she attempted all the questions and scored 240 marks, find the number of questions she attempted correctly.

(A) 124 (B) 116
(C) 130 (D) 128
(E) None of these

17. There are 3 number a, b, c. Product of a and c is 1250. Sum of a and b is 65. If c is twice that of a. Find 150% of (a +b +c).

(A) 172.5 (B) 173.5
(C) 171 (D) 174
(E) None of these

18. Find the HCF of $2^3 \times 3^3 \times 5 \times 7^3$; $2^2 \times 3^2 \times 5^2 \times 7^2$; $2^3 \times 3^3 \times 5^3 \times 7$;

(A) 1260 (B) 1280
(C) 1240 (D) 1220
(E) None of these

19. Four bells commence tolling together and toll at intervals of 15, 10, 9 and 8 seconds respectively. After how many minutes will they toll together again?

(A) 6 min (B) 5 min
(C) 8 min (D) 4 min
(E) None of these

20. Find the missing digit of the number 515_86 such that the given number is divisible by first 2-digit prime no.

(A) 0 (B) 1
(C) 2 (D) 3
(E) None of these

SOLUTIONS:

1. (B) Since the no. remains unchanged, the two digits of the number are same. Only such prime no. is 11.
Cube of 11=1331

2. (C) Largest 4-digit no. = 9999
$9999 = (30 \times 333) + 9$
333 numbers are divisible by 30.

3. (A) $1252 = (23 \times 54) + 10$
Thus, 23 - 10 = 13
13 must be added.

4. (C) Let the nos. be x, x+2, x+4, x+6.

$x + x + 2 + x + 6 = 116$
$3x + 8 = 116;$
$3x = 108;$
$x = 36$
Nos. are 36, 38, 40, 42.
Product of first & last no $= 36 \times 42$
$$= 1512$$

5. (D) A four-digit number formed by repeating a 2-digit number is always divisible by 101.

6. (B) Let the nos. be a, a+3, a+6.
$a+(a+3) + (a+6) = 99$
$3a+9=99$
$3a=90$
$a = 30$

7. (D) Sum of first 40 no's $= \dfrac{40(40+1)}{2}$
$$= \dfrac{40}{2} \times 41$$
$$= 20 \times 41$$
∴ Sum of first 40 nos. is divisible by 41.

8. (B) Let the initial sum be Rs x.
Acc. to the Qn.,
$$\left(\dfrac{x}{\frac{5}{7}}\right) - \left(x \times \dfrac{5}{7}\right) = 576$$
$$x\left(\dfrac{7}{5} - \dfrac{5}{7}\right) = 576$$
$$x = \dfrac{576 \times 35}{49-25} = \dfrac{576 \times 35}{24}$$
$x = $ Rs 840

9. (A) Let no. of friends be x.
$x \times 5x = 845$
$5x^2 = 845$
$x^2 = 169$
$x = 13$

10. (C) Let the value of land be x.
$$\dfrac{5}{7} \times x = 70,000$$
$$x = \dfrac{70,000 \times 7}{5}$$
$x = $ Rs 98,000
$$\dfrac{3}{8}x = \dfrac{3}{8} \times 98000 = \text{Rs } 36,750.$$

11. (A) LCM $= 2^2 \times 3^2 \times 5 \times 7$
$$= 4 \times 9 \times 5 \times 7$$
$$= 1260$$

12. (B) HCF $\times$ LCM of two nos.
$= $ Product of two no's
$200 \times 5 = 25 \times$ no.
No. $= \dfrac{200 \times 5}{25}$; No. $= 40$

13. (C) LCM of 4, 6, 8 $= 24$
Minimum no. of students $= 24$

14. (A) Let no. of chocolates be n and no. of children be x.
$$\dfrac{n}{x} = \dfrac{x}{8} \rightarrow x^2 = 8n$$
$$\dfrac{n}{\left(\frac{x}{2}\right)} = 16 \rightarrow \dfrac{n}{x} = 8$$
$$x = 8 \times \dfrac{n}{x} = 8 \times 8 = 64$$
$$n = \dfrac{x^2}{8} = \dfrac{64 \times 64}{8} = 64 \times 8 = 512$$

15. (D) Let the original no. be $10a + b$
Reversed no. $= 10b + a$
Acc. to the qn.,
$3(10a+b) - 2 = 10b + a$
$30a + 3b - 2 = 10b + a$
$29a - 7b = 2$
As, $b = 4a$
$29a - 7(4a) = 2$
$29a - 28a = 2$
$a = 2; b = 8$
Sum of digits $= 10$

16. (E) Let no. of questions she attempted correctly be x.
$2x - 0.5(150 - x) = 240$
$2x - 75 + 0.5x = 240$
$2.5x - 75 = 240$
$2.5x = 315; \ x = 126$

126 questions were attempted correctly.

17. (A) Given: $ac = 1250$

$$a + b = 65$$
$$c = 2a$$

Subs. $a(2a) = 1250$

$2a^2 = 1250$

$a^2 = 625; a = 25$

$\therefore b = 40, c = 50$

150 % of $(25 + 40 + 50)$
$$= \frac{150}{100}(115) = 172.5$$

18. (A) HCF $= 2^2 \times 3^2 \times 5 \times 7 = 1260$

19. (A) Required time = LCM of 15, 10, 9, 8
$$= 360 \text{ (seconds)}$$
$$= 6 \text{ minutes}$$
After 6 minutes, they toll together.

20. (A) For 515_86 to be divisible by 11:

$(5 + 5 + 8) \sim (1 + x + 6) = 0$ (or) 11

$18 \sim (7+x) = 0$ (or) 11

Only possible digit is 0.

SIMPLIFICATION & APPROXIMATION

Simplification:

Simplification means to simplify a complicated mathematical expression to get a single or direct answer.

Some basic rules of simplification:

BODMAS rule:

It defines the correct sequence in which operations are to be performed into a given mathematical expression to find the correct value. This means that to simplify an expression, the following order must be followed:

Priority wise operations:

B: Bracket
O: Order (Powers, Square roots, etc)
D: Division
M: Multiplication
A: Addition
S: Subtraction

- To solve approximation type questions correctly, you must apply the operations of brackets first. For solving the brackets, the order is (), {}, [].

- Second, evaluate exponents (powers, roots)

- Next, you should perform division & multiplication, working from left to right (division and multiplication rank equally and are done from left to right)

- Finally, you should perform addition and subtraction working from left to right (addition and subtraction rank equally and are done from left to right)

Note:

Remember to place every division symbol with multiplication symbol followed by the reciprocal of the number following the division symbol, as shown in the above illustration. This simplification trick must be applied to simplify math problems.

Approximation:

An approximation is anything that is close, but not exactly equal to something else. It is helpful to find the solution quickly by rounding off to the nearest integer, rather than solving for the exact values.

EXERCISE:

1. $0.45 + 46.43 + 643 + 3.53 + 4.43 = ?$
   (A) 697.84   (B) 684.52
   (C) 698.24   (D) 691.04
   (E) None of these

2. $\sqrt{1225} \times 28 + 203 \times 7 = ?^2$
   (A) 47   (B) 43
   (C) 49   (D) 51

(E) None of these

3. $\dfrac{(237\times237\times237)-(147\times147\times147)}{(237\times237)+(237\times147)+(147\times147)} = ?$
   (A) 89   (B) 90
   (C) 92   (D) 91
   (E) None of these

4. $4\frac{4}{5} - \frac{27}{5} + 2\frac{1}{15} = 2\frac{1}{5} \div 3 \times?$
   (A) 3   (B) 1
   (C) 4   (D) 2
   (E) None of these

5. $\sqrt{?}$ of $6 + 30\%$ of $75 = \frac{1}{2}$ of 69
   (A) 3   (B) 5
   (C) 4   (D) 6
   (E) None of these

6. $\left\{\left(\frac{11}{2}\times\frac{3}{8}\right)\div\left(\frac{28}{3}\times\frac{42}{10}\right)\right\}\%$ of $6600 = ?$
   (A) 3.02   (B) 3.47
   (C) 2.87   (D) 4.12
   (E) None of these

7. $(49)^{8.5} \times (2401)^3 \div (343)^8$
   $= (?) \times (7)^3$
   (A) 64   (B) 36
   (C) 81   (D) 49
   (E) None of these

8. $\left(3\sqrt{8}+\sqrt{32}\right)\times\left(8\sqrt{8}+\sqrt{72}\right) = ? +37$
   (A) 403   (B) 408
   (C) 397   (D) 405
   (E) None of these

9. 89.998% of $2399 + 224.057 -$
   $367.001 - 11.081 = ?^2 + 246.012$
   (A) 42   (B) 40
   (C) 38   (D) 44
   (E) None of these

10. $(7.94)^3 + (7.95)^2 = -99.98 + ?^2$
    (A) 24   (B) 28
    (C) 30   (D) 26
    (E) None of these

11. 9.98% of $399.92 = (?)^3 + 12.94$
    (A) 3   (B) 4
    (C) 1   (D) 2
    (E) None of these

12. $\sqrt{16.97 \times 44.92 + 4799.54 \div 3.98 + 59.92}$
    $=?$
    (A) 50   (B) 47
    (C) 43   (D) 45
    (E) None of these

13. $(43.74)^2 + 2021.97 \div 2.93 + ?$
    $= (14.89)^3$
    (A) 126   (B) 448
    (C) 765   (D) 890
    (E) None of these

14. $\frac{11.16}{14.12}$ of $\frac{559.12}{33.03}$ of $\frac{239.84}{499.91} = 10.02\%$ of ?
    (A) 58   (B) 64
    (C) 68   (D) 72
    (E) None of these

15. 39.86% of $601 - 300.104$
    $= ? - 70.84\%$ of 909.99
    (A) 554   (B) 564
    (C) 582   (D) 577
    (E) None of these

16. $16080 \div 12 + 13440 \div 32 + 780$
    $= 1542 + ?$
    (A) 988   (B) 998
    (C) 996   (D) 999
    (E) None of these

17. $\sqrt{841} - \sqrt{1024} + \sqrt{1296} = \sqrt{?}$
    (A) 1085   (B) 1089
    (C) 1088   (D) 1090
    (E) None of these

18. $8052 \div 6 + 53 \times 23 - 37 \times 21$
    $= ? + 11 \times 29$
    (A) 1469   (B) 1465
    (C) 1472   (D) 1462

(E) None of these

19. $\frac{195}{308} \times \frac{28}{65} + \frac{5}{22} + \frac{39}{44} = ?$
(A) $1\frac{17}{44}$ (B) $1\frac{13}{44}$
(C) $1\frac{15}{44}$ (D) $1\frac{19}{44}$
(E) None of these

20. $(17\% \text{ of } 932) + (21\% \text{ of } 1326) = ?$
(A) 436.9   (B) 435.4
(C) 436.2   (D) 437.5
(E) None of these

21. $\frac{144}{?} + 42\% \text{ of } 250 = 108$
(A) 46   (B) 42
(C) 50   (D) 48
(E) None of these

22. $? \% \text{ of } 480 + 108 = 18^2$
(A) 42%   (B) 47%
(C) 45%   (D) 50%
(E) None of these

23. $21^{5.4} \times 21^{0.4} \times 21^{3.2} \times 21^? = 21^9$
(A) 1   (B) 0
(C) 2   (D) 3
(E) None of these

24. $\sqrt[3]{1728} \times \sqrt{1024} \times \sqrt[3]{343}$
(A) 2688   (B) 2666
(C) 2866   (D) 2890
(E) None of these

25. $\sqrt{2704} + \sqrt{4624} - \sqrt{1369}$
$= ? + \sqrt{961}$
(A) 50   (B) 52
(C) 54   (D) 56
(E) None of these

26. $\sqrt{41 \times 5^3 - 75} - 17^2 = ?$
(A) 67   (B) 66
(C) 69   (D) 68
(E) None of these

27. $295 \times 34 - 1247 = ? + 3014$
(A) 5771   (B) 5766
(C) 5768   (D) 5769
(E) None of these

28. $[(729)^{1/3} + (1024)^{1/2}] = ?^2 + 5$
(A) 5   (B) 4
(C) 6   (D) 7
(E) None of these

29. $? \% \text{ of } (724.06 - 346.102 + 222.098)$
$= 522.105$
(A) 83   (B) 87
(C) 67   (D) 95
(E) None of these

30. $996.98 + 96.92 - 99.68 + 999.92 + 5.89 = 399.94 \times ?$
(A) 3   (B) 5
(C) 7   (D) 11
(E) None of these

SOLUTIONS:

1. (A) $0.45 + 46.43 + 643 + 3.53 + 4.43 = ?$
$? = 697.84$

2. (C) $\sqrt{1225} \times 28 + 203 \times 7 = ?^2$
$35 \times 28 + 1421 = ?^2$
$? = \sqrt{980 + 1421}$
$= \sqrt{2401} = 49$

3. (B) $\frac{(237 \times 237 \times 237) - (147 \times 147 \times 147)}{(237 \times 237) + (237 \times 147) + (147 \times 147)}$
$= \frac{(237)^3 - (147)^3}{(237)^2 + (237 \times 147) + (147)^2}$
$= 237 - 147 = 90$

4. (D) $4\frac{4}{5} - \frac{27}{5} + 2\frac{1}{15} = 2\frac{1}{5} \div 3 \times ?$
$\frac{24}{5} - \frac{27}{5} + \frac{31}{15} = \frac{11}{5} \times \frac{1}{3} \times ?$
$\frac{22}{15} = \frac{11}{15} \times ?$
$? = 2$

5. (C) $\sqrt{?}$ of $6 + 30\%$ of $75 = \frac{1}{2}$ of 69

$\sqrt{?} \times 6 + 22.5 = 34.5$

$\sqrt{?} \times 6 = 12$

$\sqrt{?} = 2$

$? = 4$

6. (B) $\left\{\left(\frac{11}{2} \times \frac{3}{8}\right) \div \left(\frac{28}{3} \times \frac{42}{10}\right)\right\}\%$ of $6600 = ?$

$\left(\frac{33}{16} \times \frac{15}{588}\right)\%$ of $6600 = ?$

$? = \frac{33}{16} \times \frac{5}{196} \times \frac{1}{100} \times 6600$

$= 3.47$

7. (D) $(49)^{8.5} \times (2401)^3 \div (343)^8$

$= (?) \times (7)^3$

$? = (7)^{17} \times (7)^{12} \div (7)^{24} \div (7)^3$

$= (7)^{29} \times (7)^{-27} = (7)^2 = 49$

8. (A) $\left(3\sqrt{8} + \sqrt{32}\right) \times \left(8\sqrt{8} + \sqrt{72}\right)$

$= ? + 37$

$\left(3\sqrt{8} + 2\sqrt{8}\right) \times \left(8\sqrt{8} + 3\sqrt{8}\right) = ? + 37$

$\left(5\sqrt{8} \times 11\sqrt{8}\right) = ? + 37$

$55 \times 8 = ? + 37$

$? = 440 - 37 = 403$

9. (A) 89.998% of $2399 + 224.057 -$

$367.001 - 11.081 = ?^2 + 246.012$

90% of $2400 + 224 - 367 - 11$

$\approx ?^2 + 246$

$2160 + 224 - 378 \approx ?^2 + 246$

$2010 - 246 = 1764 = ?^2$

$? = 42$

10. (D) $(7.94)^3 + (7.95)^2 = -99.98 + ?^2$

$?^2 \approx 8^3 + 8^2 + 100$

$= 512 + 64 + 100$

$= \sqrt{676} = 26$

11. (A) 9.98% of $399.92 = (?)^3 + 12.94$

10% of $400 \approx ?^3 + 13$

$?^3 \approx 40 - 13 = 27$

$? \approx 3$

12. (D)

$\sqrt{16.97 \times 44.92 + 4799.54 \div 3.98 + 59.92} = ?$

$? \approx \sqrt{17 \times 45 + 4800 \div 4 + 60}$

$\approx \sqrt{765 + 1200 + 60}$

$\approx \sqrt{2025} = 45$

13. (C) $(43.74)^2 + 2021.97 \div 2.93 + ?$

$= (14.89)^3$

$44^2 + 2022 \div 3 + ? \approx 15^3$

$? = 3375 - 1936 - 674 = 765$

14. (B) $\frac{11.16}{14.12}$ of $\frac{559.12}{33.03}$ of $\frac{239.84}{499.91} = 10.02\%$ of?

$\frac{11}{14} \times \frac{560}{33} \times \frac{240}{500} \approx 10\%$ of ?

10% of ? $= 6.4$

$? = 64$

15. (D) 39.86% of $601 - 300.104$

$= ? - 70.84\%$ of 909.99

40% of $600 - 300 \approx ? - 70\%$ of 910

$240 - 300 \approx ? - 637$

$? \approx 240 - 300 + 637 = 577$

16. (B) $16080 \div 12 + 13440 \div 32 + 780$

$= 1542 + ?$

$1340 + 420 + 780 = 1542 + ?$

$? = 2540 - 1542 = 998$

17. (B) $\sqrt{841} - \sqrt{1024} + \sqrt{1296} = \sqrt{?}$

$29 - 32 + 36 = \sqrt{?}$

$? = (33)^2 = 1089$

18. (B) $8052 \div 6 + 53 \times 23 - 37 \times 21$

$= ? + 11 \times 29$

$1342 + 1219 - 777 = ? + 319$

$? = 1784 - 319$

$? = 1465$

19. (A) $\frac{195}{308} \times \frac{28}{65} + \frac{5}{22} + \frac{39}{44} = ?$

$\frac{3}{11} + \frac{5}{22} + \frac{39}{44} = ?$

$? = \frac{12 + 39 + 10}{44} = \frac{61}{44} = 1\frac{17}{44}$

20. (A) $(17\% \text{ of } 932) + (21\% \text{ of } 1326) = ?$
$? = 278.46 + 158.44 = 436.9$

21. (D) $\frac{144}{?} + 42\% \text{ of } 250 = 108$
$\frac{144}{?} + 105 = 108$
$\frac{144}{?} = 3$
$? = \frac{144}{3} = 48$

22. (C) $? \% \text{ of } 480 + 108 = 18^2$
$? \% \text{ of } 480 = 324 - 108 = 216$
$? = 45$

23. (B) $21^{5.4} \times 21^{0.4} \times 21^{3.2} \times 21^? = 21^9$
$5.4 + 0.4 + 3.2 + ? = 9$
$? = 0$

24. (A) $\sqrt[3]{1728} \times \sqrt{1024} \times \sqrt[3]{343}$
$12 \times 32 \times 7 = 2688$

25. (B) $\sqrt{2704} + \sqrt{4624} - \sqrt{1369}$
$= ? + \sqrt{961}$
$52 + 68 - 37 = ? + 31$
$? = 83 - 31 = 52$

26. (C) $\sqrt{41 \times 5^3 - 75 - 17^2} = ?$
$= \sqrt{41 \times 125 - 75 - 289}$
$= \sqrt{5125 - 364}$
$= \sqrt{4761} = 69$

27. (D) $295 \times 34 - 1247 = ? + 3014$
$10030 - 1247 = ? + 3014$
$? = 8783 - 3014 = 5769$

28. (C) $[(729^{1/3} + (1024)^{1/2} = ?^2 + 5$
$?^2 = 9 + 32 - 5 = 36$
$? = \sqrt{36} = 6$

29. (B) $? \% \text{ of } (724.06 - 346.102 + 222.098)$
$= 522.105$
$\approx \frac{?}{100} \times (724 - 346 + 222) = 522$
$\frac{?}{100}(600) = 522$
$? = 87$

30. (B) $996.98 + 96.92 - 99.68 + 999.92 + 5.89 = 399.94 \times ?$
$\approx 997 + 97 - 100 + 1000 + 6$
$= 400 \times ?$
$? = \frac{2000}{400} = 5$

PRACTICE QUESTIONS:

1. $26 \times 42 + 43 \times 19 + 378 \div 6 = ? + 43$
(A) 1923 (B) 1932
(C) 1928 (D) 1929
(E) None of these

2. $\frac{676}{?} = \frac{?}{196}$
(A) 364 (B) 366
(C) 360 (D) 368
(E) None of these

3. $\left(6\frac{3}{5} \text{ of } \frac{5}{3} \text{ of } \frac{9}{11}\right) + ?^2 = 45$
(A) ± 5 (B) ± 7
(C) ± 6 (D) ± 8
(E) None of these

4. $\sqrt{\frac{1440}{40} + \frac{3840}{60} - \frac{1330}{70} - \frac{510}{30}} = ?$
(A) 8 (B) 7
(C) 9 (D) 6
(E) None of these

5. $\frac{1}{28} \text{ of } \frac{5}{2} \text{ of } \frac{7}{8} \text{ of } 1600 = ? - 499 + 260$
(A) 364 (B) 362
(C) 368 (D) 354
(E) None of these

6. $56\% \text{ of } 225 + 60\% \text{ of } 250 = ? - 92$
(A) 364 (B) 358
(C) 372 (D) 368
(E) None of these

7. $? \% \text{ of } 250 + 48\% \text{ of } 525 = 499$
(A) 99.2% (B) 98.8%
(C) 97.6% (D) 96.5%
(E) None of these

8. $(12)^3 + (28)^2 + (38)^2 = (65)^2 - ?$
(A) 266   (B) 279
(C) 269   (D) 272
(E) None of these

9. $\sqrt{(1331)^{1/3} - (343)^{1/3} + (125)^{1/3}} = ?$
(A) 2   (B) 3
(C) 4   (D) 5
(E) None of these

10. $(13.88)^2 - (11.02)^2 + (8.92)^2$
$= ? - 1043.122 - 1649.98$
(A) 2836   (B) 2811
(C) 2849   (D) 2855
(E) None of these

11. $(24.03)^2 + 2969 \div 2.99 - 228.9$
$= 1694.12 - ?$
(A) 128   (B) 125
(C) 130   (D) 132
(E) None of these

12. $\dfrac{(22.02)^2 + 448.928 - 33.12}{(4.98)^3 + \sqrt[3]{512.11} - ?} = 9.09$
(A) 37   (B) 23
(C) 33   (D) 40
(E) None of these

13. $\dfrac{41.98 \times 32.92 \times 4.93}{10.98 \times 14.87} + 13.89$
$= ? \% \text{ of } 279.98$
(A) 20%   (B) 25%
(C) 15%   (D) 30%
(E) None of these

14. 47.78% of $692.46 + 44.19\%$ of 913.8
$= ? + 37.87$
(A) 696   (B) 694
(C) 700   (D) 698
(E) None of these

15. $18897.68 \div 4.98 \times 1.52 + 6899.4 -$
$3698.32 = ?$
(A) 8680   (B) 9090

(C) 8870   (D) 8340
(E) None of these

16. $182.78 \times 6.926 + \sqrt{7567.42} \times 3.52$
$= 2498.61 - ?$
(A) 945   (B) 915
(C) 856   (D) 986
(E) None of these

17. $32002.45 \div 40 \times 31.95 = ? \times 79.62$
(A) 320   (B) 250
(C) 420   (D) 380
(E) None of these

18. $\dfrac{701.02}{52} \div \dfrac{11}{208.01} \times \dfrac{121}{76.98} = ?$
(A) 300   (B) 400
(C) 250   (D) 560
(E) None of these

19. 29.87% of $? + \sqrt{399.67}$
$= (15.12)^2 + 31.87$
(A) 765   (B) 810
(C) 790   (D) 750
(E) None of these

SOLUTIONS:

1. (D) $26 \times 42 + 43 \times 19 + 378 \div 6$
$= ? + 43$
$1092 + 817 + 63 = ? + 43$
$? = 1972 - 43$
$? = 1929$

2. (A) $\dfrac{676}{?} = \dfrac{?}{196}$
$? = \sqrt{676 \times 196} = 26 \times 14 = 364$

3. (C) $\left(6\dfrac{3}{5} \text{ of } \dfrac{5}{3} \text{ of } \dfrac{9}{11}\right) + ?^2 = 45$
$\dfrac{33}{5} \times \dfrac{5}{3} \times \dfrac{9}{11} + ?^2 = 45$
$?^2 = 36$
$? = \pm 6$

4. (A) $\sqrt{\frac{1440}{40} + \frac{3840}{60} - \frac{1330}{70} - \frac{510}{30}} = ?$

$\sqrt{64 + 36 - 19 - 17} = \sqrt{64} = 8$

5. (A) $\frac{1}{28}$ of $\frac{5}{2}$ of $\frac{7}{8}$ of 1600

$= ? - 499 + 260$

$\frac{1}{28} \times \frac{5}{2} \times \frac{7}{8} \times 1600 = ? - 239$

$125 = ? - 239$

$? = 125 + 239 = 364$

6. (D) 56% of 225 + 60% of 250

$= ? - 92$

$? = 126 + 150 + 92 = 368$

7. (B) ? % of 250 + 48% of 525 = 499

? % of 250 + 252 = 499

? % of 250 = 247

$? = 98.8\%$

8. (C) $(12)^3 + (28)^2 + (38)^2 = (65)^2 - ?$

$1728 + 784 + 1444 = 4225 + ?$

$? = 4225 - 3956$

$? = 269$

9. (B) $\sqrt{(1331)^{1/3} - (343)^{1/3} + (125)^{1/3}} = ?$

$\sqrt{11 - 7 + 5} = \sqrt{9} = 3$

10. (C) $(13.88)^2 - (11.02)^2 + (8.92)^2$

$= ? - 1043.122 - 1649.98$

$\approx 14^2 - 11^2 + 9^2 = ? - 1043 - 1650$

$196 - 121 + 81 = ? - 2693$

$? = 156 + 2693$

$? = 2849$

11. (A) $(24.03)^2 + 2969 \div 2.99 - 228.9$

$= 1694.12 - ?$

$\approx 24^2 + 2970 \div 3 - 229$

$= 1694 - ?$

$576 + 990 = 1694 - ?$

$? = 1694 - 1566 = 128$

12. (C) $\frac{(22.02)^2 + 448.928 - 33.12}{(4.98)^3 + \sqrt[3]{512.11} - ?} = 9.09$

$\approx \frac{(22)^2 + 449 - 33}{9} = (5)^3 + \sqrt[3]{512} - ?$

$100 = 133 - ?$

$? = 33$

13. (A) $\frac{41.98 \times 32.92 \times 4.93}{10.98 \times 14.87} + 13.89$

$= ? \% \text{ of } 279.98$

$\frac{42 \times 33 \times 5}{11 \times 15} + 14 = ? \% \text{ of } 280$

$42 + 14 = ? \% \text{ of } 280 = 20\%$

14. (A) 47.78% of 692.46 + 44.19% of 913.8

$= ? + 37.87$

48% of 692 + 44% of 914 = ? + 38

$? = 332.16 + 402.16 - 38$

$= 696.32 \cong 696$

15. (C) $18897.68 \div 4.98 \times 1.52 + 6899.4 -$

$3698.32 = ?$

$\approx 18900 \div 5 \times 1.5 + 6900 - 3700 = ?$

$1.5(3780) + 3200 = ?$

$5670 + 3200 = ?$

$? = 8870$

16. (B) $182.78 \times 6.926 + \sqrt{7567.42} \times$

$3.52 = 2498.61 - ?$

$\approx 183 \times 7 + 86.99 \times 3.5 = 2500 - ?$

$2500 - ? = 1281 + 87 \times 3.5$

$? = 2500 - 1281 - 304.5$

$? = 914.5 \approx 915$

17. (A) $32002.45 \div 40 \times 31.95 = ? \times 79.62$

$\approx \frac{32000}{40} \times 32 = ? \times 80$

$\frac{800 \times 32}{80} = 320$

18. (B) $\frac{701.02}{52} \div \frac{11}{208.01} \times \frac{121}{76.98} = ?$

$\approx \frac{700}{52} \times \frac{208}{11} \times \frac{121}{77} = ?$

$? = 400$

19. (C) 29.87% of ? $+ \sqrt{399.67}$

$= (15.12)^2 + 31.87$

$\approx$ 30% of ? $+ 20 = 15^2 + 32 = 257$

30% of ? $= 257 - 20 = 237$

$? = 79$

Unit 3

NUMBER SERIES

Number series is a sequence of numbers which follow a particular pattern.

Missing number:

A number series is given in which a specific number is missing. We need to recognise the pattern involved in the series and figure out the missing term.

Wrong number:

A number series is given and we need to identify the particular wrong number in that series.

Some of the types of no. series are

1. Arithmetic series:

Series progresses with addition or subtraction of some specific numbers. The difference between any successive terms is not very large and increases in a specific manner.

I. Constant difference between the two consecutive nos.

Ex 1: Find the missing term:

25, 31, 37, __, 49

Sol: 43 (+6 series)

$$25 \xrightarrow{+6} 31 \xrightarrow{+6} 37 \xrightarrow{+6} 43 \xrightarrow{+6} 49$$

II. Constantly increasing or decreasing difference between the two consecutive numbers.

Ex 2: Find the missing term:

40, 44, 52, 64, 80, __

Sol: 100

$$40 \xrightarrow{+4} 44 \xrightarrow{+8} 52 \xrightarrow{+12} 64 \xrightarrow{+16} 80 \xrightarrow{+20} 100$$

2. Geometric series:

Each term is multiplied by a fixed number/ specific no. pattern to get the next successive number

o Multiplication of previous number by a fixed no.

o Multiplication of previous number by the successive terms of a series itself

Ex 3: 2, 4, 8, 16, 32, __

Sol: 64

$$2 \xrightarrow{\times 2} 4 \xrightarrow{\times 2} 8 \xrightarrow{\times 2} 16 \xrightarrow{\times 2} 32 \xrightarrow{\times 2} 64$$

3. Arithmetic-Geometric series:

Combination of arithmetic & geometric series. There is an obvious difference of the successive terms.

Ex 4: 1, 2, 8, 48, __, 3840

Sol: 384

$$1 \xrightarrow{\times 2} 2 \xrightarrow{\times 4} 8 \xrightarrow{\times 6} 48 \xrightarrow{\times 8} 384 \xrightarrow{\times 10} 3840$$

4. Division series:

Each term is divided by a fixed no. or specific number pattern to get the next successive no.

Ex 5: 1875, 375, __, 15, 3

Sol: 75

$$1875 \xrightarrow[\div 5] {} 375 \xrightarrow[\div 5]{} 75 \xrightarrow[\div 5]{} 15 \xrightarrow[\div 5]{} 3$$

5. <u>Square or cube series:</u>

No. series progresses with squaring or cubing of the numbers

Ex 6: 81, 64, 49, __, 25, 16

Sol: 36

$$9^2 \; 8^2 \; 7^2 \; 6^2 \; 5^2 \; 4^2$$

6. <u>Combinational series:</u>

More than one operation is carried out to make a series.

Ex 7: 1, 3, 10, __, 144

Sol: 37

$$1 \xrightarrow[\times 4-1]{} 3 \xrightarrow[\times 4-2]{} 10 \xrightarrow[\times 4-3]{} 37 \xrightarrow[\times 4-4]{} 144$$

<u>Note:</u>

a) There is no specific sequence formula by which a series is formed.

b) If change in series is slow, it can be an arithmetic series.

c) If change in series is obvious, it can be a geometric series.

d) If change is initially slow but later becomes very fast, then it is due to addition of squared or cubed terms.

e) If number series is alternating, then maybe mixed series with two operations going on alternately.

EXERCISE:

1. 55, 61, 73, 91, __, 145
(A) 115   (B) 105   (C) 110
(D) 120   (E) None of these

2. 20, 25, 15, 30, 10, __
(A) 40   (B) 35   (C) 30
(D) 32   (E) None of these

3. 21, 23, 26, __, 38, 49

(A) 32   (B) 35   (C) 30
(D) 31   (E) None of these

4. 22, 27, 37, 54, 80, __
(A) 200   (B) 117   (C) 214
(D) 134   (E) None of these

5. 4.8, __, 24, 36, 36, 18
(A) 10   (B) 12   (C) 8
(D) 15   (E) None of these

6. 6, 7, 16, 51, __, 1045
(A) 208   (B) 200   (C) 250
(D) 212   (E) None of these

7. 5040, 840, 168, 42, 14, __
(A) 7   (B) 6   (C) 5
(D) 8   (E) None of these

8. 121, 144, 81, __, 49, 64, 25
(A) 200   (B) 121   (C) 100
(D) 81   (E) None of these

9. 120, 60, 60, 90, 180, __
(A) 540   (B) 450   (C) 400
(D) 500   (E) None of these

10. 4, 3, 4, 7, 15, __
(A) 38.5   (B) 37.5   (C) 36
(D) 37   (E) None of these

11. 50, 10, 4, 2.4, 1.92, __
(A) 1.8   (B) 1.6   (C) 1.92
(D) 1.5   (E) None of these

12. 17, 22, 32, __, 92, 172
(A) 50   (B) 64   (C) 52
(D) 58   (E) None of these

13. 2, 4, 10, 22, 42, __
(A) 72   (B) 74   (C) 70
(D) 75   (E) None of these

14. 11, 13.4, 18.2, 27.8, __, 85.4
(A) 47   (B) 45   (C) 49
(D) 42   (E) None of these

15. 1, 5, 14, 30, __ , 91
   (A) 56   (B) 54   (C) 55
   (D) 59   (E) None of these

16. 124, 127, 121, 130, __, 133
   (A) 118   (B) 115   (C) 116
   (D) 117   (E) None of these

17. 27, 35, 26, 90, 65, __
   (A) 280   (B) 284   (C) 271
   (D) 281   (E) None of these

18. 177, 160, 141, 118, __, 58
   (A) 90   (B) 89   (C) 88
   (D) 87   (E) None of these

19. 120, 240, 240, 480, __ , 960
   (A) 480   (B) 240   (C) 720
   (D) 840   (E) None of these

20. 1, 1, 4, __, 576, 14400
   (A) 48   (B) 36   (C) 32
   (D) 16   (E) None of these

21. 6250, 1250, 250, __, 10, 2
   (A) 150   (B) 50   (C) 100
   (D) 60   (E) None of these

22. 169, 121, __, 25, 9, 4
   (A) 81   (B) 36   (C) 49
   (D) 64   (E) None of these

23. 14, 9, 11, 24, __, 786
   (A) 90   (B) 96   (C) 94
   (D) 98   (E) None of these

24. 100, 10, 2, 0.6, __, 0.12
   (A) 0.24   (B) 0.36   (C) 0.34
   (D) 0.25   (E) None of these

25. 417, 432, __, 502, 577, 692
   (A) 457   (B) 453   (C) 450
   (D) 451   (E) None of these

26. 1, 2, 4, 9, 23, __

   (A) 60   (B) 68   (C) 64
   (D) 70   (E) None of these

27. 57, 63, 75, 111, 255, __
   (A) 1020   (B) 975   (C) 960
   (D) 970   (E) None of these

[15-16]
Find the wrong term in the given series:

28. 35, 40, 34, 39, 33, 42
   (A) 42   (B) 34   (C) 35
   (D) 39   (E) None of these

29. 3, 15, 200, 750, 7500, 37500
   (A) 750   (B) 15   (C) 200
   (D) 3   (E) None of these

30. 19, 30, 41, 58, 75, 94
   (A) 41   (B) 58   (C) 75
   (D) 94   (E) None of these

31. 18, 9, 9, 18, 70, 576
   (A) 576   (B) 18   (C) 70
   (D) 9   (E) None of these

32. 31, 35, 24, 42, 17, 53
   (A) 35   (B) 42   (C) 17
   (D) 24   (E) None of these

SOLUTIONS:

1. (A) $55 \underset{+6}{\to} 61 \underset{+12}{\to} 73 \underset{+18}{\to} 91 \underset{+24}{\to} 115 \underset{+30}{\to} 145$

2. (B) $20 \underset{+5}{\to} 25 \underset{-10}{\to} 15 \underset{+15}{\to} 30 \underset{-20}{\to} 10 \underset{+25}{\to} 35$

3. (D) $21 \underset{+2}{\to} 23 \underset{+3}{\to} 26 \underset{+5}{\to} 31 \underset{+7}{\to} 38 \underset{+11}{\to} 49$

4. (B) $22 \underset{+5}{\to} 27 \underset{+10}{\to} 37 \underset{+17}{\to} 54 \underset{+26}{\to} 80 \underset{+37}{\to} 117$

5. (B) $4.8 \underset{\times2.5}{\to} 12 \underset{\times2}{\to} 24 \underset{\times1.5}{\to} 36 \underset{\times1}{\to} 36 \underset{\times0.5}{\to} 18$

6. (A)

$$6 \xrightarrow[\times 1+1]{} 7 \xrightarrow[\times 2+2]{} 16 \xrightarrow[\times 3+3]{} 51 \xrightarrow[\times 4+4]{} 208 \xrightarrow[\times 5+5]{} 1045$$

7. (A) $5040 \xrightarrow[\div 6]{} 840 \xrightarrow[\div 5]{} 168 \xrightarrow[\div 4]{} 42 \xrightarrow[\div 3]{} 14 \xrightarrow[\div 2]{} 7$

8. (C) $11^2\ 12^2\ 9^2\ 10^2\ 7^2\ 8^2$

9. (B) $120 \xrightarrow[\times 0.5]{} 60 \xrightarrow[\times 1]{} 60 \xrightarrow[\times 1.5]{} 90 \xrightarrow[\times 2]{} 180 \xrightarrow[\times 2.5]{} 450$

10. (A)

$$4 \xrightarrow[\times 0.5+1]{} 3 \xrightarrow[\times 1+1]{} 4 \xrightarrow[\times 1.5+1]{} 7 \xrightarrow[\times 2+1]{} 15 \xrightarrow[\times 2.5+1]{} 38.5$$

11. (C) $50 \xrightarrow[\times 0.2]{} 10 \xrightarrow[\times 0.4]{} 4 \xrightarrow[\times 0.6]{} 2.4 \xrightarrow[\times 0.8]{} 1.92 \xrightarrow[\times 1]{} 1.92$

12. (C)

$$17 \xrightarrow[\times 2-12]{} 22 \xrightarrow[\times 2-12]{} 32 \xrightarrow[\times 2-12]{} 52 \xrightarrow[\times 2-12]{} 92 \xrightarrow[\times 2-12]{} 172$$

13. (A) $2 \xrightarrow[+2]{} 4 \xrightarrow[+6]{} 10 \xrightarrow[+12]{} 22 \xrightarrow[+20]{} 42 \xrightarrow[+30]{} 72$

14. (A)

$$11 \xrightarrow[+2.4]{} 13.4 \xrightarrow[+4.8]{} 18.2 \xrightarrow[+9.6]{} 27.8 \xrightarrow[+19.2]{} 47 \xrightarrow[+38.4]{} 85.4$$

15. (C) $1 \xrightarrow[]{+4} 5 \xrightarrow[]{+9} 14 \xrightarrow[]{+16} 30 \xrightarrow[]{+25} 55 \xrightarrow[]{+36} 91$

16. (A)

$$124 \xrightarrow[]{+3} 127 \xrightarrow[]{-6} 121 \xrightarrow[]{+9} 130 \xrightarrow[]{-12} 118 \xrightarrow[]{+15} 133$$

17. (D)

$$27 \xrightarrow[]{+8} 35 \xrightarrow[]{-9} 26 \xrightarrow[]{+64} 90 \xrightarrow[]{-25} 65 \xrightarrow[]{+216} 281$$

$$(+2^3, -3^2, +4^3, -5^2, +6^3)$$

18. (B)

$$177 \xrightarrow[]{-17} 160 \xrightarrow[]{-19} 141 \xrightarrow[]{-23} 118 \xrightarrow[]{-29} 89 \xrightarrow[]{-31} 58$$

19. (A)

$$120 \xrightarrow[]{\times 2} 240 \xrightarrow[]{\times 1} 240 \xrightarrow[]{\times 2} 480 \xrightarrow[]{\times 1} 480 \xrightarrow[]{\times 2} 960$$

20. (B) $1 \xrightarrow[]{\times 1} 1 \xrightarrow[]{\times 4} 4 \xrightarrow[]{\times 9} 36 \xrightarrow[]{\times 16} 576 \xrightarrow[]{\times 25} 14400$

21. (B) $6250 \xrightarrow[]{\div 5} 1250 \xrightarrow[]{\div 5} 250 \xrightarrow[]{\div 5} 50 \xrightarrow[]{\div 5} 10 \xrightarrow[]{\div 5} 2$

22. (C) $169 \to 121 \to 49 \to 25 \to 9 \to 4$

$$(13^2 \to 11^2 \to 7^2 \to 5^2 \to 3^2 \to 2^2)$$

23. (D)

$$14 \xrightarrow[]{\times 0.5+2} 9 \xrightarrow[]{\times 1+2} 11 \xrightarrow[]{\times 2+2} 24 \xrightarrow[]{\times 4+2} 98 \xrightarrow[]{\times 8+2} 786$$

24. (A)

$$100 \xrightarrow[]{\times 0.1} 10 \xrightarrow[]{\times 0.2} 2 \xrightarrow[]{\times 0.3} 0.6 \xrightarrow[]{\times 0.4} 0.24 \xrightarrow[]{\times 0.5} 0.12$$

25. (A)

$$417 \xrightarrow[]{+15} 432 \xrightarrow[]{+25} 457 \xrightarrow[]{+45} 502 \xrightarrow[]{+75} 577 \xrightarrow[]{+115} 692$$

$$(15 \xrightarrow[]{+10} 25 \xrightarrow[]{+20} 45 \xrightarrow[]{+30} 75 \xrightarrow[]{+40} 115)$$

26. (C) $1 \xrightarrow[]{\times 3-1} 2 \xrightarrow[]{\times 3-2} 4 \xrightarrow[]{\times 3-3} 9 \xrightarrow[]{\times 3-4} 23 \xrightarrow[]{\times 3-5} 64$

27. (B)

$$57 \xrightarrow[]{+6} 63 \xrightarrow[]{+12} 75 \xrightarrow[]{+36} 111 \xrightarrow[]{+144} 255 \xrightarrow[]{+720} 975$$

$$(6 \xrightarrow[]{\times 2} 12 \xrightarrow[]{\times 3} 36 \xrightarrow[]{\times 4} 144 \xrightarrow[]{\times 5} 720)$$

28. (D) $35 \xrightarrow[+5]{} 40 \xrightarrow[-6]{} 34 \xrightarrow[+7]{} 41 \xrightarrow[-8]{} 33 \xrightarrow[+9]{} 42$

29. (C) $3 \xrightarrow[\times 5]{} 15 \xrightarrow[\times 10]{} 150 \xrightarrow[\times 5]{} 750 \xrightarrow[\times 10]{} 7500 \xrightarrow[\times 5]{} 37500$

30. (A) $19 \xrightarrow[]{+11} 30 \xrightarrow[]{+13} 43 \xrightarrow[]{+15} 58 \xrightarrow[]{+17} 75 \xrightarrow[]{+19} 94$

31. (C) $18 \xrightarrow[]{\times 0.5} 9 \xrightarrow[]{\times 1} 9 \xrightarrow[]{\times 2} 18 \xrightarrow[]{\times 4} 72 \xrightarrow[]{\times 8} 576$

32. (D) $31 \xrightarrow[]{+4} 35 \xrightarrow[]{-9} 26 \xrightarrow[]{+16} 42 \xrightarrow[]{-25} 17 \xrightarrow[]{+36} 53$

PRACTICE QUESTIONS:

1. 7, 15, 23, _, 39, 47
    (A) 31   (B) 30
    (C) 28   (D) 32
    (E) None of these

2. 100, 111, 124, 141, 160, _, 212
    (A) 181   (B) 180
    (C) 183   (D) 185
    (E) None of these

3. 31, _, 66, 130, 255, 471
    (A) 41   (B) 39
    (C) 38   (D) 40
    (E) None of these

4. 47, 56, 74, _, 137, 182
    (A) 105   (B) 100
    (C) 98   (D) 101
    (E) None of these

5. 18, 39, 64, 97, _, 203
    (A) 126   (B) 145
    (C) 142   (D) 138
    (E) None of these

6. 100, 125, 75, 175, _, 375
    (A) -25   (B) 25
    (C) 30   (D) -30
    (E) None of these

7. _, 203, 181, 214, 170, 225
    (A) 200   (B) 192
    (C) 190   (D) 195
    (E) None of these

8. 5, 10, 40, 240, _, 19200
    (A) 1900   (B) 1910
    (C) 1800   (D) 1950
    (E) None of these

9. 4, 24, 120, _, 1440, 2880
    (A) 720   (B) 240
    (C) 480   (D) 360
    (E) None of these

10. 13, 25, 52, 100, _, 400
    (A) 212   (B) 206
    (C) 210   (D) 208
    (E) None of these

11. 750000, 150000, 15000, 1000, _2
    (A) 50   (B) 100
    (C) 5000   (D) 200
    (E) None of these

12. 64, 16, 8, 2, _, 0.25
    (A) 1.5   (B) 1
    (C) 0.5   (D) 0.75
    (E) None of these

13. 30030, 15015, 5005, 1001, _, 13
    (A) 343   (B) 151
    (C) 143   (D) 175
    (E) None of these

14. 9600000, 480000, 24000, 1200, _, 3
    (A) 80   (B) 50
    (C) 60   (D) 40
    (E) None of these

15. 121, 144, 81, _, 49, 64, 25
    (A) 64   (B) 90
    (C) 121   (D) 100
    (E) None of these

16. 128, 64, 96, 240, 840, _
    (A) 3800   (B) 3780
    (C) 3870   (D) 3760
    (E) None of these

17. _, 4, 2, 1.5, 1.5, 1.875
    (A) 12   (B) 8
    (C) 16   (D) 6
    (E) None of these

18. 4, 3, 4.5, _, 30.375, 113.9
    (A) 10.125 (B) 9.75
    (C) 10.25   (D) 10.725
    (E) None of these

19. 4, 6, 12, 30, _, 315

(A) 100   (B) 90
(C) 70   (D) 80
(E) None of these

20. 5, 12.5, 31.25, _, 195.3125, 488.281
    (A) 78.5   (B) 76.725
    (C) 77.25   (D) 78.125
    (E) None of these

21. 3, 5, 14, 48, 200, _
    (A) 1020   (B) 1000
    (C) 1040   (D) 1010
    (E) None of these

22. 10, 22, 28, 34, 43, _
    (A) 57   (B) 61
    (C) 64   (D) 63
    (E) None of these

23. 672, 668, 659, _618, 582
    (A) 620   (B) 613
    (C) 643   (D) 634
    (E) None of these

24. 4, 3, 10, 87, _, 34695
    (A) 1390   (B) 1384
    (C) 1380   (D) 1388
    (E) None of these

[25-28]

Find the wrong term:

25. 6, 6, 12, 36, 144, 700
    (A) 700   (B) 144
    (C) 12   (D) 36
    (E) None of these

26. 33696, 11232, 2808, 468, 52, 3
    (A) 52   (B) 3
    (C) 11232   (D) 2808
    (E) None of these

27. 6, 15, 29, 57, 113, 225
    (A) 6   (B) 15
    (C) 29   (D) 57
    (E) None of these

28. 2, 3, 8, 13, 32, 55
    (A) 13   (B) 55
    (C) 8   (D) 32
    (E) None of these

SOLUTIONS:

1. (A) $7 \xrightarrow{+8} 15 \xrightarrow{+8} 23 \xrightarrow{+8} 31 \xrightarrow{+8} 39 \xrightarrow{+8} 47$

2. (C)
$$100 \xrightarrow{+11} 111 \xrightarrow{+13} 124 \xrightarrow{+17} 141 \xrightarrow{+19} 160 \xrightarrow{+23} 183 \xrightarrow{+29} 212$$

3. (B) $31 \xrightarrow{+8} 39 \xrightarrow{+27} 66 \xrightarrow{+64} 130 \xrightarrow{+125} 255$
$$\xrightarrow{+216} 471$$

4. (D) $47 \xrightarrow{+9} 56 \xrightarrow{+18} 74 \xrightarrow{+27} 101 \xrightarrow{+36} 137$
$$\xrightarrow{+45} 182$$

5. (C) $18 \xrightarrow{+21} 39 \xrightarrow{+25} 64 \xrightarrow{+33} 97 \xrightarrow{+45} 142$
$$\xrightarrow{+61} 203$$

6. (A)
$$100 \xrightarrow{+25} 125 \xrightarrow{-50} 75 \xrightarrow{+100} 175 \xrightarrow{-200} -25 \xrightarrow{+400} 375$$

7. (B)
$$192 \xrightarrow{+11} 203 \xrightarrow{-22} 181 \xrightarrow{+33} 214 \xrightarrow{-44} 170 \xrightarrow{+55} 225$$

8. (E)
$$5 \xrightarrow{\times 2} 10 \xrightarrow{\times 4} 40 \xrightarrow{\times 6} 240 \xrightarrow{\times 8} 1920 \xrightarrow{\times 10} 19200$$

9. (C) $4 \xrightarrow{\times 6} 24 \xrightarrow{\times 5} 120 \xrightarrow{\times 4} 480 \xrightarrow{\times 3} 1440 \xrightarrow{\times 2} 2880$

10. (D)
$$13 \xrightarrow{\times 2-1} 25 \xrightarrow{\times 2-2} 52 \xrightarrow{\times 2-4} 100 \xrightarrow{\times 2-8} 208 \xrightarrow{\times 2-16} 400$$

11. (A)
$$750000 \xrightarrow{\div 5} 150000 \xrightarrow{\div 10} 15000 \xrightarrow{\div 15} 1000 \xrightarrow{\div 20} 50 \xrightarrow{\div 25} 2$$

12. (B) $64 \xrightarrow{\div 4} 16 \xrightarrow{\div 2} 8 \xrightarrow{\div 4} 2 \xrightarrow{\div 2} 1 \xrightarrow{\div 4} 0.25$

13. (C)
$$30030 \xrightarrow{\div 2} 15015 \xrightarrow{\div 3} 5005 \xrightarrow{\div 5} 1001 \xrightarrow{\div 7} 143 \xrightarrow{\div 11} 13$$

14. (C)
$$96,00,000 \xrightarrow{\div 20} 4,80,000 \xrightarrow{\div 20} 24,000 \xrightarrow{\div 20} 1200 \xrightarrow{\div 20} 60 \xrightarrow{\div 20} 3$$

15. (D) $121 \to 144 \to 81 \to 100 \to 49 \to 64 \to 25$

$11^2 \to 12^2 \to 9^2 \to 10^2 \to 7^2 \to 8^2 \to 5^2$

$(11^2, 9^2, 7^2, 5^2 \ \& \ 12^2, 10^2, 8^2)$

16. (B)

$$128 \xrightarrow{\times 0.5} 64 \xrightarrow{\times 1.5} 96 \xrightarrow{\times 2.5} 240 \xrightarrow{\times 3.5} 840 \xrightarrow{\times 4.5} 3780$$

17. (C)

$$16 \xrightarrow{\times 0.25} 4 \xrightarrow{\times 0.5} 2 \xrightarrow{\times 0.75} 1.5 \xrightarrow{\times 1} 1.5 \xrightarrow{\times 1.25} 1.875$$

18. (A) $4 \xrightarrow{\times 0.75} 3 \xrightarrow{\times 1.5} 4.5 \xrightarrow{\times 2.25} 10.125$

$$\xrightarrow{\times 3} 30.375 \xrightarrow{\times 3.75} 113.9$$

19. (B) $4 \xrightarrow{\times 1.5} 6 \xrightarrow{\times 2} 12 \xrightarrow{\times 2.5} 30 \xrightarrow{\times 3} 90 \xrightarrow{\times 3.5} 315$

20. (D) $5 \xrightarrow{\times 2.5} 12.5 \xrightarrow{\times 2.5} 31.25 \xrightarrow{\times 2.5} 78.125$

$$\xrightarrow{\times 2.5} 195.3125 \xrightarrow{\times 2.5} 683.594$$

21. (D)

$$3 \xrightarrow{\times 1+2} 5 \xrightarrow{\times 2+4} 14 \xrightarrow{\times 3+6} 48 \xrightarrow{\times 4+8} 200 \xrightarrow{\times 5+10} 1010$$

22. (B) $10 \xrightarrow{+12} 22 \xrightarrow{+6} 28 \xrightarrow{+6} 34 \xrightarrow{+9} 43 \xrightarrow{+18} 61$

$(12 \xrightarrow{\times 0.5} 6 \xrightarrow{\times 1} 6 \xrightarrow{\times 1.5} 9 \xrightarrow{\times 2} 18 \xrightarrow{\times 2.5} 45 \xrightarrow{\times 3} 135$

23. (C)

$$672 \xrightarrow{-4} 668 \xrightarrow{-9} 659 \xrightarrow{-16} 643 \xrightarrow{-25} 618 \xrightarrow{-36} 582$$

24. (D) $4 \xrightarrow{\times 1^2-1} 3 \xrightarrow{\times 2^2-2} 10 \xrightarrow{\times 3^2-3} 87$

$$\xrightarrow{\times 4^2-4} 1388 \xrightarrow{\times 5^2-5} 34695$$

25. (A) $6 \xrightarrow{\times 1} 6 \xrightarrow{\times 2} 12 \xrightarrow{\times 3} 36 \xrightarrow{\times 4} 144 \xrightarrow{\times 5} 700$

26. (B) $33696 \xrightarrow{\div 3} 11232 \xrightarrow{\div 4} 2808 \xrightarrow{\div 6} 468 \xrightarrow{\div 9} 52 \xrightarrow{\div 13} 4$

$(3 \xrightarrow{+1} 4 \xrightarrow{+2} 6 \xrightarrow{+3} 9 \xrightarrow{+4} 13)$

27. (A)

$$8 \xrightarrow{\times 2-1} 15 \xrightarrow{\times 2-1} 29 \xrightarrow{\times 2-1} 57 \xrightarrow{\times 2-1} 113 \xrightarrow{\times 2-1} 225$$

28. (D)

$$2 \xrightarrow{\times 2-1} 3 \xrightarrow{\times 2+2} 8 \xrightarrow{\times 2-3} 13 \xrightarrow{\times 2+4} 30 \xrightarrow{\times 2-5} 55$$

QUADRATIC EQUATIONS

An equation having term with highest degree of 2 ie, quadratic term is called quadratic equation.

General form:

A quadratic equation: $ax^2 + bx + c = 0$
a, b, c are real terms $(a \neq 0)$
If a=0 the equation will become linear.

$$x = \frac{-b \pm \sqrt{b^2 - 4ac}}{2a}$$

Methods of solving:

I. Using a standard formula:
For a general form of quadratic equation of type $ax^2 + bx + c = 0$
The solution will be

$$x = \frac{-b \pm \sqrt{b^2 - 4ac}}{2a}$$

Thus, two roots are obtained.

<u>Note:</u> This can be used for all types of quadratic equation irrespective of whether the equation can be factorised or not.

II. <u>Factorisation method:</u>
We need to find the factors of the given terms
Eg: $x^2 - 5x + 6 = 0$
$x^2 - 2x - 3x + 6 = 0$
$(x - 2)(x - 3) = 0$
$x = 2, 3$ are the roots.

<u>**Note:**</u> Though, this method is quicker, it can only be used when the given equation can be factorised.

Questions are asked based on the comparative relation between the roots of any two equations.

Comparative relations that can established between the roots are,

- $x > y$
- $x < y$
- $x \geq y$
- $x \leq y$
- $x = y$ or relation can't be established

EXERCISE:

Solve both the given equations and compare their roots (consider both of the roots in each case)

1. I. $x^2 - 18x + 81 = 0$
    II. $y^2 - 4y - 5 = 0$

2. I. $18x^2 - 117x + 189 = 0$
    II. $9y^2 - 45y + 54 = 0$

3. I. $2x^2 - 15x + 27 = 0$
    II. $y^2 - 5y + 6 = 0$

4. I. $x^2 + 18x + 77 = 0$
    II. $y^2 + 10y + 21 = 0$

5. I. $x^2 + 22x + 117 = 0$
    II. $2y^2 + 36y + 154 = 0$

6. I. $12x^2 - 7x + 1 = 0$
    II. $20y^2 - 9y + 1 = 0$

7. I. $2x^2 + 3x + 1 = 0$
II. $6y^2 + 31y + 35 = 0$

8. I. $x^2 - 2x = 0$
II. $10y^2 - y - 24 = 0$

9. I. $3x^2 - 7x + 2 = 0$
II. $3y^2 - 13y + 12 = 0$

10. I. $12x^2 - 17x + 6 = 0$
II. $6y^2 - 5y + 1 = 0$

11. I. $16x^2 = 1$
II. $3y^2 + 7y + 2 = 0$

12. I. $10x^2 - \left(18 + 5\sqrt{17}\right)x + 9\sqrt{17} = 0$
II. $3y^2 - \left(6 + \sqrt{17}\right)y + 2\sqrt{17} = 0$

13. I. $x - 5\sqrt{2x} + 12 = 0$
II. $y - 7\sqrt{2y} + 24 = 0$

14. I. $\sqrt{484}x + \sqrt{225} = 183$
II. $\sqrt{289}y - \sqrt{324} = 203$

15. I. $\sqrt{144}\,x^3 - 9x^3 = 1536$
II. $679\,y^2 - 168y^2 = 3066$

16. I. $\sqrt{x + 222} - \sqrt{36} = \sqrt{81}$
II. $14y - 25 = 59 - 7y$

17. I. $x - 1 = \sqrt{81} - 4$
II. $y + 10 = \sqrt[3]{3375}$

18. I. $3x^2 + x - 2 = 0$
II. $y = \dfrac{\sqrt{256}}{\sqrt{576}}$

19. I. $(x - 1)^2 = 121$
II. $y^2 - 24y + 144 = 0$

20. I. $x^4 = 256$
II. $y^2 - 16y + 64 = 0$

21. I. $(x + 16)^2 = 441$
II. $(y + 22)^2 = 961$

22. I. $2x + 5y = \sqrt{2601}$
II. $7x + 3y = 77$

23. I. $12x^2 = 6x$
II. $y + x^2 = 0.45$

24. I. $3x + 2y = 301$
II. $7x - 5y = 74$

25. I. $x^2 = 256$
II. $y = \sqrt{256}$

SOLUTIONS:

1. I. $x^2 - 18x + 81 = 0$
$x^2 - 9x - 9x + 81 = 0$
$(x - 9)(x - 9) = 0;$
$x = 9, 9$
II. $y^2 - 4y - 5 = 0$
$y^2 - 5y + 1y - 5 = 0$
$(y - 5)(y + 1) = 0,$
$y = 5, -1$
x > y

2. I. $18x^2 - 117x + 189 = 0$
$2x^2 - 13x + 21 = 0$
$2x^2 - 6x - 7x + 21 = 0$
$2x(x - 3) - 7(x - 3) = 0$
$(2x - 7)(x - 3) = 0$
$x = \dfrac{7}{2}, 3$
II. $9y^2 - 45y + 54 = 0$
$y^2 - 5y + 6 = 0$
$y^2 - 2y - 3y + 6 = 0$
$(y - 2)(y - 3) = 0$
$y = 2, 3$
x ≥ y

3. I. $2x^2 - 15x + 27 = 0$
$2x^2 - 6x - 9x + 27 = 0$

$2x(x-3) - 9(x-3) = 0$

$(2x-9)(x-3)$

$x = \frac{9}{2}, 3$

II. $y^2 - 5y + 6 = 0$

$y^2 - 2y - 3y + 6 = 0$

$(y-2)(y-3) = 0$

$y = 2, 3$

x ≥ y

4. I. $x^2 + 18x + 77 = 0$

$x^2 + 7x + 11x + 77 = 0$

$x(x+7) + 11(x+7) = 0$

$(x+11)(x+7) = 0$;

$x = -11, -7$

II. $y^2 + 10y + 21 = 0$

$y^2 + 3y + 7y + 21 = 0$

$y(y+3) + 7(y+3) = 0$

$(y+7)(y+3) = 0$

$y = -7, -3$

x ≤ y

5. I. $x^2 + 22x + 117 = 0$

$x + 9x + 13x + 117 = 0$

$x(x+9) + 13(x+9) = 0$

$(x+13)(x+9) = 0$;

$x = -13, -9$

II. $y^2 + 18y + 77 = 0$

$y(y+11) + 7(y+11) = 0$

$(y+7)(y+11) = 0$

$y = -7 - 11$

No relation can be established

6. I. $12x^2 - 7x + 1 = 0$

$12x^2 - 4x - 3x + 1 = 0$

$4x(3x-1) - 1(3x-1) = 0$

$(4x-1)(3x-1) = 0$

$x = \frac{1}{4}, \frac{1}{3}$

II. $20y^2 - 9y + 1 = 0$

$20y^2 - 5y - 4y + 1 = 0$

$5y(4y-1) - 1(4y-1) = 0$

$(5y-1)(4y-1) = 0$

$y = \frac{1}{5}, \frac{1}{4}$

x ≥ y

7. I. $2x^2 + 3x + 1 = 0$

$2x^2 + 2x + x + 1 = 0$

$2x(x+1) + 1(x+1) = 0$

$(2x+1)(x+1) = 0,$

$x = \frac{-1}{2}, -1$

II. $6y^2 + 31y + 35 = 0$

$6y^2 + 21y + 10y + 35 = 0$

$3y(2y+7) + 5(2y+7) = 0$

$(3y+5)(2y+7) = 0;$

$y = -\frac{5}{3}, \frac{-7}{2}$

x > y

8. I. $x^2 - 2x = 0$

$x(x-2) = 0$;

$x = 0, 2$

II. $10y^2 - y - 24 = 0$

$10y^2 - 16y + 15y - 24 = 0$

$2y(5y-8) + 3(5y-8) = 0$

$(2y+3)(5y-8) = 0;$

$y = \frac{-3}{2}, +\frac{8}{5}$

No relation can be established

9. I. $3x^2 - 7x + 2 = 0$

$3x^2 - 6x - x + 2 = 0$

$3x(x-2) - 1(x-2) = 0$

$(3x-1)(x-2) = 0;$

$x = \frac{1}{3}, \frac{1}{2}$

II. $3y^2 - 13y + 12 = 0$

$3y^2 - 9y - 4y + 12 = 0$

$3y(y-3) - 4(y-3) = 0$

$(3y-4)(y-3);$

$y = \frac{4}{3}, 3$

No relation can be established

10. I. $12x^2 - 17x + 6 = 0$

$12x^2 - 8x - 9x + 6 = 0$

$4x(3x-2) - 3(3x-2) = 0$

$(4x-3)(3x-2) = 0,$

$x = \frac{3}{4}, \frac{2}{3}$

II. $6y^2 - 5y + 1 = 0$

$6y - 2y - 3y + 1 = 0$

$2y(3y - 1) - 1(3y - 1) = 0;$

$(2y - 1)(3y - 1) = 0$

$x = \frac{1}{2}, \frac{1}{3}$

x > y

11. I. $16x^2 = 1$

$x = \pm\frac{1}{4}$

II. $3y^2 + 7y + 2 = 0$

$3y^2 + 6y + y + 2 = 0$

$(3y + 1)(y + 2) = 0$

$y = -\frac{1}{3}, -2$

x > y

12. I. $10x^2 - (18 + 15\sqrt{17})x + 9\sqrt{17} = 0$

$10x^2 - 18x - 5\sqrt{17}x + 9\sqrt{17} = 0$

$2x(5x - 9) - \sqrt{17}(5x - 9) = 0$

$(2x - \sqrt{17})(5x - 9) = 0$

$x = \sqrt{\frac{17}{2}}, \ \frac{9}{5}$

II. $3y^2 - (6 + \sqrt{17})y + 2\sqrt{17} = 0$

$3y^2 - 6y - \sqrt{17}y + 2\sqrt{17} = 0$

$3y(y - 2) - \sqrt{17}(y - 2) = 0$

$(3y - \sqrt{17})(y - 2) = 0;$

$y = \sqrt{\frac{17}{3}}, \ 2$

No relation can be established

13. I. $x - 5\sqrt{2}x + 12 = 0$

$3x - 3\sqrt{2}x - 2\sqrt{2}x + 12 = 0$

$\sqrt{x}(\sqrt{x} - 3\sqrt{2}) - 2\sqrt{2}(\sqrt{x} - 3\sqrt{2}) = 0$

$(\sqrt{x} - 2\sqrt{2})(\sqrt{x} - 3\sqrt{2}) = 0$

$\sqrt{x} = 2\sqrt{2}, 3\sqrt{2}$

$x = 8, 18$

II. $y - 7\sqrt{2y} + 24 = 0$

$y - 4\sqrt{2y} - 3\sqrt{2y} + 24 = 0$

$\sqrt{y}(\sqrt{y} - 4\sqrt{2}\ ) - 3\sqrt{2}(\sqrt{y} - 4\sqrt{2}) = 0$

$(\sqrt{y} - 3\sqrt{2}\ )(\sqrt{y} - 4\sqrt{2}\ ) = 0$

$\sqrt{y} = 3\sqrt{2}, 4\sqrt{2}$

$y = 18, 32$

x ≤ y

14. I. $\sqrt{484}x + \sqrt{225} = 183$

$22x + 15 = 183$

$22x = 168$

$x = \frac{84}{11} = 7.6$

II. $\sqrt{289}y - \sqrt{324} = 203$

$17y - 18 = 203$

$17y = 221$

$y = 13$

x < y

15. I. $\sqrt{144}\,x^3 - 9x^3 = 1536$

$12x^3 - 9x^3 = 1536$

$3x^3 = 1536$

$x^3 = 512\,;$

$x = 8$

II. $679\,y^2 - 168y^2 = 3066$

$511y^2 = 3066$

$y^2 = 6;$

$y = \pm\sqrt{6}$

x > y

16. I. $\sqrt{x + 222}\ - \sqrt{36} = \sqrt{81}$

$\sqrt{x + 222} = 9 + 6 = 15$

$x + 222 = 225$

$x = 3$

II. $14y - 25 = 59 - 7y$

$21y = 84$

$y = 4$

x < y

17. I. $x - 1 = \sqrt{81} - 4$

$x - 1 = 9 - 4 = 5$

$x = 6$

II. $y + 10 = \sqrt[3]{3375}$

$y + 10 = 15$

$y = 5$

x > y

18. I. $3x^2 + x - 2 = 0$

$3x^2 + 3x - 2x - 2 = 0$

$3x(x + 1) - 2(x + 1) = 0$

$(3x - 2)(x + 1) = 0$

$x = \frac{2}{3}, -1$

II. $y = \frac{\sqrt{256}}{\sqrt{576}}$

$y = \frac{16}{24} = \frac{4}{6} = \frac{2}{3}$

$x \leq y$

19. I. $(x - 1)^2 = 121$

$x - 1 = \pm 11$

$x = 12, -10$

II. $y^2 - 24y + 144 = 0$

$(y - 12)(y - 12) = 0;$

$y = 12, 12$

$x \leq y$

20. I. $x^4 = 256$

$x = \pm 4$

II. $y^2 - 16y + 64 = 0$

$(y - 8)(y - 8) = 0;$

$y = 8$

$x < y$

21. I. $(x + 16)^2 = 441$

$x + 16 = \sqrt{441} = \pm 21$

• $x + 16 = 21;\ \ x = 5;$

• $x + 16 = -21;\ \ x = -37$

$x = 5, -37$

II. $(y + 22)^2 = 961$

$y + 22 = \sqrt{961} = \pm 31$

• $y + 22 = 31;\ \ y = 9;$

• $y + 22 = -31;\ y = -53$

$y = 9, -53$

No relation can be established

22. I. $2x + 5y = \sqrt{2601}$

$2x + 5y = 51$

II. $7x + 3y = 77$

Solving we get $\ x = 8, y = 7$

$x = 5, -37$

$y = 9, -53$

$x > y$

23. I. $12x^2 = 6x$

$12x^2 - 6x = 0$

$6x(2x - 1) = 0;$

$x = 0, \frac{1}{2}$

II. $y + x^2 = 0.45$

Case I: $x = 0$

$y + 0 = 0.45;$

$y = 0.45$

Case II: $x = \frac{1}{2}$

$y + (0.5)^2 = 0.45;$

$y = 0.45 - 0.25$

$y = 0.2;$

$y = 0.45, 0.2$

No relation can be established

24. I. $3x + 2y = 301$

$I \times 5 + II \times 2 \rightarrow$

$15x + 10y = 1505$

$14x - 10y = 148$

$29x = 1653$

$x = 57$

II. $7x - 5y = 74$

$3(57) + 2y = 301$

$2y = 130$

$y = 65$

$x < y$

25. I. $x^2 = 256$

$x = \pm\sqrt{256} = \pm 16$

$x = 16, -16$

II. $y = \sqrt{256} = 16$

$y = 16$

$x \leq y$

PRACTICE QUESTIONS:

1. I. $x^2 - 15x + 56 = 0$

II. $y^2 - y - 30 = 0$

2. I. $x^2 + 54x + 728 = 0$

II. $y^2 + 31y + 150 = 0$

3. I. $x^2 - 45x + 506 = 0$

II. $y^2 - 9y - 360 = 0$

4. I. $2x^2 + 14x + 24 = 0$
II. $y^2 + 8y + 12 = 0$

5. I. $x^2 - 25x + 156 = 0$
II. $y^2 - 21y + 110 = 0$

6. I. $12x^2 - 7x + 1 = 0$
II. $20y^2 - 9y + 1 = 0$

7. I. $2x^2 + 11x + 15 = 0$
II. $2y^2 + 7y + 6 = 0$

8. I. $4x^2 + 23x + 33 = 0$
II. $3y^2 + 25y + 50 = 0$

9. I. $3x^2 + 20x + 32 = 0$
II. $2y^2 + 17y + 26 = 0$

10. I. $4x^2 + 33x + 65 = 0$
II. $3y^2 + 23y + 44 = 0$

11. I. $x^2 + 121 = 377$
II. $y = \sqrt[3]{4096}$

12. I. $2x + 3xy = 207$
II. $15x = \dfrac{945}{y}$

13. I. $\sqrt[3]{x - 512} = 11$
II. $y + 353 = 13$

14. I. $x^2 - 2x + 1 = 0$
II. $y - \dfrac{2}{y} = \dfrac{2}{y}$

15. I. $x^2 - 7x + 12 = 0$
II. $\dfrac{30}{y^2} = \dfrac{11}{y} - 1$

SOLUTIONS:

1. I. $x^2 - 15x + 56 = 0$
$x^2 - 7x - 8x + 56 = 0$
$x(x - 7) - 8(x - 7) = 0$
$(x - 8)(x - 7)$
$x = 7, 8$
II. $y^2 - y - 30 = 0$
$y(y - 6) + 5(y - 6) = 0$
$(y + 5)(y - 6) = 0$
$y = -5, 6$
x > y

2. I. $x^2 + 54x + 728 = 0$
$x(x + 26) + 28(x + 26) = 0$
$(x + 26)(x + 28)$
$x = -26, -28$
II. $y^2 + 31y + 150 = 0$
$y(y + 6) + 25(y + 6) = 0$
$(y + 25)(y + 6) = 0;$
$y = -25, -6$
x < y

3. I. $x^2 - 45x + 506 = 0$
$x^2 - 22x - 23x + 506 = 0$
$x(x - 22) - 23(x - 22) = 0$
$(x - 23)(x - 22) = 0$
II. $y^2 - 9y - 360 = 0$
$y^2 - 15y + 24y - 360 = 0$
$y(y - 15) + 24(y - 15) = 0$
$(y + 24)(y - 15) = 0$
No relation can be established

4. I. $2x^2 + 14x + 24 = 0$
$2x^2 + 8x + 6x + 24 = 0$
$2x(x + 4) + 6(y + 4) = 0$
$(2x + 6)(x + 4) = 0$;
$x = -3, -4$
II. $y^2 + 8y + 12 = 0$
$y^2 + 6y + 2y + 12 = 0$
$y(y + 6) + 2(y + 6) = 0$
$(y + 2)(y + 6) = 0$
$y = -2, -6$
No relation can be established

5. I. $x^2 - 25x + 156 = 0$
$x^2 - 13x - 12x + 156 = 0$
$x(x - 13) - 12(x - 13) = 0$

$(x - 12)(x - 13) = 0$

x = 13, 12

II. $y^2 - 21y + 110 = 0$

$y^2 - 11y - 10y + 110 = 0$

$y(y - 11) - 10(y - 11) = 0$

$(y - 10)(y - 11) = 0$

$y = 10, 11$

x > y

6. I. $12x^2 - 7x + 1 = 0$

$12x^2 - 4x - 3x + 1 = 0$

$4x(3x - 1) - 1(3x - 1)$

$(4x - 1)(3x - 1) = 0;$

$x = \frac{1}{4}, \frac{1}{3}$

II. $20y^2 - 9y + 1 = 0$

$20y^2 - 5y - 4y + 1 = 0$

$5y(4y - 1) - 1(4y - 1) = 0$

$(5y - 1)\ (4y - 1) = 0$

$y = \frac{1}{5}, \frac{1}{4}$

x ≥ y

7. I. $2x^2 + 11x + 15 = 0$

$2x^2 + 6x + 5x + 15 = 0$

$2x(x + 3) + 5(x + 3) = 0$

$(2x + 5)(x + 3) = 0;$

$x = -\frac{5}{2}, -3$

II. $2y^2 + 7y + 6 = 0$

$2y^2 + 4y + 3y + 6 = 0$

$2y(y + 2) + 3(y + 2) = 0$

$(2y + 3)(y + 2) = 0;$

$y = \frac{-3}{2}, -2$

x < y

8. I. $4x^2 + 23x + 33 = 0$

$4x^2 + 12x + 11x + 33 = 0$

$4x(x + 3) + 11(x + 3) = 0$

$(4x + 11)(x + 3) = 0;$

$x = -\frac{11}{4}, -3$

II. $3y^2 + 25y + 50 = 0$

$3y^2 + 15y + 10y + 50 = 0$

$3y(y + 5) + 10(y + 5) = 0$

$(3y + 10)(y + 5) = 0;$

$y = -\frac{10}{3}, -5$

x > y

9. I. $3x^2 + 20x + 32 = 0$

$3x^2 + 12x + 8x + 32 = 0$

$3x(x + 4) + 8(x + 4) = 0$

$(3x + 8)(x + 4) = 0;$

$x = -\frac{8}{3}, -4$

II. $2y^2 + 17y + 26 = 0$

$2y^2 + 8y + 9y + 36 = 0$

$2y(y + 4) + 9(y + 4) = 0$

$(2y + 9)(y + 4) = 0;$

$y = \frac{-9}{2}, -4$

x ≥ y

10. I. $4x^2 + 33x + 65 = 0$

$4x^2 + 20x + 13x + 65 = 0$

$4x(x + 5) + 13(x + 5) = 0$

$(4x + 13)(x + 5) = 0$

$x = -5, -\frac{13}{4}$

II. $3y^2 + 23y + 44 = 0$

$3y^2 + 12y + 11y + 44 = 0$

$3y(y + 4) + 11(y + 4) = 0$

$(3y + 11)(y + 4) = 0$

No relation can be established

11. I. $x^2 + 121 = 377$

$x^2 = 256$

$x = \pm 16$

II. $y = \sqrt[3]{4096}$

$y = 16$

x ≤ y

12. I. $2x + 3xy = 207$

II. $15x = \frac{945}{y}$

$15xy = 945$

$3xy = 189$

Subs. in I: $2x + 189 = 207$

$2x = 18$

$x = 9$

$$3xy = 189$$
$$27y = 189$$
$$y = \frac{189}{21} = 7$$
x > y

13. I. $\sqrt[3]{x - 512} = 11$

$x - 512 = 1331$

$x = 1843$

II. $y + 353 = 13$

$y = 2197 - 353$

$y = 1844$

x < y

14. I. $x^2 - 2x + 1 = 0$

$x^2 - x - x + 1 = 0$

$(x - 1)^2 = 0$;

$x = 1, 1$

II. $y - \frac{2}{y} = \frac{2}{y}$

$y^2 - 2 = 2$

$y^2 = 4$

$y = \pm 2$

No relation can be established

15. I. $x^2 - 7x + 12 = 0$

$x^2 - 4x - 3x + 12$

$(x - 4) - 3(x - 4)$

$(x - 3)(x - 4);$

$x = 3, 4$

II. $\frac{30}{y^2} = \frac{11}{y} - 1$

$30 = 11y - y^2$

$y^2 - 11y + 30 = 0$

$y^2 - 6y - 5y + 30 = 0$

$y(y - 6) - 5(y - 6) = 0$

$(y - 5)(y - 6) = 0$

$y = 5, 6$

x < y

PROBLEMS BASED ON AGES

If present age is x,

- Age n years ago = $x - n$
- Age n years later/hence = $x + n$
- n times present age = nx
- $\frac{1}{n}$ of age = $\frac{x}{n}$

Ages in the ratio a:b will be ax & bx respectively.

EXERCISE:

1. The present ages of Karthi & Sasi are 24 years & 16 years respectively. Before how many years, the ratio of their ages is 3:1?
   (A) 12 years   (B) 14 years
   (C) 10 years   (D) 13 years
   (E) None of these

2. The ratios of the ages of Anu & Priya after 10 years is 3:2 and the ratio of their present ages is 5:3. Find the present ages of Anu and Priya.
   (A) 30 & 50   (B) 40 & 50
   (C) 50 & 40   (D) 50 & 30
   (E) None of these

3. The ratio of present ages of P&Q is 4:5. After 5 years, the ratio of their ages will be 9:11. What will be the ratio of their ages, 5 years before?
   (A) 7:8   (B) 7:9
   (C) 9:7   (D) 8:7
   (E) None of these

4. 10 years before ratio of ages of A & B is 8:9. 10 years from now, their ages will be in the ratio of 13:14. Find the sum of present ages A & B?
   (A) 84 years   (B) 86 years
   (C) 88 years   (D) 85 years
   (E) None of these

5. Anu is as much younger to Kumar as she is older to Surya. If total age of Surya & Kumar is 54, what is the age of Anu?
   (A) 25 years   (B) 27 years
   (C) 26 years   (D) 24 years
   (E) None of these

6. 7 years ago, A's age is 6 years more than B's age. 12 years from now, the ratio of the ages of B & C will be in the ratio 5:6. If present age difference between B & C is 5 years, then what will be the present age of A?
   (A) 19 Years   (B) 18 years
   (C) 17 years   (D) 16 years
   (E) None of these

7. The ratio of the present age of girl to her brother is 4:3. The ratio of their ages, 6 years from now is 5:4. Find their present ages?
   (A) 24, 20   (B) 22, 18
   (C) 24, 18   (D) 24, 21
   (E) None of these

8. 10 years ago, the father's age is thrice the age of his daughter & the ratio of present age of mother to age of daughter is 2:1. If father is 5 years older to mother, then find the age of father.
   (A) 51 years   (B) 53 years
   (C) 57 years   (D) 55 years
   (E) None of these

9. B's age is 3 times more than A's age. B is 5 years older than C. D is 10 years older than C. The ratio of the ages C to D, 2 years ago was 5:7. What is the present age of A?
   (A) 6 years   (B) 8 years
   (C) 7 years   (D) 9 years
   (E) None of these

10. In a family, the age of father, mother and son is 46 yrs, 42 yrs and 16 yrs respectively. After 8 years, the son has married a girl whose age is two years less than his age at that time of marriage. After 2 years, they had a daughter. Find the average age of the family when the daughter is 2 years old.
    (A) 33.2 years   (B) 32.8 years
    (C) 33.6 years   (D) 34.5 years
    (E) None of these

11. The total present age of A & B is 33 years. 6 years later, the sum of ages of B and C will be 44 yrs. 3 years further, the sum of age of A & C will be 53. Find the ratio of present age A & C.
    (A) 18:17   (B) 17:16
    (C) 18:15   (D) 18:19
    (E) None of these

12. There are 5 members in a family. The average age of the family is 28. The ratio of age of youngest and eldest person in the family is 1:3. The ratio of the age of remaining three persons is 10 : 13 : 19 ,

then what is the age of the second youngest person in the family , if the youngest person is 14 years?
(A) 18 years   (B) 20 years
(C) 22 years   (D) 16 years
(E) None of these

13. A family has father, mother, son & daughter in law. 4 years ago, the son got married. Average age of the family after one year of son's marriage was 27 years and average age of family 7 years ago was 25 years. What is the present age of the daughter in law?
    (A) 23 years   (B) 22 years
    (C) 26 years   (D) 24 years
    (E) None of these

14. Sara's present age is $3/7\ th$ of her father's present age. Sara's brother is four year younger to Sara. The ratio between present ages of Sara's father and Sara's brother is 14:5. What is the present age of Sara?
    (A) 24 years   (B) 22 years
    (C) 28 years   (D) 25 years
    (E) None of these

15. The sum of present ages of a mother and her daughter is 60 years. Six years ago, mother's age was five times the age of the daughter. After 4 years, daughter's age will be.
    (A) 16 yrs   (B) 20 yrs
    (C) 17 yrs   (D) 18 yrs
    (E) None of these

16. When 6 is subtracted from the present age of P and resultant is divided by 18 then age of Q is found. R is 5 years old and Q is 2 years younger than R. What is the present age of P?
    (A) 58 yrs   (B) 60 yrs
    (C) 40 yrs   (D) 54 yrs
    (E) None of these

17. The respective ratio between karthi's age after 3 years and Shoba's age 3 years ago is 10:9 and the respective ratio between the Karthi's age 3 years ago & Shoba's age after 3 years is 17:21. What is Karthi's 1 year ago?
(A) 37 yrs   (B) 38 yrs
(C) 36 yrs   (D) 39 yrs
(E) None of these

18. The average age of a man and his wife was 25 years at the time of their marriage, who got married 4 years back. Now in the family there is a child including husband & wife and the average age of the family is 20 years. The age of child is.
(A) 2 yrs   (B) 1 yr
(C) 3 yrs   (D) 4 yrs
(E) None of these

19. Ratio of age of Raj to Sweta, 4 years ago was 5:6 while ratio of present age of Mohan to Sweta is 5:4. If 2 years later, sum of age of Raj and Mohan will be 63 years, then find the difference between present age of Raj and Sweta?
(A) 8 years   (B) 4 years
(C) 3 years   (D) 5 years
(E) None of these

20. The present age of Sasi's son is $1/3^{rd}$ of that of his age. 4 years hence, the ratio of ages of Sasi and his son will be 5:2. Find Sasi's age 5 years ago.
(A) 38 yrs   (B) 33 yrs
(C) 35 yrs   (D) 31 yrs
(E) None of these

21. In a group of 20 members, the average age is 25 years the average age of first 18 members is 24 years. What will be the average age of last 2 members?
(A) 28   (B) 40
(C) 34   (D) 32
(E) None of these

22. B is 3 years older than A & B is 3 years younger than C. 3 years hence, the ratio between the ages of A and C will be 4:5. What is the sum of present ages of A, B and C?
(A) 72 yrs   (B) 70 yrs
(C) 68 yrs   (D) 75 yrs
(E) None of these

23. Dhana's present age is $2/7^{th}$ of her father's present age. Dhana's sister is 3 years older to Dhana. The respective ratio between present ages of Dhana's father and Dhana's sister is 14:5. What is Dhana's present age?
(A) 12 yrs   (B) 14 yrs
(C) 10 yrs   (D) 11 yrs
(E) None of these

24. Sum of present ages of A & B together is 90 years and B is 4 years older than C. If present age of A is 72% of that of C, then find sum of present ages of A and C together.
(A) 90 years   (B) 76 years
(C) 86 years   (D) 84 years
(E) None of these

25. Age of Sunil 2 years later is equal to present age of Arun and ratio of present age of Ram to Sunil is 10:7. If difference between present ages of Ram and Arun is 10 years. Find sum of present ages of Sunil and Arun.
(A) 50 years   (B) 58 years
(C) 54 years   (D) 60 years
(E) None of these

SOLUTIONS

1. (A) Let the required no. of years be x.
$$\frac{24-x}{16-x} = \frac{3}{1}$$
$$24 - x = 3(16 - x)$$
$$24 - x = 48 - 3x$$

$2x = 24$

$x = 12 \; years$

2. (D) Let present ages of Anu and Priya be A and P respectively.

$\frac{A+10}{P+10} = \frac{3}{5}$ & $\frac{A}{P} = \frac{5}{3} \rightarrow A = \frac{5}{3}P$

$2A + 20 = 3P + 30$

$2A - 3P = 10$

$Subs. A, \; 2\left(\frac{5}{3}P\right) - 3P = 10$

$10p - 9p = 30$

$p = 30 \; years$

$A = \frac{5}{3} \times 30; \quad A = 50 \; years$

3. $(B)\; P = 4x; Q = 5x$

$\frac{P+5}{Q+5} = \frac{9}{11}$

$\frac{4x+5}{5x+5} = \frac{9}{11}$

$44x + 55 = 45x + 45$

$x = 10$

At present, P = 40 years; Q = 50 years

5 years before

P: Q = 35:45 = 7:9

4. (C) Acc. to the q n,

$\frac{A-10}{B-10} = \frac{8}{9}$

$\frac{A+10}{B+10} = \frac{13}{14}$

On solving we get, A = 42, B = 46

Sum of their present ages = 88 years

5. (B) Let ages of Anu, Kumar and Surya be A, K & S respectively.

$K = A + x$

$S = A - x$

$2A = K + S = 54$

$A = \frac{54}{2} = 27 years$

Age of Anu is 27 years.

6. (A) Age difference between B & C

= 5 years = 6x-5x

x = 5 years

12 years from now, the age of B = 25 years,

C = 30 years

Present ages of B = 13 years, C = 18 years

Age difference between A & B = 6 years

A = B + 6 = 13 + 6 = 19 years.

7. (C) Acc. to the Qn.,

$\frac{4x+6}{3x+6} = \frac{5}{4}$

$16x + 24 = 15x + 30$

$x = 6$

Present age of the girl = 4(6) = 24 years & her brother = 3(6) = 18 years

8. (D) F = M+5; M = F-5

10 years ago, (F-10) = 3(D-10)

M : D = 2:1

F-10 = 3D-30

3D = F+20

$D = \frac{F+20}{3}$

Subs. D & M

$\frac{F-5}{\frac{F+20}{3}} = \frac{2}{1};$

$3(F - 5) = 2(F + 20)$

3F -15 = 2F+40

F = 40 +15

F = 55 years

9. (B) Let age of A be x.

Age of B = x +3x =4x.

Age of C = 4x-5

Age of D = 4x -5+10 = 4x +5

$\frac{4x-5-2}{4x+5-2} = \frac{5}{7}$

$\frac{4x-7}{4x+3} = \frac{5}{7}$

$28x - 49 = 20x + 15$

$8x = 64$

$x = 8 \; years$

10. (C) At the time, when the daughter is 2 years old

Age of father = 46 + 8 + 4 = 58 years

Age of mother = 42 + 8 + 4 = 54 years

Age of son   = 16 + 8 + 4 = 28 years

Age of son's wife = 22 + 4 = 26 years

Required average $= \dfrac{58+54+28+26+2}{5}$

$$= \dfrac{168}{5} = 33.6 \; years.$$

11. (A) $A + B = 33$

$B + 6 + C + 6 = 44$

$B + C = 32$

$A + 9 + C + 9 = 53$

$A + C = 35$

This we get 2 (A+B+C) = 100

A + B + C = 50

A = 18, B = 15, C = 17

Ratio of present of A & C = 18:17

12. (B) Total age of family = 5 × 28 = 140

Age of youngest person = 14 years

Eldest person = $14 × 3 = 42 \; years$

Age of remaining 3 persons

= 140- (42+14) = 84

10x + 13x + 19x = 84

42x = 84; x = 2

Age of second youngest person

= 10(2)

= 20 years.

13. (D) Let present age of father, mother, son & daughter in law be a, b, c and d.

$$\dfrac{a+b+c+d-4(3)}{4} = 27$$

$$a + b + c + d = (27 × 4) + 12$$

$$= 120$$

$$\dfrac{a+b+c-3(7)}{3} = 25$$

$$a + b + c = (25 × 3) + 21 = 96$$

$$d = 120 - 96 = 24 \; years.$$

14. (A) Let Sara father's present age be x.

Sara age $\dfrac{3}{7}x$.

Sara brother's age $= \dfrac{3}{7}x - 4$

$$\dfrac{x}{\frac{3}{7}x - 4} = \dfrac{14}{5}$$

$$5x = 14\left(\dfrac{3}{7}x - 4\right)$$

$$5x = 6x - 56$$

$$x = 56$$

Sara's age $= \dfrac{3}{7}(56) = 24 \; years$

15. (D) M + D = 60

M - 6 = 5(D-6) = 5D-30

M = 5D - 30 + 6 = 5D - 24

Subs M,

5D - 24 + D = 60

6D = 84

D = 14 Years

After 4 years, daughter's age will be 18 years.

16. (B) $\dfrac{P-6}{18} = Q$

$R = 5$

$Q = R - 2 = 3 \; years$

$\dfrac{P-6}{18} = 3$

$P - 6 = 54$

$P = 60 \; years$

17. (C) Let present ages of Karthi and Shoba be a and b years respectively

$\dfrac{a+3}{b-3} = \dfrac{10}{9} \rightarrow 9a + 27 = 10b - 30$

$9a - 10b = 57 \ldots \ldots \ldots \; 1$

$\dfrac{a-3}{b+3} = \dfrac{17}{21} \rightarrow 21a - 63 = 17b + 51$

$21a - 17b = 114 \ldots \ldots \ldots 2$

On solving 1 & 2, a = 37, b = 39

Karthi's age 1 year ago = 36 years.

18. (A) At present, the sum of ages of man & wife = $(25 × 2) + 8 = 58 \; years$

At present, the sum of ages of all members $20 × 3 = 60 \; years$

Age of child   = 60 - 58 = 2 years.

19. (B) Let age of Raj and Swathi 4 years
ago be $5x$ and $6x$ respectively
2 years later, age of Raj
$$= (5x + 6) years$$
Age of Mohan, 2 years later
$$= \left(\frac{6x+4}{4} \times 5 \right) + 2$$
Acc .to the qn.,
$$(5x + 6) + \left(\frac{6x + 4}{4} \times 5 \right) + 2 = 63$$
$$20x + 24 + 30x + 20 + 8 = 252$$
$$50x + 52 = 252$$
$$50x = 200, x = 4$$
Age difference between Raj & Sweta
$= x = 4$ years.

20. (D) Let present age of Sasi and his son
be 3x and x respectively
$$\frac{3x+4}{x+4} = \frac{5}{2} \rightarrow 6x + 8 = 5x + 20$$
$$x = 12$$
Sasi's age 5years ago $= 3(12) - 5$
$= 36 - 5 = 31$ $years$

21. (C) Sum of age of all members
$= 20 \times 25 = 500$
Sum of age of first 18 members
$= 18 \times 24 = 432$
Sum of age of last 2 members
$= 500 - 432 = 68$
Average age $= \frac{68}{2} = 34$

22. (A) B=A+3; A = B -3
B = C -3;
C = B +3
Acc. to the Qn., $\frac{A+3}{C+3} = \frac{4}{5}$; $\frac{B-3+3}{B+3+3} = \frac{4}{5}$
$5B = 4B + 24$; $B = 24$
Present age of A = 21, C =27
Sum of their ages = 21+24+27
= 72 years.

23. (A) Present age of Dhana's father $=14x$
Present age of Dhana's sister $=5x$
Dhana's present age

$$= \frac{2}{7} \times 14x = 4x.$$
$$5x - 4x = 3$$
$$x = 3$$
Dhana's present age = 12 years

24. (C) Let present ages of A, B & C be a, b
and c respectively.
a + b = 90
b = c + 4
a = 0.72c
Subs Equation of b in a + b
a + c + 4 = 90
a + c = 86

25. (B) Let present age Ram & Sunil be 10x
and 7x years respectively
Present age of Arun = 7x+2
Acc. to the qn.,
$$10x - (7x + 2) = 10$$
$$3x - 2 = 10$$
$$3x = 12$$
$$x = 4$$
Required sum of ages
$= 7x+7x+2 = 58$ years

PRACTICE QUESTIONS:

1. The difference between the ages of A & B
is 16 years and their ratio between their
ages is 3:5. What is the sum of their ages
6 years hence?
(A) 76 years   (B) 78 years
(C) 74 years   (D) 80 years
(E) None of these

2. The present age of mother is 7 times of her
daughter's age ten years ago, mother's age
was 12 times of her daughter's age. Find
the present age of her daughter.
(A) 18 years   (B) 21 years
(C) 22 years   (D) 25 years
(E) None of these

3. The present ages of A & B are in the ratio of 7:4 respectively and 8 years from now, their ages after will be in the ratio 3:2. Find the average age of A and B, 4 years ago
(A) 12 years   (B) 18 years
(C) 16 years   (D) 20 years
(E) None of these

4. In a class, the average age of 15 students is 15 years. 9 students among them has 16 years and 5 students among them has the average of 14 years. What is the age of 15th student?
(A) 13 years   (B) 15 years
(C) 12 years   (D) 11 years
(E) None of these

5. The ratio of present ages of A and B is 7:9. After 6 years, B will be 8 years older than A. Find the age of A, 4 years ago.
(A) 24 years   (B) 22 years
(C) 28 years   (D) 30 years
(E) None of these

6. A's present age is $3/4\,th$ of B's present age. C is $5/8\,th$ of B's present age. If difference between the difference of C and B's age and difference of B and A's age is 6 years, then find the average of their ages (all three of them), 2 years ago.
(A) 25 years   (B) 30 years
(C) 38 years   (D) 36 years
(E) None of these

7. Three years ago, average of A, B, C is 27 years. Four years hence, ratio of A and C's age is 7:10. If B is 6 years younger than C, then find present age of A.
(A) 20 years   (B) 24 years
(C) 22 years   (D) 25 years
(E) None of these

8. Anu's age is $4/5_{th}$ of Bindu's age while age of Bindu after 5 years will be equal to twice the present age of Diana. If sum of age of all three is 37 years. Find the present age of Anu.
(A) 12 years   (B) 14 years
(C) 16 years   (D) 10 years
(E) None of these

9. The present age of a mother is twice as that of her son. 10 years ago, her age was thrice the age of her son. What will be the ratio of the ages of mother and son after 15 years from now?
(A) 12:8   (B) 11:8
(C) 11:7   (D) 7:11
(E) None of these

10. Ratio of after of Sasi and Shoba is 4:5. After 5 years their ages will be in the ratio 21:25. Find the difference of their ages.
(A) 5 years   (B) 8 years
(C) 4 years   (D) 6 years
(E) None of these

11. A person is 16 years older than his daughter. After 2 years the person's age will be double the age of his daughter, then find the age of his daughter 6 years hence.
(A) 20 years   (B) 16 years
(C) 18 years   (D) 22 years
(E) None of these

12. Present age of P is 60% more than that of Q and average of present age of Q and R is 35 years. If 5 years ago, sum of ages of P and Q is 55 years, then find the difference between present age of P and R.
(A) 2 years   (B) 4 years
(C) 8 years   (D) 5 years
(E) None of these

13. P, Q and R are members of a family. Q and R are the two sons of P. The ratio of age of P and Q is 5:2 and that of Q and R is 8:5. Also, Q is 6 years older than R. find the ratio of P, Q and R after 10 years.
(A) 26:13:10   (B) 25:13:10
(C) 24:12:7   (D) 25:12:10
(E) None of these

14. Jothi has 2 daughters named Shoba and Karthiga. The ratio of Jothi and Karthiga's age is 5:1 and the ratio between Jothi and Shoba's age 2 years ago was 3:1. If Shoba is 6 years elder than Karthiga, find Jothi's age when Shoba was born.
(A) 24 yrs   (B) 21 yrs
(C) 23 yrs   (D) 22 yrs
(E) None of these

15. Average age of a man & his wife at the time of marriage is 27 years. After 2 years and 4 years respectively, a boy child and a girl child is born. Find the average age of family after 9 years from the year they got married.
(A) 20   (B) 21
(C) 19   (D) 22
(E) None of these

SOLUTIONS

1. (A) $A \sim B = 16$
$$5x - 3x = 16$$
$$2x = 16$$
$$x = 8$$
Their ages are 24 and 40. Sum of their ages 6 years hence $= 36 + 46$
$= 76$ years.

2. (C) Let present age of mother & daughter be M & D respectively
M = 7D
M − 10 = 12(D−10) =12D −1 20
M = 12D − 110

7D = 12D−110
5D = 110
D = 22 Years

3. (B) Let present ages of A and B be 7x and 4x respectively.
$$\frac{7x+8}{4x+8} = \frac{3}{2}$$
$$14x + 16 = 12x + 24$$
$$2x = 8; x = 4 \ years$$
Age of A, 4 years ago $=7(4)-4 = 24$ years
Age of B, 4 years ago $= 4(4)-4 = 12$ years
$$Average = \frac{24+12}{2} = \frac{36}{2} = 18 \ years$$

4. (D) Required age of 15th student
$$= (15 \times 15) - [(9 \times 16) + 5(14)]$$
$$= 225 - (70 + 144)$$
$$= 225 - 214 \quad = 11 \ years$$

5. (A) $\frac{A}{B} = \frac{7}{9}$
<u>Note:</u> Age difference between any two persons remains the same, throughout the years.
B = A +8
$$\frac{A}{A+8} = \frac{7}{9} \rightarrow 9A = 7A + 56$$
2A = 56
A =28
Age of A, 4 years ago = 24 years.

6. (D) We got the ratio 3:4 & 5:8 on equalizing, can take
A's age = 6x, B's age = 8x, C's age = 5x
Acc. To the qn.,
$$(8x - 5x) - (8x - 6x) = 6$$
3x−2x=6
x=6
Required average
$$= \frac{6(6)+8(6)+5(6)-6}{3}$$
$$= \frac{36+48+30-6}{3} = 36 \ years$$

7. (B) 3 years ago, sum of their ages

$3 \times 27 = 81 \ years$

A years hence, age of $A = 7x, C = 10x,=$

$\quad B = 10x - 6$

Sum of their ages, 4 years hence

$\rightarrow 7x + 10x + 10x - 6 = 81 + 7(3)$

$27x - 6 = 81 + 21 = 102$

$\quad 27x = 108$

$\quad x = 4$

Present age of $A = 7x - 4 = 24 \ years$.

8. (A) Let present age of Anu, Bindu and Diana be A, B, D respectively

$A = \frac{4}{5}B;$

$B + 5 = 2D;$

$A + B + D = 37$

$\frac{4}{5}B + B + \frac{B+5}{2} = 37$

$\quad 8B + 10B + 5B + 25 = 370$

$23B + 25 = 370$

$B = \frac{345}{23} = 15$

Present age of Anu $= \frac{4}{5}(15)$

$\quad\quad\quad = 12 \ years.$

9. (C) M = 2S

$\quad$ M-10 = 3(S-10)

$\quad$ M-10 = 3S - 30

$\quad$ M-3S = -20

$\quad$ 2S- 3S = -20

$\quad$ S = 20 years;

$\quad$ M = 40 years

$\quad$ 15 years from now, the ratio of age of mother and son will be

$\frac{40+15}{20+15} = \frac{55}{35} = \frac{11}{7}$

10. (C) Let ages of Sasi and Shoba be 4x and 5x respectively

$\frac{4x+5}{5x+5} = \frac{21}{25}$

$100x + 125 = 105x + 105$

$5x = 20$

$x = 4 \ years$

Difference between their ages

$= x = 4$ years.

11. (A) P = 16 +D

$\quad$ P+2 = 2(D+2) = 2D+4

$\quad$ Subs., P

$\quad$ 16+D+2 = 2D +4

$\quad$ D = 14 years

$\quad$ Age of daughter 6 years hence

$\quad\quad\quad = 20$ years.

12. (D) Let present age of Q be 5x years.

Present age of P $= 5x \times \frac{160}{100}$

$\quad\quad\quad = 8x \ years.$

Present age of R $= (35 \times 2) - 5x$

$\quad\quad\quad = 70 - 5x \ years$

Acc.to the qn.,

$\quad (8x - 5) + (5x - 5) = 55;$

$\quad\quad 13x = 65$

$\quad\quad x = 5$

Required difference

$\quad = 40 \sim (70 - 25)$

$\quad = 40 \sim 45 = 5 \ years$

13. (B) P: Q = 5:2

$\quad$ Q: R = 8:5

$Q \sim R = 6 \ years$

$8x - 5x = 6$

$3x = 6; x = 2$

Age of $Q = 16, R = 10 \ years$

$P: Q = 5: 2$

Age of $P = \frac{16}{2} \times 5 = 40 \ years$.

Required ratio

$= (40+10): (16+10) :(10+10)$

$= 50: 26: 20 = 25: 13: 10.$

14. (D) Let Jothi, Shoba and Karthiga's present age be J, S and K respectively.

$\frac{J}{K} = \frac{5}{1}; \ J = 5K$

$\frac{J-2}{S-2} = \frac{3}{1} \rightarrow J - 2 = 3S - 6$

$3S - J = 4$

$S = K + 6$

Subs. S & J,

3(K+6)-5K = 4;

2K =14;

K= 7 years

S = 13 years; J = 35 years

When Shoba was born, Jothi was

35-13 = 22 years.

15.(B) Sum of age of couple at time of marriage $= 27 \times 2 = 54 \ years$

Total age of family after 9 years

$= 54 + 18 + 6 + 4 = 84$

Required average $= \dfrac{84}{4} = 21$

Unit **6**

AVERAGES

Average is generally defined as the mean value of a certain number of observations. It refers to the ratio sum of all observations divided by the total number of observations.

Formulas:

- Average $= \dfrac{Sum\ of\ observations}{Number\ of\ observations}$

- Weighted average $= \dfrac{w_1x_1 + w_2x_2 + ... + w_nx_n}{w_1 + w_2 + ... + w_n}$;

$x_1, x_2, x_3, \ldots x_n$ are averages &

$w_1, w_2, w_3, \ldots w_n$ are their respective weightages (no. of observations)

In number systems:

The average of

- First n natural nos.: $\dfrac{(n+1)}{2}$
- First n even no's: $n+1$
- First n odd no's: n
- Consecutive nos.: $\dfrac{first\ no. + last\ no}{2}$
- 1 to n odd no's: $\dfrac{last\ odd\ no. + 1}{2}$
- 1 to n even no's: $\dfrac{last\ even\ no. + 2}{2}$
- Squares of first n natural no: $\dfrac{(n+1)(2n+1)}{6}$
- Cubes of first n natural no's: $\dfrac{n(n+1)^2}{4}$
- n multiples of any no: $\dfrac{(n+1)}{2} \times number$

Note:

- If each observation is increased/decreased by a certain quantity 'n', then value of mean also increases/decreases by the same quantity 'n'.

- If each observation is multiplied/divided by a certain quantity 'n', then value of mean also gets multiplied/divided by the same quantity 'n'.

- If the same value is added to half of the quantities & the same value is subtracted from other half quantities, then there will not be any change in the final value of the average.

Methods of approach:

<u>Eg</u>: If a person with age 60 joins a group of 5 persons with average age of 48 years. What will be new average age of group?

1) <u>Standard approach:</u>
   Total age $= (5 \times 48) + 60 = 300$
   Total people $= 5 + 1 = 6$
   New average $= 300/6 = 50$

2) <u>Deviation approach:</u>
   Since 60 is 12 more than 48, by joining new person, total will increase by 12 & number of persons increase to 6, thus the average will increase by 2 $(\because \dfrac{12}{6})$

   New average is $48 + 2 = 50$

EXERCISE

1. Find the average of 10,12,14,16,18,20
   (A) 15   (B) 14
   (C) 16   (D) 13
   (E) None of these

2. What is the average of first eight multiples of 6?
   (A) 25   (B) 28   (C) 27
   (D) 26   (E) None of these

3. Find the average of all odd nos. & even nos. from 1 to 30
   (A) 16,17   (B) 14,15   (C) 14,16
   (D) 15,16   (E) None of these

4. Find the average of cubes of first 7 natural nos.
   (A) 110   (B) 112   (C) 114
   (D) 116   (E) None of these

5. Average of five consecutive positive odd integers is 13. Find the greatest number among them.
   (A) 18   (B) 16   (C) 17
   (D) 19   (E) None of these

6. The average monthly salary of non-teaching faculties is Rs 6000 & that of teaching faculties is Rs 8000. The average monthly salary of entire staffs in an office is Rs 7200. If there are 6 teaching faculties, find the no. of non-teaching faculties in the office.
   (A) 4   (B) 3   (C) 5
   (D) 7   (E) None of these

7. Average marks of 10 students is 62. If the highest & the lowest marks among them are not considered, the average is 59.5. If the lowest mark is 47, find the highest mark.
   (A) 98   (B) 95   (C) 99
   (D) 97   (E) None of these

8. Two classes A & B with 35 & 25 students respectively, have attendance percentage of 80% each on a particular day. What is the attendance average of both the classes on that day?
   (A) 75%   (B) 80%   (C) 82%
   (D) 78%   (E) None of these

9. The average monthly expenditure of a family for first four months of a year is Rs 8350, for next 5 months Rs 7560, for last three months is Rs 8070. The family saves Rs 6590 during the whole year. Find the average monthly income of the family during the whole year.
   (A) Rs 8500   (B) Rs 8000   (C) Rs 8750
   (D) Rs 8250   (E) None of these

10. The average weight of 4 men is increased by 1.5 kg, when one of them whose weight is 69 kg, is replaced by another man. What is the weight of the new man?
    (A) 74 kg   (B) 76 kg   (C) 75 kg
    (D) 72kg   (E) None of these

11. The average age of 20 students in a class is 18 years. One student aged 20 years left the class and two students came in his place whose ages differ by 4 years. If the new average in the class remains unchanged, the age of the younger new student is
    (A) 14 yrs   (B) 17 yrs   (C) 16 yrs
    (D) 19 yrs   (E) None of these

12. If average of 9, 2-digit no. is increased by 5 when the digits of one of the numbers are interchanged. The difference between the digits of that number is
    (A) 4   (B) 5   (C) 3
    (D) 6   (E) None of these

13. The average runs scored by a batsman in 25 innings is 26. After 26th innings, his average becomes 28. How many run does the batsman score in his 26th innings?
    (A) 76   (B) 75   (C) 78
    (D) 80   (E) None of these

14. The average of marks scored by students in a class is 34. The average mark of the girls in the class is 40 and that of boys is 30. What is the percentage of girls in class?
    (A) 32 %   (B) 40 %   (C) 36 %
    (D) 45 %   (E) None of these

15. Find the average of all prime nos. between 10 to 35.

(A) $143/7$ (B) $141/7$ (C) $142/7$

(D) $144/7$ (E) None of these

16. Find the average of squares of first 11 natural nos.

(A) 45 (B) 46 (C) 48

(D) 47 (E) None of these

17. The average of 4 consecutive nos. is 33.5 What is the sum of middle two nos.?

(A) 65 (B) 66 (C) 68

(D) 67 (E) None of these

18. The average of 6 numbers is 11. The average of 4 nos. among them is 10. What is the average of remaining two nos.?

(A) 13 (B) 10 (C) 12

(D) 6 (E) None of these

19. Three nos. a, b, c are given. The average of first and third nos. is 24 more than that of average of second and third nos. Find out the difference between the first and second nos.

(A) 12 (B) 24 (C) 48

(D) 36 (E) None of these

20. A man covers half of the total distance with 12 km/hr and another half distance with 24 km/hr. Find his average speed.

(A) 12 km/hr (B) 16 km/hr

(C) 14 km/hr (D) 15 km/hr

(E) None of these

21. The average monthly income of 8 members of a friends group is Rs 37,000 and the average monthly income of remaining 7 persons is Rs 40,000. Find the average monthly income of the group.

(A) Rs 38400 (B) Rs 37400

(C) Rs 37800 (D) Rs 38200

(E) None of these

22. Average score of a batsman in his initial 30 innings is `a'. In next two innings he scored 96 and 58 runs so that his average increased by 2 runs. Find his new average.

(A) 45 (B) 46 (C) 48

(D) 47 (E) None of these.

23. In a music class, an old student was replaced by a new student. It was found that the average age of five members of the class is same as it was 3 years ago. The sum of the ages of the replaced & the new members is 29. Find the age of the new member.

(A) 8 years (B) 7 years (C) 12 years

(D) 14 years (E) None of these

24. A student distributed an average of 3 chocolates per student on her birthday. When two teachers came, she gave them 16 chocolates each, the average chocolate distributed per head increased by 1. Find the no. of students.

(A) 24 (B) 25 (C) 23

(D) 22 (E) None of these

25. The average marks of 48 students in a class is 73. But after re-checking it was found that 5 students got 25 marks less & 1 student got 29 marks more than the recorded marks. If the correction is made, find the new average of the class.

(A) 70 (B) 72 (C) 75

(D) 71 (E) None of these

26. The average age of 12 students in a class was calculated as 21 years. But later, it was found that the actual age of one of the students was 26 years & not 14 years. What is the actual average age of the class?

(A) 22 yrs (B) 21 yrs (C) 23yrs

(D) 24 yrs (E) None of these

SOLUTIONS:

1. (A) $\dfrac{10+12+14+16+18+20}{6} = \dfrac{90}{6} = 15$

2. (C) $\dfrac{(n+1)\times No.}{2} = \dfrac{6\times(8+1)}{2} = \dfrac{54}{2} = 27$

3. (D) Average of odd nos. $= \dfrac{last\ odd\ no.+1}{2}$

$\qquad = \dfrac{29+1}{2} = \dfrac{30}{2} = 15$

Average of even nos. $= \dfrac{last\ even\ no.+2}{2}$

$\qquad = \dfrac{30+2}{2} = \dfrac{32}{2} = 16$

4. (B) $\dfrac{n(n+1)^2}{4} = \dfrac{7(7+1)^2}{4} = 112$

5. (C) Let nos. be x, x+2, x+4, x+6, x+8

$\qquad \therefore \dfrac{5x+20}{5} = 13$

$\qquad 5x = 65 - 20 = 45;$

$\qquad x = 9$

Greatest no. $= 9+8 = 17$

6. (A) $\dfrac{8000\times6 + 6000\times x}{6+x} = 7200$

$\qquad 48000 + 6000x = 43200 + 7200x$

$\qquad 1200\ x = 4800;$

$\qquad x = 4$

7. (D) Sum of total scores $= 10 \times 62 = 620$

$\qquad \dfrac{Total\ score - h - 1}{8} = 59.5$

$\qquad \dfrac{620 - 47 - h}{8} = 59.5$

$\qquad 573 - h = 476,$

$\qquad h = 573 - 476 = 97$

8. (B) $\therefore \dfrac{\frac{35\times80}{100} + \frac{25\times80}{100}}{60} = \dfrac{2800+2000}{100\times60}$

$\qquad = \dfrac{48000}{100 \times 60} = 80\%$

9. (A) Total income of family

$\qquad = 4(8350) + 5(7560) + 3(8070) + 6590$

$\qquad = 33400 + 37800 + 24210 + 6590$

$\qquad = Rs\ 1,02,000$

Average monthly income $= \dfrac{Rs\ 1,02,000}{12} =$ *Rs 8500*

10. (C) Total weight increased

$\qquad = 4 \times 1.5\ kg = 6kg$

Weight of new man $= 69 + 6kg$

$\qquad = 75\ kg$

11. (B) Total age of 20 students

$\qquad = 20 \times 18 = 360\ yrs$

After change, total age

$\qquad = 360 - 20 + (x+y)$

$\qquad = 340 + (x+y)$

Total age of 21 students

$\qquad = 21 \times 18 = 378\ years$

$\qquad \therefore 340 + x + y = 378;\ \ x + y = 38$

$\qquad Acc.\ to\ the\ qn.,\ \ x \sim y = 4$

$\qquad \therefore x = 21, y = 17\ years$

12. (B) Total increase $= 9\times5 = 45$

$\qquad \therefore$ Let the number be 10a + b

After reversing the digits $= 10b + a$

$\qquad 10b + a - (10a + b) = 45$

$\qquad 9b - 9a = 45$

$\qquad b - a = \dfrac{45}{9} = 5$

13. (C) Runs scored in 25 innings

$\qquad = 25\times26 = 650$

Runs scored in 26 innings $= 26\times28 = 728$

Runs scored in the 26th innings

$\qquad = 728 - 650 = 78\ runs$

14. (B) Let the number of boys & girls be x & y respectively

$\qquad \therefore 30x + 40y = 34\ (x+y)$

$\qquad 6y = 4x$

$\qquad x = \dfrac{3}{2}y$

% of girls $= \dfrac{y}{x+y} \times 100 = \dfrac{y}{\frac{3}{2}y+y} \times 100$

$\qquad = \dfrac{y}{\frac{5}{2}y} \times 100 = \dfrac{2}{5} \times 100 = 40\%$

15.(A) Prime nos. between 10 to 35 are 11,

13, 17, 19, 23, 29, 31

$$\text{Average} = \frac{11+13+17+19+23+29+31}{7} = \frac{143}{7}$$

16.(B) $\text{Average} = \frac{(n+1)(2n+1)}{6}$

$$= \frac{(11+1)[(2\times11)+1]}{6} = \frac{12\times23}{6} = 46$$

17.(D) Let nos. be x, x+1, x+2, x+3

$4x + 6 = 33.5 \times 4$

$4x + 6 = 134$

$4x = 128$

$x = 32$

Nos. are 32, 33, 34 and 35

Sum of middle nos. $= 33+34 = 67$

18.(A) Sum of 6 nos. $= 6 \times 11 = 66$

Sum of 4 nos. $= 4 \times 10 = 40$

Sum of remaining two nos.

$$= 66 - 40 = 26$$

$$\text{Average} = \frac{26}{2} = 13$$

19.(C) Acc. no the qn.,

$$\frac{a+c}{2} - \frac{b+c}{2} = 24$$

$$a + c - (b + c) = 48$$

$$a - b = 48$$

20.(B) Let total distance be 'd'.

$$\text{Average speed} = \frac{total\ distance}{total\ time}$$

$$= \frac{d}{\frac{\left(\frac{d}{2}\right)}{12} + \frac{\left(\frac{d}{2}\right)}{24}}$$

$$= \frac{d}{\frac{d}{24} + \frac{d}{48}} = \frac{48d}{3d}$$

$$= 16\ km/hr$$

21.(A) Average monthly income of the group

$$= \frac{(37,000 \times 8) + (40,000 \times 7)}{15}$$

$$= \frac{5,76,000}{15} = Rs\ 38,400$$

22.(D) Acc. to the qn.

$(30\times a) + 96 + 58 = 32(a + 2)$

$30\ a + 154 = 32a + 64$

$2a = 90$

$a = 45$

New average $= a + 2 = 47$

23.(B) Let present average be x years and age of old and new number be a and b respectively.

Total age of 5 students $= 5x$ years

$5x – a + b = 5x - 5(3)$

$5x – a + b = 5x - 15$

$a – b = 15$

Given: $a + b = 29$

$a = 22$ years

$b = 7$ years

Age of new member $= 7$ years

24.(A) Let total strength of class $= a$

No. of chocolate distributed to students

$$= 3a$$

Total chocolate she distributed

$= 3a + 16 + 16$

$= 3a + 32$

Acc. To the qn., $\frac{3a+32}{a+2} = 4;$

$3a + 32 = 4a + 8$

$a = 24$

25.(D) Total marks $= 48 \times 73 = 3504$

After correction, total marks

$= 3504 - 5(25) + 1(29) = 3408$

New average $= \frac{3408}{48} = 71$

26.(A) Total age $= 12 \times 21 = 252$

Actual total age $= 252 - 14 + 26$

$$= 264$$

Actual average $= \frac{264}{12} = 22\ years$

PRACTICE QUESTIONS

1. Find the average of the cubes of first 7 natural nos.
   (A) 110   (B) 112
   (C) 114   (D) 108
   (E) None of these

2. Find the average of odd nos. between 24 to 66.
   (A) 45   (B) 46
   (C) 44   (D) 43
   (E) None of these

3. The average of 7 consecutive even nos. is 32. The difference between the sum of the digits of the greatest and the smallest no. among them is
   (A) 4   (B) 2
   (C) 3   (D) 1
   (E) None of these

4. The average of 12 nos. is 78. What will be the new average when all the nos. are multiplied by 2?
   (A) 154   (B) 160
   (C) 152   (D) 156
   (E) None of these

5. The average monthly income of A and B is Rs 37,000; B and C is Rs 29,000; A and C is Rs 34,000. What is the monthly income of C?
   (A) Rs 26,000   (B) Rs 24,000
   (C) Rs 25,000   (D) Rs 28,000
   (E) None of these

6. A man covers half of total distance with 16 km/hr and another half distance with 32 km/hr. Find his average speed.
   (A) 65/3 km/hr   (B) 64/3km/hr
   (C) 64/5 km/hr   (D) 63/3 km/hr
   (E) None of these

7. The average runs scored by a batsman in 15 innings is 32. After 16th innings, the runs average become 34. How much runs does the batsman score in his 16th innings?
   (A) 54   (B) 60
   (C) 62   (D) 64
   (E) None of these

8. The average of 8 nos. in 52. The average of first 5 nos. is 65 and that of last 2 nos. is 34. Then the sixth no is.
   (A) 21   (B) 24
   (C) 23   (D) 27
   (E) None of these

9. The average age of 13 students and a teacher is 21 years. If the teacher's age is excluded, then the average reduced by 1 year. What is the teacher's age?
   (A) 34 years   (B) 32 years
   (C) 35 years   (D) 30 years
   (E) None of these

10. The average of 25 nos. is 62. If two nos., 74 and 86 are replaced by other 2 nos. 28 & 32. Now the average changes by
    (A) -4 unit   (B) 4 unit
    (C) -2 units   (D) 2 units
    (E) None of these

11. The average runs scored in 10 innings by a player is 42. How much he should score in next inning to raise his average by 3 more runs?
    (A) 74   (B) 72
    (C) 78   (D) 75
    (E) None of these

12. The average of 15 persons increases by 2, when a person of 52 kg is replaced with 2 new persons. Find the sum of the weight of two new persons, if the original average was 68 kg.
    (A) 150 kg   (B) 152 kg

(C) 154 kg   (D) 158 kg

(E) None of these

13. Average of series of six successive even nos. is 33. Find the average of first, third and fifth number of the series.

(A) 33   (B) 34

(C) 32   (D) 31

(E) None of these

14. A car company produces an average of 1920 car for the first 3 month. How many more cars must be produced on an average per month over the next 9 months to make an average production of 2400 cars per month over the whole year?

(A) 640   (B) 620

(C) 680   (D) 600

(E) None of these

15. A cricketer has a mean score of 68 runs in 12 innings. How many runs are to be needed in the 13th innings to raise the mean score to 71?

(A) 107   (B) 104

(C) 106   (D) 105

(E) None of these

16. If the average expenditure of a family for first half of an year is Rs 6800 & the next half of an year is Rs 6400. And the family saves Rs 12,000 during the year. What is the average monthly income of the family?

(A) Rs 7000   (B) Rs 8000

(C) Rs 8200   (D) Rs 7600

(E) None of these

SOLUTIONS

1. (B) Average of cubes of first n natural

$$\text{nos.} = \frac{n(n+1)^2}{4} = \frac{7(8)^2}{4} = 112$$

2. (A) Odd no's: 25, 27, ..., 65

$$\text{Average} = \frac{first\ no + last\ no}{2}$$

$$= \frac{25+65}{2} = \frac{90}{2} = 45$$

3. (C) Some of the nos. $7 \times 32 = 224$

Let nos. be x, x+2, x+4, x+6, x+8, x+10, x+12

Sum = 7x + 42 = 224

$7x = 182$

x = 26

Greatest no: 26 + 12 = 38

Smallest no is 26

Difference between their digits

$= (3+8) \sim (2+6) = 11 - 8 = 3$

4. (D) If every no. is multiplied by 2, then the average is also multiplied by 2.

New average = $78 \times 2 = 156$

5. (A) Monthly income of (A+B+C)

$$= \frac{2(37,000 + 29,000 + 34,000)}{2}$$

(A + B + C) = 1,00,000

Monthly income of C

= 1,00,000 - 2(37,000)

$$= Rs\ 26,000$$

6. (B) Let total distance be 'd'.

$$\text{Average speed} = \frac{Total\ distance}{Total\ time}$$

$$= \frac{d}{\left(\frac{\frac{d}{2}}{16}\right) + \left(\frac{\frac{d}{2}}{32}\right)}$$

$$= \frac{d}{\frac{d}{32} + \frac{d}{64}} = \frac{64d}{3d}$$

$$= \frac{64}{3}\ km/hr$$

7. (D) Runs scored in 15 innings

$$= 15 \times 32 = 480$$

Runs scored in 16 innings = $16 \times 34 = 544$

Runs scored in $16^{th}\ innings = 544 - 480$

$$= 64\ runs$$

8. (C) Let the sixth no. be 'x'.

Acc. to the qn.,

$(5 \times 65) + x + (2 \times 34)$

$$= (8 \times 52)$$
$$325 + x + 68 = 416$$
$$x = 416 - 393;$$
$$x = 23$$

9. (A) Total age of 13 student and teacher
$$= 14 \times 21 = 294$$
Total age of 13 students $= 13 \times 20$
$$= 260$$
Age of teacher $= 294 - 260 = 34$

10.(A) Sum of 25 nos. $= 62 \times 25 = 1550$
Acc. to the qn.,
New average $= \dfrac{1550 - 74 - 86 + 28 + 32}{25}$
$$= \dfrac{1450}{25} = 58$$
Average decreases by 4 units.

11.(D) Required score
$$= (11 \times 45) - (10 \times 42)$$
$$= 495 - 420 = 75 \; runs$$

12.(B) Let the sum of two new persons be x.
Acc. to qn.,
$$(15 \times 68) - 52 + x = 16 \times 70$$
$$1020 - 52 + x = 1120;$$
$$x = 152$$
Sum of weights of two new persons $= 152$

13. (C) Let series be x, x+2, x+4, x+6,
x+8, x + 10
$$6x + 30 = 6 \times 33$$
$$6x = 198 - 30$$
$$6x = 168;$$
$$x = 28$$
Nos. are 28, 30, 32, 34, 36, 38
Required average $= \dfrac{28 + 32 + 36}{3} = 32$

14.(A) Cars made in first 3 month
$$= 3 \times 1920 = 5760$$
No. of cars needed to be made in a year
$$= 12 \times 2400 = 28,800$$

No. of cars needed to be made in next 9 months
$$= 28,800 - 5760 = 23,040$$
Average production needed in next 9 months
$$= \dfrac{23,040}{9} = 2560$$
More cars needed to be produced per month on an average $= 2560 - 1920 = 640$

15.(A) Run scored up to 12th innings
$$= 12 \times 68 = 816$$
To raise the mean score, total score needed $= 13 \times 71 = 923$
More runs needed $= 923 - 816$
$$= 107 \; runs$$

16.(D) Total income during the year
$$= (6800 \times 6) + (6400 \times 6) + 12,000$$
$$= 40,800 + 38,400 + 12,000$$
$$= Rs \; 91,200$$
Average monthly income $= \dfrac{Rs \; 91,200}{12}$
$$= Rs \; 7600$$

Unit **7**

PERCENTAGES

'Percent' implies 'for every hundred/per hundred'

(Sign % is read as percentage)

A fraction whose denominator is 100 is called a percentage.

Eg.: 28% means $28/100 \Rightarrow 28$ parts from 100

    This can also be written as 0.28

1) <u>To express:</u>

- p % as fraction $= \dfrac{p}{100}$
- $\dfrac{p}{q}$ % as fraction $= \dfrac{p}{q} \times 100$
- $p \% \ of \ q \Rightarrow \dfrac{p}{100} \times q = \dfrac{pq}{100}$

2) <u>A quantity 'P' increasing at a rate of R% per annum for n years</u>

Its value after n years $= P\left(1 + \dfrac{R}{100}\right)^n$

Its value n years ago $= \dfrac{P}{\left(1 + \frac{R}{100}\right)^n}$

3) <u>A quantity P decreasing at a rate of R% per annum</u>

Its value after n years $= P\left(1 - \dfrac{R}{100}\right)^n$

Its value n years ago $= \dfrac{P}{\left(1 - \frac{R}{100}\right)^n}$

4) <u>**Comparison:**</u>

  i. If quantity A is R% more than B,

    Then B is less than A by $\left[\dfrac{R}{100+R} \times 100\right]\%$

  ii. If quantity A is R% less than B,

    Then B is more than A by $\left[\dfrac{R}{100-R} \times 100\right]\%$

5) Percentage error

$$= \frac{True\ value - False\ value}{False\ value} \times 100$$

EXERCISE:

1. In a bag containing balls of 3 colours, 45% of total balls are red. Number of yellow balls is 40% of red, number of green balls in 50% of yellow. If no. of green balls is 27, find the total number of balls in the bag.
   (A) 200   (B) 300   (C) 400
   (D) 350   (E) None of these

2. If 60% of P is equal to 40% of Q, P is what percentage of Q?
   (A) 66.67%   (B) 50%   (C) 64.42%
   (D) 65%   (E) None of these

3. In a small town having 12,400 people, 8184 are literate. What is the percentage of illiterate people?
   (A) 32%   (B) 40%   (C) 34%
   (D) 36%   (E) None of these

4. A's salary is 75% of salary of B and B's salary is 50% of C's salary. If C's salary is Rs 65,000. What is A's salary?
   (A) Rs 25275   (B) Rs 24350
   (C) Rs 24240   (D) Rs 24375
   (E) None of these

5. Vijay spends 35% of his income on house rent, 25% on food, 15% on entertainment & 10% on taxes. If his savings at the end of the month is Rs 2520, what is his monthly salary?

(A) Rs 17600   (B) Rs 16800
(C) Rs 16400   (D) Rs 17000
(E) None of these

6. Value of a number P is 25% more than the value of another number of Q. What percentage is value of Q less than the value of P?
(A) 20%   (B) 25%
(C) 18%   (D) 22%
(E) None of these

7. The monthly income of a person was Rs 14,500 & expenditure was Rs 6900. Next month his income will be increased by 12% and his expenditure will be increased by 10%. What will be the increase in his savings?
(A) 13.8%   (B) 13.4%   (C) 12.4%
(D) 14.2 %   (E) None of these

8. If ratio of A & B is 9:10 and C is 40% less than B and is equal to 60. How much percent is A more than that of C?
(A) 45%   (B) 48%   (C) 50%
(D) 60%   (E) None of these

9. If the price of rice is increased by 12%. By how much percent must a family reduce their consumption of rice so that their expenditure remains the same?
(A) 12 5/8 %   (B) 10 2/7 %
(C) 10 5/8 %   (D) 10 5/7 %
(E) None of these

10. If the price of sugar is increased by 18% but its consumption is decreased by 18%, the increase or decrease in the expenditure of money is
(A) 3.24%   (B) -3.24%   (C) -3.12%
(D) 3.12%   (E) None of these

11. In an examination, the student has to obtain 35% of total marks in order to pass. But a student got 30% and failed by 60 marks. The total marks is

(A) 1450   (B) 1400   (C) 1200
(D) 1250   (E) None of these

12. In an examination, B got 10% more marks than A, C got 25% less marks than B & D got 57 marks more than C. If D got 420 marks out of 500. Find the marks obtained by A.
(A) 420   (B) 480   (C) 500
(D) 440   (E) None of these

13. In an office 60% of staffs are males. 40% of males & 60% of females voted candidate A for the post of manager. The percentage of votes got by the other candidate B is
(A) 52%   (B) 50%   (C) 48%
(D) 46%   (E) None of these

14. If population of town increased by 14%, 16%, 15% during consecutive 4-year span respectively, then the overall increase in population of the town during that 12-year period is
(A) 54.026%   (B) 52.076%
(C) 51.32%   (D) 50.06%
(E) None of these

15. Monthly income of Karthi is 66 % of monthly income of Sasi. If Sasi's total monthly expenditure is Rs 14000 and he saves 30% of his salary. Find the monthly income of Karthi.
(A) Rs 12,500   (B) Rs 13,200
(C) Rs 12,800   (D) Rs 13,000
(E) None of these

16. If person A purchases a laptop & sold it to person B at 15% profit. Person B sold it to person C at 20 % loss. If person C pays Rs 69,920 to person B, then person A purchase the laptop at what cost?
(A) Rs 78,000   (B) Rs 74,000
(C) Rs 72,000   (D) Rs 76,000
(E) None of these

17. If 100 is added to a number, then it becomes 2.25 times of itself. Find 40% of the given number is what percent of 50.
    (A) 62% (B) 68%
    (C) 64% (D) 60%
    (E) None of these

18. In an examination, A got 36 % of maximum marks & failed by 48 marks, while B got 46% of maximum marks which is 12 more than passing marks. Find the maximum marks.
    (A) 800 (B) 600
    (C) 500 (D) 400
    (E) None of these

19. The salary of Varun & Vinoth are 30% and 20% less than salary of Anu respectively. By what percent is the salary of Vinoth is more than the salary of Varun
    (A) 12.8% (B) 15.25%
    (C) 14.28% (D) 16%
    (E) None of these

20. Income of P is 50% more than income of Q, find how much percent income of P is reduced so that it becomes equal to 120% of income of Q.
    (A) 15% (B) 25%
    (C) 30% (D) 20%
    (E) None of these

SOLUTIONS

1. (B) Let total no. of balls be x.
$$x \times \frac{45}{100} \times \frac{40}{100} \times \frac{50}{100} = 27$$
$$x = 300$$

2. (A) $\frac{60}{100}P = \frac{40}{100}Q$
$$P = \frac{2}{3}Q = 66.67\%$$

3. (C) No. of illiterates $= 12400 - 8184$
$$= 4216$$

% of illiterates $= \frac{4216}{12400} \times 100 = 34\%$

4. (D) B's salary $= \frac{50}{100} \times 65000$
$$= Rs\ 32500$$
A's salary $= \frac{75}{100} \times 32500$
$$= Rs\ 24375$$

5. (B) % of income goes into savings
$$= 100 - (35+25+15+10) = 15\%$$
$$15\% \text{ (income)} = 2520$$
$$\text{Income} = \frac{2520 \times 100}{15} = Rs\ 16800$$

6. (A) Percentage value less by
$$= \frac{125-100}{125} \times 100$$
$$= \frac{25}{125} \times 100$$
$$= 20\%$$

7. (A) Current savings $= 14500 - 6900$
$$= Rs\ 7600$$
New income $= \frac{112}{100} \times 14500 = Rs\ 16240$
New expenditure $= \frac{110}{100} \times 6900 = Rs\ 7590$
New savings $= 16240 - 7590 = Rs\ 8650$
Increase in percentage $= \frac{8650-7600}{7600} \times 100$
$$= \frac{1050}{7600} \times 100 \approx 13.8\%$$

8. (C) A = 9x, B = 10x
$$C = 10x \times \frac{60}{100} = 60$$
$$x = 10$$
$$\therefore A = 90, B = 100$$
Required percentage $= \frac{90-60}{60} \times 100$
$$= 50\%$$

9. (D) Required reduction in consumption
$$= \frac{x}{100+x} \times 100$$
$$= \frac{12}{100+12} \times 100$$
$$= \frac{12}{112} \times 100$$

$$= \frac{75}{7} = 10\frac{5}{7}\%$$

10.(B) Overall % change in expenditure

$$= x + y + \frac{xy}{100}$$
$$= 18 + (-18) + \frac{18(-18)}{100}$$
$$= 18 + (-18) - 3.24$$
$$= -3.24\%$$

11.(C) Let total marks be x.

30% of x + 60 = 35% of x

5% of x = 60

x = 1200

12.(D) D = C+57 = 420

C = 363

$$C = \frac{75}{100} \times B$$
$$\therefore B = \frac{363 \times 100}{75} = 484$$
$$B = \frac{110}{100} \times A$$
$$\therefore A = \frac{484 \times 100}{110} = 440$$

13.(A) Votes got by candidate A

$$= \frac{60}{100} \times \frac{40}{100} + \frac{40}{100} \times \frac{60}{100}$$
$$= \frac{24}{100} + \frac{24}{100} = 48\%$$

Votes got by candidate B

= 100 - 48 = 52%

14. (B) Effective increase in percentage

$$= x + y + \frac{xy}{100}$$

(i) Percentage increase in first 2 spans

$$= 14 + 16 + \frac{14 \times 16}{100}$$
$$= 30 + 2.24 = 32.24\%$$

(ii) Percentage increase in all 3 spans

$$= 32.24 + 15 + \frac{32.24 \times 15}{100}$$
$$= 47.24 + 4.836$$
$$= 52.076\%$$

15. (B) Monthly income of Sasi

$$= 14,000 \times \frac{100}{100-30}$$
$$= Rs\ 20,000$$

Monthly income of Karthik

$$= 20,000 \times \frac{66}{100} = Rs\ 13,200$$

16.(D) Let purchase price of laptop by person A be Rs x.

$$x \times \frac{115}{100} \times \frac{80}{100} = 69920$$
$$x = Rs\ 76,000$$

17. (C) Let the no. be x.

$$\frac{x+100}{x} = \frac{225}{100}$$

100x +10,000 = 225 x

125 x =10,000

x = 80

40% of x = 32

$$Required\ \% = \frac{32}{50} \times 100 = 64\ \%$$

18. (B) Let maximum Marks be x.

$$\left(\frac{36}{100} \times x\right) + 48$$
$$= \left(\frac{46}{100} \times 10\right) - 12$$

46x − 36x = 6000

10x = 6000

X = 600

Maximum marks is 600.

19.(C) Let salary of Anu be 100x.

Salary of

- Varun = 70x
- Vinoth = 80x

$$Required\ \% = \frac{80x-70x}{70x} \times 100$$
$$= \frac{10}{70} \times 100 = 14.28\ \%$$

20.(D) Let income of Q = Rs 100 x

Income of P = Rs 150x

120% of income of Q = Rs 120x

$$Required\ \% = \frac{150x-120\ x}{150x} \times 100$$
$$= \frac{30}{150} \times 100 = 20\%$$

PRACTICE QUESTIONS

1. 16% & 25% of departments A & B came to a competition respectively. 252 students of department A did not attend competition and total participants from department B were 500. Find the total no. of students in A & B
   (A) 2300   (B) 2400
   (C) 2500   (D) 2200
   (E) None of these

2. In a market survey, 30% and 55% opted for products A & B respectively. The remaining individuals were not certain. If the difference between those who opted for product B and those of uncertain was 840, how many individuals were covered in the survey?
   (A) 1800   (B) 2100
   (C) 2000   (D) 2400
   (E) None of these

3. In a new channel, in between the new sessions of a 30 mins news show, they telecasted 15 advertisements of 10 seconds each and 12 of 15 seconds each. What percentage of time is devoted to advertisements? (approx.)
   (A) 18.75%   (B) 18%
   (C) 17.5%   (D) 18.33%
   (E) None of these

4. A two-digit number gets reversed when one fifth of it is added to it. Find 60% of that no.
   (A) 24   (B) 30
   (C) 27   (D) 25
   (E) None of these

5. There are 60 girls in class A and 40 boys in class B. If girls in class B are 80% of girls in class A. Total students in class A are 50% more than total students in class

B. Find number of boys in class A. (Total student = No. of boys + No of girls)
   (A) 70   (B) 60
   (C) 76   (D) 72
   (E) None of these

6. The price of sugar increased by 20% and the consumption of a family decreased by $16 \frac{2}{3}$%. Find the % change in the expenditure of the family.
   (A) 0%   (B) 10%
   (C) 20%   (D) 15%
   (E) None of these

7. A spends 40% of his monthly salary on rent. Out of remaining, he spends 35% on food, 40% on furniture and remaining on a tour. Find the amount A spends on food & on the tour together if A's salary is 25% less than B's salary which is equal to Rs 32,000 per month.
   (A) Rs 8720   (B) Rs 8540
   (C) Rs 8620   (D) Rs 8640
   (E) None of these

8. If 24 is added to a number, the result becomes 130% of itself. Find the new number.
   (A) 85   (B) 80
   (C) 65   (D) 70
   (E) None of these

9. A dozen of apple costs Rs 72. A reduction in price enables the person to buy an apple for Rs 5. What is the per reduction in price of the apple? (Approx.)
   (A) 15.5%   (B) 16.5%
   (C) 16.67%   (D) 17.25%
   (E) None of these

10. A reduction of 20% in the price of wheat enables a person to buy 7 kg more wheat for Rs 770. The original price of wheat per kg is.

(A) 27.4   (B) 27.5
(C) 27.2   (D) 27.8
(E) None of these

11. The population of a village decreases at the rate of 30% per annum. If its population 2 years ago was 20,000. The present population is.
    (A) 9800   (B) 9600
    (C) 9700   (D) 10000
    (E) None of these

12. Population of a city increase by 15% and $24/23\%$ in two successive years respectively. If population of city with often two years is 24,024 then find the initial population of city.
    (A) 22,000   (B) 20,020
    (C) 20,000   (D) 18,600
    (E) None of these

13. The ratio between savings & expenditure of a person is 4:5. If his income is increased by 20% and expenditure increased by 25%, then find his savings is how much percentage increased.
    (A) 14.28%   (B) 12.25%
    (C) 13.75%   (D) 14.5%
    (E) None of these

14. Difference between 20% of a and 15% of b is 25 whereas difference between 30% of b and 25% of a is 50. Find (a + b).
    (A) 900   (B) 600
    (C) 800   (D) 1000
    (E) None of these

SOLUTIONS:

1. (A) Total students in
   (i) Dept A $= 252 \times \dfrac{100}{(100-16)} = 300$
   (ii) Dept B $= 500 \times \dfrac{100}{25} = 2000$
   Total No. of student = 2300

2. (B) % of uncertain individuals
   $= 100 - (30 + 55)$
   $= 15\%$
   Acc. To the Qn.,
   $x \times \dfrac{55 - 15}{120} = 840$
   $x = \dfrac{840 \times 100}{40} = 2100$

3. (D) Total advertisement time
   $= (15 \times 10) + (12 \times 15)$
   $= 150 + 180 = 330 \, sec$
   Required $\% = \dfrac{330}{30 \times 60} \times 100$
   $= 18.33\%$

4. (C) Let the two-digit no. be 10x +y
   Acc. To the qn.,
   10x + y + 0.2(10x+ y) = 10y + x
   12x+ 1.2y =10 y + x
   11x = 8.8 y
   x = 0.8 y
   $\dfrac{x}{y} = \dfrac{4}{5}$
   No. can only be 45 as it is a 2- digit no.
   60 % of no. = 27.

5. (D) Girls in class B $= \dfrac{80}{100} \times 60 = 48$
   Total student in class B
   $= 48 + 40 = 88$
   Total student in class A
   $= 88 + \dfrac{1}{2}(88) = 132$
   Boys in class A
   $= 132 - 60 = 72$

6. (A) Let's take price of sugar & consumption be 5x & 6x respectively
   <u>Before:</u> Price = 5x;
   Consumption = 6x
   Expenditure = 30 units
   <u>After:</u> Price $= 5x \times \dfrac{120}{100} = 6x$
   Consumption $= 6x \times \dfrac{83\frac{1}{3}}{100} = 5x$
   Expenditure = 30 units
   % Change in expenditure = 0%

7. (D) A's monthly salary $= \dfrac{75}{100} \times 32{,}000$

$\qquad = Rs\ 24{,}000$

Required amount

$\qquad = 24{,}000 \times \dfrac{60}{100} \times \dfrac{(35+25)}{100}$

$\qquad = Rs\ 8640$

8. (B) Acc. to the qn.,

$\qquad \dfrac{x+24}{x} = \dfrac{130}{100}$

$\qquad 100\,x + 2400 = 130x$

$\qquad 30\,x = 2400$

$\qquad x = 80$

The number is 80.

9. (C) Old price of 1 apple $= \dfrac{72}{12} = Rs\ 6$

New price of apple $= Rs\ 5$.

% Reduction in price

$\qquad = \dfrac{6-5}{6} \times 100 = 16.67\%$

10. (B) Reduced price $= \dfrac{20}{100} \times \dfrac{770}{7} = Rs\ 22$

Original price

$\qquad = 22 \times \dfrac{100}{80} = Rs\ 27.5$

11. (A) If population P, decreases at the rate of R% per annum

Population after n years

$\qquad = P\left[1 - \dfrac{R}{100}\right]^{n}$

$\qquad = 20{,}000\left[1 - \dfrac{30}{100}\right]^{2}$

$\qquad = 20{,}000 \times \dfrac{7}{10} \times \dfrac{7}{10} = 9800$

12. (B) Let initial population be P.

$\qquad P \times \dfrac{115}{100} \times \dfrac{2400}{2300} = 24{,}020$

$\qquad P = \dfrac{24020 \times 100}{120} = 20{,}020$

13. (C) Let expenditure & savings be Rs 5a & 4a respectively.

New income $= (5a+4a) \times \dfrac{120}{100}$

$\qquad = Rs\ 10.8a$

New expenditure $= 5a \times \dfrac{125}{100}$

$\qquad = Rs\ 6.25a$

New savings $= 10.8a - 6.25a$

$\qquad = Rs\ 4.55a$

Required % $= \dfrac{4.55a - 4a}{4a} \times 100$

$\qquad = 13.75\ \%$

14. (A) Acc. to the Qn.,

$\qquad \dfrac{20}{100}a - \dfrac{15}{100}b = 5$

$\qquad 40\,a - 30\,b = 1000 \qquad (1)\ \&$

$\qquad \dfrac{30}{100}b - \times \dfrac{25}{100}a = 50$

$\qquad 30b - 25a = 5000 \qquad (2)$

Solving (1) & (2)

$\qquad a = 400,\ b = 500$

$\qquad a + b = 900$

Unit 8

RATIO AND PROPORTION

Ratio:

A ratio is the comparison or simplified form of two quantities of same kind.

It is a relation that indicates how many times one quantity is equal to the other.

A ratio is a number which expresses one quantity as a fraction of the other.

Proportion:

Proportion, represented by '=' or '::', is an expression to say that two ratios are equal.

Note:

If ratio a:b is equal to ratio c:d, then a, b, c, d are said to be in proportion.

$$a:b \ = \ c:d \ (or) \ a:b \ :: \ c:d$$

If four terms are in proportion, then product of the two extremes (1st & 4th values) is equal to the product of two middle values (2nd & 3rd values) $\Rightarrow ad = bc$

- d is called the fourth proportional to a, b, c
- c is called the third proportional to a, b
- Mean proportional between a & b $= \sqrt{ab}$
- In continued proportion,
- e.g., $a:b = b:c, b^2 = ac$
- b is said to be mean proportional to the other two extreme terms.

Reminder:

Order of terms in ratios is very important as it indicates how many times one quantity is contained by other.

Parts of a quantity expressed in its ratio:

- A divided in ratio a:b (2 parts)

  1st part $= \dfrac{a}{a+b} \times A$

  2nd part $= \dfrac{b}{a+b} \times A$

  A divided to form parts, those are of 'a' parts & 'b' parts each.

- A divided into n parts in ratio a: b: c…: n

  Value of 1st part $= \dfrac{a}{a+b+\cdots+n} \times A$

  Value of nth part $= \dfrac{n}{a+b+\cdots+n} \times A$

  Value of any part $= \dfrac{\text{its related term}}{a+b+\cdots+n} \times A$

EXERCISE:

1. b: c $= 6:7$, c: d $= 3:2$, find b: d.
    (A) 7:9   (B) 1:2
    (C) 9:7   (D) 3:7
    (E) None of these

2. If a: b $= 7:4$, b: c $= 8:11$, then a: b: c $= ?$
    (A) 12:8:11   (B) 14:8:11
    (C) 14:9:11   (D) 10:12:11
    (E) None of these

3. If $(a + b):(b + c):(c + a) = 3:6:7$, find $a:b:c$.
(A) 3:2:5   (B) 4:3:2
(C) 1:4:3   (D) 2:1:5
(E) None of these

4. If $a:b :: b:c$. then $a:c = ?$
(A) $a^2:b^2$ (B) $a:b^2$
(C) $a^2:b$ (D) $a:b$
(E) None of these

5. The number to be added to each of the numbers 1,4,13,25 to make the numbers in proportion is:
(A) 3   (B) 2
(C) 4   (D) 1
(E) None of these

6. Rs 18,000 is divided between A, B, C in the ratio 3:2:4. Find C's share.
(A) Rs 7500   (B) Rs 7000
(C) Rs 9000   (D) Rs 8000
(E) None of these

7. A collection of 315 coins consisting of Rs 1, 50 paise and Rs 2 coins have their values in the ratio of 7:3:4. No. of each type of coins respectively are
(A) 145, 121, 40   (B) 138, 130, 41
(C) 147, 126, 42   (D) 147, 124, 42
(E) None of these

8. P, Q and R started a business with investment ratios 4:8:5 respectively. After 1 year, P increased her capital by 25% of her investment and Q withdrew 50% of her capital. After two years, in what ratio should the earned profit be distributed among P, Q and R respectively?
(A) 9:14:10   (B) 9:12:10
(C) 12:8:14   (D) 10:8:9
(E) None of these

9. A sum of Rs 5400 is divided among A, B, C, D such that B receives half of what C & D receive together and A receives thrice of what B receives. What is A's share?
(A) Rs 2500   (B) Rs 2900
(C) Rs 3000   (D) Rs 2700
(E) None of these

10. In a 3 ½ hrs examination, there are 300 questions. Among that, 120 are from Electrical Engg., 100 are from GK & 80 are from English. A student spent twice as much as time on each Electrical Engg. question as for each other questions. How many minutes did she spend on Electrical Engg. questions?
(A) 140 mins   (B) 160 mins
(C) 120 mins   (D) 100 mins
(E) None of these

11. A person leaves Rs 32,200 to be divided among his 4 sons, 2 daughters and his 3 brothers. If each son receives twice as much as each of the person's brothers and each daughter receives thrice as much as each son. Find the share of each son, daughter & his brother.
(A) Rs 2800, Rs 8400, Rs 1400
(B) Rs 2600, Rs 8200, Rs 1400
(C) Rs 3800, Rs 8400, Rs 1200
(D) Rs 2500, Rs 8000, Rs 1200
(E) None of these

12. If $x:y = y:z$ then $x^4 : y^4 = ?$
(A) $z^2:x^2$ (B) $x^2:z^2$
(C) $y^2:z^2$ (D) $z^2:y^2$
(E) None of these

13. If $p:q = 3:4$ and $q:r = 3:5$, find $q^2:pr:p^2$.
(A) 16:20:11   (B) 20:16:9
(C) 16:20:9   (D) 16:9:20
(E) None of these

14. Rs 1300 is divided in the ratio 1/4: 1/3: 1/2. Find the lowest share.
    (A) Rs 300 (B) Rs 45
    (C) Rs 250 (D) Rs 400
    (E) None of these

15. Instead of dividing Rs 1000 among P & Q in the ratio of 1/2 : 1/3, it was divided in the ratio 2:3 by mistake. Who gained in this?
    (A) P gained
    (B) Neither P nor Q gained
    (C) Q gained
    (D) Can't be determined
    (E) None of these

16. A box contains coins of Rs 1, Rs 2, Rs 5, Rs 10 denomination in the ratio 3:4:5:6. If total amount is Rs 480, find the number of coins of Rs 5 denomination.
    (A) 25 (B) 28
    (C) 30 (D) 22
    (E) None of these

17. A sum of money is divided among A, B and C in the ratio 2:3:7. If share of B is Rs 3270 more than share of A, how much does C receive more than B?
    (A) Rs 13,250 (B) Rs 13,080
    (C) Rs 13,560 (D) Rs 12,280
    (E) None of these

18. In a company, the ratio of male technical to male non-technical staff is 5:4. There are 64% females in the company. Males in technical are half of females in technical. What is the ratio of male technical staff to that of female non-technical staff?
    (A) 5:4 (B) 6:7
    (C) 6:5 (D) 5:6
    (E) None of these

19. The ratio of first-class fare to second class fare is 4:1. No. of tickets booked of first class to second class is in the ratio 2:3. Total fare collected was Rs 4400. Find fare collected from passengers of second class.
    (A) Rs 1200 (B) Rs 800
    (C) Rs 2400 (D) Rs 1600
    (E) None of these

20. In a class, the ratio of failed to passed students is 1:9. If 6 more student have failed among the total students in that class, then their ratio would be 4:21. Find the total no. of student in the class.
    (A) 80 (B) 100
    (C) 90 (D) 104
    (E) None of these

21. The ratio of income of P, Q & R is 7:4:3 & ratio of expenditure is 2:5:4. If R saves Rs 600 out of Rs 5400, find the average expenditure of P, Q & R (in Rs)
    (A) Rs 4400 (B) Rs 4000
    (C) Rs 4800 (D) Rs 5200
    (E) None of these

22. A, B & C entered into a partnership. Ratio of investment of A & B is 4:x & that of B & C is 3:4. If at the end of 2 years, C received Rs 3700 as profit out of Rs 7400. Then find the value of x.
    (A) 10 (B) 12
    (C) 8 (D) 16
    (E) None of these

23. The monthly income of A & B is Rs 8000 & Rs 6000 respectively. A saves Rs 250 per month & B saves Rs 500 per month, what is the ratio of their expenditure respectively?
    (A) 24:31 (B) 22:13
    (C) 31:22 (D) 22:31
    (E) None of these

24. If the ratio of the speeds of the two persons is 7:13. Then the ratio of their time periods is

(A) 14:23   (B) 7:14

(C) 7:13   (D) 13:7

(E) None of these

25. A certain amount of money has to be divided between two persons A & B in the ratio 5:3. But it was divided in the ratio 3:2. Thereby, A loses by Rs 30. What is the total amount?

(A) Rs 120   (B) Rs 240

(C) Rs 80   (D) Rs 480

SOLUTIONS:

1. (C) $\dfrac{b}{d} = \dfrac{b}{c} \times \dfrac{c}{d} = \dfrac{6}{7} \times \dfrac{3}{2} = \dfrac{9}{14}$

$b:d = 9:14$

2. (B) LCM of common (b) = 8

Equalising the ratio based on the common term $\Rightarrow 14:8:11$

3. (D) $(a + b) + (b + c) + (c + a)$

$= 2(a + b + c)$

$A + b + c = \dfrac{(a+b)+(b+c)+(c+a)}{2}$

$= \dfrac{3+6+7}{2} = \dfrac{16}{2} = 8$

$a = (a + b + c+) - (b + c)$

$= 8 - 6 = 2$

$b = (a + b + c+) - (a + c)$

$= 8 - 7 = 1$

$c = (a + b + c+) - (a + b)$

$= 8 - 3 = 5$

$\therefore a: b: c = 2: 1: 5$

4. (A) $ac = b^2; c = \dfrac{b^2}{a}$

$\therefore \dfrac{a}{c} = \dfrac{a}{\left(\frac{b^2}{a}\right)} = \dfrac{a^2}{b^2}$

$a: c = a^2: b^2$

5. (A) Formula: $\dfrac{bc-ad}{(a+d)-(c+b)}$

$= \dfrac{(4\times13)-(1\times25)}{(1+25)-(4+13)}$

$= \dfrac{52-25}{26-17} = \dfrac{27}{9} = 3$

6. (D) Sum of ratios $= 3 + 2 + 4 = 9$

C's share $= \dfrac{4}{9} \times 18000 = $ Rs 8000

7. (C) Value of coins

$= $ Denomination $\times$ Ratio of coins

Ratio of coins $= \dfrac{7}{1} : \dfrac{3}{0.5} : \dfrac{4}{2} = 7:6:2$

Total no. of coins $= 315$

No. of Rs 1 coins $= \dfrac{7}{15} \times 315 = 147$

No. of 0.5 paise coins $= \dfrac{6}{15} \times 315$

$= 126$

No. of Rs 2 coins $= \dfrac{2}{15} \times 315 = 42$

8. (B) Investment for first year $\rightarrow 4:8:5$

Second year capital:

P $= 4 + 25\%$ of $4 = 5$

Q $= 8 - 50\%$ of $8 = 4$

Profit ratio

$= (4 + 5): (8 + 4): (5 + 5)$

$= 9:12:10$

9. (D) Let share of C & D together be 2x.

Required ratio of A:B:C+D

$= 3x:1x:2x$

$= 3:1:2$

A's share $= \dfrac{3}{6} \times 5400 = $ Rs 2700

10. (C) Ratio of questions on Electrical Engg. & other $=120:180 = 2:3$

Ratio of time spent $= (2 \times 2): (3:1)$

$= (3 \times 1) = 4:3$

Time spent on Electrical Engg. qns

$= \dfrac{4}{7} \times 210 = 120$ mins

11. (A) Let share of each of his brother be x.

Share ratio of sons, daughters, brothers

$= 4 \times 2x: 2 \times 6x: 3 \times x$

$= 8x:12x:3x = 8:12:3$

Shares of them $= \frac{8}{23} \times 32{,}200;$

$\frac{12}{23} \times 32{,}200; \frac{3}{23} \times 32{,}200$

$= $ Rs 11200; Rs 16800; Rs 4200

Shares of each one of them

$= \frac{11200}{4}, \frac{16800}{2}, \frac{4200}{3}$

$=$ Rs 2800, Rs 8400, Rs 1400

12. (B) $y^2 = xz$

$\frac{x^4}{y^4} = \frac{x^4}{(xz)^2} = \frac{x^4}{x^2 z^2} = \frac{x^2}{z^2}$

$x^4 : y^4 = x^2 : y^2$

13. (C) LCM of common term (q) = 12

p: q: r = 9:12:20

$q^2 : pr : p^2 = (12)^2 : 9 \times 20 : 9^2 =$

$144 : 180 : 81 = 16 : 20 : 9$

14. (B) LCM of 4,3,2=12

Ratio 1/4 :1/3 :1/2 = 3:4:6

Lowest share $= \frac{3}{13} \times 1300 =$ Rs 300

15. (C) Actual ratio = 1/2:1/3=3:2

P's share = 3/5×1000 = Rs 600

Q's share = 2/5×1000 = Rs 400

Mistaken ratio = 2:3

P's share = Rs 400

Q's share = Rs 600

Q gained

16. (A) Value of coins

$= $ Denominator $\times$ Ratio of coins

Ratio of their values

$= 3 \times 1 : 4 \times 2 : 5 \times 5 : 6 \times 10$

$= 3 : 8 : 25 : 60$

Sum of ratio of values

$= 3 + 8 + 25 + 60 = 96$

For a value of Rs 96, there are 5 five-rupee coins

For a value of Rs 480

$= \frac{480}{96} \times 5 = 5 \times 5 = 25$

There are 25 five-rupee coins

17. (B) A: B: C = 2:3:7

B's share $-$ A's share = 1x

= Rs 3270

C's share $-$ A's share = 7x $-$ 3x

= 4x = 4×3270 = Rs 13,080

18. (D) Let total employees in the company be 100x.

Females $= \frac{64}{100} \times 100x = 64x$

Males = 100x $-$ 64x = 36x

Males in technical $= \frac{5}{9} \times 36x = 20x$

Females in technical = 2 × 20x = 40x

Females in non-technical

$= 64x - 40x = 24x$

Required ratio $= \frac{20x}{24x} = 5 : 6$

19. (A) Let fare for first class & second class be 4x & x respectively.

Let no. of tickets booked for first & second class be 2y & 3y respectively

Total fare for

First class = 4x × 2y = 8xy

Second class = x × 3y = 3xy

Fare collected from second class

$= \frac{3xy}{11xy} \times 4400 =$ Rs 1200

20. (B) Let failed & passed no. of students be x & 9x respectively.

$\frac{x+6}{9x-6} = \frac{4}{21}$

21x + 126 = 36x $-$ 24

15x = 150; x = 10

Total no. of students = 10x = 100

21. (A) Expenditure of R = Rs 4800

Expenditure of P $= \frac{4800}{4} \times 2$

$= $ Rs 2400

Expenditure of Q $= \frac{4800}{4} \times 5$

$= $ Rs 6000

Average $= \frac{4800+2400+6000}{3} = 4400$

22.(B) Ratio of their investment (A: B: C)

$$= (4 \times 3) : (x \times 3) : (4 \times x)$$

Radio of their profits

$$= (12 \times 24) : (3x \times 24) : (4x \times 24)$$

$$= 12 : 3x : 4x$$

$$\frac{4x}{7x+12} = \frac{3700}{7400};$$

$$8x = 7x + 12x; \; x = 12$$

23.(C) Ratio of their expenditure

$$= \frac{8000 - 250}{6000 - 500}$$

$$= \frac{7750}{5500} = \frac{31}{22}$$

24.(D) Time period $\propto \dfrac{1}{speed}$

Required radio $= \dfrac{1}{7} : \dfrac{1}{13}$

$$= 13 : 7$$

25.(A) Difference $= \dfrac{5}{8} - \dfrac{3}{5} = \dfrac{1}{40}$

Total amount = Rs 30×40

$$= \text{Rs } 120$$

PRACTICE:

1. If p: q = 6:5, q: r = 2:3, then p: q: r = ?
(A) 10:12:15   (B) 12: 10:15
(C) 12:10:6   (D) 12:5:15
(E) None of these

2. The number of students speaking Tamil & English are in the ratio 5:4. If the number of students speaking English increased by 20% & those speaking Tamil increased by 35%. What would be the new respective ratio?
(A) 35:32   (B) 32:35
(C) 34:35   (D) 35:34
(E) None of these

3. Karthi has Rs 8000 which he wants to donate to 4 organizations. If on the day of donation, he decided to donate only 90% of the amount he decided, what would be the difference of the largest & smallest amount he donates, if the ratio of donation to 4 organization is 4:5:2:1
(A) Rs 2200   (B) Rs 2600
(C) Rs 2400   (D) Rs 2000
(E) None of these

4. Edward's income & savings are in the ratio 16:3. If the expenditure increases by 1/2 & his savings increases by 1/3. Find the ratio of new income to earlier income.
(A) 46:31   (B) 32:47
(C) 47:34   (D) 47:32
(E) None of these

5. The population of city is 11,39,500. The ratio of men & women is 20:23. If there are 24% literate among men & 20% literate among women, the total no. of literate persons in the city is?
(A) 24,94,000   (B) 24,91,000
(C) 24,96,000   (D) 24,81,000
(E) None of these

6. Profit earned by company is divided among two departments A & B in the ratio 3:5. If the number of employees in dept. A is 80 & that of dept. B is 45. If the share obtained by each employee of dept. B is Rs 25,000. What was the total amount of profit earned?
(A) 18 lakhs   (B) 13 lakhs
(C) 12.75 lakhs   (D) 23.5 lakhs
(E) None of these

7. The ratio of passed & failed students in an exam is 6:1. The ratio would have been 9:1 if 6 more students had been passed. The total no. of students is
(A) 120   (B) 100
(C) 140   (D) 160
(E) None of these

8. Ratio of two nos. is 7:5. If 30 is added to each no, the ratio become 4:3. Find the ratio of the number if 10 is subtracted from each no.
(A) 7:9   (B) 9:7
(C) 10:7   (D) 7:10
(E) None of these

9. P & Q earn in the ratio 1:2. They spend in the ratio 3:5 & save in the ratio 1:4. If the total monthly savings of both P & Q are Rs 5,000. The income of P is
(A) Rs 7000   (B) Rs 6500
(C) Rs 6800   (D) Rs 7200
(E) None of these

10. The ratio of squares of a number to cube of another number is 16:125. The ratio of first & second no. is?
(A) 4:5   (B) 5:4
(C) 4:3   (D) 3:4
(E) None of these

11. The present ages of the A & B are 4:6. Ten years age their ages were in the ratio 3:5. Find the present age of A.
(A) 36 years   (B) 40 years
(C) 38 years   (D) 42 years
(E) None of these

12. In a class, the ratio of the number of girls to boys is 8:5. If there are 40 girls, the total number of students in the class is
(A) 62   (B) 64
(C) 65   (D) 66
(E) None of these

13. If a: b = 3:1, find the value of (a + 2b): (3a +7 b)
(A) 16:5   (B) 5:16
(C) 16:7   (D) 7:16
(E) None of these

14. What must be added to each of the numbers 8, 11, 28 & 36. So that the resultant numbers are in proportion?
(A) 3   (B) 4
(C) 6   (D) 5
(E) None of these

15. A box has 420 coins of denomination one rupee & two rupees only. The ratio of their respective value is 9:10. The number of 2-rupee coin is
(A) 200   (B) 270
(C) 180   (D) 150
(E) None of these

16. The sum of two no's is 60 & their difference is 12. Then the ratio of the nos. is
(A) 2:3   (B) 3:5
(C) 3:2   (D) 4:3
(E) None of these

SOLUTIONS

1. (B) LCM of common (q) =10
Equalizing the ratio based on the common term = 12 : 10 : 15

2. (A) New no. of student speaking
(i) Tamil = $5x \times \frac{135}{100}$
(ii) English = $4x \times \frac{120}{100}$
New ratio $= \frac{5x \times \frac{135}{100}}{4x \times \frac{120}{100}} = 35:32$

3. (C) Donated amount
$= 8000 \times \dfrac{90}{100} = $ Rs 7200
Required different $\dfrac{5x - 1x}{12x} \times 7200$
$= \dfrac{7200}{3} = $ Rs 2400

4. (D) Let his income & savings be 16x & 3x respectively
Expenditure = 16x- 3x =13 x

New expenditure $= 13x + \frac{1}{2}(13x)$

$\quad$ = Rs 19.5x

New savings $= 3x + 1/3(3x) =$ Rs 4x

New income $=$ Rs 4x + Rs 14.5x

$\quad$ = Rs 23.5x

Ratio $= = \frac{23.5x}{16x} = 47:32$

5. (B) Literal population

$= \left(1134500 \times \frac{20}{43} \times \frac{24}{100}\right) +$

$\quad \left(1139500 \times \frac{23}{43} \times \frac{20}{100}\right)$

$= 127200 + 121900 = 249100$

6. (A) Total profit

$= (25{,}000 \times 45) + \left(25{,}000 \times 45 \times \frac{3}{5}\right)$

$= 18{,}00{,}000$

7. (C) $\frac{6x+6}{7x} = \frac{9}{10}$

$\quad 60x + 60 = 63x$

$\quad 3x = 60$

$\quad x = 20$

Total no. of students

$= 7x = 7 \times 20$

$= 140$

8. (D) Let two nos. be 7x & 5x respectively

$\frac{7x+30}{5x+30} = \frac{4}{3}$

$21x + 90 = 20x + 120$

$x = 30$

Two nos. are 210 & 150 respectively.

Required ratio $= \frac{210-10}{150-10} = \frac{200}{140} = \frac{10}{7}$

9. (A) Let earnings of P & Q be x & 2x respectively.

$\frac{1x-3x}{2x-5y} = \frac{1}{4}$

$4x - 12y = 2x - 5y$

$2x = 7y;$

$x = 7/2\ y$

$(2x - 5y) + (x-3y) = 5000$

Subs. x, y = 2000; x = 7000

Income of P = Rs 7000

10. (A) $\frac{a^2}{b^3} = \frac{16}{125}$

$\frac{a}{b} = \frac{(16)^{1/2}}{(125)^{1/3}} = 4:5$

11. (B) $\frac{4x-10}{6x-10} = \frac{3}{5}$

$20x - 50 = 18x - 30$

$2x = 20\ ;\ x = 10$

Present age of A = 4(10) = 40 years

12. (C) 8x = 40

$x = 5$

Total no. of students = 13x

$\quad = 13(5) = 65$ student

13. (B) Let a & b be 3x & x respectably

Required radio $= \frac{3x+2x}{9x+7x}$

$= \frac{5x}{16x} = 5:16$

14. (B) Formula $= \frac{bc-ad}{(a+d)-(b+c)}$

Here

$a = 8, b = 11, c = 28\ \&\ d = 36$

$x = \frac{11(28)-8(36)}{(8+36)-(11+28)} = \frac{308-288}{44-39} = \frac{20}{5} = 4$

4 must be added

15. (D) Their value = 9:10

The ratio of no. of coins

$= \frac{9}{1} : \frac{10}{2}$

$= (9 \times 2):10$

$= 18:10$

No. of two-rupees coin

$= \frac{10}{28} \times 420 = 150$

16. (C) Let the nos. be a & b

$a + b = 60$

$a - b = 12$

$2a = 72$

$a = 36$

$b = 24$

Ratio of the no's = 36:24 = 3:2

MIXTURE AND ALLEGATION

Allegation is a rule that enables us to find the ratio in which two or more ingredient at the given price must be mixed to produce a mixture of desired price.

<u>Mean price:</u> The price of a unit quantity of the mixture. Its value will be an intermediate between the price of dearer & cheaper quantity.

1. **Allegation method 1:**

   It is a modified form of finding the weighted average. Two products are mixed in a ratio, then mean price is given by

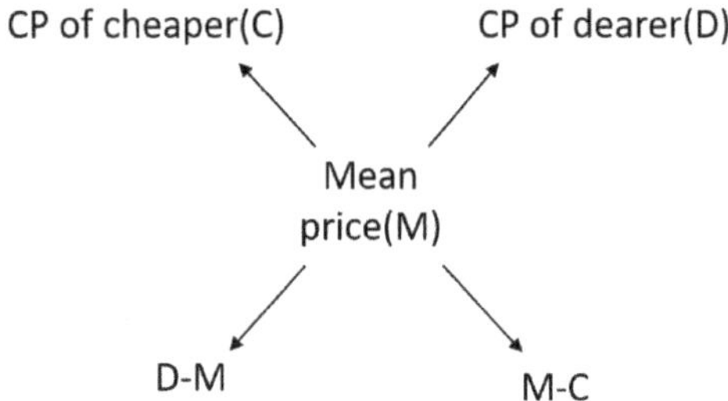

$$\frac{\text{Quantity of cheaper product}}{\text{Quantity of dearer product}}$$
$$= \frac{\text{CP of dearer} - \text{Mean price}}{\text{Mean price} - \text{CP of cheaper}}$$
$$= \frac{D - M}{M - C}$$

2. **Allegation method 2: (Replacement of part of solution)**

   It is a method used for repeated dilution. This is used to calculate pure quantity left after 'n' no. of processes of repeated replacements is done on the pure quantity.

If a container contains 'x' units of a liquid from which 'y' units are taken out & replaced by water. After 'n' operations quantity of pure liquid remaining is:
$$x\left(1 - \frac{y}{x}\right)^n$$

Final amount of ingredient that is not replaced

$$= \text{Initial amount} \times \left(\frac{\text{Volume after removal}}{\text{Volume after replacing}}\right)^n$$
$$= x\left(1 - \frac{y}{x}\right)^n$$

3. If mixture 'a' having 2 ingredients A & B in ratio a:b is added with 'x' litres of B, then ratio, becomes a:c (as quantity of A remains unchanged)
   Quantity of A in original mixture
   $$= \frac{a}{c - b} \times x \text{ litres}$$
   Quantity of B in original mixture
   $$= \frac{b}{c - b} \times x \text{ litres}$$

4. If 2 mixtures having 2 ingredients A & B in the ratio a:b & c:d are mixed, then the ratio of A:B in new mixture is
   $$\left(\frac{a}{a + b} + \frac{c}{c + d}\right) : \left(\frac{b}{a + b} + \frac{d}{c + d}\right)$$

5. If 'n' mixtures having 2 ingredients A & B in the ratio $a_1:b_1$, $a_2:b_2$, ... $a_n:b_n$, respectively are mixed,
   Then ratio of A & B in new mixture
   $$= \frac{\text{Quantity of A}}{\text{Quantity of B}} = \frac{\frac{a_1}{a_1 + b_1} + \frac{a_2}{a_2 + b_2} + \cdots \frac{a_n}{a_n + b_n}}{\frac{b_1}{a_1 + b_1} + \frac{b_2}{a_2 + b_2} + \cdots \frac{b_n}{a_n + b_n}}$$

EXERCISE:

1. 120 kg of an alloy A is mixed with 300 kg of alloy B to make a new alloy. If alloy A has metal P and metal Q in the ratio 1:2 & alloy B has metal Q & metal R in the ratio 1:2, then what will be the amount of metal Q in the new alloy?
(A) 160 kg   (B) 120 kg
(C) 150 kg   (D) 180 kg
(E) None of these

2. Two mixture A & B contain water and milk in the ratio 4:5 & 5:3 respectively. 45 litres of mixture A and 40 litres of mixture B are mixed to obtain a new mixture. Then find the ratio of water to milk in the new mixture.
(A) 9:8   (B) 8:9
(C) 8:7   (D) 7:8
(E) None of these

3. A milkman buys 30 litres of milk at Rs 35 per litre and also buys some amount of milk at Rs 25 per litre. He mixes and sells the mixture at Rs 37.5 per litre at a profit of 25%. Then how many litres of milk he buys for Rs 25 per litre?
(A) 35 litres   (B) 30 litres
(C) 25 litres   (D) 20 litres
(E) None of these

4. Two glasses contain milk and water in the ratio 3:4 & 2:5 respectively. If the entire mixture from both the glasses is mixed together in another glass, find the ratio of water to milk in the new container.
(A) 5:9   (B) 6:5
(C) 9:5   (D) 5:7
(E) None of these

5. Two containers A and B contain milk & water in the ratio 2:3 & 5:2 respectively. Calculate the ratio in which these to be mixed to obtain a new mixture in which the ratio of milk & water is 4:3?
(A) 6:5   (B) 5:6
(C) 2:3   (D) 3:4
(E) None of these

6. A 500 gm mixture of acid and base contains 40% of acid. If 100 gm of base is added, then what % of base weight is in the new mixture?
(A) 66 2/3%   (B) 33 1/3%
(C) 62%   (D) 72.25%
(E) None of these

7. Two alloys contain copper and tin in the ratio 1:3 & 4:1. What quantities of second alloy should be mixed to prepare tin being 60% in 11 kg?
(A) 2 kg   (B) 3 kg
(C) 4 kg   (D) 2.5 kg
(E) None of these

8. A person purchases milk at Rs 40/litre and mixes 9 litres of water to it. By selling the resultant mixture at the rate of Rs 30/litre, he earns a profit of 20%. What was the minimum amount of mixture he had with him to sell?
(A) 8 litres   (B) 16 litres
(C) 24 litres   (D) 4 litres
(E) None of these

9. A 100 litres mixture contain 30% of water & remaining juice. How many litres of water should be mixed to make 50% of water in the mixture?
(A) 40 litres   (B) 30 litres
(C) 35 litres   (D) 25 litres
(E) None of these

10. Three identical containers contain milk & water in the ratios 2:1, 3:2 & 1:5 respectively. All the three containers are emptied completely into a big container.

The ratio of milk to water in the big container is

(A) 49:43   (B) 47:43
(C) 43:47   (D) 49:47
(E) None of these

11. Mixture A contains milk & water in the ratio 3:5 & mixture B contains milk & water in the ratio 4:1. A & B is mixed in the ratio 4:5. If the quantity of milk in the resultant mixture is 66 litres, find the total quantity of resultant mixture.

(A) 108 litres   (B) 104 litres
(C) 112 litres   (D) 100 litres
(E) None of these

12. There are two vessels of equal volume. The first vessel contains 60% of liquor and the rest water. The second vessel contains liquor and water in the ratio 7:3. The mixture contained in the two vessels is mixed. The ratio of liquor and water in the final mixture is

(A) 7:12   (B) 7:13
(C) 13:7   (D) 6:13
(E) None of these

13. 60 litres of a solution contain milk & water in the ratio 3:1. If some amount of mixture is taken out then the ratio of milk & water in the remaining mixture is unchanged. Find the amount of mixture replaced.

(A) 10 litres   (B) 20 litres
(C) 30 litres   (D) Can't be determined
(E) None of these

14. 140 litres of milk & water mixture contains 35% of milk in it. How much amount of milk should be added so as to make it 45% milk in the solution? (approx.)

(A) 25.5 litres   (B) 27.5 litres
(C) 22.7 litres   (D) 26.8 litres
(E) None of these

15. 50 litres of mixture contain juice and water in the ratio of 2:3. When some amount of the mixture is taken out & the same amount of water is added to the mixture, the ratio becomes 8:17. How much amount of water is added to the mixture?

(A) 5 litres   (B) 30 litres
(C) 20 litres   (D) 10 litres
(E) None of these

16. A vessel contains 75 litres of mixture that contains coke and water in the ratio of 13:12. If 11 litres of coke is added & x litres of water is added in the mixture, the ratio will become 10:9. Find the value of x.

(A) 7 litres   (B) 10 litres
(C) 9 litres   (D) 11 litres
(E) None of these

17. A vessel contains 50 litres of alcohol. 10 litres of alcohol is drawn off & same amount of water is replaced in the vessel. This process is repeated for one more time. Find sub-duplicate ratio of alcohol to water in the vessel.

(A) 16:9   (B) 8:19
(C) 9:19   (D) 9:20
(E) None of these

18. In 200 litres mixture of milk & water, milk is 136 litres more than that of water. When 'a' litres of milk is taken out and (a+30) litres of water is added, milk becomes 50% more than that of water. Find the value of 'a'.

(A) 30 litres   (B) 15 litres
(C) 20 litres   (D) 40 litres
(E) None of these

19. A container contains mixture of milk & water in the ratio 3:2. If 8 litres of milk is added in it then ratio of milk to water

becomes 2:1. Find the initial quantity of total mixture.
(A) 50 litres   (B) 30 litres
(C) 40 litres   (D) 45 litres
(E) None of these

20. In 4 kg mixture of copper and zinc, 30% is copper. How much zinc powder should be added to the mixture so that the quantity of copper becomes 20%?
(A) 1 kg   (B) 2 kg
(C) 1.5 kg   (D) 2.5 kg
(E) None of these

SOLUTION

1. (D) Quantity of metal Q in 120 kg of alloy A $= 120 \times \frac{2}{3} = 80$ kg

   Quantity of metal Q in 300 kg of alloy B $= 300 \times \frac{1}{3} = 100$ kg

   Quantity of metal Q in new alloy $= 80 + 100 = 180$ kg

2. (A) Required ratio
   $$= \left(45 \times \frac{4}{9} + 40 \times \frac{5}{8}\right) : \left(45 \times \frac{5}{9} + 40 \times \frac{3}{8}\right)$$
   $$= (20 + 25) : (25 + 15)$$
   $$= 45 : 40 = 9 : 8$$

3. (B) Cost of the mixture
   $$= 37.5 \times \frac{100}{125} = \text{Rs } 30$$

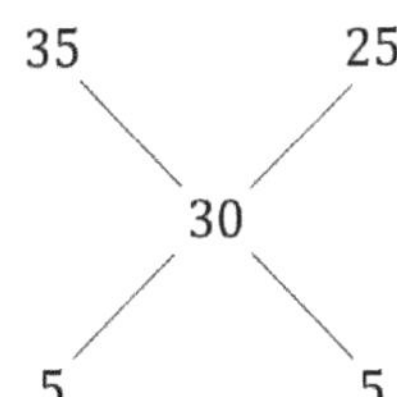

   Ratio is 1:1
   30 liters of milk he buys at Rs 25 per liter.

4. (C) Required ratio $= \left(\frac{4}{7} + \frac{5}{7}\right) : \left(\frac{3}{7} + \frac{2}{7}\right)$
   $$= \frac{9}{7} : \frac{5}{7} = 9 : 5$$

5. (B) Equating the quantity of milk in the given 3 mixture

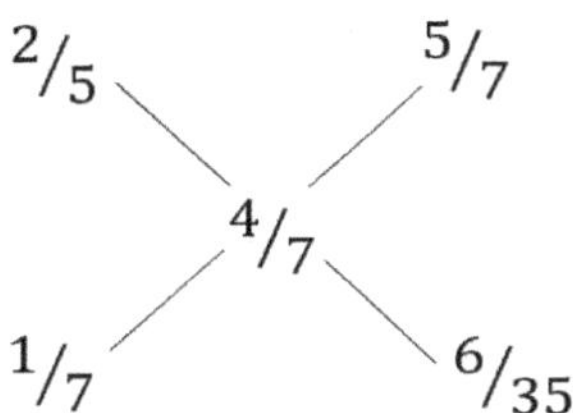

   Ratio is 5:6
   This can be found using the quantities of water also.

6. (A) Amount of base in mixture
   $$= \frac{(100-40)}{100} \times 500 = 300 \text{ gm}$$
   New amount of base
   $$= 300 + 100 = 400 \text{ gm}$$
   Required percentage
   $$= \frac{400}{500+100} \times 100 = \frac{4}{6} \times 100 = 66\frac{2}{3}\%$$

7. (B) Taking the proportion of tin in the mixture

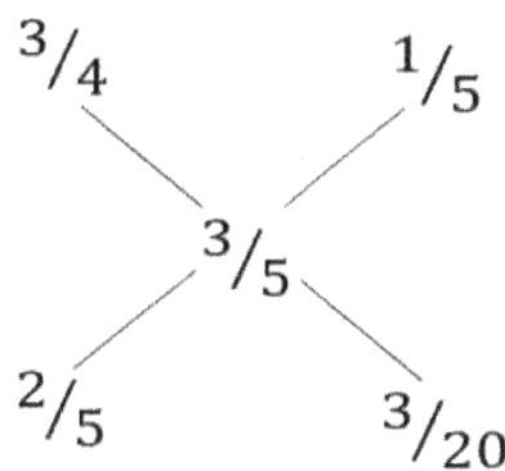

   Ratio is 8:3
   Required quantity $= 11 \times \frac{3}{11} = 3$ kg

8. (C) Cost price $= 30 \times \frac{100}{120} = \text{Rs } 25$
   Equating the proportion of milk in the mixture

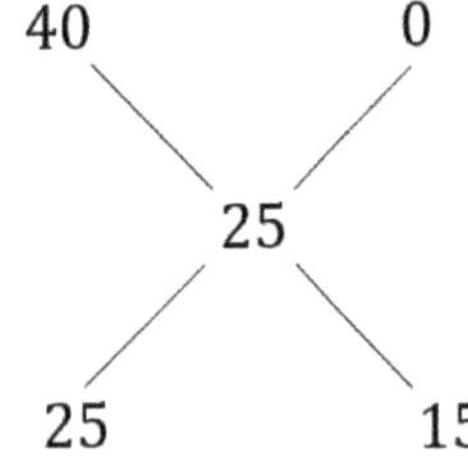

Ratio is 5:3

3 litres of water & 5 liters of milk in the mixture

Minimum mixture of water is 24 liters.

9. (A) In 100 litres of mixture,

30% of water = 30L

70% of juice = 70L

Let the water needed to be added be 'x' litres.

$$\frac{x+30}{70} = \frac{^{50}/_{100}}{^{50}/_{100}} = 1$$

$x + 30 = 1$

$x = 40$ litres

10. (C) If capacity of 1 container is 1, capacity of 3 containers is 3.

Total amount of milk in all three containers

$$= \frac{2}{3} + \frac{3}{5} + \frac{1}{6} = \frac{20+18+5}{30} = \frac{43}{30}$$

Total water $= 3 - \frac{43}{30} = \frac{47}{30}$

Required ratio $= \frac{43}{30} : \frac{47}{30} = 43:47$

11. (A) Ratio of milk & water in the resultant mixture $= \left(\frac{3}{8} \times 4 + \frac{4}{5} \times 5\right) : \left(\frac{5}{8} \times 4 + \frac{1}{5} \times 5\right) = \frac{11}{2} : \frac{7}{2} = 11:7$

Required quantity $= \frac{66}{11} \times (11 + 7) =$

6×18

$\qquad = 108$ litres

12. (C) Amount of

• Liquor in final mixture $= \frac{60}{100} + \frac{7}{10}$

$$= \frac{3}{5} + \frac{7}{10} = \frac{13}{10}$$

• Water in final mixture $= \frac{40}{100} + \frac{3}{10} = \frac{7}{10}$

Required ratio $= \frac{12}{10} : \frac{7}{10} = 13:7$

13. (B) Whatever the amount of mixture is taken out, the ratio will remain unchanged. So, the amount of mixture replaced can't be determined.

14. (A) In 40 litres of mixture,

• Amount of milk $= 140 \times \frac{35}{100}$

$\qquad = 49$ litres

• Amount of milk $= 140 \times \frac{65}{100}$

$\qquad = 91$ litres

Let amount of water added be x.

$$\frac{49+x}{91} = \frac{45}{55} = \frac{9}{11}$$

$539 + 11x = 819$

$11x = 280$

$x = 25.45 \approx 25.5$ litres

15. (D) Let x litres of mixture be taken out & same amount of water is added to mixture.

$$\frac{20 - \frac{2x}{5}}{30 - \frac{3x}{5} + x} = \frac{8}{17}$$

$$\frac{100 - 2x}{150 + 2x} = \frac{8}{17}$$

$x = 10$ litres

16. (C) In 75 L of mixture,

• Amount of coke $= \frac{13}{25} \times 75$

$\qquad = 39$ litres

• Amount of water $= \frac{12}{25} \times 75$

$\qquad = 36$ litres

Acc. To the Qn.,

$$\frac{39+11}{36+x} = \frac{10}{9}$$

$50(9) = 10(36 + 3)$

$10x + 360 = 450$

$10x = 90$

$x = 9$ litres

17. (A) After 1st replacement:

Mixture = 40 litres of alcohol +

10 litres of water

Ratio of alcohol to water = $4:1$

After 1st replacement:

Mixture = $\left[40 - \frac{4}{5}(10)\right]$ litres of alcohol

$+ \left[10 - \frac{1}{5}(10)\right]$ litres of water

$+ 10$ litres of water

= 32 litres of alcohol + 18 litres of water

Required ratio = $\frac{32}{18} = 16:9$

18. (A) Let quantity of milk & water be x & y respectively.

$x + y = 200$

$x - y = 136$

$x = 168, \ y = 32$

$\frac{168 - a}{32 + a + 30} = \frac{3}{2}$

$336 - 2a = 186 + 3a$

$5a = 150$

$a = 30$ litres

19. (C) Let initial quantity of milk & water be x & y litres respectively.

$\frac{x}{y} = \frac{3}{2} \Rightarrow x = \frac{3}{2}y$

$\frac{x+8}{y} = \frac{2}{1} \Rightarrow x - 2y + 8 = 0$

$\frac{3}{2}y - 2y + 8 = 0$

$\frac{1}{2}y = 8; \ y = 16$

$x = 24$ litres

Total quantity = $24 + 16 = 40$ litres

20. (B) In 4 kg,

- Copper = $\frac{30}{100} \times 4 = 1.2$ kg

- Zinc = $\frac{70}{100} \times 4 = 2.8$ kg

$\frac{1.2}{2.8 + a} = \frac{2}{8} = \frac{1}{4}$

$4.8 = 2.8 + a$

$a = 4.8 - 2.8 = 2$ kg

Thus, 2 kg of zinc needed to be added.

PRACTICE:

1. In what ratio must rice at Rs 35 per kg be mixed with another rice at Rs 45 per kg so that the mixture be worth Rs 41 per kg?
   (A) 2:5 (B) 2:3
   (C) 3:2 (D) 5:2
   (E) None of these

2. A container has 50 litres of milk. 10 litres of milk is taken out and replaced by an equal amount of water. If 10 litres of newly formed mixture is taken out of the container, what is the final quantity of milk left in the container?
   (A) 36 litres (B) 34 litres
   (C) 32 litres (D) 28 litres
   (E) None of these

3. From a 5:4 solution of milk & water, 25% taken out & replaced by milk. How many times should this process be done to make the ratio of milk to water as 13:3?
   (A) 1 time (B) 4 times
   (C) 2 times (D) 3 times
   (E) None of these

4. In the first mixture, quantity of milk was 12 litres more than that of water. After adding 80 litres of second mixture (having ratio of water to milk 3:5) to the first mixture, ratio of water to milk in the final mixture becomes 5:7. Find the total quantity of water in the final mixture.
   (A) 55 litres (B) 50 litres
   (C) 40 litres (D) 60 litres
   (E) None of these

5. In a mixture of juice & water, juice is 25% more than water. This is mixed with another mixture having juice & water in the ratio 7:2. If these two are mixed in the ratio 4:3. Find the ratio of juice & water in the final mixture.

(A) 41:22   (B) 43:21
(C) 41:21   (D) 40:23
(E) None of these

6. A container is full of 60 litres milk. If 15 litres of content is replaced by water and the same process is further repeated for two times, then find the quantity of milk left in the final solution (approx.)
(A) 25 litres   (B) 21 litres
(C) 28 litres   (D) 32 litres
(E) None of these

7. In a mixture of wine and water, 40 litres of water is mixed due to which ratio changes from 3:5 to 1:3. Find the initial quantity of mixture (in litres)
(A) 90 litres   (B) 60 litres
(C) 70 litres   (D) 80 litres
(E) None of these

8. In what ratio, should tea costing Rs 72 per kg should be mixed with tea costing Rs 58 per kg so that a profit of 20% is earned when the mixture is sold at Rs 78 per kg
(A) 1:2   (B) 3:1
(C) 1:1   (D) 2:3
(E) None of these

9. A mixture has milk and water in the ratio of 3:4. If 5 litres of water is added to the mixture, then total quantity of water is increased by 25%. Find the quantity of milk in the mixture.
(A) 18 litres   (B) 15 litres
(C) 25 litres   (D) 20 litres
(E) None of these

10. Tin and copper are mixed in different ratios to form two alloys, alloy A & alloy B. Alloy A contains 30% tin and alloy B contains 40% copper. Both are further mixed in a certain ratio 'a' to form a new alloy which contains 60% copper. Find the ratio 'a'.
(A) 2:1   (B) 1:2
(C) 2:3   (D) 3:1
(E) None of these

11. A mixture contains alcohol and water in the ratio 3:4. On adding 23 litres of water, the ratio of alcohol to water becomes 7:17. Actual quantity of alcohol in the mixture is
(A) 18 litres   (B) 25 litres
(C) 14 litres   (D) 21 litres
(E) None of these

12. Two types of alloys possess gold & silver in the ratio 8:9 and 7:10. In what ratio should they be mixed so as to have a new alloy in which gold & silver would exist in the ratio 12:5?
(A) 2:3   (B) 5:4
(C) 4:5   (D) 3:2
(E) None of these

13. One type of liquid contains 30% of water & the second type of liquid contains 25% of water. A glass is filled with 8 parts of first liquid & 4 parts of second liquid. The percentage of water in the new mixture in the glass is
(A) 28 1/3%   (B) 27 2/3%
(C) 26%   (D) 29 1/2%
(E) None of these

14. In a mixture of acid & water, 50 litres of water is added due to which the ratio of milk & water changes from 4:5 to 2:5. Find the initial quantity of mixture.
(A) 110 litres   (B) 45 litres
(C) 90 litres   (D) 80 litres
(E) None of these

15. A vessel contains x litres of milk & water in the ratio 4:5. 36 litres of mixture is taken out from the vessel & replaced by water. Thus, water becomes 81.25% more than the milk in the vessel now. What is the value of 'x'?

(A) 190 litres   (B) 135 litres
(C) 90 litres   (D) 180 litres
(E) None of these

16. A person purchased 60 kg of rice at Rs 35 per kg and another 30 kg rice at a certain rate. He mixed the two and sold the entire quantity at the rate of Rs 37.2 per kg and made 20% overall profit. At what price per kg did he purchase the lot of another 30 kg rice?

(A) Rs 26   (B) Rs 23
(C) Rs 27.5   (D) Rs 21
(E) None of these

SOLUTION:

1. (B) Required ratio = $2:3$

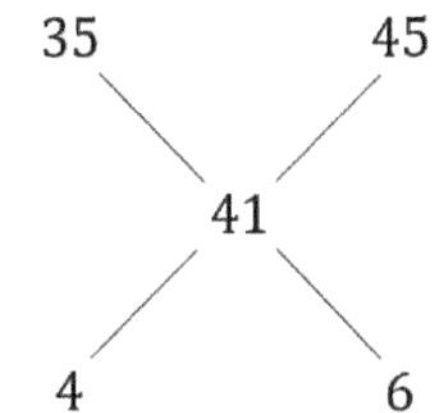

2. (C) Required quantity $= 50\left(1 - \dfrac{10}{50}\right)^2$

$$= 50 \times \dfrac{4}{5} \times \dfrac{4}{5} = 32 \text{ litres}$$

3. (D) Let the no. of times of the repeating process be 'n'. Equating the volume of water

$$\dfrac{4}{(5+4)} \times \left(\dfrac{75}{100}\right)^n = \dfrac{3}{(13+3)}$$

$$\dfrac{4}{9} \times \left(\dfrac{3}{4}\right)^n = \dfrac{3}{16}$$

$$\left(\dfrac{3}{4}\right)^n = \dfrac{3}{16} \times \dfrac{9}{4} = \left(\dfrac{3}{4}\right)^3$$

$$n = 3 \text{ times}$$

4. (B) In first mixture,

- Quantity of water = x litres
- Quantity of milk = (x + 12) litres

Quantity of second mixture added,

- Water $= 80 \times \dfrac{3}{8} = 30$ litres
- Milk $= 80 \times \dfrac{5}{8} = 50$ litres

$$\dfrac{x+30}{x+12+50} = \dfrac{5}{7}$$

$$7x + 210 = 5x + 310$$

$$2x = 100$$

$$x = 50 \text{ litres}$$

5. (A) Mixture 1:

Juice: Water $= \dfrac{125}{100} \times 100 : 100 = 5:4$

Final mixture:

$$\dfrac{\text{Juice}}{\text{Water}} = \dfrac{(5\times4)+(7\times3)}{(4\times4)+(2\times3)} = \dfrac{20+21}{16+6} = \dfrac{41}{22}$$

6. (A) Required quantity $= 60\left(1 - \dfrac{15}{60}\right)^3$

$$= 60 \times \left(\dfrac{3}{4}\right)^3 = 25.3125 \approx 25 \text{ litres}$$

7. (D) Let initial quantity of wine & water be 3x & 5x litres respectively.

$$\dfrac{3x}{5x+40} = \dfrac{1}{3}$$

$$9x = 5x + 40$$

$$4x = 40$$

$$x = 10$$

Initial volume $= (3 + 5)10$

$$= 80 \text{ litres}$$

8. (C) CP of mixture $= 78 \times \dfrac{100}{120} = $ Rs 65

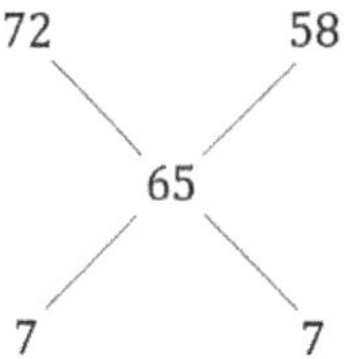

Ratio $= 1:1$

9. (B) As given,

$$4x + 5 = \dfrac{125}{100} \times 4x$$

$$4x + 5 = 5x$$

$$x = 5$$

Quantity of milk = $3 \times 5 = 15$ litres

10. (A) Fraction of copper in
- Alloy A $= \dfrac{70}{100} = \dfrac{7}{10}$
- Alloy B $= \dfrac{40}{100} = \dfrac{4}{10}$
- New alloy $= \dfrac{60}{100} = \dfrac{6}{10}$

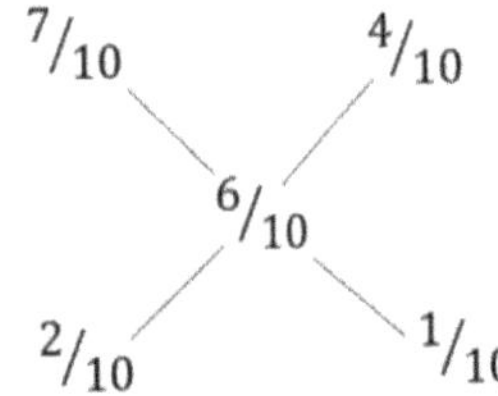

Required ratio $= 2:1$

11. (D) Acc. To the Qn.,

$$\frac{3x}{4x+23} = \frac{7}{17}$$
$$51x = 28x + 161$$
$$23x = 161$$
$$x = 7$$

Quantity of alcohol $= 7 \times 3$
$$= 21 \text{ litres}$$

12. (B)

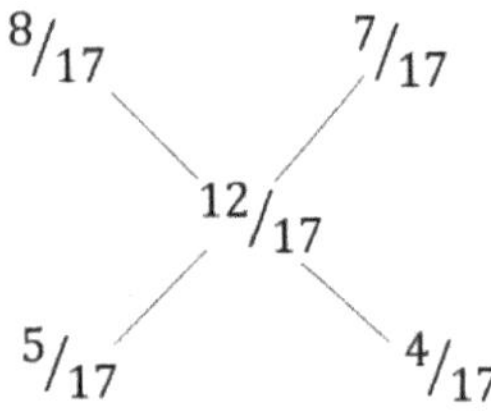

Required ratio $= 5:4$

13. (A) Amount of water in
- 1st liquid $= \dfrac{30}{100} \times 8$
$$= 2.4 \text{ parts}$$
- 2nd liquid $= \dfrac{25}{100} \times 4$
$$= 1 \text{ part}$$

In new mixture,

Water $= \dfrac{2.4+1}{8+4} \times 100 = \dfrac{3.4}{12} \times 100$
$$= 28\,{}^{1}/_{3}\,\%$$

14. (C) $\dfrac{4x}{5x+50} = \dfrac{2}{5}$
$$20x = 10x + 100$$
$$10x = 100$$
$$x = 10 \text{ litres}$$

Initial quantity of mixture $= 9x$
$$= 9(10)$$
$$= 90 \text{ litres}$$

15. (D) $\dfrac{4x-\left(36\times\frac{4}{9}\right)}{5x-\left(36\times\frac{5}{9}\right)+36} = \dfrac{181.25}{100}$

$$\frac{4x-16}{5x-20+36} = \frac{725}{400} = \frac{29}{16}$$
$$116x - 464 = 80x + 256$$
$$36x = 720$$
$$x = 20 \text{ litres}$$

Initial quantity $= 9x = 9(20)$
$$= 180 \text{ litres}$$

16. (B) Let he purchase 30 kg lot at Rs x kg

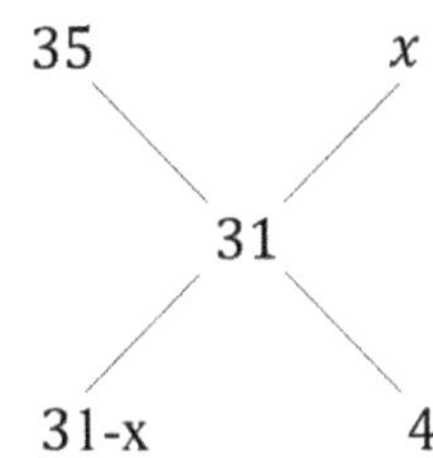

ATQ, $\dfrac{31-x}{4} = \dfrac{60}{30}$

$$x = 23$$

SIMPLE INTEREST & COMPOUND INTEREST

Unit 10

SIMPLE INTEREST:

Simple interest is based on the principal amount of a loan or deposit, while compound interest is based on the principal amount and the interest that accumulates on it in every period.

Key terms:
- Principle:
The money borrowed or lent out for a certain period of time
- Interest:
Extra amount of money paid by the borrower to the lender for usage of that money.
- Rate of interest:
Interest per year expressed as percentage of principle.
- Amount:
Total money summed by after its return.

Amount = Principle + Interest

Note: SI is calculated only on the principal amount or portion of the principal amount which remains unpaid)

Formulas:
1) $SI = \frac{P \times R \times T}{100}$
P-Principal/sum borrowed or lent out
R-Rate of interest
T-Time for which sum is borrowed / lent out

2) Amount(A) = Principal + SI
$= P + \frac{PRT}{100}$
$= P(1 + \frac{RT}{100})$

Remainder: In SI, every year, the interest will be the same

COMPOUND INTEREST:

During the process of interest calculation, the interest is added to the principal at the end of each period to arrive at the new period for the next period.

Under compound interest, the amount at the end of the first year will become principal for the second year. The amount at the end of the second year becomes the principle for the third year & so on.

(Time period can be of monthly/quarterly, 6months (half yearly), 12months(yearly)

P-Principle/sum
n - No. of years
R-Rate percent per annum
A-Amount

1) Compounded Yearly:
Interest is added to principle every 12 months (1year)
- Amount after n years: $P \times [1 + \frac{R}{100}]^n$
- Interest I = Amount − Principle
$$= P \times [\left(1 + \frac{R}{100}\right)^n - 1]$$

- When rates are r_1, r_2, r_3…r_n percent for interest
  1st, 2nd, 3rd… n^{th} year,
  Amount equals
  $$P\left(1 + \frac{r1}{100}\right)\left(1 + \frac{r2}{100}\right)\left(1 + \frac{r3}{100}\right)…\left(1 + \frac{rn}{100}\right)$$

2) <u>Compounded half yearly or semi-annually:</u>

The interest is added to principle every 6 month,

- Amount $= P \times [1 + \frac{R/2}{100}]^{2n}$

3) <u>Compounded quarterly:</u>

Interest is calculated and added four times in a year

$$A = P[1 + \frac{R/4}{100}]^{4n}$$

4) Difference between SI & CI for 2 years, considering principle & rate of interest as same

- For a period of 2 years: Difference
  $= P(\frac{R}{100})^2$

  If SI's given, difference $= SI \times \frac{R}{100}$

- For a period of 3 years: Difference
  $= P\left(\frac{R}{100}\right)^2 (\frac{R}{100} + 3)$

- In case of paying sum in instalments ie., in parts
  Then,
  $$P = [\frac{x}{1 + \frac{R}{100}} + \frac{x}{(1 + \frac{R}{100})^2} + \frac{x}{(1 + \frac{R}{100})^3}$$
  $$+ ….+ \frac{x}{(1 + \frac{R}{100})^n})$$

  x = Value of each instalment
  Total amount paid in instalments $\rightarrow$ A
  $$= P(1 + \frac{R}{100})^n$$
  n$\rightarrow$ no. of installments

- If a certain sum at CI becomes 'a' times in n_1 year & 'b' times in n_2 years,
  Then, $a^{\frac{1}{n1}} = b^{\frac{1}{n2}}$

EXERCISE:

SIMPLE INTEREST:

1. What is the simple interest obtained on a sum of Rs 15,600 for 7 months at 4% p.a.?
   (A) Rs 348   (B) Rs 326
   (C) Rs 420   (D) Rs 364
   (E) None of these

2. Shoba invested Rs 8500 at 7% p.a. simple interest for 3 years. Karthi invested Rs 9600 at 11% p.a. for 2 years. Find the total interest obtained by both of them.
   (A) Rs 3796   (B) Rs 3897
   (C) Rs 3954   (D) Rs 3840
   (E) None of these

3. Ajay invested a sum for half a year at 12% p.a. At the end of 6 months, he got a total amount of Rs 4240. Find the sum.
   (A) Rs 4000   (B) Rs 4500
   (C) Rs 3800   (D) Rs 4200
   (E) None of these

4. A invested Rs 18,250 at 10% p.a. SI for 200 days & B invested Rs 7,300 for 100 days at 12% pa. Find the total amount received.
   (A) Rs 26,620   (B) Rs 26,840
   (C) Rs 26,790   (D) Rs 26,750
   (E) None of these

5. Raj invested Rs 9500 at 14% p.a. for 3 years & Rs 7000 at R% p.a. for 4 years. He got a total amount of 22,730. Find the rate of interest (R%).
   (A) 6%   (B) 8%
   (C) 10%   (D) 9%
   (E) None of these

6. If a sum of money quadruples in 15 years. Find the rate of interest.
   (A) 20%   (B) 25%

(C) 12% (D) 18%
(E) None of these

7. Sasi invested Rs 4500 at R% p.a. SI for 8 years & Rs 5000 at R/2% p.a. SI for 5 years. Difference between the interests earned from the two instalments is Rs 2115. Find rate of interest (R).
(A) 8% (B) 7%
(C) 9% (D) 10%
(E) None of these

8. Kumar invested a certain sum at 5% p.a. SI for 3 years & he invested $2/3^{rd}$ of the sum at 6% p.a. SI for 4 years. He got a total interest of Rs 4464. After that, he invested the total amount in bank that offers SI at 10% p.a. for 5 years. Find the interest he earned from bank.
(A) Rs 14,323 (B) Rs 14,232
(C) Rs 14,252 (D) Rs 14,848
(E) None of these

9. Varun borrowed Rs 4000 from his friend at 5% p.a. SI for 7 years. Varun lent that money at 12% p.a. SI for 4 years. After 4 years, he lent the total amount at 10% p.a. SI for 3 years. Find the profit earned by Varun.
(A) Rs 2304 (B) Rs 2280
(C) Rs 2345 (D) Rs 2296
(E) None of these

10. A sum is borrowed at 4.5% pa SI for 4 years. If an amount of Rs 10,325 is returned back, what is the interest returned.
(A) Rs 1585 (B) Rs 1580
(C) Rs 1570 (D) Rs 1575
(E) None of these

11. Simple interest on a certain amount is $1/4^{th}$ of the principal. If the numbers representing the rate of interest in percent & time of years be equal then time for which the principal is lent out is?
(A) 8 years (B) 5 years
(C) 6 years (D) 4 years
(E) None of these

12. A certain money becomes $5/4^{th}$ of itself in 5 years at a certain rate of simple interest find the rate of interest (in %)
(A) 4% (B) 4.5%
(C) 5% (D) 5.5%
(E) None of these

13. A certain sum of money is amounted to Rs 1200 at 5% in a time duration in which Rs 800 amounted to Rs 960 at the same rate. If rate of interest is simple, then what is the sum?
(A) Rs 1050 (B) Rs 1200
(C) Rs 800 (D) Rs 1000
(E) None of these

14. A sum becomes 3 times in 2 years at a rate of simple interest. If twice of that sum is invested, then in how many years the sum will become 6 times of initial sum at same rate of interest?
(A) 1 year (B) 1.5 years
(C) 2.5 yeas (D) 2 years
(E) None of these

15. Bhuvana invests a sum of Rs 30,664 in two schemes for 2 years, one at 5% pa & other at 10% pa SI & got total interest of Rs 4669.6 (after 2 years). Find the sum invested at 10% per annum.
(A) Rs 15,462 (B) Rs 16,032
(C) Rs 16,132 (D) Rs 16,064
(E) None of these

COMPOUND INTEREST

16. A person invested Rs 20,000 for 2 years at an interest of 12% p.a. compounded

annually. What is the compound interest that the person gets after 2 years?
(A) Rs 5092   (B) Rs 5084
(C) Rs 5044   (D) Rs 5088
(E) None of these

17. Sasi lends Rs 1000 at 10% compound interest every year. How much will he get back after 3 years?
(A) Rs 3651   (B) Rs 3631
(C) Rs 3641   (D) Rs 3621
(E) None of these

18. At what rate percent per annum of compound interest will Rs 13,125 amounts to Rs 15,309 in 2 years?
(A) 6%   (B) 8%
(C) 12%   (D) 10%
(E) None of these

19. In how many years, Rs 62,500 become Rs 70,304 at 4% p.a. compound interest, calculated annually?
(A) 3 years   (B) 4 years
(C) 2 years   (D) 2.5 years
(E) None of these

20. P invests Rs 30,000 for half year at 8% pa compounded quarterly. Find the total amount (in Rs)
(A) Rs 31,208   (B) Rs 31,220
(C) Rs 31,212   (D) Rs 31,218
(E) None of these

21. If certain sum of money invested for 3 years compounded annually gets 5 times itself. In how many years it will amount to 25 times itself?
(A) 3 years   (B) 5 years
(C) 4 years   (D) 6 years
(E) None of these

22. Dhana borrowed certain sum of money on compound interest and returned it in 3 annual instalments in 3 years. If annual instalment is Rs 4968 and rate of interest is 20% per annum. Find the sum.
(A) Rs 10,465   (B) Rs 10,460
(C) Rs 10,425   (D) Rs 10, 475
(E) None of these

23. A person interested certain sum of money in scheme A For 2 years at 10% per annum compound interest. Interest earned in scheme A is Rs 920 less than the scheme B's compound interest on Rs 4000 for 2 years at 20% per annum. Find the sum invested in scheme A.
(A) Rs 3500   (B) Rs 4000
(C) Rs 3000   (D) Rs 4500
(E) None of these

24. A person with a sum of Rs 67,700 wants to deposit this sum in the bank account of his two daughters, so that after 5 years and 7 years respectively at the rate of 8% gets compounded annually to equal amounts. Find the part of amount deposited into the account of first daughter whose share was deposited for 5 years.
(A) Rs 36,450   (B) Rs 36, 540
(C) Rs 35,000   (D) Rs 37,250
(E) None of these

25. Sasi invested Rs P in scheme A offering 20% p.a. CI compound annually for 2 years and Rs (P + 4000) in Scheme B offering 10% p.a. CI compounding annually for 2 years. If interest received by Sasi from scheme B is Rs 265 more than that received by him from scheme A, then find P.
(A) Rs 2450   (B) Rs 2800
(C) Rs 2500   (D) Rs 2600
(E) None of these

COMBINED SI & CI

26. A sum of money was invested for 12 years in scheme A which offers simple interest at a rate of 6% p.a. The amount received from scheme A after 12 years was then invested for two years in scheme B which offers compound interest (compounded annually) at a rate of 10 % p.a. If the interest received from scheme B was Rs. 5418 what was the sum invested in scheme A?
(A) Rs 15,500   (B) Rs 14,000
(C) Rs 15,000   (D) Rs 16,000
(E) None of these

27. A person invested Rs. P and Rs (P+350) each at the rate of 20% of p.a. on CI and SI respectively for two years. If ratio of interest received by the person is 44:75. Then find amount invested by the person on SI?
(A) Rs 750   (B) Rs 650
(C) Rs 725   (D) Rs 700
(E) None of these

28. Edward invested Rs X in scheme A offering R% p.a. at SI for 4 years. Edward also invested Rs X in scheme B offering 20% p.a. at CI compounding annually for 2 years. If interest received by Edward from scheme A & B is Rs 9600 and Rs 6600 respectively, then find R.
(A) 16%   (B) 17%
(C) 14%   (D) 15%
(E) None of these

29. Difference between interest received when a sum is invested at 15% p.a. at CI compounded annually for 2 years & that of, when that sum is invested at 30% pa. at SI for 1 year is Rs 1080. Find the SI when the same sum invested for 2.5 years at 22% p.a.
(A) Rs 26,500   (B) Rs 26,300

(C) Rs 26,400   (D) Rs 26,200
(E) None of these

30. Find ratio between SI & CI on a sum of money invested for 3 years at 20% rate of interest per annum?
(A) 74:91   (B) 75:91
(C) 75:92   (D) 91:75
(E) None of these

SOLUTIONS:

1. (D) $SI = 15{,}600 \times \frac{4}{100} \times \frac{7}{12} = Rs\ 364$

2. (B) Total interest obtained
$= 8500 \times \dfrac{7}{100} \times 3 + 9600 \times \dfrac{11}{100} \times 2$
$= 1785 + 2112$
$= Rs\ 3897$

3. (A) Let the sum be P.
$4240 = P + (P \times \frac{6}{12} \times \frac{12}{100})$
$4240 = P\left(1 + \frac{6}{100}\right) = P\left(\frac{106}{100}\right)$
$P = \frac{4240 \times 100}{106} = Rs\ 4000$

4. (C) Total interest
$= 18250 \times \dfrac{10}{100} \times \dfrac{200}{365}$
$\qquad\qquad + 7300 \times \dfrac{100}{365} \times \dfrac{12}{100}$
$= 1000 + 240 = 1240$
Total amount $= 18250 + 7300 + 1240$
$\qquad\qquad = Rs\ 26{,}790$

5. (B) Total interest
$= 22730 - (9500 + 7000) = 6230$
Thus,
$9500 \times \frac{14}{100} \times 3 + 7000 \times \frac{R}{100} \times 4 = 6230$
$3990 + 280R = 6230$
$280R = 2240$
$R = 8\%$

6. (A) $4P = P + \dfrac{P \times R \times 15}{100}$

$$3P = \frac{P \times R \times 15}{100}$$
$$R = 20\%$$

7. (C) Let rate of interest be R.
$$4500 \times \frac{R}{100} \times 8 \sim 5000 \times \frac{R}{200} \times 5 = 2115$$
$$R(360 - 125) = 2115$$
$$R = \frac{2115}{235} = 9\%$$

8. (B) Let the sum be P.
$$P \times \frac{5}{100} \times 3 + \frac{2P}{3} \times \frac{6}{100} \times 4 = 4464$$
$$P\left(\frac{15}{100} + \frac{16}{100}\right) = 4464;$$
$$P\left(\frac{31}{100}\right) = 4464$$
$$P = 14400$$
Total sum
$$= 14400 + \frac{2}{3}(14400) + 4464$$
$$= 28{,}464$$
Interest $= 28{,}464 \times \frac{10}{100} \times 5$
$$= \text{Rs } 14{,}232$$

9. (D) Money to be returned after 7 years =
$$4000 \times \frac{5}{100} \times 7 + 400 = 1400 +$$
$$4000 = \text{Rs } 5400$$
Money lent:
For 4 yrs.: $4000 \times 4 \times \frac{12}{100} = 1920$,
Amount $= 4000 + 1920 = \text{Rs } 5920$
For 3 yrs.: $5920 \times 3 \times \frac{10}{100} = 1776$,
Amount $= 5920 + 1776 = \text{Rs } 7696$
Profit earned by Varun $= 7696 - 5400$
$$= \text{Rs } 2296$$

10. (D) $P \times \frac{4.5}{100} \times 4 + P = 10325$
$$P\left(\frac{18}{100} + 1\right) = 10325$$
$$P = \frac{10325 \times 100}{118} = \text{Rs } 8750$$
Interest $= 10325 - 8750 = \text{Rs } 1575$

11. (B) Let the principal x
$$SI = \frac{1}{4}x$$

Let rate = a % & time = a years
$$\frac{x \times a \times a}{100} = \frac{1}{4}x$$
$$a^2 = \frac{100}{4} = 25; \quad a = 5$$
Time = 5 years

12. (C) Let the amount be x & rate of interest be R%
Interest $= \frac{5}{4}x - x = \frac{1}{4}x$
$$\frac{1}{4}x = \frac{x \times R \times 5}{100}$$
$$R = \frac{100}{5 \times 4} = 5\%$$

13. (D) According to the Qn.
$$960 - 800 = \frac{800 \times 5 \times T}{100}$$
$$T = \frac{160 \times 100}{800 \times 5} = 4 \text{ years}$$
T = 4 years, R = 5%, Amount = Rs 1200
$$1200 - P = \frac{P \times 5 \times 4}{100}$$
$$\frac{P}{5} + P = 1200;$$
$$P = \text{Rs } 1000$$

14. (D) Acc. to the qn.,
$$3P - P = \frac{P \times 2 \times R}{100}; R = 100\%$$
$$(6P - 2P) = \frac{2P \times T \times 100}{100}$$
$$T = \frac{4P}{2P} = 2 \text{ years}$$

15. (B) Let sum invested at 10% per annum be Rs x.
$$\frac{x \times 2 \times 10}{100} + \frac{(30664 - x) \times 5 \times 2}{100} = 4669.6$$
$$20x + 306640 - 10x = 466960$$
$$10x = 160320$$
$$x = \text{Rs } 16{,}032$$

16. (D) CI $= P[(1 + \frac{R}{100})^n - 1]$
$$= 20{,}000 \left[(1 + \frac{12}{100})^2 - 1\right]$$
$$= 20{,}000\left[(1 + \frac{112}{100})^2 - 1\right]$$
$$= 20000 \left[\frac{28^2 - 25^2}{25^2}\right]$$
$$= 32(159) = \text{Rs } 5088$$

17. (C) Amount

$$= 1000 \times \frac{110}{100} + 1000 \times \left(\frac{110}{100}\right)^2 +$$
$$1000 \times \left(\frac{110}{100}\right)^3$$
$$= 1100 + 1210 + 1331$$
$$= \text{Rs } 3641$$

18. (B) Let rate be R%

$$15309 = 13125 \left[(1 + \frac{R}{100})\right]^2$$

$$(1 + \frac{R}{100})^2 = \frac{15309}{13125} = \frac{729}{625}$$

$$1 + \frac{R}{100} = \sqrt{\frac{729}{625}} = \frac{27}{25}$$

$$\frac{R}{100} = \frac{27}{25} - 1 = \frac{2}{25}$$

$$R = \frac{200}{25} = 8\%$$

19. (A) Let the no. of years be n.

$$70304 = 62500 \left[(1 + \frac{4}{100})^n\right]$$

$$(1 + \frac{4}{100})^n = \frac{70304}{62500} = \frac{17576}{15625}$$

$$\left(\frac{26}{25}\right)^n = \frac{17576}{15625}$$

$$N = 3 \text{ years}$$

20. (C) Amount $= P \left(1 + \frac{\frac{R}{4}}{100}\right)^2$

$$= 30000 \left(1 + \frac{\frac{8}{4}}{100}\right)^2$$

$$= 30000 \left(\frac{102}{100}\right)^2$$

$$= 3 \times (102)^2$$

$$= \text{Rs } 31,212$$

21. (D) $x^{1/n_1} = y^{1/n_2}$

When x & y are sum and n_1 & n_2 are years

$$5^{1/3} = 25^{1/n_2}$$

$$\frac{1}{3} = \frac{2}{n_2} \text{ (equating the powers)}$$

$$n_2 = 6 \text{ years}$$

22. (A) Sum $= \left[\frac{x}{1 + \frac{r}{100}} + \frac{x}{\left(1 + \frac{r}{100}\right)^2} + \frac{x}{\left(1 + \frac{r}{100}\right)^3}\right]$

Where x is instalment -

$$= x\left[\frac{100}{100 + r} + \frac{100^2}{(100 + r)^2} + \frac{100^3}{(100 + r)^3}\right]$$

$$= 4968\left[\frac{100}{120} + \frac{100^2}{120^2} + \frac{100^3}{120^3}\right]$$

$$= 4968\left[\frac{5}{6} + \frac{25}{36} + \frac{125}{216}\right]$$

$$= 4968 \times \frac{455}{216} = \text{Rs } 10465$$

23. (B) For scheme B

$$4000 \times \left(1 + \frac{20}{100}\right)^2 - 400$$

$$4000 \left(\frac{36}{25} - 1\right) = \text{Rs } 1760$$

For scheme A

$$840 = P \left[(1 + \frac{10}{100})^2 - 1\right]$$

$$P \left(\frac{121}{100} - 1\right) = P \times \frac{21}{100}$$

$$P = \frac{840 \times 100}{21} = \text{Rs } 4000$$

24. (A) Let the amount be P1 & P2 whose time periods are 5 years & 7 years respectively.

$$P1 \left(1 + \frac{8}{100}\right)^5 = P2 \left(1 + \frac{8}{100}\right)^7$$

$$\frac{p_1}{p_2} = \frac{\left(\frac{27}{25}\right)^7}{\left(\frac{27}{25}\right)^5}$$

$$= \left(\frac{27}{25}\right)^2 = \frac{729}{625}$$

$$P1 = \frac{729}{1354} \times 67,700$$

$$= \text{Rs } 36,450$$

25. (C) Acc. To the Qn.,

$$(P + 4000)(1 + \frac{10}{100})^2 - 1] - P\left[(1 + \frac{20}{100})^2 - 1\right]$$

$$(P + 4000)\left[\frac{121 - 100}{100}\right] - P\left[\frac{36 - 25}{25}\right] = 340$$

$$(P + 4000)\frac{21}{100} - P\left(\frac{11}{25}\right) = 265$$

$$21P + 84000 - 44P = 26500$$

$$23P = 57500$$

$$P = \text{Rs } 2500$$

26. (C) Let the amount invested in scheme A be Rs x.

$$SI = \frac{x \times 6 \times 12}{100} = \frac{72x}{100}$$

Amount invested in scheme B

$$= x + \frac{72x}{100} = \frac{172x}{100}$$

$$CI = P \left[1 + (\frac{R}{100})^t - 1\right]$$

$$= \frac{172x}{100}\left[(1 + \frac{10}{100})^2 - 1\right]$$

$$= \frac{172x}{100}\left[\frac{121}{100} - 1\right]$$

$$= \frac{172x \times 21}{10000}$$

$$\frac{172x \times 21}{10000} = 5418$$

$$x = \frac{5418 \times 10000}{172 \times 21} = Rs\ 15,000$$

27. (D) Equivalent CI at rate of 20% for 2 years

$$= 20 + 20 + \frac{20 \times 20}{100} = 44\ \%$$

Total CI received $= P \times \frac{44}{100} = \frac{44P}{100}$

Total SI received $= (P+350) \times \frac{40}{100}$

$$= \frac{40P + 14000}{100}$$

Acc. to the Qn.,

$$\frac{44P}{40P + 14000} = \frac{44}{75}$$

$75P = 40P + 1400$

$35P = 1400$

$P = Rs\ 400$

Amount invested on SI $= 400 + 350$

$= Rs\ 700$

28. (A) Equivalent rate of interest at 20% p.a. CI for 2 years

$$= 20 + 20 + \frac{20 \times 20}{100} = 44\%$$

$$= x \times \frac{44}{100} = 6600$$

$x = 15,000$

$$\frac{15000 \times R \times 4}{100} = 9600$$

$$R = \frac{9600}{100 \times 4}$$

$R = 16\%$

29. (C) Let the sum be Rs x.

Equivalent rate of interest at 15 % p.a. CI

$$= 15 + 15 + \frac{(15 \times 15)}{100} = 32.25\%$$

Acc.to. the Qn.,

$$x = \frac{32.25}{100} - x \times \frac{30}{100} = 1080$$

$$x = \frac{1080 \times 100}{2.25}$$

$x = Rs\ 48,000$

Required interest $= \dfrac{48000 \times 22 \times 2.25}{100}$

$$= Rs\ 26,400$$

30. (B) Required ratio $= \dfrac{\frac{P \times 20 \times 3}{100}}{P\left(1 + \frac{20}{100}\right)3 - P}$

$$= \frac{\frac{3P}{5}}{P\left[\left(\frac{6}{5}\right)3 - 1\right]} = \frac{3}{5\left[\frac{216}{125} - 1\right]}$$

$$= \frac{3 \times 125}{5 \times 91} = \frac{75}{91}$$

PRACTICE:

1. Surya invested Rs 12,500 at 6% p.a. for 4 years. After 4 years, he invested total amount at R% SI for 4 more years. Finally, he got a total amount of Rs 20,460. Find rate of interest.
   (A) 4% (B) 6%
   (C) 10% (D) 8%
   (E) None of these

2. A borrowed a sum of Rs 26,000 at 4% p.a. for 3.5 years from B. A also borrowed a sum of Rs 18,000 at 5% p.a. for a certain time period from C. If the total amount paid back by A is 49,890. Find the time period of the borrowing from C.
   (A) 2.5 years (B) 2 years
   (C) 3 years (D) 1.5 years
   (E) None of these

3. Karthi invested a certain sum (P) at 12% p.a. for 7 years. After 7 years he invested the total amount at 8% p.a. SI for 5 years. Finally, he got a total amount of Rs 87,584. If he invested the sum(P) at 6% p.a. SI for 2 years, find the interest he would have received.
   (A) Rs 4200 (B) Rs 4100

(C) Rs 4080 (D) Rs 4050
(E) None of these

4. Ratio of sum invested in 2 schemes A & B is 10:11. Ratio of their rates of SI is 4:5 and ratio of their investment period is 2:3. Find the ratio of their SI received.
(A) 16:33 (B) 33:16
(C) 32:17 (D) 17:32
(E) None of these

5. Priya invested a certain sum at 12% p.a. SI for 4 years & she invested 3/4th of the sum at 10% p.a. for 5 years. She got a total interest of Rs 4617. After that she invested the total amount in another scheme which offers SI at 10% p.a. for 5 years. Find interest earned from the last scheme.
(A) Rs 7033.5 (B) Rs 7076.5
(C) Rs 6946.2 (D) Rs 7155.2
(E) None of these

6. A deposited Rs 12,400 at fixed deposit at 8% SI for 2 years. After 2 years, A adds the interest to the principle. What is the total interest earned after 5 years?
(A) Rs 5346.16 (B) Rs 5436.16
(C) Rs 5234.16 (D) Rs 5468.16
(E) None of these

7. Karthi invests an amount of Rs 19,070 at a rate of 4% pa to obtain a total amount of Rs 22,884 on   simple interest after a certain period. for how many years did he invest the amount to obtain the total sum?
(A) 6 years (B) 8 years
(C) 4 years (D) 5 years
(E) None of these

8. In what time Rs 8000 at 3% simple interest p.a. will produce the same amount of interest as Rs 6000 does in 5 years at 8% simple interest per annum?

(A) 10 years (B) 8 years
(C) 9 years (D) 6 years
(E) None of these

9. Sasi invested an amount for 3 years at a simple interest rate of 9% p.a. He got an amount of Rs 38,100 at the end of 3 years. What principal amount did he invest?
(A) Rs 29,500 (B) Rs 30,000
(C) Rs 30,500 (D) Rs 32,000
(E) None of these

10. A person deposits an equal amount of Rs 24,000 in two different banks on different interest rates. After 6 years, the difference between the interest received from these two banks Rs 576. What is the difference between their interest rates?
(A) 0.6 % (B) 0.2%
(C) 0.4% (D) 0.8%
(E) None of these

11. If a certain sum becomes twice in 3 years at certain rate of SI, then find simple interest earned on Rs 3000 after 4 years at the same rate of interest.
(A) Rs 4000 (B) Rs 4500
(C) Rs 3800 (D) Rs 3600
(E) None of these

12. Simple interest become what times of principal of Rs 5000 after 8years at the rate of 22.5% per amount at SI?
(A) 1.6 (B) 1.2
(C) 1.8 (D) 2.2
(E) None of these

13. A person invests his money in 2 schemes. He invests Rs (P + 2000) in scheme A at 10 % SI for 3 years & Rs P in scheme B at 15% SI for 3 years. If after 3 years, he got a total of Rs 3600 interest. find the value of P.
(A) Rs 4200 (B) Rs 4000

(C) Rs 3500   (D) Rs 3000
(E) None of these

14. Shobana has certain money. She spends 15% on paying bills, 20% on loan instalment & interest 35% on simple interest at rate of 25% per annum & saves remaining Rs 2520. Find interest earned by her after 1 year?
(A) Rs 735   (B) Rs 740
(C) Rs 732   (D) Rs 748
(E) None of these

15. Edward bought a laptop under a scheme of down payment of Rs 28,000 & the rest amount at 8% per annum SI for 2 years. In this way, he paid Rs 58,160 in total find the actual price of the laptop?
(A) Rs 54,000   (B) Rs 52,000
(C) Rs 58,000   (D) Rs 48,000
(E) None of these

16. Jothi interest Rs 5600 at simple interest and after a year he got Rs 6076. Find the rate of interest (in %)
(A) 8%   (B) 7.8%
(C) 8.5%   (D) 8.6 %
(E) None of these

17. Karthi interest Rs 40,000 for one year at 6% pa compounded half yearly. Find the total amount (in Rs)
(A) Rs 42,432   (B) Rs 42,436
(C) Rs 42,420   (D) Rs 42,442
(E) None of these

18. A certain sum amounts to Rs 37,044 in 3 years and to Rs 35,280 in 2 years in CI compounded annually. Find the sum.
(A) Rs 33,000   (B) Rs 32,000
(C) Rs 31,000   (D) Rs 30,000
(E) None of these

19. Shoba invested certain sum of money at 25% compound interest. After how many years it get more than double?
(A) 4 years   (B) 3 years
(C) 2 years   (D) 5 years
(E) None of these

20. A sum of Rs 8856 was taken as a loan. This is to be repaid in two annual instalments. The rate of interest is 25%, which is compounded annually. Find the value of each instalment (in Rs)
(A) Rs 6150   (B) Rs 6250
(C) Rs 6100   (D) Rs 6050
(E) None of these

21. How much more would Rs 24000 make, after two years, if it is invested at 20% p.a. compound interest payable half yearly, than if it is invested 20% p.a. compound interest payable yearly (in Rs.)
(A) Rs 580.5   (B) Rs 576.2
(C) Rs 578. 4   (D) Rs 582.6
(E) None of these

22. Each year, Mahesh spent 60% of his annual income and remaining he invested at 16% p.a. compound interest, compounded annually. How much will it become at the end of three years, Mahesh's annual income is Rs. 8 lakhs (approx.)
(A) 10 lakhs   (B) 12 lakhs
(C) 15 lakhs   (D) 13 lakhs
(E) None of these

23. Edward invested certain sum of money which amounts to Rs 10,609 in 6 months at the rate of 12% p.a. when the interest compounded quarterly. After that, she invested same sum in scheme A which offer 6% p.a. compounded annually. Find the interest earned by Edward from scheme A.

(A) Rs 545   (B) Rs 708

(C) Rs 960   (D) Rs 1050

(E) Data insufficient

24. Bhuvana invested Rs 10,000 with rate of interest 20% per annum. The interest was compounded half yearly for first one year and in the next year it was compounded yearly. What will be the total interest earned at the end of two years?

(A) Rs 4520   (B) Rs 4560

(C) Rs 4450   (D) Rs 4525

(E) None of these

25. Interest earned on a sum in 20 months is Rs 126, rate of interest is 12% per annum at CI. Find the sum if interest is calculated after every 10 months?

(A) Rs 580   (B) Rs 600

(C) Rs 550   (D) Rs 650

(E) None of these

26. An amount of (P + 5000) is invested on CI at the rate (R+4) % for two years. If total interest obtained on principal is 44%, then find the value of R.

(A) 15%   (B) 14%

(C) 18%   (D) 16%

(E) None of these

27. The respective ratio of the sums invested for 2 years each, in scheme A offering 20% per annum compound interest (compounded annually) and in scheme B offering 7% p.a. simple interest is 1:4. Different between the interests earned from both the scheme is Rs 2940. How much was invested in scheme A?

(A) Rs 24,500   (B) Rs 24,000

(C) Rs 25,500   (D) Rs 24,750

(E) None of these

28. The simple interest accrued on an amount of Rs 50,000 at the end of 4 years is Rs 16,000. What would be the compound interest accrued on the same amount at the same rate in the same period (approx.)

(A) Rs 18028   (B) Rs 18024

(C) Rs 18030   (D) Rs 18016

(E) None of these

29. Sasi invested a sum of money 'P' for 2 years in scheme A at 20% p.a. CI. The amount received at end of two years from scheme A, reinvested in scheme B for 4 years that offers 25% p.a. SI. If total interest received from scheme B is Rs 33,000 more than P, then find 'P'?

(A) Rs 76,000   (B) RS 74,000

(C) Rs 75,000   (D) Rs 73,000

(E) None of these

30. The difference between SI & CI on a sum of money interested for 2 years is Rs 100. Find rate of interest per annum if sum of money invested is Rs 50,625. (approx.)

(A) 4%   (B) 4.44%

(C) 4.78%   (D) 5.55%

(E) None of these

31. What will be the difference between simple interest & compound interest at 10% p.a. on the sum of Rs 1000 after 4 years? (approx.)

(A) Rs 66   (B) Rs 62

(C) Rs 68   (D) Rs 64

(E) None of these

SOLUTION:

1. (D) $SI = 12500 \times 4 \times \frac{6}{100} = 3000$

Total amount $= 12500 + 3000$

$$= 15500$$

Final amount $= 20460$

Interest $= 20460 - 15500 = 4960$

$15500 \times \frac{R1}{100} \times 4 = 4960$

$$R1 = \frac{4960}{155 \times 4} = 8\%$$

2. (A) Total interest equals
$$49890 - (26000 + 18000) = 5890$$
$$26{,}000 \times \frac{4}{100} \times 3.5 + 18000 \times \frac{5}{100} \times N = 5890$$
$$3640 + 900N = 5890$$
$$900N = 2250$$
$$N = 2.5 \text{ years}$$

3. (C)
$$\left[\left(P \times \frac{12}{100} \times 7 + P\right) \times \frac{8}{100} \times 5\right] + \left[P \times \frac{12}{100} \times 7 + P\right] = 87584$$
$$\left[\left(P \times \frac{84}{100} + P \times \frac{40}{100}\right)\right] + \left[P \times \frac{84}{100} + P\right] = 87584$$
$$P\left[\frac{184}{100} \times \frac{40}{100} + \frac{184}{100}\right] = 87584$$
$$P = \frac{87584 \times 10000}{25760} = 34{,}000$$

Interest he would have received
$$= 34000 \times \frac{6}{100} \times 2 = \text{Rs } 4080$$

4. (A) Ratio of SI
$$= 10 \times 2 \times 4 : 11 \times 3 \times 5$$
$$= 80 : 165$$
$$= 16 : 33$$

5. (A) Let the sum be P.
$$P \times \frac{12}{100} \times 4 + \frac{3P}{4} \times \frac{10}{100} \times 5 = 4617$$
$$P\left(\frac{48}{100} + \frac{75}{200}\right) = 4617$$
$$P(171/200) = 4617$$
$$P = \text{Rs } 5400$$

Total amount $= 5400 + \frac{3}{4}(5400) + 4617$
$$= 14067$$

Interest from last scheme $= 14067 \times \frac{10}{100} \times 5$
$$= \text{Rs } 7033.5$$

6. (B) SI $= 12400 \times 2 \times \frac{8}{100} = \text{Rs } 1984$

Amount $= 12400 + 1984 = \text{Rs } 14{,}384$

$$SI = 14384 \times 3 \times \frac{8}{100} = 3452.16$$
Total interest $= 3452.16 + 1984$
$$= \text{Rs } 5436.16$$

7. (D) $SI = \frac{19070 \times 4 \times T}{100}$
$$= (22884 - 19070)$$
$$3814 = \frac{19070 \times 4 \times T}{100}$$
$$T = \frac{3814 \times 100}{19070 \times 4} = 5 \text{ years}$$

8. SI is same
$$\frac{8000 \times 3 \times T}{100} = \frac{6000 \times 8 \times 5}{100}$$
$$T = \frac{6000 \times 8 \times 5}{8000 \times 3} = 10 \text{ years}$$

9. (B) $38100 - P = \frac{P \times 9 \times 3}{100} = \frac{27}{10}$
$$\frac{27P}{100} + P = 38100$$
$$127P = 38100 \times 100$$
$$P = \frac{38100 \times 100}{127}$$
$$P = \text{Rs } 30{,}000$$

10. (C) Let the interest rates be R1 & R2.
$$\frac{24{,}000 \times 6 \times R1}{100} - \frac{24{,}000 \times 6 \times R2}{100} = 576$$
$$R1 - R2 = \frac{576}{240 \times 6} = 0.4\%$$

11. (A) According to the qn.,
$$2P - P = \frac{P \times 3 \times R}{100}$$
$$R = \frac{100}{3}\%$$
$$\text{Required interest} = \frac{300 \times 4 \times \frac{100}{3}}{100}$$
$$= \text{Rs } 4000$$

12. (C) $SI = \frac{5000 \times 8 \times 22.5}{100} = 9000$
$$\text{Required value} = \frac{9000}{5000} = 1.8 \text{ times}$$

13. (B) Acc. to the qn.,
$$\frac{(P+2000) \times 3 \times 10}{100} + \frac{P \times 3 \times 15}{100} = 3600$$
$$30P + 60{,}000 + 45P = 3600 \times 100$$

$$75P = 3,00,000$$
$$P = \text{Rs } 4000$$

14. (A) Percentage of money she saved

$$= 100 - (15 + 20 + 35)$$
$$= 100 - 70 = 30\%$$

30% *of* $x = 2520$

$x = 8400$

35% *of* $x = Rs\ 2940$

$$\text{Required interest} = \frac{2940 \times 25 \times 1}{100}$$
$$= Rs\ 735$$

15. (A) Let actual price of laptop be Rs x

$$58160 - x = \frac{(x-28000) \times 8 \times 2}{100}$$
$$58,16,000 - 100x$$
$$= 16x - 4,48,000$$
$$116x = 62,64,000$$
$$x = \text{Rs } 54,000$$

16. (C) Let rate of interest be R %

$$(6076 - 5600) = \frac{5600 \times 1 \times R}{100}$$
$$R = \frac{476 \times 100}{5600} = 8.5\ \%$$

17. (B) Amount $= P\left(1 + \frac{\frac{R}{2}}{100}\right)^2$

$$= 40,000\left(1 + \frac{\frac{6}{2}}{100}\right)^2$$
$$= 40,000\left(\frac{103}{100}\right)^2$$
$$= 4 \times (103)^2$$
$$= \text{Rs } 42,436$$

18. (B) SI between 2nd, 3rd year

$$= 37044 - 35280$$
$$= 1764$$
$$\text{Rate} = \frac{100 \times 1764}{35280} = 5\%$$

Let Sum be Rs x

$$x(1 + 5/100)^2 = 35280$$
$$\frac{35280 \times (100)^2}{(105)^2} = \text{Rs } 32,000$$

19. (A) $P\left(1 + \frac{R}{100}\right)^n > 2P$

$$\left(1 + \frac{25}{100}\right)^n > 2$$
$$(1.25)^n > 2$$
$$n = 4 \text{ years}$$

20. (A) Let the present worth of loan be Rs x.

Present worth of Rs x due n years hence

$$= \frac{x}{\left(1 + \frac{R}{100}\right)^n}$$

Let x = Annual payment

Worth of x1 years hence + Worth of x2 years hence

$$= \text{Rs}\left(\frac{x}{1 + \frac{25}{100}}\right) + \left(\frac{x}{1 + \frac{25}{100}}\right)^2 = 8856$$
$$= \left(\frac{x}{\frac{5}{4}}\right) + \left(\frac{x}{\frac{5}{4}}\right)^2 = 8856$$
$$= \frac{4x}{5} + \frac{46x}{25} = 8856$$
$$x = \frac{8856 \times 25}{36} = \text{Rs } 6150$$

21. (C) Required difference

$$= 24000\left(1 + \frac{20/2}{100}\right)^4 - 24000\left(1 + \frac{20}{100}\right)^2$$
$$= 24000\left(\frac{11}{10}\right)^4 - 24000\left(\frac{6}{5}\right)^2$$
$$= 35138.4 - 34560$$
$$= \text{Rs } 578.4$$

22. (A) The amount invested in CI

$$= 8,00,000 \times \frac{40}{100}$$
$$= \text{Rs } 3,20,000$$

Required amount:

$$= 3,20,000\left[\left(1 + \frac{16}{100}\right) + \left(1 + \frac{16}{100}\right)^2 + \left(1 + \frac{16}{100}\right)^3\right]$$
$$= 3,20,000\left[\frac{29}{25} + \left(\frac{29}{25}\right)^2 + \left(\frac{29}{25}\right)^3\right]$$
$$= 13,01,278.72 = 13 \text{ lakhs}$$

23. (E) Since the data related to no. of years, the sum is invested in scheme A is not given, the problem cannot be solved.

24. (A) $\underline{1^{st}\ year:}$

$CI = 10{,}000\ [1+\frac{\frac{2}{2}}{100}]^2$

$=10000[\frac{11}{10}]^2$

$= Rs\ 12{,}100$

$\underline{2^{nd}\ year:}$
$P = Rs\ 12{,}100$

$CI = 12{,}100\ [1+\frac{20}{100}]^1$

$= 12100 \times \frac{6}{5} = Rs\ 14520$

Total interest $= 14520 - 10000$
$= Rs\ 4520$

25. (B) Let the sum be Rs x.
Rate of interest for 10 months

$=12 \times \frac{10}{12} = 10\%$

$126 = x\ [(1+\frac{10}{100})^2 -1]$

$126 = x\ [(\frac{11}{10})^2 -1]$

$126 = x \times \frac{21}{100}$

$x = \frac{12600}{21} = Rs\ 600$

26. (D) $(P+5000) \times \frac{144}{100}$

$= (P + 5000)(1+\frac{(R+4)^2}{100})$

$(1 + \frac{(R+4)}{100})^2 = \frac{144}{100}$

$1 + \frac{(R+4)}{100} = \frac{12}{10};$

$\frac{R+4}{100} = \frac{12}{10} - 1 = \frac{2}{10}$

$R + 4 = \frac{100}{5} = 20$

$R = 20 - 4 = 16\%$

27. (A) Let amount invested in scheme A &
B be x & 4x respectively

$CI = P[(1 + \frac{R}{100})^T -1]$

$= x\ [(1+\frac{20}{100})^2 -1]$

$= \frac{11x}{25}$

$= \frac{4x \times 2 \times 7}{100} = \frac{56x}{100}$

$\frac{56x}{100} - \frac{11x}{25} = 2940$

$\frac{12x}{100} = 2940$

$x = \frac{2940 \times 100}{12} = Rs\ 24{,}500$

28. (B) Rate $= \frac{16{,}000 \times 100}{50{,}000 \times 4} = 8\%$

$CI = 50{,}000[(1 + \frac{8}{100})^4 -1]$

$= 50{,}000\ [(\frac{108}{100})]^4 -1$

$= 50{,}000\ [(\frac{27}{25})]^4 -1$

$= 50{,}000\ [\frac{531441}{390625} - 1]$

$= 50{,}000 \times 0.36049$

$= Rs\ 18024.448$

$= Rs\ 18024$

29. (C) Amount invested in scheme B

$= P\ [1+\frac{20}{100}]^2 = \frac{36P}{25}$

$SI = \frac{36P}{25} \times \frac{25}{100} \times 4 = \frac{36P}{25}$

$\frac{36P}{25} - P = 33{,}000$

$P \times \frac{11}{25} = 33{,}000$

$P = 3000 \times 25$
$= Rs\ 75{,}000$

30. (B) Difference between SI & CI on a sum
of money invested for 2 years $= P(\frac{R}{100})^2$

$50{,}625\ (\frac{R}{100})^2 = 100$

$R^2 = \frac{100 \times 100 \times 100}{50625}$

$R = \frac{1000}{225} = 4.44\%$

31. (D) $SI = \frac{1000 \times 10 \times 4}{100} = Rs\ 400$

$CI = 1000[1 + \frac{10}{100}]^4 -1000$

$= 1000\ [(\frac{11}{10})^4 -1]$

$= 1000\ [\frac{14{,}641 - 10{,}000}{10{,}000}]$

$= \frac{4641}{4} = Rs\ 464.1$

$CI - SI = 464.1 - 400$
$= Rs\ 64.1$
$\approx Rs\ 64$

PROFIT & LOSS

It is an application-oriented concept dealing with day-to-day transactions that happens in one's life.

Profit & loss occurs when goods are purchased from a seller or sold to a buyer.

Key terms:
- Cost price CP: Price at which goods are brought
- Selling price SP: Price at which goods are sold
- Profit: The extra money made when SP is greater than CP
- Loss: The part of trader needs to invest from his part due to less money a seller gets on selling an article. SP is less than CP
- Profit%: Profit expressed as percentage of CP
- Loss%: Loss expressed as percentage of CP

(Note: Profit & loss% calculated as percentage of CP unless mentioned in the question)

- Marked price/ List price MP/LP: Price marked on the product or quoted in the price list
- Discount: The reduction given on marked price by the seller. It is calculated on MP/LP.

Formula:
1) Gain/Profit = SP - CP

2) Loss = CP - SP

3) $\text{Gain} \% = \dfrac{\text{Gain} \times 100}{\text{CP}}$

4) $\text{Loss} \% = \dfrac{\text{Loss} \times 100}{\text{CP}}$

5) Discount = MP - SP

6) $\text{Discount} \% = \dfrac{\text{Discount}}{\text{Marked price}} \times 100$

7) If two similar articles are sold at same SP, one at a gain of A% & one at the loss of A%, the seller always incurs a percentage loss of $\left(\dfrac{A}{10}\right)^2$

$$\text{Loss} \% = \left(\frac{\text{Common value of profit/loss}}{10}\right)^2$$

$$= \left(\frac{A}{10}\right)^2$$

8) If a seller claims to sell at cost price but uses false weights, then

$$\text{Gain} \% = \frac{\text{True value} - \text{Given value}}{\text{Given value}} \times 100\%$$

$$= \frac{\text{Error}}{\text{True value} - \text{Error}} \times 100\%$$

(True Value – Given Value = Error)

9) If two similar are of same CP, one sold at A% profit & other at A% loss. The overall profit or loss% is 'zero'

(As overall profit or loss = 0)

EXERCISE:

1. Raj sells his mobile phone at a profit of 35% and gives the discount of 75%. If the marked price of his mobile phone is Rs 8100, then what is the cost price of his mobile phone?
(A) Rs 5400   (B) Rs 4800
(C) Rs 4500   (D) Rs 4400
(E) None of these

2. A discount of 20% is given on the marked price of a book. The shopkeeper charges tax of 10% on the discounted price. If the selling price is Rs 792. What is the marked price of the book?
(A) Rs 920   (B) Rs 800
(C) Rs 950   (D) Rs 900
(E) None of these

3. A person sells a table at Rs 5781 by giving successive discount of 18% and 6% over the marked price. Find the marked price of the table.
(A) Rs 7600   (B) Rs 7500
(C) Rs 7300   (D) Rs 7400
(E) None of these

4. Amir sold a chair at a profit of 20%. If he had sold it for Rs 160 more, he would have gained 40%. Find the cost price of the chair.
(A) Rs 800   (B) Rs 900
(C) Rs 1000   (D) Rs 700
(E) None of these

5. A person bought two motorbikes at Rs 50,000 each. He sells one at 25% profit and another at 20% discount. Find the total selling price, if the marked price of a motorbike is 20% above the cost price.
(A) Rs 1,10,600   (B) Rs 1,10,500
(C) Rs 1,11,000   (D) Rs 1,10,000

(E) None of these

6. Karthi sold his car for Rs 6,05,000 hence gained a certain amount. Had the car been sold for Rs 5,60,000, he would have suffered loss equal to 50% of the gain in the first case. Find the cost price of the bike.
(A) Rs 5,75,000   (B) Rs 5,50,000
(C) Rs 5,75,500   (D) Rs 5,25,000
(E) None of these

7. The cost price of 3 kg of bananas is equal to the cost price of 5 kg of oranges. 15 kg of oranges is Rs 450. Find the selling price of bananas per kg, if the seller aims for a profit of 30%.
(A) Rs 70   (B) Rs 55
(C) Rs 60   (D) Rs 65
(E) None of these

8. Ranjit marked the price of a book 25% more than its cost price. If he allows a discount of 40%, then find his profit/loss percent.
(A) -16   (B) -20
(C) -25   (D) -22
(E) None of these

9. The cost price of two items is Rs 100 each. The shopkeeper sold one at 25% profit and another at 10% profit. Find the overall profit percentage.
(A) 19%   (B) 16%
(C) 18.5%   (D) 17.5%
(E) None of these

10. The selling price of a tablet is Rs 14,000. A person bought it at an availing discount of 8%, after 5 months it was sold with a further discount of 10%, what was his loss percentage?
(A) 20%   (B) 8%
(C) 10%   (D) 12%

(E) None of these

11. A man marks an article 20% above the cost price and allows two successive discounts of 10% & 8%, find the overall percentage of profit or loss.
(A) -1.2%   (B) 0.64%
(C) 1.2%   (D) -0.64%
(E) None of these

12. Selling price of a product is 5 times of the profit, then find out the profit percentage.
(A) 25%   (B) 20%
(C) 30%   (D) 40%
(E) None of these

13. A reduction of 25% in the price of sugar would enable a purchaser to get 2 kg more sugar for Rs 240. Find the original price per kg of sugar (in Rs.)
(A) Rs 60   (B) Rs 45
(C) Rs 30   (D) Rs 40
(E) None of these

14. A reduction of 20% in the price of oranges enables a person to purchase 15 more oranges for Rs 300. The price of oranges per dozen after reduction in price is
(A) Rs 42   (B) Rs 48
(C) Rs 56   (D) Rs 60
(E) None of these

15. A shopkeeper offers successive discounts of 12% & 20% on the marked price of an product and he gains 10% on selling the same. Find the profit percentage if the discount is 32% on the marked price.
(A) 5.5%   (B) 7.2%
(C) 6.25%   (D) 6.9%
(E) None of these

16. The marked price of a computer is Rs 45,000. If successive discounts of 10%, 12% & 14% be allowed, then what is the selling price of the computer? (approx.)
(A) Rs 29,880   (B) Rs 30,650
(C) Rs 31,750   (D) Rs 32,300
(E) None of these

17. The overall loss or gain percentage on selling two items of same selling price, one at 5% gain and the other at 5% loss is
(A) -0.25%   (B) 0.25%
(C) 2.5%   (D) -2.5%
(E) None of these

18. A trader purchased calculators at the rate of Rs 600 each from the market. He raised the price by 25% and then allowed a discount of 12% on each calculator. His profit% will be
(A) 15%   (B) 12%
(C) 8%   (D) 10%
(E) None of these

19. A person buys 10 apples for Rs 18 and sells them at 8 apples for Rs 15. What is the profit/loss percentage?
(A) 5.17%   (B) 4.167%
(C) 4.54%   (D) 3.67%
(E) None of these

20. Nandhini bought a laptop at Rs 40,000 and a sofa at Rs 20,000. She spent Rs 1000 on transportation and Rs 2500 on service of these items. What should be the selling price of both items if she wants to make 20% profit?
(A) Rs 75,500   (B) Rs 63,500
(C) Rs 76,200   (D) Rs 72,400
(E) None of these

21. The cost price of two articles is same, a shopkeeper got a profit of 40% on the first article, selling price of the second article is 10% less than the first article, then find the overall profit percentage.

(A) 33%   (B) 31%
(C) 35%   (D) 36%
(E) None of these

22. Persons A and B bought two bikes for Rs 70,000 each. Person A gives a discount of 25% on whole, while person B gives a discount of 15% on the first Rs 40,000 and 10% on the rest Rs 30,000. What is the difference between their selling prices?

(A) Rs 7500   (B) Rs 8500
(C) Rs 9000   (D) Rs 8000
(E) None of these

23. The cost price of 24 items is same as the selling price of 'n' items. If the profit is 20%, find the value of n (in Rs.)

(A) 20   (B) 18
(C) 15   (D) 22
(E) None of these

SOLUTION:

1. (C) Selling price of mobile phone
$$= 8100 \times \frac{75}{100} = Rs\ 6075$$
Cost price of mobile phone
$$= 6075 \times \frac{100}{135} = Rs\ 4500$$

2. (D) Let marked price of the book be Rs x.
$$\text{Selling price} = x \times \frac{80}{100} \times \frac{110}{100}$$
$$\frac{88x}{100} = 792$$
$$x = \frac{792 \times 100}{88} = Rs\ 900$$

3. (B) Let the marked price be x.
$$x \times \frac{82}{100} \times \frac{94}{100} = 5781$$
$$x = \frac{5781 \times 100 \times 100}{82 \times 94} = Rs\ 7500$$

4. (A) Let cost price be Rs x.
$$x \times \frac{20}{100} + 160 = \frac{40}{100} \times x$$
$$\frac{(40-20)}{100} \times x = 160$$
$$\frac{20}{100} \times x = 160$$
$$x = \frac{160 \times 100}{20} = Rs\ 800$$

5. (B) Selling price
$$= 50,000 \left(\frac{125}{100}\right) + \left(50,000 \times \frac{120}{100} \times \frac{80}{100}\right)$$
$$= 62,500 + 48,000 = Rs\ 1,10,500$$

6. (A) If the loss is Rs x in second case, then the profit in the first case is Rs 2x.
Difference $= x + 2x = 3x$
$3x = (6,05,000 - 5,60,000)$
$3x = 45,000$
$x = 15,000$
Cost price $= Rs\ 5,60,000 + 15,000$
$= Rs\ 5,75,000$

7. (D) CP of 1kg of oranges $= \frac{450}{15}$
$$= Rs\ 30$$
CP of 5 kg of oranges $= 5 \times 32$
$$= Rs\ 150$$
CP of 3 kg of bananas $= Rs\ 150$
CP of 1 kg of bananas $= \frac{150}{3} = Rs\ 150$
For a profit of 30%
$$SP = 50 \times \frac{130}{100} = Rs\ 65$$

8. (C) Overall profit/loss percentage
$$= x + y + \frac{xy}{100}$$
$$= 25 - 40 + \frac{25(-40)}{100}$$
$$= -15 - 10 = -25\%$$

9. (D) Total profit
$$= 100 \times \frac{25}{100} + 100 \times \frac{10}{100}$$
$$= 25 + 10 = Rs\ 35$$
Overall profit percentage
$$= \frac{35}{200} \times 100 = 17.5\%$$

10. (C) He sold with a discount of 10%, his loss percentage is 10%

11. (D) Let cost price be Rs 100

Marked price $= 100 \times \frac{120}{100} =$ Rs 120

SP $= 120 \times \frac{90}{100} \times \frac{92}{100} = 99.36$

Required % $= \frac{100-99.36}{100} \times 100$

Loss% $= 0.64\%$

12. (A) Let profit be 'x'

SP $= 5x$

CP $= 5x - x = 4x$

Profit% $= \frac{x}{4x} \times 100 = 25\%$

13. (D) Let cost per kg of sugar be Rs x.

Reduced cost $= \frac{75}{100}x = \frac{3}{4}x$

Acc. To the qn.,

$\frac{240}{\frac{3}{4}x} - \frac{240}{x} = 2$

$\frac{240 \times 4}{3x} - \frac{240}{x} = 2$

$\frac{960-720}{3x} = 2$

$6x = 240$

$x =$ Rs 40

14. (B) 15 oranges are purchased for 20% of the price of Rs 300.

Price of 15 oranges $= \frac{20}{100} \times 300$

$=$ Rs 60

Price of 12 oranges $= \frac{60}{15} \times 12$

$=$ Rs 48

15. (C) Let cost price be Rs 100

Selling price $=$ Rs 110

Marked price $= 110 \times \frac{100}{88} \times \frac{100}{80}$

$=$ Rs 156.25

If discount is 32%, SP $= 156.25 \times \frac{68}{100}$

$=$ Rs 106.25

Profit percentage $= \frac{6.25}{100} \times 100 = 6.25\%$

16. (B) Selling price

$= 45000 \times \frac{90}{100} \times \frac{88}{100} \times \frac{86}{100}$

$=$ Rs 30650.4

17. (A) Loss % $= \frac{x^2}{100}$

(where x is the common percentage of gain/loss)

Loss% $= \frac{5^2}{100} = 0.25\%$

18. (D) CP $=$ Rs 600

MP $=$ Rs $600 \times \frac{125}{100} =$ Rs 750

Selling price $= 750 \times \frac{88}{100} =$ Rs 660

Profit percentage $= \frac{660-600}{600} \times 100$

$= 10\%$

19. (B) For buying 'a' items for Rs x & selling 'b' items for Rs y.

Gain/loss percent $= \frac{ay-bx}{bx} \times 100\%$

$= \frac{10 \times 15 - 8 \times 18}{8 \times 18} \times 100$

$= \frac{150-144}{144} \times 100 = 4.167\%$

20. (C) Total CP

$= 40,000 + 20,000 + 1000 + 2500$

$=$ Rs 63,500

Selling price $= 63,500 \times \frac{120}{100}$

$=$ Rs 76,200

21. (A) Let CP of each article be Rs 100

SP of 1st article $=$ Rs 140

SP of 2nd article $= 140 \times \frac{90}{100}$

$=$ Rs 126

Overall profit

$= \frac{(140+126)-200}{200} \times 100\%$

$= \frac{66}{200} \times 100 = 33\%$

22. (B) SP of person A's bike

$$= 70{,}000 \times \frac{75}{100} = \text{Rs } 52500$$

SP of person B's bike

$$= 40{,}000 \times \frac{85}{100} + 30{,}000 \times \frac{90}{100}$$

$$= 34{,}000 + 27{,}000 = \text{Rs } 61{,}000$$

Required difference = Rs 8500

23. (A) $24 \times CP = n \times SP$

$$\frac{CP}{SP} = \frac{n}{24}$$

On equation, $CP = n$, $SP = 24$

$$\text{Profit\%} = \frac{SP - CP}{CP} \times 100$$

$$= \frac{24 - n}{n} \times 100 = 20$$

$$\frac{24}{n} - 1 = \frac{20}{100} = \frac{1}{5}$$

$$\frac{24}{n} = \frac{6}{5}$$

$$n = \frac{24 \times 5}{6} = 20$$

PRACTICE:

1. The marked price of watch is Rs 2000. A retailer purchases it for Rs 1620 on two successive discounts. The one among them is 10%, then another discount is
(A) 25%   (B) 15%
(C) 20%   (D) 10%
(E) None of these

2. Two TV sets were purchased for Rs 8000. The first one was sold at 40% profit and the second one was sold at 40% loss. If the selling price of both are same, then what is the difference in their cost price?
(A) Rs 3200   (B) Rs 3000
(C) Rs 2800   (D) Rs 3300
(E) None of these

3. A salesman sells goods to a customer at a profit of P % over the cost price, besides if he cheats his customer by giving 880 g only instead of 1 kg. Thus, his overall profit percentage is 25%. Find the value of P.
(A) 15%   (B) 10%
(C) 12%   (D) 8%
(E) None of these

4. A trader sold two watches, each for Rs 990. If he gained 20% on one watch and suffered a loss of 20% on the other, then what is the loss/gain percentage in the transaction?
(A) 1%   (B) 2%
(C) -1%   (D) -2%
(E) None of these

5. A movie ticket was worth Rs 300. When the price of the ticket was lowered, the sale of the ticket increased by 50% while the collections recorded a decrease of 34%. Find the deduction in the ticket price.
(A) 56%   (B) 44%
(C) 84%   (D) 28%
(E) None of these

6. What will be the single discount equivalent to two successive discounts of 20% and 15%?
(A) 30%   (B) 32%
(C) 38%   (D) 35%
(E) None of these

7. An article is listed at Rs 130. A customer bought this article for Rs 112.32 and got two successive discounts of which the first one is 10%, the other rate of discount that was allowed was
(A) 5%   (B) 6%
(C) 8%   (D) 4%
(E) None of these

8. A shopkeeper sells a product after two successive discounts of 10% and 20% on it. Find the profit percent if the profit is

30% of the price by which the product is marked up.
(A) 25% (B) 10%
(C) 20% (D) 30%
(E) None of these

9. Marked price of an article is Rs 180 more than its cost price. If profit earned is equal to the discount given, then find the profit earned.
(A) Rs 120 (B) Rs 90
(C) Rs 45 (D) Rs 180
(E) None of these

10. A headphone was sold at Rs 1600. If it was sold at Rs 200 more, then the profit percent will be 16% more. Find the cost price of the headphone.
(A) Rs 1250 (B) Rs 1000
(C) Rs 1300 (D) Rs 1500
(E) None of these

11. A man sells two pipes at Rs 24 each. He gains 20% on one and loses 20% on the other. In the whole transaction, there is
(A) Loss of Rs 1 (B) Loss of Rs 2
(C) Profit of Rs 1 (D) Profit of Rs 2
(E) Neither Loss nor gain

12. Vinoth purchases a computer and sold it to Raj at 15% profit. Raj sold it to Arun at 20% loss. If Arun pays Rs 34,960 to Raj, then Vinoth purchases the computer at what price?
(A) Rs 38,000 (B) Rs 36,000
(C) Rs 40,000 (D) Rs 39,000
(E) None of these

13. A shopkeeper marked up the price of a book 25% above the cost price and sold the book at 10% discount. Find his profit percentage
(A) 11.5% (B) 10.5%
(C) 12.5% (D) 13.5%

(E) None of these

14. By selling an article at Rs 1800, a trader gets a loss of 25%. Find for how much he should sell the article to make a profit of 20%.
(A) Rs 2840 (B) Rs 2940
(C) Rs 2670 (D) Rs 2880
(E) None of these

15. When an item is sold at certain loss % and profit % then the ratio of loss to profit becomes 3:2 and ratio of the selling price at loss and at profit is 7:12. Find the profit percentage.
(A) 18% (B) 20%
(C) 25% (D) 15%
(E) None of these

16. If a book is marked 40% above the cost price and sold at 15% discount. Find the ratio of discount given to profit earned.
(A) 21:19 (B) 19:21
(C) 18:19 (D) 19:23
(E) None of these

17. When an article was sold at 4/5th of the marked price, the loss percentage was 10%. The article should be sold at what fraction of marked price to earn 10% profit?
(A) 44/49 (B) 23/25
(C) 41/48 (D) 44/45
(E) None of these

18. A dishonest trader sells cloth at the cost price but uses false scale which measures 80 cm in lieu of 1m. Find his gain percentage.
(A) 20% (B) 25%
(C) 15% (D) 30%
(E) None of these

19. Hari sold a car to Raj at 20% profit. Raj sold it to Anu at 10% profit. If Anu paid Rs 6,60,000 for the car then, at what price Hari purchased it?
(A) 5.5 lakhs   (B) 4 lakhs
(C) 5 lakhs   (D) 4.5 lakhs
(E) None of these

20. Two articles were sold at same price. The person earned a profit of 10% on one of them and a loss of 10% on the other. Find the total percentage profit or loss in the entire transaction.
(A) 2%   (B) 0.5%
(C) 1%   (D) 4%
(E) None of these

SOLUTION:

1. (D) $2000 \times \frac{90}{100} \times \frac{x}{100} = 1620$
$x = \frac{1620 \times 100 \times 100}{2000 \times 90} = 90$
Discount% = 100 - 90 = 90%

2. (A) $\frac{100}{140} \times SP + \frac{100}{60} \times SP = 8000$
$SP = \frac{8000 \times 42}{100} = Rs\ 3360$
Difference in CP
$= \frac{100}{60}(3360) - \frac{100}{140}(3360)$
$= 5600 - 2400 = Rs\ 3200$

3. (B) $\frac{100+25}{100+P} = \frac{1000}{880}$
$125 \times 880 = 1000 \times (100 + P)$
$100 + P = 110$
$P = 10\%$

4. (C) Loss/gain %
$= 10 - 10 - \frac{10 \times 10}{100}\% = -1\%$

5. (A) Let the price of the ticket is lowered by a %
Resultant percentage $= a + b + \frac{ab}{100}$

$-34 = -a + 50 - \frac{50a}{100}$
$-a + 50 - \frac{a}{2} = -34$
$-\frac{3}{2}a = -34 - 50 = -84$
$a = \frac{84 \times 2}{3} = 56\%$
Price of the ticket decreased by
$= \frac{56}{100} \times 300 = Rs\ 168$

6. (B) Equivalent discount
$= R1 + R2 + \frac{R1R2}{100}$
$= -20 - 15 + \frac{(-20)(-15)}{100}$
$= -35 + 3 = -32\%$

7. (D) Price of article after 1st discount
$= 130 - 13 = Rs\ 117$
Second discount $= \frac{117 - 112.32}{117} \times 100$
$= 4\%$

8. (C) Let marked price be Rs 100x.
$SP = 100x \times \frac{90}{100} \times \frac{80}{100} = Rs\ 72x$
Let cost price be Rs y.
$\frac{72x - y}{100x - y} = 0.3$
$y = 60x$
Profit percentage $= \frac{12x}{60x} \times 100 = 20\%$

9. (B) Marked price = Rs (CP+180)
$(CP + 180) - SP = SP - CP$
$CP - SP + 180 = SP - CP$
$2SP - 2CP = 180$
$SP - CP = Rs\ 90$

10. (A) Acc. To the qn., 16% = 200
$CP = 100\% = \frac{200}{16} \times 100 = Rs\ 1250$

11. (B) Total SP = 24 + 24 = Rs 48
Total CP $= \frac{100}{80} \times 24 + \frac{100}{120} \times 24$
$= 30 + 20 = 50$
Loss = 50 - 48 = Rs 2

12. (A) Let Vinoth purchase the computer at Rs 100x.

$$100x \times \frac{115}{100} \times \frac{80}{100} = 34960$$

$$x = \frac{34960 \times 100}{115 \times 80} = Rs\ 38,000$$

13. (C) Let the cost price be Rs 100x.

Marked price $= 100x \times \frac{125}{100}$

$$= Rs\ 125x$$

Selling price $= 125x \times \frac{90}{100}$

$$= Rs\ 112.5x$$

Required profit percentage

$$= \frac{112.5x - 100x}{100x} \times 100 = 12.5\%$$

14. (D) Let cost price of the article be Rs x.

$$x \times \frac{75}{100} = 1800$$

$$x = Rs\ 2400$$

Required selling price $= 2400 \times \frac{120}{100}$

$$= Rs\ 2880$$

15. (B) Let profit earned & loss incurred be Rs 3x & Rs 2x respectively.

$$\frac{CP - 3x}{CP + 2x} = \frac{7}{12}$$

$$12CP - 36x = 7CP + 14x$$

$$5CP = 14x + 36x = 50x$$

$$CP = 10x$$

Required profit $\% = \frac{2x}{10x} \times 100 = 20\%$

16. (A) Let cost price be Rs 100x.

Marked price $= 100x \times \frac{140}{100} = Rs\ 140x$

Selling price $= 140x \times \frac{85}{100} = Rs\ 119x$

Required ratio

$$= (140 - 119) : (119 - 100)$$

$$= 21 : 19$$

17. (D) Let the marked price be Rs x.

$$SP = \frac{4}{5} \times x = 0.8x$$

$$Loss = 10\%$$

$$CP = 0.8x \times \frac{100}{90} = \frac{8}{9}x$$

SP at 10% profit $= \frac{110}{100} \times \frac{8}{9}x = \frac{44}{45}x$

18. (B) Percentage gain

$$= \frac{20}{80} \times 100 = 25\%$$

19. (C) Required cost price

$$= \frac{100}{120} \times \frac{100}{110} \times 6,60,000 = 5,00,000$$

20. (C) Required loss $\% = \left(\frac{x}{10}\right)^2 \%$

$$= \left(\frac{10}{10}\right)^2 \%$$

$$= 1\%$$

PARTNERSHIP

Partnership refers to a business association between two or more than 2 persons who run a business together & share the total profit at an agreed proposition.

The persons who enter into a partnership are called partners.

Simple partnership:

A partnership in which each partner invests capital for the same period.

Compound partnership:

A partnership in which each partner invests their capital for different periods.

Formulas:

- If 2 partners invest capital Rs C1 & C2 for 'same period' & earn a total profit Rs P.

  The ratio of their profits = C1: C2

  Share of the partners in profit

  Rs $\frac{C1}{C1+C2} \times P$ & Rs $\frac{C2}{C1+C2} \times P$

- If 2 partners invest capital Rs C1 & Rs C2 for 'different period' T1 & T2 respectively & earn a total profit Rs P.

  The ratio of their profits = $\frac{C1T1}{C2T2}$

  Share of the partners in profit are

  Rs $\frac{C1T1}{C1T1+C2T2} \times P$ & Rs $\frac{C2T2}{C1T1+C2T2} \times P$

- If 3 partners invest capital Rs C1, Rs C2 & Rs C3 for 'same period' & earn a total profit Rs P.
    - The ratio of their profits: C1: C2: C3
    - Share of the partners in profit:

      $\frac{C1}{C1+C2+C3} \times P$, $\frac{C2}{C1+C2+C3} \times P$,

      $\frac{C3}{C1+C2+C3} \times P$

- If 3 partners invest capital Rs C1, Rs C2, Rs C3 for 'different period' T1, T2 & T3 & earn a total profit Rs P.
    - The ratio of their profits: C1T1: C2T2: C3T3
    - Share of the partners in profit:

      $\frac{C1T1}{C1T1+C2T2+C3T3} \times P$,

      $\frac{C2T2}{C1T1+C2T2+C3T3} \times P$,

      $\frac{C3T3}{C1T1+C2T2+C3T3} \times P$

- If C1: C2: C3 is ratio of capital investment

  & T1: T2: T3 is ratio of time investment

  & P1: P2: P3 is ratio of their profits

  Then,

  T1: T2: T3 $= \frac{P1}{C1}:\frac{P2}{C2}:\frac{P3}{C3}$ (if ratio of profits & capital investments is given)

  C1: C2: C3 $= \frac{P1}{T1}:\frac{P2}{T2}:\frac{P3}{T3}$ (if ratio of profits & time period is given)

EXERCISE:

1. A, B & C start a business by investing Rs 8000, Rs 4000 & Rs 16000 respectively. Find the ratio of their share of profits after 1 year.
   (A) 2:3:4   (B) 2:1:4
   (C) 3:1:4   (D) 2:1:3
   (E) None of these

2. P & Q jointly start a business. The investment of P is equal to six times the investment of Q. Find the share of P in the annual profit of Rs 28,700.
   (A) Rs 24,600   (B) Rs 22,800
   (C) Rs 24,400   (D) Rs 25,580
   (E) None of these

3. P, Q & R start a business together. Q invests 1/5th of the total capital while investment of P & R is equal. If the annual profit on this investment is Rs 25,000. Find the difference between the share of profits of Q & R.
   (A) Rs 4500   (B) Rs 6000
   (C) Rs 5500   (D) Rs 5000
   (E) None of these

4. A, B & C started a business by entering into a partnership. B received 3/7 of the profit. A & C distributed the remaining profit equally. If C got Rs 1400 less than B, the total profit is
   (A) Rs 9600   (B) Rs 9000
   (C) Rs 9800   (D) Rs 10,000
   (E) None of these

5. P, Q & R invested their capital in the ratio 3:4:5. They invested for the time periods, in the ratio of 1:2:3. Find the ratio of profit share of P, Q & R respectively.
   (A) 2:6:15   (B) 3:8:15
   (C) 2:8:15   (D) 3:10:15

6. P, Q & R invested different capitals for the time periods in the ratio 3:2:3. At the end of their business periods, they received the profit in the ratio 8:7:9. Find the ratio of their investment capitals.
   (A) 16:21:18   (B) 15:20:18
   (C) 16:20:9   (D) 16:21:16
   (E) None of these

7. Ram & Leela entered into a business with initial investments in the ratio 5:3 & their annual profits were in the ratio 2:3. If Ram invested the money for 8 months, then for what time period Leela invested the money?
   (A) 20 months   (B) 18 months
   (C) 24 months   (D) 15 months
   (E) None of these

8. A & B jointly started a business and after 8 months B left the business. At the end of the year their profit ratio is 2:1. If B invests Rs 57,000 initially, find the capital investment of A.
   (A) Rs 72,000   (B) Rs 78,000
   (C) Rs 76,000   (D) Rs 74,000
   (E) None of these

9. Three persons A, B & C started a business & invested in the ratio 2:3:5. After 6 months each of them added Rs 1000. If at the end of the year, A received Rs 1000 less than the profit share of B. Find the total profit.
   (A) Rs 28,000   (B) Rs 28,000
   (C) Rs 25,000   (D) Rs 24,000
   (E) None of these

10. A, B & C start a business with investment of Rs 60,000, Rs 80,000 &

Rs 1 lakh respectively. After another 3 months, A additionally invest 20% of his initial investment. After another 3 months, B withdrew 25% of his initial investment. After 8 months, C left the partnership and at the end of 10 months, A withdrew 50% of his total investment at that time. Find the ratio of their profit.
(A) 189:195:210 (B) 191:195:200
(C) 189:190:205 (D) 189:210:200
(E) None of these

11. Raj started a business with Rs 2000. After 2 months of starting, Kumar joined with Rs 4500. After 6 months, Raj added Rs 1000 more to his capital. For the last 3 months, Karthi invested Rs 7000. At the end of the year, the business gave a profit of Rs 64,000. What is the difference between the profit share of Kumar & Karthi?
(A) Rs 15,500 (B) Rs 14,000
(C) Rs 16,800 (D) Rs 16,000
(E) None of these

12. A & B entered into a partnership investing Rs 2400 & Rs 5600 respectively. After 1 year, A & B accrues capital by Rs 3200 & Rs 2400 respectively. At the end of three years, there was a profit of Rs 4400. What is the share of B?
(A) Rs 2700 (B) Rs 3600
(C) Rs 2500 (D) Rs 2250
(E) None of these

13. P, Q & R jointly started a business with shares in the ratio 5/2: 4/3: 7/4. After 6 & 8 months, Q & R left the partnership respectively. Find the ratio of their profit shares at the year-end respectively.
(A) 15:4:6 (B) 15:4:7

(C) 14:4:7 (D) 15:3:7
(E) None of these

14. Ravi, Sam & Madhan enter into a partnership. Sam invests one-third of Madhan's capital & Ravi invests two-fifth of Sam's capital. At the end of the year, they got a profit of Rs 6600. Find the profit share of Sam.
(A) Rs 1800 (B) Rs 1000
(C) Rs 2000 (D) Rs 1500
(E) None of these

15. A & B invest in the ratio 6:5. After 6 months, C enters the business with the investment of half the investment to that of A. What will be the ratio of the profits of A, B & C at the end of the year?
(A) 12:10:5 (B) 12:8:3
(C) 12:10:3 (D) 10:10:3
(E) None of these

16. Five persons P, Q, R, S & T entered into a partnership. T invests 2 times of what R invests. P invests 1/3 of T invests. Q & S invest equal amount. The total investment is Rs 40,000 & R invests Rs 6000. Find the difference between the profit share of P and (Q & S) together at the end of the year, if total profit is Rs 10,000.
(A) Rs 3500 (B) Rs 3200
(C) Rs 7000 (D) Rs 4000
(E) None of these

17. P, Q & R enter into a partnership with the investment of Rs 3000, Rs 4000 & Rs 5000 respectively. After 2 months, P withdraws 1/3rd of the capital, Q invests additionally 1/4th of his investment. After 6 months, P adds Rs 3000 to his existing capital & R adds Rs 1000 to his capital. At the end of the

year, they received a profit of Rs 16,800. Find the profit share of R.
(A) Rs 7600   (B) Rs 6600
(C) Rs 6000   (D) Rs 5500
(E) None of these

18. If Sushma and Geetha enter into a partnership with their capitals in the ratio 8:5. At the end of 6 months, Geetha withdraws her capital. If they receive the profits in the ratio 4:3, find how long Sushma's capital was used in the business?
(A) 5 months   (B) 6 months
(C) 4 months   (D) 8 months
(E) None of these

19. A started a business with an investment of Rs 72,000. After few months B joined him with an investment of Rs 90,000. If at the end of the year, they share the profit in the ratio 16:15 (A: B), then find after how much time B joined business?
(A) 4 months   (B) 3 months
(C) 6 months   (D) 9 months
(E) None of these

20. Dhana invests twice the sum invested by Karthi and withdraws half of sum after 4 months and again withdraws half of the remaining sum after 4 months. Find the ratio of profit share of Dhana to Karthi at the end of the year.
(A) 6:5   (B) 6:7
(C) 7:6   (D) 5:6
(E) None of these

21. A and B invested Rs 5000 and Rs 8000 in a business respectively and after 4 months B withdrew 50% of his initial investment and again after 4 months, he reinvested 50% of amount of what he had withdrawn. After a year, they got

total profit of Rs 1,05,270. Find profit share of B.
(A) Rs 58,420   (B) Rs 56,800
(C) Rs 57,400   (D) Rs 57,420
(E) None of these

22. Arun and Anu invested Rs 3000 and Rs 4000 respectively in a partnership. After 4 months Arun increased his amount by $33\frac{1}{3}\%$ and at the end of the year, difference between their profit shares is Rs 1500. Find the profit share of Anu.
(A) Rs 15,000   (B) Rs 18,000
(C) Rs 12,500   (D) Rs 16,000
(E) None of these

SOLUTION:

1. (B) Ratio of their profits
$= (8000\times1) :(4000\times1) :(16000\times1)$
$= 2:1:4$

2. (A) Profit share $\propto$ Investment
Profit ratio of P & Q = 6:1
Profit share of P $= \frac{6}{7} \times 28{,}700$
$= Rs\ 24{,}600$

3. (D) Investment ratio = 2:1:2
Required difference $= \frac{2x-1x}{5x} \times 25{,}000$
$= \frac{1}{5} \times 25{,}000 = Rs\ 5000$

4. (C) Profit ratio $= \frac{2}{7}:\frac{3}{7}:\frac{2}{7} = 2:3:2$
R got Rs 1400 less than Q.
$3x - 2x = Rs\ 1400$
$x = Rs\ 1400$
Total profit $= 7x = 7\times1400 = Rs\ 9800$

5. (B) Profit share $\propto$ (Investment capital $\times$ Time period of investment)
Profit share $= (3\times1) :(4\times2) :(5\times3)$
$= 3:8:15$

6. (A) Investment $\propto \dfrac{\text{Profit share}}{\text{Time period}}$

 Ratio of their investments $= \dfrac{8}{3} : \dfrac{7}{2} : \dfrac{9}{3}$

$$= 16 : 21 : 18$$

7. (A) Profit share $\propto$ (Capital $\times$ Time period)

 Acc. To the Qn.,

$$\dfrac{5 x \times 8}{3 x \times T} = \dfrac{2}{3}$$

$$T = \dfrac{5 \times 8 \times 3}{3 \times 2}$$

 T = 20 months

8. (C) Acc. To the Qn.,

$$\dfrac{I \times 12}{57{,}000 \times 8} = \dfrac{2}{1}$$

$$I = \dfrac{57{,}000 \times 8 \times 2}{12} = 76{,}000$$

 Investment of A is Rs 76,000.

9. (B) Profit ratio

$$= (2x \times 6) + [6 \times (2x + 1000)]:$$
$$(3x \times 6) + [6 \times (3x + 1000)]:$$
$$(5x \times 6) + [6 \times (5x + 1000)]$$
$$= 24x + 6000:$$
$$36x + 6000:$$
$$60x + 6000$$

 Acc. To the Qn.,

$$(36x + 6000) - (24x + 6000)$$
$$= 1000$$

 $12x = 1000$

 Total profit $= 120x + 18{,}000$
$$= Rs\ 28{,}000$$

10. (C) Profit share ratio in 1000's

$$= [(60 \times 3) + (72 \times 7) + (36 \times 2)]:$$
$$[(80 \times 6) + (60 \times 6)]:$$
$$(100 \times 8)]$$
$$= (180 + 504 + 72):$$
$$(480 + 360):$$
$$800$$
$$= 756 : 840 : 800$$
$$= 189 : 210 : 200$$

11. (D) Profit share ratio

$$= [(2000 \times 6) + (3000 \times 6)]:$$
$$(4500 \times 10):$$
$$(7000 \times 3)$$
$$= 30{,}000 : 45{,}000 : 21{,}000$$
$$= 10 : 15 : 7$$

 Required difference $= \dfrac{(15-7)}{32} \times 64{,}000$

$$= \dfrac{64000}{4} = Rs\ 16{,}000$$

12. (A) Profit ratio

$$= [(2400 \times 1) + (5600 \times 2)]:$$
$$[(5600 \times 1) + (8000 \times 2)\}$$
$$= 13600 : 21600 = 17 : 27$$

 Share of B $= \dfrac{27}{44} \times 4400 = Rs\ 2700$

13. (B) Profit ratio

$$= \left(\dfrac{5}{2} \times 12\right) : \left(\dfrac{4}{3} \times 6\right) : \left(\dfrac{7}{4} \times 8\right)$$
$$= 30 : 8 : 14$$
$$= 15 : 4 : 7$$

14. (D) Profit ratio $= \left(\dfrac{2}{5}\left(\dfrac{1}{3}x\right)\right) : \left(\dfrac{1}{3}x\right) : x$

$$= 2 : 5 : 15$$

 Sam's profit share $= \dfrac{5}{22} \times 6600$
$$= Rs\ 1500$$

15. (C) Profit share ratio

$$= 6x \times 12 : 5x \times 12 : 3x \times 6$$
$$= 12 : 10 : 3$$

16. (A) Investment of

- R = Rs 6000
- T = 2 $\times$ 6000 = Rs 12,000
- P $= \dfrac{1}{3} \times 12{,}000 = RS\ 4000$
- Q = S $= \dfrac{1}{2}[40{,}000 - (6000 + 12{,}000 + 4000)]$

$$= \dfrac{1}{2}(40{,}000 - 22{,}000)$$
$$= Rs\ 9000$$

 Profit ratio (in 1000's) = P: Q: R: S: T
$$= 4 : 9 : 6 : 9 : 12$$

Required difference

$$= \frac{4 \sim (9+9)}{40} \times 10{,}000$$

$$= \frac{14}{40} \times 10{,}000$$

$$= Rs\ 3500$$

17. (B) Profit ratio (in 1000's) : (P: Q: R)

$$= [(3 \times 2) + (2 \times 4) : (5 \times 6)] : [(4 \times 2) + (5 \times 10)] : [(5 \times 6) + (6 \times 6)]$$

$$= (6 + 8 + 30) : (8 + 50) : (30 + 36)$$

$$= 44 : 58 : 66 = 22 : 29 : 33$$

Profit share of C $= \frac{33}{84} \times 16{,}800$

$$= Rs\ 6600$$

18. (A) Let Sushant's investment period be T.

$$\frac{8x \times T}{5x \times 6} = \frac{4}{3}$$

$$T = \frac{4 \times 30}{3 \times 8} = 5\ months$$

19. (B) Let time period of B's investment be T months.

$$\frac{72{,}000 \times 12}{90{,}000 \times T} = \frac{16}{15}$$

$$T = \frac{72 \times 12 \times 15}{90 \times 16} = 9\ months$$

B joined after 3 months

20. (C) Let investment of Karthi be Rs 4x. Investment of Dhana = Rs 8x.

Required ratio $= [(8x \times 4) + (4x \times 4) + (2x \times 4)] : (4x \times 12)$

$$= 14 : 12 = 7 : 6$$

21. (D) Ratio of profit share

$$= (5000 \times 12) : (8000 \times 4) + [(4000 \times 4) + (6000 \times 4)]$$

$$= 60{,}000 : (32{,}000 + 16{,}000 + 24{,}000)$$

$$= 60{,}000 : 72{,}000 = 5 : 6$$

Profit share of B $= \frac{6}{11} \times 1{,}05{,}270$

$$= Rs\ 57{,}420$$

22. (B) Profit ratio of Arun & Anu

$$= [(3000 \times 4) + (4000 \times 8)] : (4000 \times 12) = 11 : 12$$

$$11x \sim 12x = 1500$$

$$x = Rs\ 1500$$

Profit share of Anu

$$= 12x = 12 \times 1500$$

$$= Rs\ 18{,}000$$

PRACTICE:

1. Reshma left Rs 34,400 for his 4 daughters, 5 sons & 2 nieces. If amount got by each daughter is four times that of each niece and amount got by each son is five times that of each niece, then what will be the share of each daughter?
(A) Rs 3200   (B) Rs 6400
(C) Rs 1600   (D) Rs 3600
(E) None of these

2. P & Q started a business with the investments in the ratio 3:5 respectively. After 6 months from the start of the business, R joined them and the respective ratio between the investments of P & R was 2:3. If the annual profit earned by them was Rs 49,200, what was the difference between P's share and R's share in the profit?
(A) Rs 3200   (B) Rs 3800
(C) Rs 3600   (D) Rs 4000
(E) None of these

3. If the ratio of time periods of investment of A and B is 5:4, profit at the end of the year is Rs 50,000 and A's share is Rs 10,000, then what is the ratio of A's and B's investment?
(A) 5:1   (B) 1:5
(C) 4:1   (D) 1:4
(E) None of these

4. Karthi invested Rs (x+1500) and Sasi invested Rs (x+2500) in a partnership.

If profit at the end of the year is Rs 24,000 and value of Sasi's share in it is Rs 14,000, then find the value of x. (in Rs)
(A) Rs 1500   (B) Rs 500
(C) Rs 2000   (D) Rs 1000
(E) None of these

5. A invested Rs 75,000 and B invested Rs 25,000 in a business and ratio of time in which they invest is 4:7. If the difference between their profit Rs 1000, then what is the total profit?
(A) Rs 3600   (B) Rs 3800
(C) Rs 1900   (D) Rs 1600
(E) None of these

6. P, Q & R invested Rs 85,000, Rs 60,000 & Rs 70,000 respectively in a partnership for 2 years. After 2 years, Q and R increased their investments by Rs 15,000 and Rs 20,000 respectively and P decreased his investment by Rs 20,000. At the end of 3 years, total profit received by them is Rs 2,64,000. Then find Q's profit share.
(A) Rs 78,000   (B) Rs 76,000
(C) Rs 80,000   (D) Rs 72,000
(E) None of these

7. X & Y started a business with some amount. After 9 months Y left the business & Z joins the business with Rs 24,000 and remains in business till the end of the year. At the end of the year, profit share of X, Y and Z is Rs 960, Rs 960 and Rs 480 respectively. Find the sum of the amount (in Rs.) invested by X & Y together in the business.
(A) Rs 26,000   (B) Rs 16,000
(C) Rs 28,000   (D) Rs 14,000
(E) None of these

8. A and B entered into a business with the capital of Rs 4000 &Rs 3000 respectively. After 6 months C joined them with capital of Rs P and after another four months A left the business. If after 1 year, profit sharing ratio of A, B & C is 10:9:9 respectively, then find P.
(A) Rs 4000   (B) Rs 6000
(C) Rs 6500   (D) Rs 4500
(E) None of these

9. A & B invested Rs 30,000 & Rs 40,000 respectively. After 6 months, B increased his investment by 25% and after another 2 months A increased his investment by 60%. If at the end of the year total profit is Rs 81,000, then find profit share of B at the end of the year.
(A) Rs 36,000   (B) Rs 54,000
(C) Rs 90,000   (D) Rs 45,000
(E) None of these

10. P and Q enters into a partnership with a total capital of Rs 23,000. After 4 months, A increases his capital by Rs 4000. Find the initial amount invested by P if ratio of profit share of P to that of Q at the end of the year is 5:6.
(A) Rs 9000   (B) Rs 4500
(C) Rs 18,000   (D) Rs 8000
(E) None of these

11. Karthi, Sasi and Shoba started a business by investing money in the ratio 37:23:31 for a year. If the difference between Karthi & Sasi's share of profit at the end of 1 year was Rs 13,520. Find the total profit earned by three of them at the end of a year?
(A) Rs 83,680   (B) Rs 87,880
(C) Rs 86,970   (D) Rs 82,500
(E) None of these

12. P, Q & R invested in the ratio 5:8:7 in a business. They got an annual profit of Rs 68,400. If R and P withdrew their amount at the end of 3 months and 7 months respectively, then find the difference between Q and R's share of profit.
(A) Rs 33,750   (B) Rs 32,500
(C) Rs 33,250   (D) Rs 33,500
(E) None of these

13. Shoba and Jothi invested in the ratio 8:7 in a business. They got an annual profit of Rs 68,900. If Jothi withdrew her entire amount at the end of 9 months, then find the difference between their share in profit?
(A) Rs 14,200   (B) Rs 14,500
(C) Rs 14,300   (D) Rs 14,600
(E) None of these

14. A, B & C started a business with Rs 8000, Rs 16000 & Rs 12000 respectively. After an year if all three divide the profit equally, then time period of B in partnership is what percent of the time period of C in the partnership?
(A) 60%   (B) 75%
(C) 25%   (D) 80%
(E) None of these

15. A and B invested in a partnership Rs 50,000 and Rs P for half and two-third of time respectively and profit share of A is 20% more than profit share of B. Find P.
(A) Rs 31,500   (B) Rs 31,750
(C) Rs 32,250   (D) Rs 31,250
(E) None of these

16. If an amount of Rs 84,840 is distributed to three persons such that share of R is half of P and Q together and share of Q is one-third of P and R together. Find the share of Q and R together.
(A) Rs 63,630   (B) Rs 49,490
(C) Rs 21,210   (D) Rs 42,420
(E) None of these

17. Two persons P and Q invested in a partnership for 2/5th and 2/3rd of the investment time respectively. If P and Q invested Rs 10000 and Rs 4000 respectively. Find profit share of Q is how much percent more/less than profit share of P?
(A) 33 1/3%   (B) 36%
(C) 66 2/3%   (D) 50%
(E) None of these

18. Ram and Vinoth invested in a partnership and Ram is active partner, so he got 10% of total profit and remaining profit is distributed in the ratio of theirs investments. Ram invested Rs 24000 and after 4 months Vinoth joined with Rs 60,000 and at the end of the year, Ram got Rs 7000 as profit share, find the share of Vinoth.
(A) Rs 10,000   (B) Rs 18,000
(C) Rs 12,000   (D) Rs 9,000
(E) None of these

SOLUTION:

1. (A) Let share amount received by each daughter, son & niece be a:b:c respectively.
If $c = x, a = 4x, b = 5x$
$a : b : c = 4 : 5 : 1$
Ratio of total amount = 16:25:2
Share of daughters $= \frac{16}{43} \times 34,400$
$= $ Rs 12,800
Share of each daughter $= \frac{12,800}{4}$
$= $ Rs 3200

2. (C) Investment ratio:
   - $P : Q = 3 : 5$
   - $P : R = 2 : 3$
   - $Q : P : R = 10 : 6 : 9$
   - $P : Q : R = 6 : 10 : 9$

   Profit ratio for a year
   $$= (6x \times 12) : (10x \times 12) : (9x \times 6)$$
   $$= 12 : 20 : 9$$
   Required difference $= \dfrac{12-9}{41} \times 49,200$
   $$= \text{Rs } 3600$$

3. (B) Let the ratio of A & B's investment be a and b.
   Ratio of investment period $= 5{:}4$
   Acc. To the qn.,
   Profit share $= 5x \times a : 4x \times b = 5a : 4b$
   $$\dfrac{5a}{(5a+4b)} = \dfrac{10,000}{50,000}$$
   $$25a = 5a + 4b$$
   $$20a = 4b$$
   $$a : b = 1 : 5$$

4. (D) Profit share of Karthi & Sasi
   $$= (x + 1500) \times 12 : (x + 2500) \times 12$$
   $$= x + 1500 : x + 2500$$
   Acc. To the Qn.,
   $$\dfrac{x+2500}{(x+1500+x+2500)} = \dfrac{14000}{24000}$$
   $$\dfrac{x+2500}{2x+4000} = \dfrac{7}{12}$$
   $$12x + 30,000 = 14x + 28,000$$
   $$2x = 2000$$
   $$x = 1000$$

5. (B) Ratio of their profits (A : B)
   $$= 75,000 \times 4x : 25,000 \times 7x = 12 : 7$$
   $$\dfrac{12-7}{19} \times \text{Total profit} = 1000$$
   $$\text{Total profit} = \dfrac{1000 \times 19}{5} = \text{Rs } 3800$$

6. (A) Profit ratio A:B:C
   $$= [(85,000 \times 2) + (65,000 \times 1)] : [(60,000 \times 2) + (75,000 \times 1)] : [(70,000 \times 2) + (90,000 \times 1)]$$

$= 235 : 195 : 230 = 47 : 39 : 46$
Q's profit share $= \dfrac{39}{132} \times 2,64,000$
$$= \text{Rs } 78,000$$

7. (C) Let amount invested by X and Y be a & b respectively.
   Profit ratio of X, Y & Z
   $$= a \times 12 : b \times 9 : 24,000 \times 3$$
   $$= 4a : 3b : 24,000$$
   Acc. To the Qn.,
   $$\dfrac{3b}{24,000} = \dfrac{960}{480}$$
   $$b = \text{Rs } 16,000$$
   $$\dfrac{4a}{3b} = \dfrac{960}{960} = 1$$
   $$a = \dfrac{3 \times 16,000}{4} = \text{Rs } 12,000$$
   Required sum $= 16,000 + 12,000$
   $$= \text{Rs } 28,000$$

8. (B) Profit sharing of A, B & C
   $$= 4000 \times 10 : 3000 \times 12 : P \times 6$$
   $$= 40,000 : 36,000 : 6P$$
   Acc. To the Qn., profit ratio of (C:A)
   $$\dfrac{6P}{40,000} = \dfrac{9}{10}$$
   $$P = \text{Rs } 6000$$

9. (D) Profit ratio of A & B
   $$= [(30,000 \times 8) + (48,000 \times 4)] : [(40,000 \times 6) + (50000 \times 6)]$$
   $$= (240 + 192) : (240 + 300)$$
   $$= 432 : 540 = 4 : 5$$
   Profit share of B $= \dfrac{5}{9} \times 81,000$
   $$= \text{Rs } 45,000$$

10. (A) Let the capital of P be Rs x.
    Capital of Q $= \text{Rs } (23,000 - x)$
    Profit ratio of P & Q $= [(x \times 4) + [(x + 4000) \times 8]] : (23,000 - x) \times 12$
    $$= 12x + 32,000 : 2,76,000 - 12x$$
    $$= 3x + 8000 : 69,000 - 3x$$
    Acc. To the Qn.,
    $$\dfrac{3x+8000}{69,000-3x} = \dfrac{5}{6};$$
    $$x = \text{Rs } 9000$$

11. (C) Let total profit be Rs x.

$$\frac{37-23}{(37+23+31)} \times x = 13520$$

$$x = \frac{13520 \times 91}{14}$$

x = Rs 87,880

12. (A) Ratio of profit sharing of P, Q & R

$= (5 \times 7):(8 \times 12):(7 \times 3)$

$= 35:96:21$

Required difference

$= \frac{96-21}{152} \times 68,400 =$ Rs 33,750

13. (C) Ratio of their profits

$= (8 \times 12):(7 \times 9)$

$= 32:21$

Required difference

$= \frac{32-21}{(32+21)} \times 68,900$

$= \frac{11}{53} \times 68,900$

= Rs 14,300

14. (B) Let time periods of A, B, C be a, b, c respectively.

Profit ratio of A, B & C

$= 8000 \times a:16,000b:12,000 \times c$

$= 2a:4b:3c$

Acc. to the Qn., $2a:4b:3c = 1:1:1$

$a:b:c = \frac{1}{2}:\frac{1}{4}:\frac{1}{3} = 6:3:4$

Required % $= \frac{3}{4} \times 100 = 75\%$

15. (D) Let time of investment of A & B be $\frac{1}{2}x$ & $\frac{2}{3}x$ respectively

$$\frac{\text{Profit share of A}}{\text{Profit share of B}} = \frac{120}{100}$$

$$\frac{50,000 \times \frac{1}{2}x}{P \times \frac{2}{3}x} = \frac{120}{100}$$

$$\frac{50,000 \times 3}{4P} = \frac{6}{5}$$

$6P = 12,500 \times 3 \times 5$

P = Rs 31,250

16. (B) Let profit share of P, Q, R be a, b & c respectively.

$c = \frac{a+b}{2}; a+b = 2c$

$b = \frac{a+c}{3}; a+c = 3b$

On solving a: b: c = 5:3:4

Share of Q & R $= \frac{3+4}{5+3+4} \times 84,840$

$= $ Rs 49,490

17. (A) Let total time of investment be x months.

Profit ratio $= 10,000 \times \frac{2}{5}x:4000 \times \frac{2}{3}x$

$= 4000:\frac{8000}{3}$

$= 12,000:8000$

$= 3:2$

Required % $= \frac{2 \sim 3}{3} \times 100$

$= \frac{100}{3} = 33\,{}^{1}\!/_{3}\%$

18. (D) Ratio of profit share of Ram & Vinoth $= 24,000 \times 12:60,000 \times 8$

$= 3:5$

Let total profit be x.

$x \times \frac{90}{100} \times \frac{3}{8} + x \times \frac{10}{100} = 7000$

$x = \frac{7000 \times 800}{270+80} = $ Rs 16,000

Share of Vinoth

$= 16,000 - 7000 = $ Rs 9000

TIME AND DISTANCE

Time and distance:

It deals with moving objects. Time, distance & speed are inter-related keywords.

Speed is the measure of how quickly an object moves from a place to another in a period of time.

Reminder:

Units (generally used)

- Distance: km, m

  $1 \text{ km} = 1000 \text{ m}$

- Time: hr, min, sec

  $1 \text{ hr} = 60 \text{ min}$

  $1 \text{ min} = 60 \text{ sec}$

- Speed: km/hr, m/s

  $1 \text{ km/hr} = \dfrac{1000 \text{ m}}{60 \times 60 \text{ sec}} = \dfrac{5}{18} \text{ m/s}$

  $1 \text{ m/s} = \dfrac{\frac{1}{1000}}{\frac{1}{60 \times 60 \text{ sec}}} = \dfrac{18}{5} \text{ km/hr}$

Formulas:

For an object, covering specific distance in a specific period of time:

1. $\text{Speed} = \dfrac{\text{Distance travelled}}{\text{Time taken}}$

   $\text{Time} = \dfrac{\text{Distance}}{\text{Speed}}$

   $\text{Distance} = \text{Speed} \times \text{time taken}$

2. At constant conditions:
   - If time is constant: $\text{Distance} \propto \text{Speed}$
   - If speed is constant: $\text{Distance} \propto \text{Time}$

- If distance is constant: $\text{Speed} \propto \dfrac{1}{\text{Time}}$
- If ratio of two speeds is $a : b$

  then ratio of their time taken $= \dfrac{1}{a} : \dfrac{1}{b}$

  $= b : a$

3. **Average speed:**

   Varying speed at different intervals of time If object travels d1, d2, d3,... dn metres with speeds s1, s2, s3,...sn seconds respectively,

   then, average speed of overall journey

   $= \dfrac{\text{Total distance}}{\text{Total time taken}}$

   $= \dfrac{d1 + d2 + d3 + \cdots + dn}{t1 + t2 + t3 + \cdots + tn} \text{ m/s}$

Case1:

If 2 equal distance 'a' covered at x & y km/hr respectively then, average speed

$$= \dfrac{a}{\dfrac{a/2}{x} + \dfrac{a/2}{y}} = \dfrac{1}{\dfrac{1}{2x} + \dfrac{1}{2y}} = \dfrac{2xy}{x+y}$$

Note: distance is equal in each frame

Case2:

If total distance is divided into x parts, & each part is covered. If object will take same equal time to cover different distance frames d1, d2, d3...,dn, with different speeds s1, s2, s3, ...dn respectively....,then, average speed $=$

$$\dfrac{1}{\dfrac{1}{d1s1} + \dfrac{1}{d2s2} + \dfrac{1}{d3s3} + \cdots \dfrac{1}{dnsn}}$$

Note: Time is equal in each frame

4. <u>Relative speed:</u>

If two objects are moving with speeds a & b km/hr respectively, the relative speed of two objects:

- When moving in opposite direction (towards each other) $\Rightarrow$ (a + b) km/hr (speed gets added up)
- When moving in same direction with each other $\Rightarrow$ (a − b) km/hr (Their speeds get differenced)

5. If 2 persons, A & B start from 2 places P & Q at the same time, with speed a & b km/hr respectively meet each other at point R & takes further time of t1 & t2 hours to reach their destination from R.

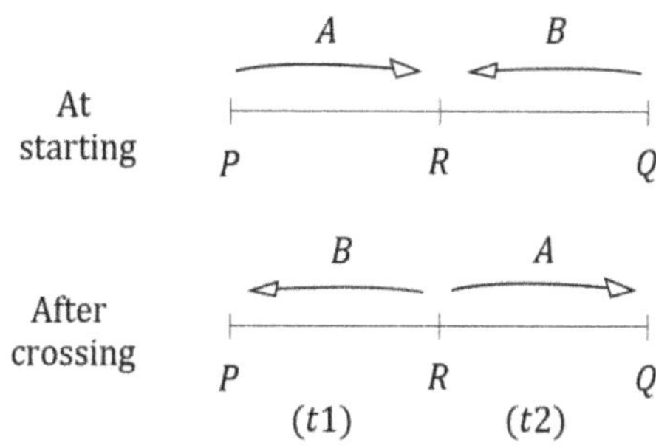

1) $\dfrac{A's\ speed}{B's\ speed} = \dfrac{a}{b} = \sqrt{\dfrac{T2}{T1}}$

2) Time taken for each person from their start to reach R (before crossing)
$= \sqrt{T1 \times T2}$ hours

BASED ON TRAIN:

It is an application of time & distance concept taking movement of trains into case. The movement of train is relatively compared with other stationary or moving train or object

1. <u>Train vs stationary object</u>
   <u>Case 1:</u>
   <u>Stationary object of no length:</u>
   Pole, standing man, building, etc.

<u>Note:</u> Consider, train of length L metre, Time taken by train to cross the stationary object = Time taken by train to cover 'L' metre

Speed of train
$= \dfrac{\text{Length of train}}{\text{TIme taken to cross stationary object}}$

<u>Case2:</u>
<u>Stationary object of certain length:</u>
<u>Eg:</u> Another stationary train, railway platform, bridge, etc.

Speed of train
$= \dfrac{\text{Length of (train+stationary object)}}{\text{TIme taken to cross stationary object}}$

<u>Note:</u> Consider train of length passing a stationary object of length 'x' metre. Time taken by train to cross the stationary object = Time taken by train to cover (L + x) metre.

2. <u>Train vs Moving object:</u>
   <u>Case1:</u>
   <u>Moving object of no length</u>
   Eg: Walking man
   Consider a train & man with x& y m/s respectively, moving in

- Opp. Direction:
  Relative speed:
  $x + y = \dfrac{\text{Length of train}}{\text{TIme taken to cross each other}}$
- Same direction:
  Relative speed:
  $x - y = \dfrac{\text{Length of train}}{\text{TIme taken to cross each other}}$

<u>Case2:</u>
<u>Moving object of certain length</u>
Eg: Another moving train
Consider 2 moving trains with speed x & y m/s moving in

- <u>Opposite direction:</u>
  Relative speed: $x + y$
  $= \dfrac{\text{Length of (train1+train2)}}{\text{TIme taken to cross each other}}$

- **Same direction:**
  Relative speed: $x - y$
  $$= \frac{\text{Length of (train1+train2)}}{\text{TIme taken to cross each other}} \ (x > y)$$

3. If 2 trains starting at same time from 2 places A & B moving towards, B & A respectively, cross each other at place R

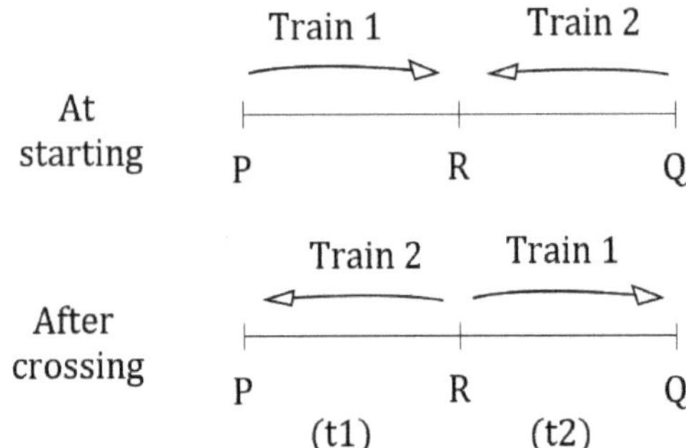

& takes further time of t1 & t2 hours respectively to reach their destination after crossing

Then, $\dfrac{\text{Speed of train1}}{\text{Speed of train2}} = \sqrt{\dfrac{t2}{t1}}$

Time taken for each train to reach their crossing places from their start
$= \sqrt{t1 \times t2} \text{ hours}$

4. Stoppage & Non-stoppage case:
   If a train travels a certain distance a speed of x km/hr without stoppage & covers same distance with stoppage at a speed of y km/hr
   Stoppage time per hour
   $$= \frac{\text{Difference in speeds}}{\text{Speed without stoppage}}$$
   $$= \frac{x-y}{x} \quad (x > y)$$

BOATS & STREAMS:

It is also an application of time & distance concept, taking moving boats & its parameters involved, into case.

Key terms:

- **Still water:** Speed of water in river $= 0$

- **Stream water:** Water in river is moving & its speed is not zero
- **Motion in still water:** Moving in water when water current is zero. Motion will be of uniform speed.
- **Downstream motion:** Motion against the stream ie., opposite to the direction in which water in stream flowing.
- **Upstream motion:** Motion along the stream ie., in the direction in which water in the stream is flowing.

Formulas:
Let speed of boat in still water: B kmph
   Speed of water in the stream: W kmph
   Speed of boat in upstream: U kmph
   Speed of boat in downstream: D kmph

- Speed of boat along/with the stream: Downstream speed, $D = B + W$ kmph
- Speed of boat against the stream: Upstream speed, $U = B - W$ kmph
- Speed of boat/man in still water
  $$= \frac{1}{2}(D + U) \text{ kmph}$$
- Speed of boat/man in stream
  $$= \frac{1}{2}(D - U) \text{ kmph}$$

EXERCISE:

1. Convert 108 km/hr to m/s
   (A) 30 m/s   (B) 28 m/s
   (C) 20 m/s   (D) 32 m/s
   (E) None of these

2. Convert 25 m/s to km/hr
   (A) 60 m/s   (B) 180 m/s
   (C) 45 m/s   (D) 90 m/s
   (E) None of these

3. A person has to travel from P to Q in certain time. Travelling at a speed of 6 km/hr. She reaches the office 35 mins late, while at a speed of 12 km/hr. She

reaches 45 mins early. What is the distance between P & Q?
(A) 8 km   (B) 16 km
(C) 32 km   (D) 12 km
(E) None of these

4. Driving 3/4 of his usual speed, a person is 40 mins late to his office. Find the usual time he takes to cover the distance.
(A) 2 hrs   (B) 3 hrs
(C) 2.5 hrs   (D) 1.5 hrs
(E) None of these

5. A van covers four successive 10 km distances at speeds 10 km/hr, 20 km/hr, 30 km/hr, 40 km/hr respectively. Its average speed in the whole journey is
(A) 18.5 kmph   (B) 19.2 kmph
(C) 19.6 kmph   (D) 20 kmph
(E) None of these

6. If a person goes at an average speed of 25 km/hr & then returns at the average speed of 15 km/hr. Find his average speed during the whole journey.
(A) 18.75 kmph   (B) 18.25 kmph
(C) 17.5 kmph   (D) 18.5 kmph
(E) None of these

7. Find the diameter of the wheel that makes 413 revolutions to go 5192 metres (Use pi=22/7)
(A) 4 m   (B) 3 m
(C) 2 m   (D) 5 m
(E) None of these

8. A policeman noticed a thief at a distance of 250 m. The thief starts running & the policeman chases him. The thief & the policeman run at the rate of 8 km/hr & 9 km/hr respectively. What is the distance between them after six minutes?

(A) 100 m   (B) 150 m
(C) 200 m   (D) 180 m
(E) None of these

9. A car completed a certain journey in 6 hours. It covers one-fourth distance at 40 km/hr & the rest at 60 km/hr. The length of the journey is
(A) 300 km   (B) 180 km
(C) 160 km   (D) 320 km
(E) None of these

10. If a person reduces his speed by 2/3 of his normal speed then he takes 2 hours more in walking certain distance. The time (in minutes) to cover the distance with normal speed is
(A) 50 min   (B) 40 min
(C) 60 min   (D) 30 min
(E) None of these

11. A passenger counts the poles nearby the railway track. If poles are situated 60 metres apart and the speed of the train is 54 km/hr, then how many poles will he count in one minute?
(A) 16 poles   (B) 15 poles
(C) 17 poles   (D) 18 poles
(E) None of these

12. A person starts from P to reach Q which is 40 kms apart, a speed of 10 km/hr. By what percent should he increase his speed in order to shorten the journey time by 60%?
(A) 120%   (B) 150%
(C) 100%   (D) 160%
(E) None of these

13. A & B have their speeds in the ratio 6:5. If both start from two places P & Q, 220 kms away, towards each other. How much distance A had travelled more

than B, when they meet for first time, if both start at the same time?
(A) 20 kms   (B) 18 kms
(C) 15 kms   (D) 16 kms
(E) None of these

14. Two cars P and Q, start from places A & B having distance 120 km between them and meet in 75 minutes. If the speed of the car P is 45 km/hr, then the speed of car Q is
(A) 45 kmph   (B) 48 kmph
(C) 53 kmph   (D) 51 kmph
(E) None of these

TRAINS

15. A train crosses a 100 m long platform in 40 seconds. If the speed of the train is 5 m/s, what is the length of the train?
(A) 200 m   (B) 100 m
(C) 150 m   (D) 50 m
(E) None of these

16. A train 160 m long is moving at a speed of 60 kmph. What is the time taken by the train to cross a platform of 90 m long?
(A) 30 sec   (B) 10 sec
(C) 15 sec   (D) 20 sec
(E) None of these

17. A train 150 metres long takes 5 second to pass a standing man. Find the time taken by the train in crossing a railway platform of 360 metre in length.
(A) 17 sec   (B) 15 sec
(C) 16 sec   (D) 14 sec
(E) None of these

18. A train running at the speed of 15 m/s crosses a pole in 24 seconds less than the time it requires to cross a platform three times its length at the same speed. What is the length of the train?
(A) 150 m   (B) 140 m

(C) 60 m   (D) 120 m
(E) None of these

19. A train of 180 m length, passes a tree in 9 seconds and another train of the same length travelling in the opposite direction in 6 secs. The speed of the second train is
(A) 144 kmph   (B) 121 kmph
(C) 156 kmph   (D) 136 kmph
(E) None of these

20. Two trains, each 250 m long move towards each other on parallel tracks with velocities 30 km/hr and 20 km/hr respectively. What is the time that elapses when they first meet until they have cleared each other?
(A) 16 sec   (B) 72 sec
(C) 32 sec   (D) 36 sec
(E) None of these

21. Excluding stoppage time, the speed of a train is 68 km/hr and including the stoppages the speed of a train is 51 km/hr. For each hour the train stops for how many minutes?
(A) 12 min/hr   (B) 20 min/hr
(C) 15 min/hr   (D) 30 min/hr
(E) None of these

22. Two trains from P to Q and another from Q to P, start simultaneously. After they meet, the trains reach their destinations after 25 hours and 16 hours respectively. The ratio of their speed is
(A) 4:5   (B) 5:3
(C) 5:4   (D) 3:5
(E) None of these

23. A train covered a certain distance at a uniform speed. If the train have been 6 km/hr faster, it would have taken 1 hour less than the scheduled time. And if the train was slower by 6 km/hr, the train would have taken 3 hours more than the scheduled time. Find the length of the journey is.

(A) 42 km   (B) 24 km
(C) 30 km   (D) 36 km
(E) None of these

24. Two trains of lengths 180 m and 120 m run on parallel tracks. When running in the same direction, faster train crosses slower one in 30 sec. When running in opposite direction at their same speeds they pass each other completely in 10 seconds. Find the speed of the slower train.

(A) 12 m/s   (B) 8 m/s
(C) 10 m/s   (D) 16 m/s
(E) None of these

25. The distance between two stations X and Y is 580 km. One train leaves station X towards station Y at an average speed of 80 km/hr. After half an hour, another train leaves station Y towards X, at the average speed of 100 km/hr. The distance from station X where the two trains meet is

(A) 280 km   (B) 260 km
(C) 300 km   (D) 320 km
(E) None of these

26. Two trains leave station A at 10 AM and 10.30 AM respectively and travel at 60 km/hr and 70 km/hr respectively. How many kilometres from station A will the two-trains meet?

(A) 240 km   (B) 230 km
(C) 210 km   (D) 180 km
(E) None of these

27. 'L' metres long train cross a 210-meter-long tunnel in 15 sec, running at the speed of 72 km/hr. If the train crosses a

man running in opposite direction in 15/4 seconds, find the speed of the man.

(A) 3 m/s   (B) 4 m/s
(C) 6 m/s   (D) 8 m/s
(E) None of these

28. Train A travelling at 126 km/hr speed, completely crosses train B in 18 seconds. Train B is half the length of train A and is travelling at a speed of 90 km/hr in the opposite direction towards train A. How much will train B takes to cross a platform of length 340 metres?

(A) 24 sec   (B) 28 sec
(C) 30 sec   (D) 26 sec
(E) None of these

BOATS & STREAMS

29. A person can row downstream at 12 km/hr and upstream at 8 km/hr. Find the speed of person at still water and speed of the stream.

(A) (10,1) kmph   (B) (8,3) kmph
(C) (10,2) kmph   (D) (4,4) kmph
(E) None of these

30. A boat covers a distance of 60 kms upstream in 5 hours while it takes only 2 hours to cover the same distance downstream. What is the speed of the boat in still water in kmph?

(A) 30 kmph   (B) 21 kmph
(C) 42 kmph   (D) 25 kmph
(E) None of these

31. A boat covers 50 km downstream and 28 km upstream in 12 hours. It covers 40 km downstream and 48 km upstream in 16 hours. What is the speed of the boat in still water?

(A) 3 kmph   (B) 4 kmph
(C) 6 kmph   (D) 7 kmph
(E) None of these

32. A man takes five times as much as time to cover a distance against the stream as to cover the same distance with the stream. Find the ratio between the speed of the man in still water to that of the speed of the stream.
(A) 2:3   (B) 3:5
(C) 3:2   (D) 5:3
(E) None of these

33. A boat covers a distance of 54 km along a river in 6 hours. If it takes 18 hours to cover the same distance upstream, then what is the difference between the speed of the flow of the river and speed of the boat in still water?
(A) 4 kmph   (B) 5 kmph
(C) 6 kmph   (D) 3 kmph
(E) None of these

34. A boat covers total distance of 176 km. The boat covers a certain distance upstream in 12 hours and covers a certain distance in downstream in 8 hours. The speed of boat in still water is 10 km/hr. Find the speed of the stream.
(A) 8 kmph   (B) 5 kmph
(C) 6 kmph   (D) 4 kmph
(E) None of these

35. A man covers a certain distance along the stream in 3 hours and he covers the same distance against the stream in 6 hours. What is the speed of the stream, if the speed of the boat in still water is 12 kmph?
(A) 6 kmph   (B) 5 kmph
(C) 9 kmph   (D) 4 kmph
(E) None of these

36. A man can row a distance of 2km downstream in 10 minutes and 2 km upstream in 15 minutes. How much time will he take to row the same

distance upstream if due to a tide the speed of the current gets tripled?
(A) 30 min   (B) 40 min
(C) 50 min   (D) 45 min
(E) None of these

37. A boat covers 30 km in upstream in 5 hours. Speed of boat in still water is 3/8 times less than the speed of the boat in downstream. Find the time taken by boat to cover 96 km in downstream.
(A) 4.5 hours   (B) 3.5 hours
(C) 3 hours   (D) 4 hours
(E) None of these

38. The speed of a boat in still water is 10 kmph, rate of current is 5 kmph. While moving with the stream, the boat covers 105 km, then find out how much distance can be covered in same time while moving against the stream (in km)?
(A) 38 km   (B) 35 km
(C) 32 km   (D) 40 km
(E) None of these

39. A boat can go at 12 kmph in still water. If the speed of the river is 3 kmph, the boat takes 12 hours more in upstream than to go downstream for the same distance. How far is the place?
(A) 270 km   (B) 240 km
(C) 540 km   (D) 250 km
(E) None of these

40. Speed of a boat in upstream is 70% of speed of boat in downstream. If speed of current is 6 km/hr. Find time taken by boat in downstream to cover 360 km.
(A) 8 hours   (B) 6 hours
(C) 9 hours   (D) 10 hours
(E) None of these

41. A boat runs at 9.6 km/hr in still water and it takes twice as much time to travel up than as to travel down the same distance in river. The speed of the water current is

(A) 3 kmph   (B) 9.6 kmph

(C) 3.2 kmph   (D) 4.8 kmph

(E) None of these

SOLUTION:

TIME & DISTANCE:

1. (A) $x \frac{km}{hr} = \left(x \times \frac{5}{18}\right)$ m/s

$$108 \times \frac{5}{18} = 30 \text{ m/s}$$

2. (D) $x \frac{m}{s} = \left(x \times \frac{18}{5}\right)$ km/hr

$$25 \times \frac{18}{5} = \frac{450}{5} = 90 \text{ m/s}$$

3. (B) Distance

$$= \frac{S1 \times S2}{S1 - S2} \times \text{Difference of the timings}$$

$$\text{Distance} = \frac{12 \times 6}{12 - 6} \times \frac{80}{60} = 16 \text{ km}$$

4. (A) Distance covered remains the same. Let it be 's' and actual time taken be 't'.

$$\frac{3}{4} s \left(t + \frac{40}{60}\right) = st$$

$$t + \frac{2}{3} = \frac{4t}{3}$$

$$t = 2 \text{ hours}$$

5. (B) Average speed $= \frac{4 \times 10}{\frac{10}{10} + \frac{10}{20} + \frac{10}{30} + \frac{10}{40}} =$

$$\frac{40}{250} \times 120 = 19.2 \text{ kmph}$$

6. (A) Average speed for cases with for two equal distance $= \frac{2xy}{x+y}$

$$= \frac{2 \times 25 \times 15}{25 + 15} = \frac{750}{40}$$

$$= 18.75 \text{ kmph}$$

7. (A) Circumference of the wheel $= 2\pi r$

$$413 \times 2\pi r = 5192$$

$$r = \frac{5192}{2 \times \frac{22}{7} \times 413} = 2 \text{ m}$$

Diameter of wheel $= 4$ m

8. (B) Relative speed of policeman

$$= 9 - 8$$

$$= 1 \text{ kmph} = \frac{5}{18} \text{ m/s}$$

Distance reduced in 6 minutes

$$= 6 \times \frac{5}{18} \times 60 = 100 \text{ m}$$

Remaining distance $= 250 - 100$

$$= 150 \text{ m}$$

9. (D) Let total distance be x km.

Time taken $= 6$ hrs

$$\left(x \times \frac{1}{4} \times \frac{1}{40}\right) + \left(x \times \frac{3}{4} \times \frac{1}{60}\right) = 6$$

$$\frac{x}{160} + \frac{x}{80} = 6$$

$$\frac{3x}{160} = 6$$

$$x = 2 \times 160 = 320 \text{ km}$$

10. (C) Let his actual speed and time be 's' km/hr and 'T' hours respectively. As speed remains constant.

$$sT = \frac{1}{3}s(T + 2)$$

$$T = \frac{T}{3} + \frac{2}{3}$$

$$\frac{2}{3}T = \frac{2}{3}$$

$$T = 1 \text{ hour} = 60 \text{ minutes}$$

11. (A) Distance travelled in 1 minute

$$= 54 \times \frac{5}{18} \times 60 = 900 \text{ m}$$

No. of poles counted $= \frac{900}{60} + 1$

$$= 15 + 1$$

$$= 16 \text{ poles}$$

12. (B) Actual time taken $= \frac{40}{10} = 4$ hours

New journey time $= 40\%$ (Actual time)

$$= \frac{40}{100} \times 4 = 1.6 \text{ hours}$$

New speed $=\dfrac{40}{1.6} = 25$ kmph

Required % $=\dfrac{25-10}{10} \times 100 = 150\%$

13. (A) Distance covered $\propto$ speed

Let the distance covered by A & B be 6x & 5x respectively.

When they start at same time, they cover distance in the ratio of their speeds.

Required distance $=\dfrac{6x\sim 5x}{(6x+5x)} \times 220$

$\qquad = 20$ kms

14. (D) Time taken $=\dfrac{75}{60} = \dfrac{5}{4}$ hours

Relative speed $=\dfrac{120}{5/4} = \dfrac{480}{5}$

$\qquad = 96$ kmph

Speed of car Q = 96 - 45 = 51 kmph

TRAINS:

15. (B) Speed $=\dfrac{\text{Distance}}{\text{TIme taken}}$

Speed of train $=$

$\dfrac{\text{Lenght of (train+platform)}}{\text{TIme taken}}$

$5 = \dfrac{(L+100)}{40}$

$L = 200 - 100 = 100$ m

16. (C) Time taken $=\dfrac{\text{Distance}}{\text{Speed}} = \dfrac{160+90}{60\times\frac{5}{18}}$

$\qquad = \dfrac{250 \times 18}{60 \times 5} = 15$ seconds

17. (A) Speed of the train $=\dfrac{150}{5} = 30$ m/s

Time taken $=\dfrac{360+150}{30} = \dfrac{510}{30}$

$\qquad = 17$ seconds

18. (D) Let length of the train be x metres.

Length of platform = 4x metres

Acc. To the qn.,

Time taken to cover

- $[(x + 4x) - x]$ metres = 3x metres

$\qquad = 24$ seconds

- x metres $=\dfrac{24}{3} = 8$ seconds

- Length of train $= 8 \times 15 =$ 120 metres

19. (A) Speed of first train $=\dfrac{180}{9} = 20$ m/s

Relative speed of 2 trains $=\dfrac{180+180}{6}$

$\qquad = 60$ m/s

Speed of the second train = 60-20

$= 40$ m/s $= 40 \times \dfrac{18}{5} = 144$ kmph

20. (D) Total distance $= 250 \times 2 = 500$ m

Relative speed $= 30 + 20 = 50$ kmph

$\qquad = 50 \times \dfrac{5}{18}$ m/s

Required time $=\dfrac{500}{50\times\frac{5}{18}} = 2 \times 18$

$\qquad = 36$ seconds

21. (C) Time spent on stoppages (per hour)

$=$ Time in which the train could have travelled in (68 -51) km

17 km $=\dfrac{17}{68} \times 60 = 15$ min/hr

22. (A) Speed of train1: Speed of train2

$\qquad = \sqrt{T2}:\sqrt{T1}$

where T1 & T2 are time taken by the two trains to reach their destinations from the point of their meeting

Required ratio $= \sqrt{16}:\sqrt{25} = 4:5$

23. (D) Let total distance be d km and the normal speed be x km/hr.

$\dfrac{d}{x} - \dfrac{d}{x+6} = 1; \quad \dfrac{d}{x-6} - \dfrac{d}{x} = 3$

Solving we get, x = 12, d = 36 km

Length of the journey = 36 km

24. (C) Train lengths: L1 = 180 m, L2 $\qquad = 120$ m

Time periods:
$$T1 = 30 \text{ secs}, T2 = 10 \text{ secs}$$

Speed of trains:

- $S1 = \dfrac{L1+L2}{2} \times \dfrac{T1+T2}{T1 \times T2}$

$$= \dfrac{180 + 120}{2} \times \left(\dfrac{30 + 10}{30 \times 10}\right)$$

$$= 20 \text{ m/s}$$

- $S2 = \dfrac{L1+L2}{2} \times \dfrac{T1-T2}{T1 \times T2}$

$$= \dfrac{180 + 120}{2} \times \left(\dfrac{30 - 10}{30 \times 10}\right)$$

$$= 10 \text{ m/s}$$

25. (A) Distance covered by the first train in half an hour $= \dfrac{1}{2} \times 80 = 40$ km

Remaining distance $= 580 - 40$
$$= 540 \text{ km}$$

Relative speed $= 80 + 100$
$$= 180 \text{ km/hr}$$

Both trains meet in $= \dfrac{540}{180} = 3$ hr

In three hours, first train covers 3×80
$$= 240 \text{ km}$$

Required distance $= 40 + 240$ km
$$= 280 \text{ km}$$

26. (C) The time taken after 10.30 AM they meet be 'T' hours.
$$(0.5 \times 60) + (60 + T) = 70 \times T$$
$$30 + 60T = 70T$$
$$10T = 30$$
$$T = 3 \text{ hours}$$

Required distance $= 3 \times 70$
$$= 210 \text{ km from station A}$$

27. (B) Speed of train $= 72 \times \dfrac{5}{18} = 20$ m/s

$$\dfrac{L+210}{15} = 20$$

$$L = 300 - 210 = 90 \text{ metres}$$

Let speed of man be x m/s

$$(20 + x) = \dfrac{90}{15/4} = 24$$

$$x = 4 \text{ m/s}$$

28. (B) Let length of train A & B be 2x & x metres respectively.

$$(126 + 90) \times \dfrac{5}{18} = \dfrac{3x}{18}$$

$$3x = 1080$$

$$x = 360 \text{ m}$$

Time taken $= \dfrac{360+340}{90 \times \frac{5}{18}} = \dfrac{700 \times 18}{90 \times 5}$

$$= 28 \text{ seconds}$$

BOATS & STREAMS:

29. (C) Speed in still water
$$= \dfrac{1}{2}(\text{upstream} + \text{downstream})$$
$$= \dfrac{1}{2}(12 + 8) = 10 \text{ kmph}$$

Rate of stream
$$= \dfrac{1}{2}(\text{upstream} - \text{downstream})$$
$$= \dfrac{1}{2}(12 - 8) = 2 \text{ kmph}$$

30. (B) Upstream speed $= \dfrac{60}{5} = 12$ kmph

Downstream speed $= \dfrac{60}{2} = 30$ kmph

Speed in still water $= \dfrac{1}{2}(30 + 12)$
$$= 21 \text{ kmph}$$

31. (D) Let x & y be speed of boat in still water & speed of stream respectively.

Acc. To the qn.,
$$\dfrac{50}{x+y} + \dfrac{28}{x-y} = 12$$
$$\dfrac{40}{x+y} + \dfrac{48}{x-y} = 16$$

On solving we get,
$$x = 7 \text{ kmph}, y = 3 \text{ kmph}$$

Speed of boat in still water $= 7$ kmph

32. (C) Let upstream & downstream time be 5x & x respectively.

Required ratio
$$= \dfrac{1}{2}(5x + x) : \dfrac{1}{2}(5x - x) = 3:2$$

33. (D) Speed of downstream $= \dfrac{54}{6}$

$\qquad\qquad\qquad = 9$ kmph

Speed of upstream $= \dfrac{54}{18} = 3$ kmph

Speed of the flow of the river

$\qquad = \dfrac{1}{2}(9 - 3) = 3$ kmph

Speed of boat in still water $= \dfrac{1}{2}(9 + 3)$

$\qquad\qquad\qquad\qquad = 6$ kmph

Required difference $= 6 \sim 3 = 3$ kmph

34. (C) Let speed of the stream be x kmph

$8(10 + x) + 12(10 - x) = 176$

$80 + 8x + 120 - 12x = 176$

$4x = 24$

$x = 6$ kmph

35. (D) Let speed of the stream be x kmph.

$3(12 + x) = 6(12 - x)$

$36 + 3x = 72 - 6x$

$9x = 36$

$x = 4$ kmph

Speed of the stream is 4 kmph.

36. (A) Let speed of man and water current be x & y kmph respectively.

$\dfrac{2}{x+y} = \dfrac{10}{60}$ & $\dfrac{2}{x-y} = \dfrac{15}{60}$

$x + y = 12$ & $x - y = 8$

$x = 10$ & $y = 2$

Required time $= \dfrac{2}{10-6} = \dfrac{2}{4} = \dfrac{1}{2}$ hour

$\qquad\qquad\qquad = 30$ minutes

37. (D) Let the speed of boat in downstream be x kmph.

Speed of boat in still water

$\qquad =$ Downstream speed $-$ Speed of stream

$\qquad = x - \dfrac{3}{8}x = \dfrac{5}{8}x$

Speed of stream

$=$ Downstream speed - Speed of boat

$= \left(x - \dfrac{5}{8}x\right)$

Speed of boat in upstream

$=$ Speed of boat $-$ speed of stream

$= \dfrac{5}{8}x - \left(x - \dfrac{5}{8}x\right)$

$= \dfrac{5}{8}x - \dfrac{3}{8}x = \dfrac{2}{8}x$ kmph

Acc. To the qn.,

$\dfrac{30}{5} = \dfrac{2}{8}x$

$x = 24$

Required time $= \dfrac{96}{24} = 4$ hours

38. (B) Upstream speed $= 10 - 5$

$\qquad\qquad\qquad = 5$ kmph

Downstream speed $= 10 + 5$

$\qquad\qquad\qquad = 15$ kmph

Time taken by boat while moving

along the stream $= \dfrac{105}{15} = 7$ hours

Distance covered in 7 hours while

moving upstream $= 7 \times 5 = 35$ km

39. (A) Let the distance be D kms.

$\dfrac{D}{12-3} - \dfrac{D}{12+3} = 12$

$5D - 3D = 12 \times 45$

$2D = 540$

$D = 270$ kms

40. (C) Let speed of boat in still water & speed of current be x & y kmph respectively.

$x - y = \dfrac{70}{100}(x + y)$

$10x - 10y = 7x + 7y$

$3x = 17y$

$x = \dfrac{17y}{3} = \dfrac{17 \times 6}{3} = 34\dfrac{\text{km}}{\text{hr}}$

Required time $= \dfrac{360}{34+6} = 9$ hours

41. (C) Let the distance & speed of current be D & x respectively.

Acc. To the Qn.,

$2 \times \dfrac{D}{(9.6+x)} = \dfrac{D}{(9.6-x)}$

$19.2 - 2x = 9.6 + x$

$3x = 9.6;$

$x = 3.2$ km/hr

PRACTICE:

1. A person runs 800m in 100 seconds. His speed in km/hr is
   (A) 57.6 kmph   (B) 27.5 kmph
   (C) 28.8 kmph   (D) 30 kmph
   (E) None of these

2. A car covers first 101 km in 100 mins & the remaining 123 km in 140 mins. What is the average speed of the car?
   (A) 48 kmph   (B) 52 kmph
   (C) 56 kmph   (D) 60 kmph
   (E) None of these

3. A person travels 90 km at 15 km/hr, next 96 km at 32 km/hr and remaining 160 km/hr. Find his average speed(approx.)
   (A) 25 kmph   (B) 30 kmph
   (C) 24 kmph   (D) 27 kmph
   (E) None of these

4. The radius of each wheel of a car is 35 cm. If each wheel rotates 450 times per minute, then the speed of the car (in km/hr) is
   (A) 58.6 kmph   (B) 60.5 kmph
   (C) 59.4 kmph   (D) 62 kmph
   (E) None of these

5. The diameter of the wheel is 56 cm. How many revolutions will it make in travelling 1056 m? (Use pi=22/7)
   (A) 500 rev   (B) 600 rev
   (C) 300 rev   (D) 700 rev
   (E) None of these

6. Person A saw person B at a distance of 300 m. Person B started running & person A chases him. Person A & person B run at the rate of 12 km/hr & 9 km/hr respectively. How long will it take for the person A to catch person B?
   (A) 6 min   (B) 12 min
   (C) 3 min   (D) 5 min
   (E) None of these

7. A person is walking at a speed of 8 km/hr. After every km, he takes rest for 10 mins. How much time will be taken to cover a distance of 24 kms?
   (A) 420 mins   (B) 400 mins
   (C) 410 mins   (D) 415 mins
   (E) None of these

8. A bus starts from A to B and another bus starts from B to A, they meet at the exact middle of the places of A & B. After meeting they complete the journey in 3 hrs and 2 hrs 40 mins respectively. The ratio of the time taken by them to complete the whole journey is
   (A) 9:8   (B) 8:9
   (C) 8:7   (D) 7:8
   (E) None of these

9. Sasi walks at a speed of 6 kmph for half an hour and rides a cycle at 12 kmph for next 20 minutes and finally in a van at 60 kmph for 10 minutes. Find his average speed during the entire journey (in kmph)
   (A) 18 kmph   (B) 15 kmph
   (C) 16 kmph   (D) 17 kmph
   (E) None of these

10. Karthi walks at a speed of 6 km/hr and he runs at a speed of 14 km/hr. How much time will he take to cover a distance of 84 km, if he covers equal distance by walking & running?
    (A) 12 hrs   (B) 8 hrs
    (C) 10 hrs   (D) 14 hrs
    (E) None of these

11. A 640-metre train is running at the average speed of 144 km/hr. How long will it take to pass a tree?
(A) 20 sec   (B) 11 sec
(C) 12 sec   (D) 16 sec
(E) None of these

12. What is the ratio between time taken by a train of 160 m length to cross an electric pole and a bridge of 80 m length?
(A) 2:3   (B) 3:2
(C) 4:3   (D) 3:4
(E) None of these

13. A 140-metre-long train crosses a platform twice its length in 20 seconds. What is the speed of the train?
(A) 42 m/s   (B) 21 m/s
(C) 20 m/s   (D) 40 m/s
(E) None of these

14. Two trains are running in opposite directions with the same speed. If the length of each train is 150 metres & they cross each other in 15 seconds, the speed of each train (in km/hr)
(A) 66 m/s   (B) 60 m/s
(C) 72 m/s   (D) 84 m/s
(E) None of these

15. Two trains of lengths 120 m and 140 m are travelling in opposite directions at speeds of 60 kmph and 70 kmph respectively. What is the time taken by them to cross each other?
(A) 9 sec   (B) 7.2 sec
(C) 6 sec   (D) 8 sec
(E) None of these

16. A train is running at 55 km/hr but due to stoppages it could cover a certain distance at 44 km/hr. For each hour the train stops for how many minutes?

(A) 10 min/hr   (B) 12 min/hr
(C) 6 min/hr   (D) 16 min/hr
(E) None of these

17. The speed of three trains are in the ratio 3:5:2. What is the ratio between the time taken by the trains to cover the same distance?
(A) 10:6:15   (B) 10:8:15
(C) 8:6:15   (D) 10:6:12
(E) None of these

18. The distance between two places P & Q is 345 km. A train starts from P at 6 AM, at 75 kmph, moving towards Q. Another train starts from Q at 7AM and travels towards P at 60 kmph. At what time do they meet?
(A) 10.30 AM   (B) 9 AM
(C) 9.30 AM   (D) 10 AM
(E) None of these

19. The distance between P and Q is 1200 km. Train A leaves place P at 2 PM and runs at a speed of 60 km/hr. Train B leaves place Q at 3 PM and runs at a speed of 75 kmph. If the train A stops on the way for 50 minutes and the train B stops on the way for 40 minutes, then what is the total time taken by both the trains to reach their destinations from their starting points?
(A) 3 hrs 50 mins (B) 4 hrs 20 min
(C) 4 hrs   (D) 4 hrs 10 min
(E) None of these

20. Train A is 240 metre long and train B is 180 metre long. Train A has a speed 40 kmph and train B has a speed of 30 kmph. If the trains move in opposite directions, then in what time will train B pass train A completely?
(A) 21.6 sec   (B) 20 sec
(C) 21.2 sec   (D) 22.2 sec

(E) None of these

21. A train can cross a platform of length 400 m in 12 seconds while a tree in 8 seconds. In what time the train can cross a platform of length 150 m?
(A) 5 sec   (B) 4 sec
(C) 6 sec   (D) 7 sec
(E) None of these

22. The rate of stream is 16 kmph and the ratio between the speed of boat in upstream and the speed of the boat in downstream is 9:5. What is the speed of the boat in still water?
(A) 56 kmph   (B) 48 kmph
(C) 52 kmph   (D) 45 kmph
(E) None of these

23. A person can swim 6 kmph in still water. If the velocity of the stream is 3 kmph, the time taken by the person to swim 27 km upstream and back is?
(A) 9 hours   (B) 12 hours
(C) 10 hours   (D) 14 hours
(E) None of these

24. A boat travels downstream in 5 hours and upstream in 3 hours. The speed of the boat in still water is 40 km/hr and speed of the stream is 15 km/hr. Find the total distance travelled by the boat.
(A) 350 km   (B) 275 km
(C) 380 km   (D) 360 km
(E) None of these

25. A boat running downstream covers a distance of 40 km in 5 hours while coming back the boat takes twice the time it took for downstream. What is the speed of the boat?
(A) 4 kmph   (B) 6 kmph
(C) 5 kmph   (D) 8 kmph
(E) None of these

26. The speed of a person along the river is 6 kmph and against the river is 2 kmph. If he covers 30 kms in upstream and same distance in downstream, what is the distance covered by him in 7 hours, if he swims at an average speed?
(A) 21 km   (B) 20 km
(C) 18 km   (D) 24 km
(E) None of these

27. A boat in downstream covers 14 km in same time as it covers 11 km in upstream. Find speed of stream is what percent of the speed of boat in still water.
(A) 10%   (B) 15%
(C) 12%   (D) 8%
(E) None of these

28. A man rows 3 kmph in still water. If the speed of the stream is 1 kmph, it takes him 45 minutes to row to a place and back. How far is the place?
(A) 3 km   (B) 0.5 km
(C) 2 km   (D) 1 km
(E) None of these

29. A boat covers 175 km upstream in 7 hours and takes 4 hours to cover 300 km in downstream. If speed of boat in still water is increased by 10% then find time takes by boat to cover 200 km in downstream.
(A) 2 hours   (B) 2.5 hours
(C) 3 hours   (D) 1.5 hours
(E) None of these

30. A man can row 8 kmph in still water. If the speed of the stream is 6 kmph, he takes 30 hours more to go upstream than to go downstream for the same distance. What is the distance?
(A) 70 km   (B) 60 km
(C) 75 km   (D) 65 km
(E) None of these

SOLUTION:

1. (C) Speed $= \dfrac{\text{distance}}{\text{time taken}}$

Required speed $= \dfrac{800}{1000}$

$= \dfrac{800}{1000} \times \dfrac{3600}{100}$

$= 28.8$ kmph

2. (C) Average speed $= \dfrac{\text{Total distance}}{\text{Total time taken}}$

$= \dfrac{101 + 123}{\left(\dfrac{100 + 140}{60}\right)} = \dfrac{224 \times 60}{240}$

$= 56$ kmph

3. (D) Average speed $= \dfrac{\text{Total distance}}{\text{Total time taken}}$

$= \dfrac{90 + 96 + 160}{\left(\dfrac{90}{15}\right) + \left(\dfrac{96}{32}\right) + \left(\dfrac{160}{40}\right)} = \dfrac{346}{6 + 3 + 4}$

$= \dfrac{346}{13}$

$= 26.61$ kmph $\cong 27$ kmph

4. (C) Circumference of wheel

$= 2 \times \dfrac{22}{7} \times 35 = 2.2$ m

Distance covered by wheel

• Per minute $= 450 \times 2.2 = 990$ m

• Per second $= \dfrac{990}{60} = 16.5$ m

Speed $= 16.5 \times \dfrac{18}{5} = 59.4$ kmph

5. (B) Circumference of wheel $= 2\pi r$

$= 2 \times \dfrac{22}{7} \times 28 = 176$ cm

No. of revolutions $= \dfrac{1056 \times 100}{176}$

$= 600$ revolutions

6. (A) Person A can make (12-9)

$= 3$ km/hr

He can cover 300 m in 6 minutes.

7. (C) Time taken to cover 24 km $= \dfrac{24}{8}$

$= 3$ hours

He takes rest 23 times

$\therefore$ 3 hours + 23(10)mins

$= 3$ hours + 230 mins

$= (180 + 230)$mins

$= 410$ mins

8. (A) Time taken by 2 buses to cover equal distances is 3 hrs & 2 hrs 40 mins respectively.

Ratio of time taken $= 180 : 160$

$= 9 : 8$

9. (D) Total distance $= \left(6 \times \dfrac{30}{100}\right) +$

$\left(12 \times \dfrac{20}{60}\right) + \left(60 \times \dfrac{10}{60}\right)$

$= 3 + 4 + 10 = 17$ kms

Total time taken $= 30+20+10$

$= 17$ kms

Average speed $= \dfrac{\text{Total distance}}{\text{Total time taken}}$

$= \dfrac{17}{1}$

$= 17$ kmph

10. (C) Distance covered by karthi

• While walking $= \dfrac{84}{2}$

$= 42$ km

• While running $= 42$ km

Total time required $= \dfrac{42}{6} + \dfrac{42}{14}$

$= 7 + 3 = 10$ hours

11. (D) Time taken $= \dfrac{640}{144 \times \frac{5}{18}}$

$= 16$ seconds

12. (A) Speed of the train is same

Required ratio $= 160 : (160 + 80)$

$= 160 : 240 = 2 : 3$

13. (B) Length of platform

$= 2 \times 140 = 280$ m

Speed of train $= \dfrac{140 + 280}{20} = \dfrac{420}{20}$

$= 21$ m/s

14. (C) Total distance $= 150 \times 2$

$$= 300 \text{ m}$$

Relative speed $= \dfrac{300}{15} = 20 \text{ m/s}$

Speed (in kmph) $= 20 \times \dfrac{18}{5}$

$$= 72 \text{ m/s}$$

15. (B) Relative speed $= 60 + 70$

$$= 130 \text{ m/s}$$

Total distance $= 120 + 140 = 260 \text{ m}$

Required time $= \dfrac{260}{130} \times \dfrac{18}{5}$

$$= 7.2 \text{ seconds}$$

16. (B) Time spent on stoppages (per hour) = Time in which the train could have travelled (55-44) km ie., 11 km

$$= \dfrac{11}{55} \times 60 = 12 \text{ min/hr}$$

17. (A) Time taken $\propto \dfrac{1}{\text{speed}}$

Required time ratio $= \dfrac{1}{3} : \dfrac{1}{5} : \dfrac{1}{2}$

$$= 10 : 6 : 15$$

18. (B) Distance travelled by first train in 1 hour = 75 km

Remaining distance $= 345 - 75$

$$= 270 \text{ km}$$

Relative speed $= 75 + 60$

$$= 135 \text{ km}$$

Time taken $= \dfrac{270}{135} = 2 \text{ hours}$

Required time = 7 AM + 2 hours

$$= 9 \text{ AM}$$

19. (D) Travel time of

- Train P $= \dfrac{1200}{60} = 20 \text{ hours}$
- Train Q $= \dfrac{1200}{75} = 16 \text{ hours}$

Total time taken by

- Train P = 20 hours 50 minutes
- Train Q = 16 hours 40 minutes

Require difference

$= 20$ hours 50 minutes ~ 16 hours 40 minutes

$= 4$ hours 10 minutes

20. (A) Total distance $= 240 + 180 = 420 \text{ m}$

Relative speed $= (40 + 30) = 70 \text{ kmph}$

Required time $= \dfrac{420}{70 \times \frac{5}{18}} = 21.6 \text{ seconds}$

21. (D) Let length of train be 'L' m.

Speed of train is constant.

$\therefore \dfrac{L+400}{12} = \dfrac{L}{4}$

$L + 400 = 3L$

$2L = 400$

$L = 200 \text{ m}$

Speed of train $= \dfrac{200}{4} = 50 \text{ m/s}$

Required time $= \dfrac{200+150}{50} = \dfrac{350}{50}$

$$= 7 \text{ seconds}$$

22. (A) Rate of stream $= \dfrac{1}{2}(9x - 5x) = 16$

$$x = 8$$

Speed of boat in still water

$= \dfrac{1}{2}(9x - 5x)$

$= \dfrac{1}{2} \times 14 \times 8 = 56 \text{ kmph}$

23. (B) Required time $= \dfrac{27}{6+3} + \dfrac{27}{6-3} = 9 + 3$

$$= 12 \text{ hours}$$

24. (A) Downstream speed $= 40 + 15$

$$= 55 \text{ kmph}$$

Upstream speed $= 40 - 15 = 25 \text{ kmph}$

Total distance $= (55 \times 5) + (25 \times 3)$

$$= 275 + 75 = 350 \text{ km}$$

25. (B) Downstream speed $= \dfrac{40}{5} = 8 \text{ kmph}$

Upstream speed $= \dfrac{40}{10} = 4 \text{ kmph}$

Speed of the boat $= \dfrac{1}{2}(8 + 4) = 6 \text{ kmph}$

26. (A) Distance covered = $30 + 30 = 60$ kms

Total time taken $= \dfrac{30}{6} + \dfrac{30}{2} = 5 + 15$

$\qquad\qquad\qquad = 20$ hours

Average speed $= \dfrac{60}{20} = 3$ kmph

Distance covered in 7 hours $= 7 \times 3$

$\qquad\qquad\qquad = 21$ kms

27. (C) Let time taken be t & x and y be speed of boat in still water and stream respectively.

$\dfrac{11}{x-y} = \dfrac{14}{x+y} = t$

$\dfrac{x}{y} = \dfrac{25}{3}$

Required % $= \dfrac{3}{25} \times 100 = 12\%$

28. (D) Let the distance be D.

$\dfrac{D}{3-1} + \dfrac{D}{3+1} = \dfrac{45}{60}$

$\dfrac{D}{2} + \dfrac{D}{4} = \dfrac{3}{4}$

$3D = 3$

$D = 1$ km

29. (B) Let speed of boat in still water and stream speed be x & y kmph respectively.

$x + y = \dfrac{300}{4} = 75$

$x - y = \dfrac{175}{7} = 25$

$x = 50$ & $y = 25$

Required time $= \dfrac{200}{\left(50 \times \frac{110}{100}\right) + 25} = \dfrac{200}{80}$

$\qquad\qquad\qquad = 2.5$ hours

30. (A) Let the distance be x km.

$\dfrac{x}{8-6} - \dfrac{x}{8+6} = 30$

$\dfrac{x}{2} - \dfrac{x}{14} = 30$

$7x - x = 30 \times 14$

$6x = 30 \times 14$

$x = 70$ km

TIME & WORK

Work is defined as something which could produce an effect or outcome.

The basic concept of time & work is the concept of proportionality

$$\text{Efficiency} \propto \frac{1}{\text{TIme taken}}$$

Efficiency: Rate of doing work

i. If a person does a piece of work in n days.
    Then, $\text{efficiency} = \frac{\text{Total workdone}}{\text{Total time taken}} = \frac{1}{n}$
    Then, the person does $1/n^{th}$ work in one day (for a work, done in 'n' days)
    The person needs to work at a uniform rate of $1/n^{th}$ work a day.

ii. If $1/n^{th}$ of a work is done by a person in one day, then the person takes n days to complete the entire work (considering the person work's at an uniform rate)

iii. If A can complete piece of work in x days & B can complete the same work in y days, both A & B working together can finish the same work in $\frac{xy}{x+y}$

iv. If a person is x times as efficient as the others, then he will take 1/x of the time taken by the other to finish a piece of work.

v. If A can work x times faster than B,
    • Ratio of work done by A & B for same duration of time = x : 1
    • Ratio of time taken by A & B for same amount of work = 1 : x

vi. If A, B, C can do a work in D1, D2 & D3 days respectively, If they work for a1, a2, a3 days respectively.
    Work done by A in a1 days $= \frac{a1}{D1}$
    work done by B in a2 days $= \frac{a2}{D2}$
    work done by C in a3 days $= \frac{a3}{D3}$
    So total amount of work done by A, B, C together $= \frac{a1}{D1} + \frac{a2}{D2} + \frac{a3}{D3}$
    We usually consider the total work as 1.

vii. Per day work $= \frac{\text{Total work}}{\text{No. of days}}$

viii. If A takes 'a' hours more, and B takes 'b' hours more, than the time taken by A & B working together to complete a piece of work. Then, time taken by A & B to complete that piece of work is $\sqrt{ab}$ hours, (ie., $\sqrt{}$(Extra time taken by 1st person × Extra time taken by 2nd person))
    Unit can be hours or days, based on the unit of time used in the problem.

ix. Wages are directly proportional to the work done by individual
    $$\text{Wage} \propto \frac{1}{\text{Time taken by individual}}$$
    Total wage = one person's per day wage × no. of persons × no. of days

PIPES & CISTERNS:

It is an application of time & work, involving filling & emptying a tank or cistern using inlet & outlet pipes respectively

Analogy of keywords:

TIME & WORK	PIPES & CISTERNS
Amount of work done	Part of tank filled/emptied
Time taken to do a piece of work	Time taken to fill or empty a tank completely or to desired level
Per day work	Per hour filling

Inlet pipe: A pipe which is connected to fill a tank/cistern

Outlet pipe: A pipe which is connected to empty a tank/cistern

i. If an inlet connected to a tank, fills it in x hours

Part of tank filled in one hour = 1/x

ii. If an outlet connected to a tank, empties it in y hours

Part of tank emptied in one hour = 1/y

iii. If an inlet which can fill a tank in x hours & an outlet which will empty a tank in y hours are opened at the same time, provided y > x,

- Net part of tank filled in 1 hr $= \dfrac{1}{x} - \dfrac{1}{y}$
- Time taken to fill the whole tank $= \dfrac{1}{\frac{1}{x}-\frac{1}{y}} = \dfrac{xy}{y-x}$

iv. If 2 inlets can fill a tank separately in x & y hours and if they are opened together at same time,

- The net part of tank filled in 1hr = $\dfrac{1}{x} + \dfrac{1}{y}$
- Time taken to fill the whole tank = $\dfrac{1}{\frac{1}{x}+\frac{1}{y}} = \dfrac{xy}{x+y}$

v. If 2 outlets can empty a tank separately in x & y hrs respectively and if they are opened together at same time,

- The net part of tank emptied in 1hr $= \dfrac{1}{x} + \dfrac{1}{y}$
- Time taken to empty the whole tank $= \dfrac{1}{\frac{1}{x}+\frac{1}{y}} = \dfrac{xy}{x+y}$

EXERCISE:

1. A alone can do a piece of job in 12 days and B alone can do the same job in 4 days. If they work together, in how many days can they complete the same job?
   (A) 5 days   (B) 3 days
   (C) 4 days   (D) 2 days
   (E) None of these

2. A alone can do a piece of work in 6 days. If A & B work together, they can complete the same work in 4 days. In how many days B alone can complete the same work?
   (A) 12 days   (B) 24 days
   (C) 8 days   (D) 16 days
   (E) None of these

3. P & Q together can complete the work in 15 days and R & S together can complete the work in 30 days. They work in alternate days, on the first day P & Q work together and the next day R & S work together the process is going on until the work is completed. In how many days the work will be completed?
   (A) 30 days   (B) 15 days

(C) 10 days   (D) 20 days
(E) None of these

4. P, Q & R alone can complete a work in 5, 8 & 10 days respectively. If they worked together for 2 days, what is the fraction of the work that is left?
(A) 3/40   (B) 3/20
(C) 17/20   (D) 17/40
(E) None of these

5. A, B, C and D can do a piece of work in 4, 5, 6 & 8 days respectively. A, B and C started working together and after 1 days, A and B left. After one day of C & D working, C also left & D completed the remaining work. How many days was required for completing the whole work? (approx.)
(A) 3.2 days   (B) 2.45 days
(C) 4.16 days   (D) 2.73 days
(E) None of these

6. If 3 men, 4 women & 2 girls can do a piece of work in 6 days, then in how many days 6 men, 8 women & 4 girls can complete the same work?
(A) 3 days   (B) 4 days
(C) 2 days   (D) 2.5 days
(E) None of these

7. If 6 men complete a piece of work in 15 days and 5 women can do the same work in 18 days, then in how many days 5 men & 4 women can complete the work?
(A) 5 days   (B) 10 days
(C) 12 days   (D) 9 days
(E) None of these

8. P & Q can complete one-fourth of a work in 5 days, Q & R can complete one-fifth of the work in 5 days and P & R together can complete half of the work in 5 days. In how many days P, Q & R together can complete three-fourth of the work?
(A) 7 5/6 days   (B) 6 2/3 days
(C) 7 17/19 days   (D) 7 21/29 day
(E) None of these

9. P, Q & R together can complete three-fourth work in 9 days, Q & R together can complete one-half of the work in 8 days. In how many days P alone can complete three-fourth of the work?
(A) 16 days   (B) 36 days
(C) 48 days   (D) 24 days
(E) None of these

10. A alone can do a piece of work in 40 days. A is 75% more efficient than B. In how many days A & B together can complete the work?
(A) 26 1/7   (B) 25 2/3
(C) 24 3/8   (D) 25 5/11
(E) None of these

11. N number of persons working 6 hours per day can build 80 m road in 18 days. If 5 more persons join them, by working 8 hours per day they can build a 60 m road in 8 days. How many persons were there at the beginning?
(A) 4 men   (B) 5 men
(C) 8 men   (D) 6 men
(E) None of these

12. A alone can do a piece of work in 6 days an B alone can do the same work in 12 days. With the help of C, they can complete the entire work in 3 days. If the wage for the total work is Rs 4800, find C's share.
(A) Rs 2400   (B) Rs 3600
(C) Rs 1200   (D) Rs 1500
(E) None of these

13. A alone can do a piece of work in 6 days, B alone can do the same work in 4 days more than the time taken by A alone. They work together & get a total wage of Rs 5600. What is the share of B?
(A) Rs 2400   (B) Rs 2800
(C) Rs 3000   (D) Rs 2100
(E) None of these

14. 16 students can complete a task in 24 days working 4 hours a day. Find in what time 10 men will complete the same task with 60% more efficiency than that of a student & working 6 hours a day?
(A) 16 days   (B) 18 days
(C) 14 days   (D) 12 days
(E) None of these

PIPES & CISTERNS

15. Pipe A empties a tank & Pipe B fills the tank. Both the pipes are open. It takes 20 hours to fill the tank. If pipe B takes 4 hours individually to fill the tank, then what is the time taken by pipe A to empty the tank?
(A) 5 hours   (B) 4 hours
(C) 3 hours   (D) 6 hours
(E) None of these

16. Pipe A can fill a tank in 40 minutes when it works at 40% efficiency. Pipe B is 2 times as efficient as pipe A. If both the pipes are opened and they work at 80% efficiency, then in how many minutes the tank will be filled?
(A) 6 8/9 mins   (B) 5 2/5 mins
(C) 6 2/3 mins   (D) 7 mins
(E) None of these

17. Pipes A & B together can fill a tank in 12 minutes. Pipes B & C together can fill the tank in 18 minutes. Pipes A & C

together can fill the tank in 24 minutes. If all the pipes are opened simultaneously, how many minutes are required to fill the tank?
(A) 12 1/3 mins   (B) 11 8/9 mins
(C) 10 2/5 mins   (D) 11 1/3 mins
(E) None of these

18. Pipes A, B & C can fill a tank in 3, 6 & 9 hours respectively. Pipe D can empty the tank in 6 hours. If all the four pipes are opened, at what time will the tank be full?
(A) 2 hrs   (B) 2 hrs 15 min
(C) 2 hrs 45 mins   (D) 2 hrs 30 min
(E) None of these

19. Three inlet pipes - Pipe A, Pipe B & Pipe C fill a tank in 4 hours, 6 hours & 8 hours respectively. An outlet pipe will empty the tank in certain hours. When all the pipes are opened simultaneously, the tank is filled in 24 hours. Find the time taken to empty the tank by the outlet pipe.
(A) 1 hour   (B) 3 hours
(C) 2 hours   (D) 2.5 hours
(E) None of these

20. A, B & C are three inlet pipes. Time taken by A & B together to fill the tank is same as the time taken by pipe C alone to fill one-third of the tank. If A, B & C together can fill the tank in 18 hours, then find the time taken by pipe C alone to fill the tank.
(A) 64 hours   (B) 72 hours
(C) 48 hours   (D) 30 hours
(E) None of these

21. A pipe can fill a tank in 4 hours but due to a leak it takes 6 hours to completely fill up the tank. If the pipe is closed, the leak will empty 48 litres in 4 hours, what is the capacity of the tank?

(A) 216 litres   (B) 144 litres

(C) 288 litres   (D) 120 litres

(E) None of these

22. Pipes A, B & C together can fill an empty tank in 5 hours. Pipes A & B together and B & C together can fill the same tank in 10 hours & 6 hours respectively. Find the time taken by pipe B alone to fill the tank.

(A) 14 hours   (B) 16 hours

(C) 12 hours   (D) 15 hours

(E) None of these

23. Pipe A and B alone can fill a tank in 'a' hours and 'a+15' hours respectively. If both pipes together fill the tank in 10 hours, then find the time taken by A alone to fill the tank is what percent of that of B alone?

(A) 150%   (B) 200%

(C) 50%   (D) 100%

(E) None of these

24. Two pipes A alone & B alone can fill a tank in 'x' hours and 'x+6' hours respectively. If both together fill the same tank in 7 1/5 hours, then find the time taken by pipe B alone to fill the tank.

(A) 21 hours   (B) 18 hours

(C) 15 hours   (D) 12 hours

(E) None of these

25. Ratio of time taken by pipe A to pipe B to fill a tank is 4:3 and efficiency of another pipe C is twice of B. If A and B are opened for first 5 minutes and C is opened, then the tank in filled in 20 minutes. Find the time taken by pipe C to fill the tank.

(A) 32.75 mins   (B) 31.25 mins

(C) 33 mins   (D) 32.5 mins

(E) None of these

26. A pipe can fill a tank in 10 hours. Due to a leak, it took 13 hours for the pipe to fill the tank. Find the time in which the full tank can be drained out by the leak.

(A) 65/3 hours   (B) 130/3 hours

(C) 130 hours   (D) 65/3 hours

(E) None of these

27. Pipe A and pipe B can fill a cistern together in 54 minutes. Pipe A is 50% more efficient than pipe B. Find the capacity of cistern, if it is given that pipe B fills the cistern at a speed of 12 litres/min.

(A) 1620 litres   (B) 810 litres

(C) 1215 litres   (D) 1350 litres

(E) None of these

28. A tank can be filled with water by two pipes A & B together in 68 4/7 minutes. If the pipe B was stopped after 1 hour, rest of the tank is filled in 20 minutes. The pipe B can alone fill the tank in

(A) 1 hours   (B) 2 hours

(C) 2.5 hours   (D) 1.5 hours

(E) None of these

SOLUTION:

1. (B) One day output of A & B

$$= \frac{1}{12} + \frac{1}{4} = \frac{1+3}{12} = \frac{4}{12}$$

No. of days $= \frac{12}{4} = 3$ days

2. (A) One day output of A & B together is $\frac{1}{4}$, ie.

$$\frac{1}{6} + \frac{1}{x} = \frac{1}{4}$$

$$\frac{1}{x} = \frac{1}{4} - \frac{1}{6} = \frac{6-4}{24} = \frac{2}{24}$$

$$x = \frac{24}{2} = 12 \text{ days}$$

3. (D) One day work of

- $P \& Q = \dfrac{1}{15}$
- $R \& S = \dfrac{1}{30}$

Total work $= \dfrac{1}{15} + \dfrac{1}{30} = \dfrac{3}{30} = \dfrac{1}{10}$

No. of pair of days (alternate days)

$= 10 = 1 + 1 + 0.73$ days

Total no. of days$= 10 \times 2 = 20$ days

4. (B) Let the total work be 40 units (LCM)

One day work of

- $P = \dfrac{40}{5} = 8$ units
- $Q = \dfrac{40}{8} = 5$ units
- $R = \dfrac{40}{10} = 4$ units

Total work completed in 2 days

$= (8 + 5 + 4) \times 2 = 17 \times 2$

$= 34$ units

Fraction of work that is left $= \dfrac{40 - 34}{40}$

$$= \dfrac{6}{40} = \dfrac{3}{20}$$

5. (D) Let total work be 120 units (LCM)

1 day work of85

- $A = \dfrac{120}{4} = 30$ units
- $B = \dfrac{120}{5} = 24$ units
- $C = \dfrac{120}{6} = 20$ units
- $D = \dfrac{120}{8} = 15$ units

Work completed in

- First day $= (30 + 24 + 20)$

  $= 74$ units
- 2nd day $= 20 + 15 = 35$ units
- Remaining work

  $= 120 - (74 + 46)$

  $= 120 - (74 + 35) = 120 - 109$

  $= 11$ units

C takes $\dfrac{11}{15} = 0.73$ days to complete the remaining work alone.

Total no. of days required

$= 2.73$ days

6. (A) Per day work of 3 men, 4 women & 2 girls $= \dfrac{1}{6}$

Per day work of 6 men, 8 women & 4 girls $= 2 \times \dfrac{1}{6} = \dfrac{1}{3}$

No. of days$= 3$ days

7. (B) Per day work of

- 1 man $= \dfrac{1}{6 \times 15}$
- 1 woman $= \dfrac{1}{5 \times 18}$

Per day work of 5 men & 4 women

$= \dfrac{5}{6 \times 15} + \dfrac{4}{5 \times 18} = \dfrac{9}{90} = \dfrac{1}{10}$

No. of days $= 10$ days

8. (C) Time to complete entire work

- $P \& Q = 5 \times 4 = 20$
- $Q \& R = 5 \times 5 = 25$
- $P \& R = 2 \times 5 = 10$

Per day work of

- $P \& Q = \dfrac{1}{20}$
- $P \& R = \dfrac{1}{10}$
- $Q \& R = \dfrac{1}{25}$
- $P, Q \& R = \dfrac{1}{2}\left(\dfrac{1}{20} + \dfrac{1}{25} + \dfrac{1}{10}\right)$

  $= \dfrac{19}{2 \times 100}$

Required days $= \dfrac{2 \times 100}{19} \times \dfrac{3}{4} = 7\dfrac{17}{19}$ days

9. (B) Time taken by P, Q, R to complete total work $= 9 \times \dfrac{4}{3} = 12$ days

Per day work of P, Q & R $= \dfrac{1}{12}$

Q & R together can complete the entire work $= 8 \times \dfrac{2}{1} = 16$ days

Per day work of Q & R $= \dfrac{1}{16}$

Per day work of Q & R $= \dfrac{1}{16}$

Per day work of P $= \dfrac{1}{12} - \dfrac{1}{16} = \dfrac{1}{48}$

Required days $= 48 \times \dfrac{3}{4} = 36$ days

10. (D) Efficiency ratio of A & B

$= 175 : 100 = 7 : 4$

Ratio of no. of days of A & B $= 4 : 7$

B alone can do the work $= \dfrac{40}{4} \times 7$

$\qquad\qquad = 70$ days

A & B together can complete the work

in $\dfrac{1}{40} + \dfrac{1}{70} = \dfrac{11}{280}$

No. of days $= \dfrac{280}{11} = 25\dfrac{5}{11}$

11. (A) Total work done is constant.

$N \times 6 \times 80 \times 18 = (N + 5) \times 8 \times 60 \times 8$

$\dfrac{N}{N+5} = \dfrac{8 \times 60 \times 8}{6 \times 80 \times 18} = \dfrac{8}{18}$

$18N = 8N + 40$

$10N = 40$

$N = 4$

12. (C) C's output per day $= \dfrac{1}{4} - \left(\dfrac{1}{6} + \dfrac{1}{12}\right)$

$= \dfrac{1}{4} - \left(\dfrac{3}{12}\right) = \dfrac{1}{3} - \left(\dfrac{1}{4}\right) = \dfrac{1}{12}$

Ratio of A, B & C's output per day

$= \dfrac{1}{6} : \dfrac{1}{12} : \dfrac{1}{12} = 2 : 1 : 1$

C's share $= 4800 \times \dfrac{1}{4} = $ Rs 1200

13. (D) B's per day work $= 6 + 4 = 10$ days

Efficiency ratio of A to B $= \dfrac{1}{6} : \dfrac{1}{10} = 5 : 3$

Share of B $= \dfrac{3}{8} \times 5600 = $ Rs 2100

14. (A) Let efficiency of student be a.

Time taken by 10 men be 'x'.

Total work done is same in both the cases.

$16a \times 24 \times 4 = 10(1.6a) \times x \times 6$

$x = \dfrac{24 \times 4}{6} = 16$ days

15. (A) Let time taken by pipe A to empty the tank be x hours.

$\dfrac{1}{20} = \dfrac{1}{4} - \dfrac{1}{x}$

$\dfrac{1}{x} = \dfrac{1}{4} - \dfrac{1}{20} = \dfrac{4}{20} = \dfrac{1}{5}$

$x = 5$ hours

16. (C) To fill a tank:

A, at 40% efficiency, takes 40 minutes.

A, at 80% efficiency, takes 20 minutes.

B has 2 times efficiency than A.

B, at 40% efficiency takes 20 minutes.

B, at 80% efficiency takes 10 minutes.

$\dfrac{1}{20} + \dfrac{1}{10} = \dfrac{3}{20} = \dfrac{20}{3} = 6\dfrac{2}{3}$

A & B can fill in $6\dfrac{2}{3}$ minutes.

17. (D) (A+B)'s output $= \dfrac{1}{12}$ I

(A+B)'s output $= \dfrac{1}{18}$ II

(A+B)'s output $= \dfrac{1}{24}$ III

Adding I, II & III,

$2(A + B + C)$'s output

$= \dfrac{1}{12} + \dfrac{1}{18} + \dfrac{1}{24}$

$= \dfrac{6+4+3}{72} = \dfrac{13}{72}$

$(A + B + C)$'s output $= \dfrac{13}{144}$

Time taken $= \dfrac{144}{13} = 11\dfrac{1}{13}$ minutes

18. (B) The part of the tank all four pipes can fill per hour $= \left(\dfrac{1}{3} + \dfrac{1}{6} + \dfrac{1}{9} - \dfrac{1}{6}\right) = \dfrac{4}{9}$

Required time $= \dfrac{9}{4}$ hours

$\qquad\qquad = 2$ hours 15 mins

19. (C) Input by all the 3 inlet pipes

$= \dfrac{1}{4} + \dfrac{1}{6} + \dfrac{1}{8} = \dfrac{13}{24}$

Work done by outlet pipe to empty the tank $= \frac{13}{24} - \frac{1}{24} = \frac{12}{24} = \frac{1}{2}$

Time taken by the outlet pipe to empty the tank = 2 hours

20. (B) $A + B = 3C$

$A + B + c = \frac{1}{18}$

$4C = \frac{1}{18}$

$C = \frac{1}{18 \times 4} = \frac{1}{72}$

C takes 72 hours to fill the tank.

21. (B) In 2 hours,

- Pipe can fill $= \frac{2}{4} = \frac{1}{2}$ part of tank

- Pipe & leakage can fill $= \frac{2}{6}$

  $= \frac{1}{3}$ part of tank

- Leakage can empty $= \frac{1}{2} - \frac{1}{3}$

  $= \frac{1}{6}$ part of tank

which is $\left(\frac{48}{2}\right) = 24$ litres

$\frac{1}{6}$ part of tank = 24

Total capacity $= 24 \times 6 = 144$ litres

22. (D) Let total work be 60 units.

Efficiency of

- $A + B = \frac{60}{10} = 6$ units

- $B + C = \frac{60}{6} = 10$ units

- $A + B + C = \frac{60}{5} = 12$ units

- $B = \left[(A + B) + (B + C)\right] - (A + B + C)] = 6 + 10 - 12 = 4$ units

Time taken by B alone $= \frac{60}{4}$

$= 15$ hours

23. (C) Acc. To the Qn.,

$\frac{1}{a} + \frac{1}{a+15} = \frac{1}{10}$

$\frac{(a+15) \times a}{a + (a+15)} = 10$

$a^2 + 15a = 20a + 150$

$a^2 - 5a - 150 = 0$

$(a - 15)(a + 10) = 0$

$a = 15 \text{ or} - 10$

$a = 15,$

$a + 15 = 30$

Required % $= \frac{15}{30} \times 100 = 50\%$

24. (B) Acc. To the qn.,

$\frac{1}{x} + \frac{1}{x+6} = \frac{1}{36/5} = \frac{5}{36}$

$\frac{x(x+6)}{x+(x+6)} = \frac{36}{5}$

$5x^2 + 30x = 72x + 216$

$5x^2 - 42x - 216 = 0$

$5x^2 - 60x + 18x - 216 = 0$

$(5x + 18)(x - 12) = 0$

$x = -\frac{18}{5} \text{ or } 12$

$x = 12, \ x + 6 = 18$ hours

25. (D) Ratio of time taken=4:3

Ratio of their efficiencies=3:4

Efficiency of C=4x× 2 = 8x units/min

Total capacity=20(7x) + 15(8x)

$= 140x + 120x = 260x$

Required time $= \frac{260x}{8x} = 32.5$ mins

26. (B) Let the leak drain the tank in T hours.

$\frac{1}{10} - \frac{1}{T} = \frac{1}{13}$

$\frac{1}{T} = \frac{1}{10} - \frac{1}{13} = \frac{13-10}{130} = \frac{3}{130}$

$T = \frac{130}{3}$ hours

27. (A) Let pipe B fill the cistern in x minutes.

Pipe A fills the tank in $x \times \frac{100}{150}$

$= \frac{2x}{3}$ minutes

$\frac{1}{x} + \frac{1}{\frac{2x}{3}} = \frac{5}{2x}$

$\frac{5}{2x} = \frac{1}{54}$

$x = \frac{54 \times 5}{2} = 135$

Capacity of cistern $= 135 \times 12$
$$= 1620 \text{ litres}$$

28. (B) Let pipe A & pipe B alone can fill the tank in 'x' & 'y' respectively.

$$\frac{1}{x} + \frac{1}{y} = \frac{1}{480/_7} = \frac{7}{480}$$

$$\frac{80}{x} + \frac{60}{y} = 1$$

On solving,
$x = 160$, $y = 120$ minutes

PRACTICE:

1. A starts a work and completes one-third of the work in 3 days and B alone completes the remaining work in 4 days. In how many days B alone can complete the entire work?
(A) 6 days   (B) 8 days
(C) 5 days   (D) 7 days
(E) None of these

2. P is 2 times as efficient as Q. Q is 5 times as efficient as R. If R alone can do a piece of work in 20 days, how many days required by P, Q & R together to complete 4 times the entire work?
(A) 6 days   (B) 5 days
(C) 4 days   (D) 3 days
(E) None of these

3. Priya alone can complete a piece of work in 8 days and Raj alone can complete the work in 16 days. If they worked with 75% efficiency, how many days are required by them if they work together to complete the entire work?
(A) 3 days   (B) 6 days
(C) 4 days   (D) 5 days
(E) None of these

4. If 12 men & 16 women can construct a building in 42, then in how many days 9 men & 12 women can build the same building, if the efficiencies of individual man and individual woman are equal?
(A) 64 days   (B) 56 days
(C) 60 days   (D) 52 days
(E) None of these

5. If 11 girls & 10 boys can complete a project work in 27 days working 8 hours/day. In how many days 14 girls & 13 boys can complete the same project work working 6 hours/day if efficiency of a girl is equal to the efficiency of a boy?
(A) 28 days   (B) 24 days
(C) 32 days   (D) 27 days
(E) None of these

6. P alone can do a piece of work in 4 days, Q alone can do the same work in 8 days. R alone can do the same work in 16 days. If they work together, they get a total wage of Rs 2100/day. What is the per day share of P & Q together?
(A) Rs 1500   (B) Rs 1800
(C) Rs 2000   (D) Rs 1600
(E) None of these

7. A & B can complete a work in 15 days, B & C complete the same work in 12 days and C & A in 10 days. In how many days will A alone complete the work?
(A) 24 days   (B) 20 days
(C) 18 days   (D) 28 days
(E) None of these

8. A, B and C working alone can finish a work in 50 days, 80 days & 90 days respectively. A worked on it alone for 22 days, then B took over from A. B worked on it alone for 21 days, then C took over from B. In how many days will C finish the remaining work? (in days)

(A) $27 \frac{23}{40}$ (B) $26 \frac{13}{37}$
(C) $26 \frac{31}{40}$ (D) $25 \frac{11}{24}$
(E) None of these

9. 25 male workers can finish a work in 24 days and 15 female workers can finish the work in 30 days. If all of them work together, then in how many they will finish the same work?
   (A) 13 2/7 days (B) 14 2/5 days
   (C) 12 2/3 days (D) 13 1/3 days
   (E) None of these

10. Rajesh can complete a work in 10 days and Suresh can complete the same work in 15 days. If Rajesh worked for 6 days and left the work, then find how many days will Suresh alone takes to complete the remaining work?
    (A) 7 days (B) 6 days
    (C) 5 days (D) 8 days
    (E) None of these

11. A, B and C can complete a work in 15 days, 24 days and 20 days respectively. If they all work together till the completion of work, find the share of C's wage, if the total wage for the work is Rs 3800.
    (A) Rs 1500 (B) Rs 1000
    (C) Rs 1200 (D) Rs 1400
    (E) None of these

12. A is 25% more efficient than B while C is 40% less efficient than A. If B alone can complete the work in 15 days then in how many days A & C can complete the work?
    (A) 8.4 days (B) 7.5 days
    (C) 6.5 days (D) 8 days
    (E) None of these

13. Tap A can fill a tank in 30 minutes, tap B can fill the same tank in 24 minutes & another tap C can empty half of the tank in 10 minutes. If tap A & tap B are opened together & after 8 minutes tap C is also opened, then find the total time taken to fill the remaining tank.
    (A) 16 mins (B) 20 mins
    (C) 18 mins (D) 15 mins
    (E) None of these

14. A cistern has two pipes. One can fill it with water in 15 hours and other can empty it in 12 hours. In how many hours will the cistern be emptied if both the pipes are opened together when 1/4th of the cistern is already full of water?
    (A) 35 hours (B) 40 hours
    (C) 50 hours (D) 45 hours
    (E) None of these

15. A tank is normally filled in 5 hours but due to a leak in it, it takes 4 hours more to be filled. If the tank is completely filled, then the leak will empty it in? (in hours)
    (A) 11.25 hours (B) 10.5 hours
    (C) 12.75 hours (D) 11.75 hours
    (E) None of these

16. There are 2 inlet pipes and 1 outlet pipe assigned to fill a tank. If inlet pipe 1 & outlet pipe 2 can fill the tank in 10 hours & 5 hours respectively and outlet pipe can empty the tank in 30 hours, then what will be the time taken by all three pipes together to fill the tank?
    (A) 4 2/3 hours (B) 3 2/3 hours
    (C) 3 3/4 hours (D) 4 3/4 hours
    (E) None of these

17. A tank is filled in 10 hours by three pipes A, B & C. The pipe A is twice as fast as B and B is twice as fast as C.

How much time will pipe C alone take to fill the tank?

(A) 70 hours   (B) 50 hours

(C) 35 hours   (D) 75 hours

(E) None of these

18. A cistern can be filled by a tap in 5 hours while it can be emptied by another tap in 9 hours. If both the taps are opened simultaneously, then after how much time will cistern will get filled?

(A) 12.15 hours   (B) 10.5 hours

(C) 11.25 hours   (D) 11.75 hours

(E) None of these

SOLUTION:

1. (A) B completes $\frac{2}{3}$ of work in 4 days

No. of days $= \frac{3}{2} \times 4 = 6$ days

2. (B) Time to complete entire work

- $R = 20$ days
- $Q = \frac{20}{5} = 4$ days
- $P = \frac{4}{2} = 2$ days
- $P + Q + R = \dfrac{1}{\frac{1}{20}+\frac{1}{4}+\frac{1}{2}} = \dfrac{1}{\frac{16}{20}}$

$$= \frac{20}{16} = \frac{5}{4}$$

For four times the entire work

$$= \frac{5}{4} \times 4 = 5 \text{ days}$$

3. (C) Output work per day of Priya &

$\text{Raj} = \dfrac{1}{\left(8\times\frac{75}{100}\right)} + \dfrac{1}{\left(16\times\frac{75}{100}\right)} = \dfrac{1}{6} + \dfrac{1}{12}$

$$= \frac{3}{12} = \frac{1}{4}$$

No. of days = 4 days

4. (B) Since, both men & women have same efficiencies,

Total no. of workers $= 12 + 16 = 28$

Since total work done is constant

$28 \times 4 = (9 + 12) \times x$

$x = \frac{28 \times 42}{21} = 56$ days

5. (A) Total work done is same. Since, efficiencies are same, total no. of workers in both the cases

$= (11 + 10, 14 + 13)$

$= (21, 27)$

$21 \times 27 \times 8 = 27 \times 6 \times x$

$x = \frac{21 \times 27 \times 8}{27 \times 6} = 28$ days

6. (B) Ratio of output work per day of P,

Q & R $= \frac{1}{4} : \frac{1}{8} : \frac{1}{16} = 4 : 2 : 1$

Total share of P & Q $= \frac{6}{7} \times 2100$

$$= \text{Rs } 1800$$

7. (A) One day work of

- $A + B + C = \frac{1}{2}\left(\frac{1}{15} + \frac{1}{12} + \frac{1}{10}\right)$

$$= \frac{1}{2} \times \frac{15}{60} = \frac{1}{8}$$

- $A = \frac{1}{8} - \left(\frac{1}{12}\right) = \frac{3-2}{24} = \frac{1}{24}$

A can complete the work in 24 days.

8. (C) Total work = 3600 units (LCM of 50, 80, 90)

One day work output of

- $A = \frac{3600}{50} = 72$
- $B = \frac{3600}{80} = 45$
- $C = \frac{3600}{90} = 40$

Total work completed by A & B

$= (72 \times 22) + (45 \times 21)$

$= 2529$ units

Remaining work $= 3600 - 2529$

$$= 1071$$

No. of days required $= \frac{1071}{40}$

$$= 26\frac{31}{40} \text{ units}$$

9. (D) Since no. of male & female workers remains the same in both the cases, they can be considered as single entity separately.

One day work of

- 25 male workers $= \dfrac{1}{24}$

- 15 female workers $= \dfrac{1}{30}$

- 25 male & 15 workers $= \dfrac{1}{24} + \dfrac{1}{30}$

$$= \dfrac{5+4}{120}$$

$$= \dfrac{9}{120} = \dfrac{3}{40}$$

No. of days $= \dfrac{40}{3} = 13\dfrac{1}{3}$ days

10. (B) Total work = 30 units (LCM)

One day work of

- Rajesh $= \dfrac{30}{10} = 3$ units

- Suresh $= \dfrac{30}{15} = 2$ units

Work completed by

- Rajesh in 6 days $= 6 \times 3$
- $ = 18$ units

Remaining work $= 30 - 18$

$$= 12 \text{ units}$$

No. of days required by Suresh to complete the remaining work $= \dfrac{12}{2}$

$$= 6 \text{ days}$$

11. (C) Total work = 120 units

One-day output of

- $A = \dfrac{120}{15} = 8$

- $B = \dfrac{120}{24} = 5$

- $C = \dfrac{120}{20} = 6$

Ratio of their work output = 8:5:6

Share of C $= \dfrac{6}{(8+5+6)} \times 3800$

$$= \dfrac{6}{19} \times 3800$$

$$= \text{Rs } 1200$$

12. (B) No. of days required for completing the work by

- B = 15 days (as given)

- $A = 15 \times \dfrac{100}{125} = 12$ days

- $C = 12 \times \dfrac{100}{60} = 20$ days

- A & C together $= \dfrac{1}{\frac{1}{12}+\frac{1}{20}} = \dfrac{1}{\frac{8}{60}} = \dfrac{60}{8}$

$$= 7.5 \text{ days}$$

13. (A) Let total capacity = 120 units (LCM of all 3 taps)

Efficiency of tap

- $A = \dfrac{120}{30} = 4$ units/min

- $B = \dfrac{120}{24} = 5$ units/min

- $C = \dfrac{120}{2(10)} = 6$ units/min

Tank filled by tap A & B in 8 mins

$$= 8 \times (4+5) = 72 \text{ units}$$

Remaining = 48 units

Required time $= \dfrac{48}{(4+5)-6} = \dfrac{48}{3}$

$$= 16 \text{ mins}$$

14. (D) Let capacity of cistern be 60L.

¼ of capacity $= {}^{1}/_{4}(60) = 45\text{L}$

Filling rate $= \dfrac{60}{15} = 4$ L/hr

Emptying rate $= \dfrac{60}{12} = 5$ L/hr

Effective emptying rate = 5 - 4

$$= 1 \text{ L/hr}$$

The cistern will get empty in $\dfrac{45}{1}$

$$= 45 \text{ hours}$$

15. (A) Let leak empty the tank in x hours.

$$\dfrac{1}{5} - \dfrac{1}{x} = \dfrac{1}{9}$$

$$\dfrac{1}{x} = \dfrac{1}{5} - \dfrac{1}{9} = \dfrac{4}{45}$$

$$x = \dfrac{45}{4} = 11.25 \text{ hours}$$

16. (C) Part of tank filled by all 3 pipes together in 1 hour $= \dfrac{1}{10} + \dfrac{1}{5} - \dfrac{1}{30}$

$$= \frac{8}{30} = \frac{4}{15}$$

Total time taken $= \frac{15}{4}$ hours

$$= 3\frac{3}{4} \text{ hours}$$

17. (A) Ratio of efficiencies of A: B: C

$$= 4{:}2{:}1$$

Efficiency of C $= \frac{1}{7}$

Time taken by C alone $= 7 \times 10$

$$= 70 \text{ hours}$$

18. (C) Let the required time be T.

$$\frac{1}{T} = \frac{1}{5} - \frac{1}{9} = \frac{4}{45}$$

$$T = \frac{45}{4} = 11.25 \text{ hours}$$

PERMUTATIONS & COMBINATIONS

It basically refers to arrangement of objects in a particular order.

Factorial:

It is the product of the number (for which we are finding the factorial) by its successor till it reaches to one.

$$n! = n(n-1)(n-2) \dots 1$$

Permutation:

It refers to number of ways a particular set can be arranged when order of the arrangement matters. If r objects are to be chosen from n objects, $(n \geq r)$
permutation of n objects taken r at a time,

$$nPr = \frac{n!}{(n-r)!}, \qquad r \leq n$$
$$= n(n-1)(n-2)(n-3) \dots (n-r+1)$$

Combination:

It refers to the number of ways a particular set can be arranged, where order of the arrangement does not matter which means for a combination of n number of things, there may be different orders.

If r objects are to be chosen from n,
Combination of n objects taken r at a time,

$$nCr = \frac{n!}{r! \, (n-r)!}, \qquad r \leq n$$

Useful relations:

- $0! = 1! = 1$ (As an empty set can arrange in one way only)
- $n! = n \times (n-1)!$

- $nPr = \dfrac{n!}{(n-r)!}$
- $(n+1) \times nPr = {}^{(n+1)}P_{(r+1)}$
- $nCr = \dfrac{nPr}{r!}$
- $nCr = nC(n-r)$
- $nC0 = \dfrac{n!}{0! \times n!} = \dfrac{1}{0!} = 1$
- $(n-1)C(r-1) + (n-1)Cr = nCr$

(If any event can occur in m ways & after it happens in any one of these ways, a second event can occur in n ways, then both the events together can occur in m × n ways)

EXERCISE:

1. If 8 men and 8 women are to sit around a circular table, so that there is one man between two women. Find the number of ways they can sit.
   (A) 7! × 6!   (B) 8! × 8!
   (C) 8! × 7!   (D) 8! × 6!
   (E) None of these

2. How many 4-digit numbers can be formed without repetition from the digits - {2,3,5,6,8,9}
   (A) 360   (B) 240
   (C) 720   (D) 480
   (E) None of these

3. How many 4-digit odd numbers can be formed with repetition from the digits - {1,2,4,5,7,8}?
   (A) 432   (B) 648
   (C) 1296   (D) 216

(E) None of these

4. How many 4-digit numbers greater than 5000 can be formed without repetition from the digits - {1,3,4,5,6,7}
(A) 90   (B) 270
(C) 360   (D) 180
(E) None of these

5. How many different selections can be made to form a 5-member team out of a 10 people?
(A) 252   (B) 360
(C) 120   (D) 200
(E) None of these

6. Find the number of ways in which 5 girls and 5 boys be seated in a row, so that all the girls sit together and all the boys sit together?
(A) $2(4!)^2$ (B) $2(5!)^2$
(C) $2(6!)^2$ (D) $2(3!)^2$
(E) None of these

7. Out of 6 boys and 2 girls, a group of 3 is to be formed. In how many ways can it be formed if at least one girl is to be included?
(A) 48   (B) 24
(C) 36   (D) 30
(E) None of these

8. How many different letters arrangement can be made from the letters of the word 'DIRECTION' so that all the vowels occur together?
(A) $\dfrac{6!\times3!}{2!}$ (B) $\dfrac{6!\times5!}{2!}$
(C) $\dfrac{5!\times4!}{2!}$ (D) $\dfrac{6!\times4!}{2!}$
(E) None of these

9. Find the number of different words that can be formed from the word 'CHERRY'.
(A) 360   (B) 240
(C) 300   (D) 400

(E) None of these

10. How many three letter words can be formed using the letters of the word 'BAND' if repetition of letters is allowed?
(A) 64   (B) 48
(C) 50   (D) 68
(E) None of these

11. How many 3-letter words with (or) without meaning, can be formed using all the letters of the word 'ANOTHER' if repetition of letters is not allowed?
(A) 250   (B) 200
(C) 420   (D) 210
(E) None of these

12. In how many ways can 6 members form a group out of 12 be selected, so that 3 particular members must not be selected?
(A) 86   (B) 84
(C) 92   (D) 78
(E) None of these

13. In how many ways 4 persons form a committee out of 9 to be selected so that two particular persons must not be included?
(A) 30   (B) 14
(C) 35   (D) 42
(E) None of these

14. A round table meeting is to be held between 12 persons. In how many ways can they be seated if 2 persons wish to sit together?
(A) $9! \times 4!$ (B) $10! \times 2!$
(C) $10! \times 3!$ (D) $9! \times 2!$
(E) None of these

15. Find the number of combinations of three things selected out of 8 things.
(A) 56   (B) 48
(C) 50   (D) 64

(E) None of these

16. In how many ways can 5 letter words can be formed from 2nd, 5th, 6th, 8th and 9th letters of the word 'METICULOUS'?
(A) 30   (B) 80
(C) 70   (D) 60
(E) None of these

17. In how many 5 boys can be seated among 8 girls around a circular desk such that no two boys sit together?
(A) 8P5 × 7!   (B) 8P5 × 6!
(C) 8P6 × 5!   (D) 8P6 × 7!
(E) None of these

18. In how many ways letters of the word 'ACCESS' be arranged such that word always starts with a vowel?
(A) 61   (B) 62
(C) 60   (D) 64
(E) None of these

19. Sasi has 10 friends out of which 6 are his classmates. In how many ways he can invite 5 friends such that at least 3 of them are his classmates?
(A) 192   (B) 176
(C) 180   (D) 186
(E) None of these

20. How many 4-digit nos. can be formed using digits from 0 to 9 if repetition is not allowed, such that the unit digit of the number will always be 4?
(A) 446   (B) 448
(C) 452   (D) 440
(E) None of these

21. Find all the possible four-digit number which are divisible by 5 if repetition of digits are not allowed (use digits from 0 to 9).
(A) 952   (B) 948
(C) 930   (D) 960

22. If 2 cards taken out randomly from a pack of 52 cards, then in how many ways we can select two black cards?
(A) 300   (B) 325
(C) 320   (D) 340
(E) None of these

23. In how many ways can 8 persons be arranged in a linear row if all are facing south and 2 specific people never sit together?
(A) 7! × 8   (B) 6! × 7
(C) 7! × 6   (D) 8! × 7
(E) None of these

24. If four different chocolates are to be distributed among seven students. If no student gets more than one chocolate, then the number of ways possible to do is?
(A) 640   (B) 720
(C) 900   (D) 840
(E) None of these

25. How many four-letter words containing at least one vowel & one consonant can be formed using the letters of the word 'DRAKE' so that no letter is repeated in the word formed?
(A) 125   (B) 100
(C) 160   (D) 120
(E) None of these

26. In how many different ways can the letters of the word 'INVITATION' be arranged so that the vowels always come together?
(A) 3600   (B) 1800
(C) 3200   (D) 4000
(E) None of these

27. How many words can be formed using the letters of the word 'MISSISSIPPI'?
(A) 34,620   (B) 34,650

(C) 34,560   (D) 34,660
(E) None of these

28. From a group of 5 men & 4 women, five persons are to be selected to form a committee in which there should be at least 3 men. In how many ways it can be done?
(A) 100   (B) 64
(C) 78   (D) 81
(E) None of these

29. In how many ways can 5 prizes be distributed to 8 students if each student can get any number of prizes?
(A) 5^8 (B) 7^5
(C) 8^5 (D) 5^7
(E) None of these

30. In how many ways 3 boys & 5 girls be arranged in a row all facing same direction such that no two boys sit together?
(A) 240^2 (B) 100^2
(C) 120^2 (D) 80^2
(E) None of these

SOLUTION:

1. (C) Permutation for circular seating
$= n! \times (n-1)!$
No. of ways $= 8! \times 7!$

2. (A) Total no. of ways without repetition
$= 6 \times 5 \times 4 \times 3$
$= 360$ ways

3. (B) Unit place must be $\{1,5,7\}$
Unit place can be placed only in 3 ways
Total no. of ways $= 6 \times 6 \times 6 \times 3$
$= 648$ ways

4. (D) In 1st position, only $\{5,6,7\}$ can be replaced.
Total no. of ways $= 3 \times 5 \times 4 \times 3$
$= 180$ ways

5. (A) Total no. of selections $=$ nCr
$= 10C5 = \dfrac{10 \times 9 \times 8 \times 7 \times 6}{1 \times 2 \times 3 \times 4 \times 5}$
$= 252$ ways

6. (B) No. of ways $= 2 \times 5! \times 5!$
$= 2 \times (5!)^2$

7. (C) Possible ways $= 2$ boys $+ 1$ girl
(or) 1 boy $+ 2$ girls
No. of ways $= (6C2 \times 2C1) +$
$(6C1 \times 2C2)$
$= (15 \times 2) + (6 \times 1)$
$= 30 + 6 = 36$ ways

8. (D) The word 'DIRECTION' has 4 vowels & 5 consonants. Since, the vowels occur together, they can be treated as 1 letter.
$5 + 1 = 6$ letters. I is repeated twice.
No. of ways $= \dfrac{6! \times 4!}{2!}$

9. (A) No. of letters is 6, R occur twice
No. of words $= \dfrac{6!}{2!} = 6 \times 5 \times 4 \times 3$
$= 360$ words

10. (A) No. of words $= 4 \times 4 \times 4$
$= 64$ words

11. (D) No. of words $= 7 \times 6 \times 5$
$= 210$ words

12. (B) As 3 members are excluded, no. of members $= 12 - 3 = 9$
No. of ways $= 9C6 = \dfrac{9!}{6!3!} = \dfrac{9 \times 8 \times 7}{1 \times 2 \times 3}$
$= 84$ ways

13. (C) 2 persons excluded
No. of persons $= 9 - 2 = 7$

No. of ways = 7C4 $= \dfrac{7!}{4!3!} = \dfrac{7 \times 6 \times 5}{1 \times 2 \times 3}$
$\qquad$ = 35 ways

14. (B) For circular arrangement, no. of arrangements = (n-1)!
Since, 2 persons sit together. They can be considered as 1.
No. of ways = $(11 - 1)! \times 2!$
$\qquad$ $= 10! \times 2!$

15. (A) No. of combinations = 8C3
$= \dfrac{8!}{3!\,5!} = \dfrac{8 \times 7 \times 6}{1 \times 2 \times 3} = 56$ ways

16. (D) No. of words $= \dfrac{5!}{2!} = 60$
('U' is repeated twice)

17. (A) No. of places for boys among 8 girls = 8
No. of ways = $8P5 \times (8 - 1)!$
$\qquad$ $= 8P5 \times 7!$

18. (C) No. of ways $= \dfrac{2 \times 5!}{2! \times 2!} = 60$ ways

19. (D) Possible cases:
- 3 classmates + 2 non-classmates
- 4 classmates + 1 non-classmates
- 5 classmates

No. of ways
$= (6C3 \times 4C2) +$
$\quad (6C4 \times 4C1) +$
$\quad (6C5)$
$= (20 \times 6) + (15 \times 4) + 6$
$= 186$

20. (B) No. of numbers formed
$= 8 \times 8 \times 7 \times 1 = 448$ numbers

21. (A) Total possible numbers when the unit digit Is
- 0: $9 \times 8 \times 7 \times 1 = 504$
- 5: $8 \times 8 \times 7 \times 1 = 448$

Total numbers = 504 + 448 = 952

22. (B) No. of ways = 26C2 $= \dfrac{26 \times 25}{1 \times 2}$
$\qquad$ = 325 ways

23. (C) Total no. of ways = 8!
No. of ways when 2 specific people always sit together = $7! \times 2!$
Required no. of ways
$= 8! - (7! \times 2!)$
$= 7! (8 - 2!)$
$= 7! \times 6$

24. (D) No. of way = 7P4
$\qquad$ $= 7 \times 6 \times 5 \times 4$
$\qquad$ $= 840$ ways

25. (D) It can either be
- 1 vowel & 3 consonants
- 2 vowel & 2 consonants

Total no. of ways
$= [(2C1 \times 3C3) + (2C2 \times 3C2)] \times 4!$
$= (2 + 3) \times 24 = 120$

26. (A) No. of ways $= \dfrac{6!}{2!2!} \times \dfrac{5!}{3!}$
$\qquad$ $= 3600$ ways

27. (B) Required no. of words $= \dfrac{11!}{4!\,4!\,2!}$
$\qquad$ $= 34,650$ ways

28. (D) No. of ways
$= (5C5) + (5C4 \times 4C1) +$
$\quad (5C3 \times 4C2)$
$= 1 + (5 \times 4) + (10 \times 6)$
$= 1 + 20 + 60$
$= 81$ ways

29. (C) No. of ways = 8^5

30. (A) Ways to arrange girls = 5!
In alternate order, 6 places will be available to arrange boys, ie., 6P3
Total ways = $5! \times 6P3 = 120^2$

PRACTICE:

1. Find the number of ways in which 8 boys & 8 girls can be seated in a row, so that all the girls sit together and all the boys sit together?
(A) $2(6!)^2$ (B) $2(5!)^2$
(C) $2(6!)(5!)$ (D) $2(5!)(4!)$
(E) None of these

2. A team of 5 players to be selected from a group of 11 players. How many different selections can be made?
(A) 478   (B) 460
(C) 456   (D) 462
(E) None of these

3. There are 12 students in a class. In how many ways can the first five ranks be allotted to them?
(A) 95,020   (B) 95,040
(C) 95,080   (D) 95,060
(E) None of these

4. The number of arrangements that can be made with the letters of the word 'STYLE' so that letter 'S' will occupy always the first place?
(A) 3!   (B) 5!
(C) 4!   (D) 2!
(E) None of these

5. The number of arrangements of the word 'MOUSER', so that the vowels always occupy even positions, is?
(A) 3P3 × 2!   (B) 3P2 × 2!
(C) 3P3 × 3!   (D) 3P3
(E) None of these

6. What is the number of words formed from the letters of the word 'ROAD' so that the vowels & consonants alternate?
(A) 8   (B) 6
(C) 7   (D) 5
(E) None of these

7. In how many different ways a group of 3 men and 2 women can be formed out of 6 men & 5 women?
(A) 250   (B) 180
(C) 150   (D) 200
(E) None of these

8. How many rectangles can be formed on a chess board?
(A) 1298   (B) 1294
(C) 1296   (D) 1280
(E) None of these

9. In how many ways 5 balls can be put in 3 buckets during a game?
(A) 81   (B) 243
(C) 27   (D) 125
(E) None of these

10. In how many ways can letters of the word 'EQUATION' be arranged so that each word begins with 'A' and ends with 'T'?
(A) 8!   (B) 7!
(C) 5!   (D) 6!
(E) None of these

11. In how many ways can 6 prices be given away to 9 students when each student is eligible for every prize?
(A) 6^8 (B) 9^6
(C) 9^5 (D) 6^9
(E) None of these

12. In how many ways can a team of 4 people be formed from 4 boys & 5 girls such that girls are never less than boys and team has both boys & girls?
(A) 100   (B) 110
(C) 120   (D) 90
(E) None of these

13. How many words can be formed with the letters of the word 'MONSTROUS' such that no two vowels come together?

(A) 37,700   (B) 37,900
(C) 37,800   (D) 37,600
(E) None of these

14. How many different 4 letter words can be formed from 'WORKLIST' using all letters only once?
(A) 1720   (B) 1600
(C) 1640   (D) 1680
(E) None of these

15. In how many ways letters of the word 'LOWKEY' be arranged such that consonants always come together?
(A) $3! \times 4!$ (B) $3! \times 5!$
(C) $4! \times 2!$ (D) $5! \times 4!$
(E) None of these

16. How many 6 letter words can be formed using the word 'FATTER' in which no T's come together?
(A) 240   (B) 200
(C) 280   (D) 220
(E) None of these

17. What are the ways in which a committee of 7 people can be formed from a group of 5 girls and 6 boys such that the committee will always have more number of boys than girls?
(A) 200   (B) 215
(C) 210   (D) 230
(E) None of these

18. In how many different ways can letters of the word 'COMPLAINT' be arranged in such a way that vowels occupy the odd positions?
(A) 43400   (B) 43250
(C) 43200   (D) 43000
(E) None of these

SOLUTION:

1. (A) No. of ways $= 2 \times 6! \times 6!$

$$= 2(6!)^2$$

2. (D) No. of selections $= nCr = 11C5$
$$= \frac{11!}{5!\,6!} = \frac{11 \times 10 \times 9 \times 8 \times 7}{1 \times 2 \times 3 \times 4 \times 5}$$
$$= 462 \text{ ways}$$

3. (B) In case of ranks, the order of persons is also considered
No. of ways $= 12P5 = \dfrac{12!}{(12-5)!} = \dfrac{12!}{7!}$
$$= 12 \times 11 \times 10 \times 9 \times 8$$
$$= 95040 \text{ ways}$$

4. (C) So, remaining four letters can be arranged in 4! ways.

5. (C) 3 vowels to be arranged in 3 even places $= 3P3$
3 consonants to be arranged in 3 places $= 3!$
No. of ways $= 3P3 \times 3!$

6. (A) No. of ways (starting with vowel/consonant)
$$= (2 \times 2!) + (2 \times 2!)$$
$$= 4 + 4 = 8 \text{ ways}$$

7. (D) No. of ways $= 6C3 \times 5C2$
$$= \frac{6 \times 5 \times 4}{1 \times 2 \times 3} \times \frac{5 \times 4}{1 \times 2} = 20 \times 10$$
$$= 200 \text{ ways}$$

8. (C) There are 9 horizontal & 9 vertical lines on a chess board.
No. of rectangles $= 9C2 \times 9C2$
$$= \frac{9 \times 8}{1 \times 2} \times \frac{9 \times 8}{1 \times 2} = 1296$$

9. (B) Since things exceed the places, No. of ways
$$= (\text{Repeating element})^{\text{Non-repeating element}}$$
$$= (3)^5 = 243$$

10. (D) First & last letters are fixed.
No. of ways $= 6!$

11. (B) Each of the 6 prices can be given to any of the 9 students.

No. of ways $= 9 \times 9 \times 9 \times 9 \times 9 \times 9$

$\qquad\qquad = 9^6$ ways

12. (A) Possible cases:

- (1 boy, 3 girls) $= 4C1 \times 5C3 = 40$
- (2 boys, 2 girls) $= 4C2 \times 5C2 = 60$

Total no. of ways $= 40 + 60 = 100$

13. (C) It means vowels come at alternate place

No. of ways $= 7C3 \times \dfrac{3!}{2!} \times \dfrac{6!}{2!} = 37{,}800$

14. (D) No. of ways $= 8C4$

$= 8 \times 7 \times 6 \times 5 = 1680$

15. (A) No. of ways $= 3! \times 4!$

16. (A) No. of ways $= \dfrac{6!}{2!} - 5!$

$= 360 - 120 = 240$

17. (B) No. of ways $= (6C6 \times 5C1) +$
$(6C5 \times 5C2) + (6C4 \times 5C3)$
$= (1 \times 5) + (6 \times 10) + (15 \times 10)$
$= 5 + 60 + 150$
$= 215$ ways

18. (C) No. of ways $= 5P3 \times 6!$
$= 5 \times 4 \times 3 \times 6!$
$= 60 \times 720$
$= 43{,}200$

PROBABILITY

Probability is the measure of the likelihood/chances for the occurrence of some event. It is a quantitative measure of certainty.

Probability of an event always lies between 0 to 1.

Key terms:

- Deterministic experiment:

    An experiment in which outcome is certain.

- Random experiment:

    An experiment in which outcome is not unique and can be one amongst many possible outcomes.

- Sample space:

    It is the set of all possible outcomes of an experiment.

- Event:

    One or more outcomes of an experiment is called an event. It is a subset of the sample space.

- Biased and unbiased experiment:

    If the chance of occurrence of one outcome is more than other outcomes, then their experiment is biased.

Probability, P of an event

$$= \frac{\text{Number of cases favourable to the event}}{\text{Number of possible outcomes}}$$

For an event A, the probability of the happening of a certain event is denoted by p & that of not happening by q. p, q is non-negative & cannot exceed unity

$$0 \leq p \leq 1 \ \& \ 0 \leq q \leq 1$$

EXERCISE:

1. Two dices are thrown simultaneously. Then the probability that the sum of numbers on its top face is 6 is
(A) 5/36   (B) 4/36
(C) 1/6   (D) 1/12
(E) None of these

2. From a pack of 52 cards, two cards are drawn together at random. What is the probability of both the cards being Jacks?
(A) 1/223   (B) 2/221
(C) 1/221   (D) 3/221
(E) None of these

[3-5]

Study the given information carefully and answer the questions that follow.

A bag contains 3 white, 4 black and 5 purple balls.

3. If three balls are picked at random, what is the probability that either all are black or white?
(A) 1/66   (B) 1/44
(C) 1/22   (D) 1/33
(E) None of these

4. If two balls are drawn at random, what is the probability that both are purple?
(A) 5/36   (B) 3/44
(C) 5/22   (D) 5/33
(E) None of these

5. If three balls are picked at random, what is the probability that at least one is black?
(A) 31/54   (B) 41/55
(C) 31/55   (D) 41/54
(E) None of these

6. A bag contains 12 gold coins and 8 silver coins. Two coins are drawn at random, what is the probability that they are of the same colour?
(A) 47/95   (B) 1/2
(C) 47/97   (D) 43/95
(E) None of these

7. A bag contains 4 blue, 5 green and 6 red coloured balls. 2 balls are drawn at random one after another without replacement, then what is the probability that at least one ball is green?
(A) 5/7   (B) 3/7
(C) 1/7   (D) 2/7
(E) None of these

8. P speaks truth in 60% of cases and Q speaks truth in 75% of the cases. In what percentage of cases are they likely to contradict each other, while narrating the same incident happened?
(A) 60%   (B) 55%
(C) 50%   (D) 45%
(E) None of these

9. In a box containing one dozen of apples, one third have become bad. If 3 apples are taken out from the box at random, what is the probability that at least one apple out of the three apples picked up is good?
(A) 54/55   (B) 53/55
(C) 3/11   (D) 1/55
(E) None of these

10. Three-digit numbers are formed from the digits {5,6,7,8,9}. What is the probability that the number formed will be divisible by 2?
(A) 3/5   (B) 4/5
(C) 2/5   (D) 1/5
(E) None of these

11. H hits the target accurately 3 out of five times, whereas K succeeds 2 out of four times. Both tried to hit the target. What is the probability that the target will be hit?
(A) 3/5   (B) 4/5
(C) 2/5   (D) 1/5
(E) None of these

[12-14]

Based on the given data, answer the following questions:

Two coins are tossed simultaneously, what is the probability of getting,

12. At most one tail?
(A) 1/4   (B) 1/2
(C) 1   (D) 3/4
(E) None of these

13. Exactly two heads?
(A) 1   (B) 1/2
(C) 1/4   (D) 3/4
(E) None of these

14. At least one head?
(A) 3/4   (B) 1/4
(C) 1   (D) 1/2
(E) None of these

[15-18]

Based on the given data, answer the following questions:

A card is drawn from a well shuffled pack of 52 cards. What is the probability of getting

15. A red card?
    (A) 2/13   (B) 1/4
    (C) 1/2   (D) 1/13
    (E) None of these

16. Not a diamond card?
    (A) 3/4   (B) 1/4
    (C) 1/13   (D) 1/2
    (E) None of these

17. A queen or jack card?
    (A) 1/13   (B) 3/13
    (C) 1/4   (D) 2/13
    (E) None of these

18. A king?
    (A) 2/13   (B) 1/13
    (C) 3/13   (D) 4/13
    (E) None of these

19. A storekeeper has 2 types of cards ie., 10 blue cards and 15 green cards. If he sold 3 cards, what is the probability that these are either all blue or all green?
    (A) 3/10   (B) 1/4
    (C) 3/25   (D) 1/2
    (E) None of these

20. There are 5 pens in a bag which are green and red in colour. A pen is drawn at random. The probability of getting a red pen is 0.6. Find no. of green pens in the bag.
    (A) 2   (B) 4
    (C) 3   (D) 1
    (E) None of these

21. 3 coins are tossed up simultaneously. Find the probability of getting at least 2 tails.
    (A) 1/4   (B) 2/3
    (C) 1/3   (D) 1/2
    (E) None of these

22. There are 4 red coins and 6 blue coins in a bag. If three coins are drawn from the bag, then find the probability of getting at least 1 red coin.
    (A) 1/6   (B) 5/6
    (C) 2/3   (D) 1/2
    (E) None of these

23. A bag contains 5 gold balls, 6 silver balls and 8 copper balls. If 2 balls are taken out from the bag randomly, then find the probability of both balls being silver or copper balls.
    (A) 43/171   (B) 41/171
    (C) 43/169   (D) 47/163
    (E) None of these

24. A committee of 3 members is to be selected out of 3 women and 2 men. What is the probability that the committee has at least one man?
    (A) 9/20   (B) 1/10
    (C) 9/10   (D) 9/16
    (E) None of these

25. Find the probability of selecting two face cards or two number cards from a pack of 52 cards?
    (A) 60:221   (B) 116:221
    (C) 125:221   (D) 72:121
    (E) None of these

26. What is the probability of getting 2 tails and 6 when two coins and a dice are tossed simultaneously?
    (A) 2/25   (B) 1/24
    (C) 1/36   (D) 1/12
    (E) None of these

SOLUTION:

1. (A) Total no. of outcomes = 36
No. of favourable outcome
$= \{(1,5), (2,4), (3,3), (4,2), (5,1)\} = 5$
Probability $= \dfrac{5}{36}$

2. (C) No. of Jack cards $= 4$

$$\text{Probability} = \frac{4C2}{52C2} = \frac{\frac{4\times3}{1\times2}}{\frac{52\times51}{1\times2}}$$

$$= \frac{1}{13\times17} = \frac{1}{221}$$

3. (B) Probability that all are either black or white $= \dfrac{3C3+4C3}{12C3} = \dfrac{\frac{3\times2\times1}{1\times2\times3}+\frac{4\times3\times2}{1\times2\times3}}{\frac{12\times11\times10}{1\times2\times3}}$

$$= \frac{6+24}{1320} = \frac{30}{1320} = \frac{1}{44}$$

4. (D) Probability $= \dfrac{5C2}{12C2} = \dfrac{5}{33}$

5. (B) No. of events which do not contain black ball $= 3$ balls out of $8 = 8C3 = 56$

$$P(E) = 1 - \frac{56}{12C3} = 1 - \frac{56}{220} = \frac{164}{220} = \frac{41}{55}$$

6. (A) Probability $= \dfrac{12C2+8C2}{20C2} = \dfrac{\frac{12\times11}{1\times2}+\frac{8\times7}{1\times2}}{\frac{20\times19}{1\times2}}$

$$= \frac{132+56}{380} = \frac{188}{380} = \frac{47}{95}$$

7. (C) Probability that no ball is green
$$= \frac{10C1\times9C1}{15C2} = \frac{10\times9}{\frac{15\times14}{2}} = \frac{90}{105} = \frac{6}{7}$$

Required probability $= 1 - \dfrac{6}{7} = \dfrac{1}{7}$

8. (D) Probability of
- P speaks truth $= \dfrac{60}{100} = \dfrac{3}{5}$
- Q speaks truth $= \dfrac{3}{4}$
- P lies $= \dfrac{2}{5}$
- Q lies $= \dfrac{1}{4}$

P (P & Q contradict) = [P lies & Q true]
or [P true & Q lies] $= \left(\dfrac{2}{5}\times\dfrac{3}{4}\right) + \left(\dfrac{3}{5}\times\dfrac{1}{4}\right)$

$$= \frac{6+3}{20} = \frac{9}{20}$$

Required percentage $= \dfrac{9}{20}\times100 = 45\%$

9. (A) Probability that all 3 apples are bad
$$= \frac{4C3}{12C3}$$

Probability that at least one apple is good
$$= 1 - \frac{4C3}{12C3} = 1 - \frac{1}{55} = \frac{54}{55}$$

10. (C) For the number to be divisible, the last digit must be even ie.,$\{6,8\}$
$$P(E) = \frac{2}{5}$$

11. (B) Probability of not hitting the target
$$= \frac{2}{5}\times\frac{2}{4} = \frac{1}{5}$$
Probability of hitting the target
$$= 1 - \frac{1}{5} = \frac{4}{5}$$

12. (D) $P(E) = \dfrac{3}{4}$

13. (C) $P(E) = \dfrac{1}{4}$

14. (A) $P(E) = \dfrac{3}{4}$

15. (C) No. of red cards $= 26$
$$P(E) = \frac{26}{52} = \frac{1}{2}$$

16. (A) No. of diamond cards $= 13$
No. of non-diamond cards $= 52 - 13$
$$= 39$$
$$P(E) = \frac{39}{52} = \frac{3}{4}$$

17. (D) No. of queen and jack cards
$$= 4 + 4 = 8$$
$$P(E) = \frac{8}{52} = \frac{2}{13}$$

18. (B) No. of king cards $= 4$
$$P(E) = \frac{4}{52} = \frac{1}{13}$$

19. (B) Required probability $= \dfrac{10C3+15C3}{25C3}$
$$= \frac{\frac{10\times9\times8}{1\times2\times3}+\frac{15\times14\times13}{1\times2\times3}}{\frac{25\times24\times23}{1\times2\times3}} = \frac{120+455}{2300} = \frac{1}{4}$$

20. (A) Let no. of red pens $= x$
$$\frac{x}{5} = 0.6; \quad x = 3$$

No. of green pens $= 5 - 3 = 2$

21. (D) Total no. of outcomes $= 8$
No. of favourable outcomes
$= \{TTT, TTH, THT, HTT\}$
Required probability $= \dfrac{4}{8} = \dfrac{1}{2}$

22. (C) Probability of getting no red coin
$= \dfrac{6C2}{10C2}$
$= \dfrac{30}{90} = \dfrac{1}{3}$
Probability of getting at least 1 red coin
$= 1 - \dfrac{1}{3} = \dfrac{2}{3}$

23. (A) Required probability $= \dfrac{6C2 + 8C2}{19C2}$
$= \dfrac{\frac{6 \times 5}{1 \times 2} + \frac{8 \times 7}{1 \times 2}}{\frac{19 \times 18}{1 \times 2}} = \dfrac{43}{171}$

24. (C) Required probability
$= \dfrac{2C1 \times 3C2 + 2C2 \times 3C1}{5C3}$
$= \dfrac{2 \times 3 + 1 \times 3}{10} = \dfrac{9}{10}$

25. (B) No. of face cards $= 4 \times 3 = 12$
No. of number cards $= 9 \times 4 = 36$
Required probability $= \dfrac{12C2 + 36C2}{52C2} = \dfrac{116}{221}$

26. (B) Total no. of possible outcomes
$= 6 \times 4 = 24$
Required no. of outcome (TT6) $= 1$
Required probability $= \dfrac{1}{24}$

PRACTICE:

[1-2]

Based on the given data, answer the following questions:
Three coins are tossed, what is the probability of getting

1. At least one head?
(A) 3/8   (B) 1/8
(C) 5/8   (D) 7/8
(E) None of these

2. At most one tail?
(A) 1/2   (B) 1/4
(C) 3/8   (D) 1/8
(E) None of these

[3-5]

Based on the given data, answer the following questions:

When 2 dice are thrown, what is the probability of getting,

3. A sum of 8?
(A) 1/12   (B) 1/9
(C) 5/36   (D) 5/18
(E) None of these

4. A product of 24?
(A) 1/12   (B) 1/18
(C) 1/9   (D) 1/36
(E) None of these

5. Both outputs are odd number?
(A) 1/4   (B) 1/9
(C) 1/36   (D) 1/12
(E) None of these

[6-7]

Based on the given data, answer the following questions:

Two cards are drawn from a well- shuffled pack of 52 cards. What is the probability that

6. Both are diamond cards?
(A) 1/51   (B) 1/17
(C) 3/17   (D) 1/13
(E) None of these

7. One is spade card and the other is diamond card?
(A) 169/204   (B) 7/51
(C) 13/102   (D) 13/51
(E) None of these

[8-12]

Based on the given data, answer the following questions: A and B appear for an interview in an office. The probability of A's selection is 1/4 and that of B's selection is 1/3.

8. What is the probability that exactly one of them gets selected?
   (A) 7/12　　　　(B) 3/7
   (C) 1/3　　　　(D) 5/12
   (E) None of these

9. What is the probability that none of them gets selected?
   (A) 1/2　　　　(B) 1/3
   (C) 3/8　　　　(D) 1/12
   (E) None of these

10. What is the probability that at least one of them gets selected?
    (A) 1/4　　　　(B) 1/12
    (C) 1/2　　　　(D) 1/3
    (E) None of these

11. What is the probability that at most one of them gets selected?
    (A) 3/8　　　　(B) 11/12
    (C) 3/4　　　　(D) 1/12
    (E) None of these

12. What is the probability that both of them get selected?
    (A) 1/12　　　　(B) 1/6
    (C) 1/4　　　　(D) 1/3
    (E) None of these

[13-15]

Study the given information and answer the given questions:
A bag contains 2 red, 3 green, 4 yellow and 5 green balls.

13. If two balls are picked randomly, what is the probability of both of them to be green?
    (A) 20/91　　　　(B) 5/91
    (C) 10/13　　　　(D) 10/91
    (E) None of these

14. Three balls are picked randomly. What is the probability that one is blue and two are yellow?
    (A) 9/91　　　　(B) 6/182
    (C) 9/182　　　　(D) 3/182
    (E) None of these

15. Four balls are picked randomly, what is the probability that at least one ball is yellow?
    (A) 113/143　　　　(B) 30/143
    (C) 103/143　　　　(D) 11/13
    (E) None of these

16. Find the probability of selecting two face cards or two number cards from a pack of 52 cards.
    (A) 121/221　　　　(B) 116/221
    (C) 125/221　　　　(D) 61/221
    (E) None of these

17. What is the probability of getting 2 tails and 3 when two coins and a dice are tossed simultaneously?
    (A) 1/24　　　　(B) 1/12
    (C) 1/16　　　　(D) 1/6
    (E) None of these

18. If two dices are rolled simultaneously, then find the probability of getting a sum of 8?
    (A) 1/12　　　　(B) 1/6
    (C) 5/36　　　　(D) 7/36
    (E) None of these

19. There are 6 men and 8 women in a group. From this group, 3 persons are selected

randomly, then what is the probability that 2 men and 1 woman are selected?

(A) 55/91   (B) 29/91
(C) 15/91   (D) 30/91
(E) None of these

20. A bag contains 30 balls numbered 1 to 30. Two balls are selected randomly without replacement. Find the probability that both balls are even numbered balls.

(A) 6/29   (B) 7/29
(C) 5/29   (D) 8/29
(E) None of these

SOLUTION:

1. (D) Total no. of outcomes $= 2^3 = 8$
At least 1 head = {TTH, THT, HTT, HHT, HTH, THH, HHH}
$P(E) = \dfrac{7}{8}$

2. (A) At most 1 tail
= {HHH, HHT, HTH, THH}
$P(E) = \dfrac{4}{8} = \dfrac{1}{2}$

3. (C) No. of outcomes = 36
A sum of 8
= {(2,6), (6,2), (3,5), (5,3), (4,4)}
$P(E) = \dfrac{5}{36}$

4. (B) A product of 24 = {(4,6), (6,4)}
$P(E) = \dfrac{2}{36} = \dfrac{1}{18}$

5. (A) Both outputs are odd no.
= {(1,1),(1,3),(1,5),
(3,1),(3,3),(3,5),
(5,1),(5,3),(5,5)}
$P(E) = \dfrac{9}{36} = \dfrac{1}{4}$

6. (B) $P(E) = \dfrac{13C2}{52C2} = \dfrac{\frac{13\times12}{1\times2}}{\frac{52\times51}{1\times2}} = \dfrac{1}{17}$

7. (C) $P(E) = \dfrac{13C1\times13C1}{52C2} = \dfrac{13\times13}{\frac{52\times51}{1\times2}} = \dfrac{13}{102}$

[8-12]
Probability of
- A being selected $= \dfrac{1}{4}$
  A not selected $= \dfrac{3}{4}$
- B being selected $= \dfrac{1}{3}$
  B not selected $= \dfrac{2}{3}$

8. (D) $P(E) = \left[\left(\dfrac{1}{4}\times\dfrac{2}{3}\right) + \left(\dfrac{3}{4}\times\dfrac{1}{3}\right)\right]$
$= \dfrac{2}{12} + \dfrac{3}{12} = \dfrac{5}{12}$

9. (A) $P(E) = \dfrac{3}{4}\times\dfrac{2}{3} = \dfrac{6}{12} = \dfrac{1}{2}$

10. (C) $P(E) = 1 - [P(\text{None of them gets selected})]$
$= 1 - \dfrac{1}{2} = \dfrac{1}{2}$

11. (B) $P(E) = 1 - [P(\text{Both of them gets selected})] = 1 - \left(\dfrac{1}{4}\times\dfrac{1}{3}\right) = 1 - \dfrac{1}{12} = \dfrac{11}{12}$

12. (A) $P(E) = \dfrac{1}{4}\times\dfrac{1}{3} = \dfrac{1}{12}$

[13-15]
Total no. of balls $= 2 + 3 + 4 + 5 = 14$

13. (D) $P(E) = \dfrac{5C2}{14C2} = \dfrac{\frac{5\times4}{1\times2}}{\frac{14\times13}{1\times2}} = \dfrac{10}{91}$

14. (C) $P(E) = \dfrac{3C1\times4C2}{14C3} = \dfrac{3\times6}{\frac{14\times13\times12}{1\times2\times3}} = \dfrac{9}{182}$

15. (A) $P(E)$
$= 1 - [P(\text{None of the balls is yellow})]$
$= 1 - \left(\dfrac{10C4}{14C4}\right) = 1 - \left(\dfrac{30}{143}\right) = \dfrac{113}{143}$

16. (B) $P(E) = \dfrac{12C2 + 36C2}{52C2} = \dfrac{\frac{12\times11}{1\times2} + \frac{36\times35}{1\times2}}{\frac{52\times51}{1\times2}}$
$= \dfrac{1392}{2652} = \dfrac{116}{221}$

17. (A) Total outcomes $= 6 \times 4 = 24$
Required outcome {TT3} = 1
$P(E) = \dfrac{1}{24}$

18. (C) No. of favourable outcomes
= {(2,6), (6,2), (3,5), (5,3), (4,4)} = 5

$$P(E) = \frac{5}{36}$$

19. (D) $P(E) = \dfrac{6C2 \times 8C1}{14C3} = \dfrac{15 \times 8}{\frac{14 \times 13 \times 12}{1 \times 2 \times 3}} = \dfrac{30}{91}$

20. (B) Total no. of even nos. = 15

$$P(E) = \frac{15C2}{30C2} = \frac{15 \times 14}{30 \times 29} = \frac{7}{29}$$

MENSURATION

Mensuration is the study of measurement of geometric figures & their parameters like length, volume, shape, surface area, lateral surface area, etc.

It deals with the study of different geometrical shapes, their areas & volume. It is all about the process of measurement.

Formulas:

2 DIMENSIONAL FIGURES:

1. **Square:**
   a-length of each side
   d-diagonal

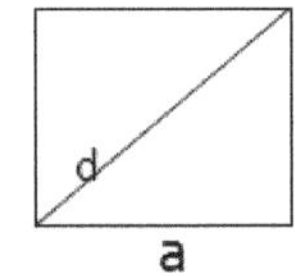

- Area (A) $= a^2 = \frac{1}{2}d^2$
- Diagonal (d) $= \sqrt{2}a$
- Perimeter $= 4a$

2. **Rectangle:**
   l-length
   b-breadth
   d-diagonal

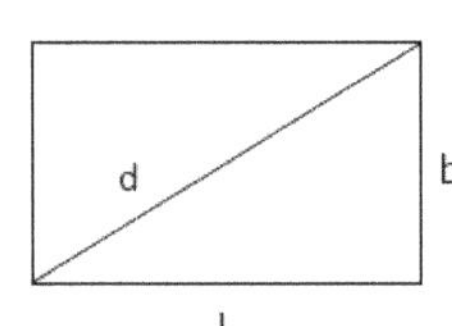

- Area = Base × Height
- Diagonal (d) $= \sqrt{l^2 + b^2}$

- Perimeter $= 2(l + b)$

3. **Rhombus:**
   d1, d2 - length of the diagonals

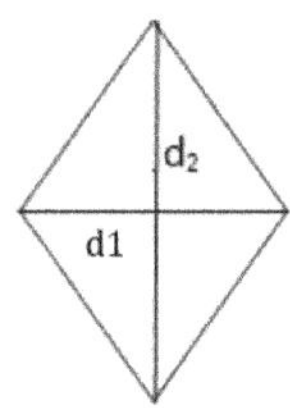

- Area $= \frac{1}{2} \times d1 \times d2$
- Diagonal $= \frac{2 \times Area}{Other\ diagonal}$
- Perimeter $= 4(Side)$

4. **Parallelogram:**
   h-height
   l-length
   b-breadth
   (d1 ≠ d2)

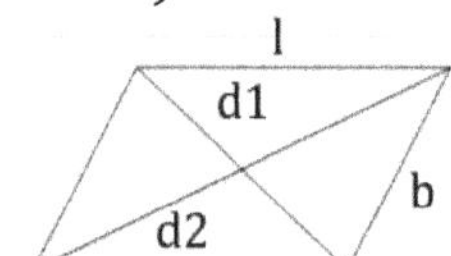

- Area = Length × Height
- Perimeter $= 2(l + b)$

5. **Triangle:**
   a, b, c - length of sides
   h-height

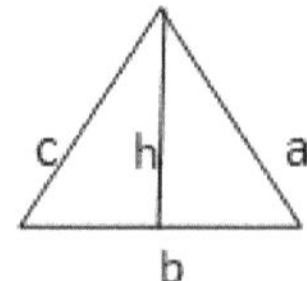

- Area $= \frac{1}{2} \times b \times h$

$$= \sqrt{s(s-a)(s-b)(s-c)}$$

where $s = \frac{a+b+c}{2}$

- Perimeter $= a + b + c$

6. Equilateral triangle:
a - length of each side
h – height

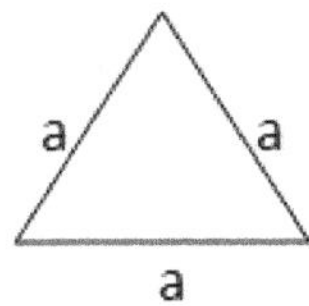

- Area $= \frac{\sqrt{3}}{4}a^2 = \frac{h^2}{\sqrt{3}}$

where $h = \frac{\sqrt{3}}{2}a$

- Perimeter $= 3a$

7. Trapezium:
a, b-length of parallel sides
h-height

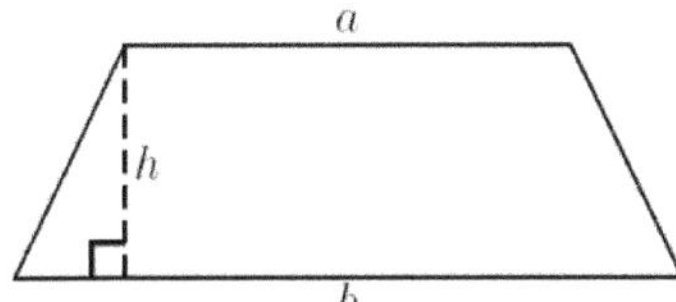

- Area $= \frac{1}{2}h(a+b)$
- Perimeter = Sum of four sides

8. Circle:
r – radius
- Diameter $= 2r$

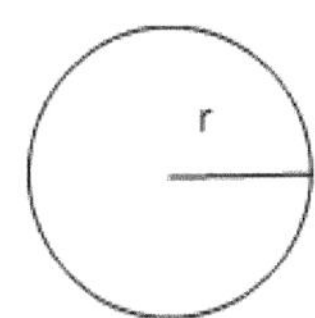

- Circumference $= 2\pi r$
- Area $= \pi r^2$

9. Semicircle:
r-radius

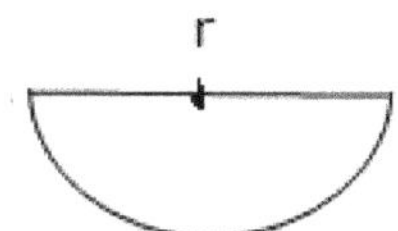

- Area $= \frac{1}{2}\pi r^2$
- Circumference $= \pi r + 2r$

10. Sector:

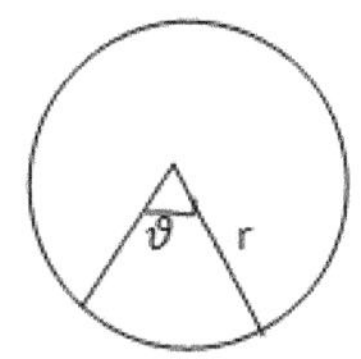

- Area $= \frac{\theta}{360°} \times \pi r^2$
- Circumference

$$= \left(\frac{\theta}{360°} \times 2\pi r\right) + 2r$$

3 DIMENSIONAL FIGURES:

11. Cube:
a-length of each cube

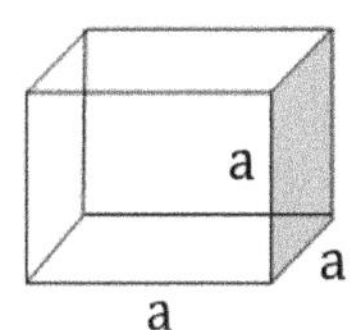

- Volume $= a^3$ cubic units
- Lateral surface area $= 4a^2$ sq. units
- Total surface area $= 6a^2$ sq. units
- Diagonal $= \sqrt{3}a$

12. Cuboid:
l-length
b-breadth
h-height

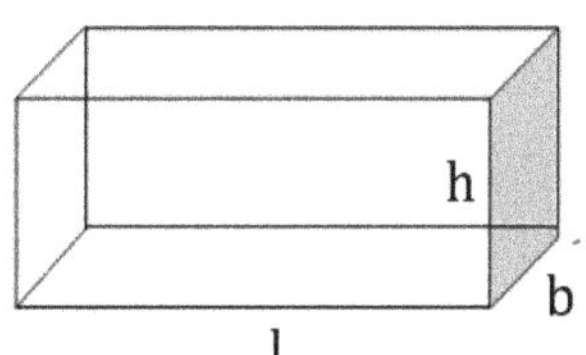

- Volume = l × b × h cubic units
- Lateral surface area
  = 2h(l + b) sq. units
- Total surface area
  = 2(lb + bh + lh) sq. units
- Diagonal = $\sqrt{l^2 + b^2 + h^2}$

13. Cylinder:
r-radius of base
h-height

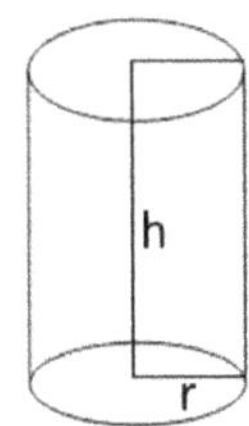

- Volume = $\pi r^2 h$ cubic units
- Lateral surface area = $2\pi rh$ sq. units
- Total surface area
  = $2\pi(r + h)$ sq. units

14. Cone:
r - radius of base
h - height
l - slant height of cone

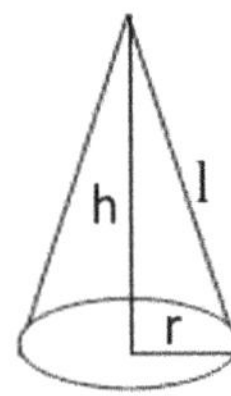

- Slant height (l) = $\sqrt{h^2 + r^2}$ units
- Volume (V) = $\frac{1}{3}\pi r^2 h$ cubic units
- Curved surface area = πrl sq. units
- Total surface area = $\pi r(r + l)$ sq. units

15. Sphere:
r-radius

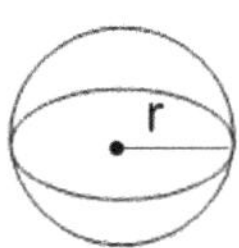

- Volume (V) = $\frac{4}{3}\pi r^3$ cubic units
- Total surface area = $4\pi r^2$ sq. units

16. Hemisphere:
r-radius

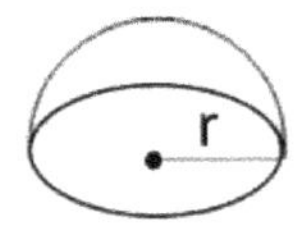

- Volume (V) = $\frac{2}{3}\pi r^3$ cubic units
- Curved surface area = $2\pi r^2$ sq. units
- Total surface area = $3\pi r^2$ sq. units

EXERCISE:

SQUARE

1. The perimeter & area of a square are equal, side of the square (in cm) is
   (A) 5 cm　　　　　(B) 4 cm
   (C) 2 cm　　　　　(D) 6 cm
   (E) None of these

2. If all the sides of a square are decreased by 20%, its area will be decreased by
   (A) -38%　　　　　(B) -40%
   (C) -44%　　　　　(D) -36%
   (E) None of these

3. A path of uniform width runs outside a square field. If the width of the path is 1.5m and the area of the path is 39 m², find the area of the field.
   (A) 49 m²　　　　　(B) 25 m²
   (C) 16 m²　　　　　(D) 36 m²
   (E) None of these

RECTANGLE

4. The length and breadth of a rectangle are in the ratio 4:3. The perimeter and the area of the rectangle are in the ratio 7:6. What is the length of the rectangle?
(A) 4 units   (B) 8 units
(C) 2 units   (D) 12 units
(E) None of these

5. A cow is tied on the corner of a rectangular field of length 50 and breadth 40 m by a 21 m long rope. The area of the region, that the cow cannot graze is (use $\pi = 22/7$)
(A) 1294 m²   (B) 1653.5 m²
(C) 1382 m²   (D) 1504 m²
(E) None of these

6. What will be the cost of gardening 2m broad boundary around a rectangular plot having perimeter of 1020 m at the rate of Rs 10 per square meter?
(A) Rs 36,750   (B) Rs 28,200
(C) Rs 42,500   (D) Rs 20,560
(E) None of these

TRIANGLE

7. Initially, three sides of a triangle are 2 cm, 3 cm & 5 cm (using 2 cm as base & 3 cm as its height). Then, the altitude of the triangle, using the largest side as base will be
(A) 1.6 cm   (B) 2 cm
(C) 1.2 cm   (D) 1.4 cm
(E) None of these

8. The altitude drawn to the base of an isosceles triangle is 6 cm & the perimeter is 36 cm. The area of the triangle is
(A) 72 cm²   (B) 48 cm²
(C) 24 cm²   (D) 36 cm²
(E) None of these

CIRCLE

9. A sector of 270° cut out from a circle, has an area of 462 sq.cm, the radius of the circle is (Use pi = 22/7)
(A) 14 cm   (B) 10 cm
(C) 7 cm   (D) 21 cm
(E) None of these

10. If a wheel covers a distance of 600 m in 25 rotations, then the radius of the wheel is (Use $\pi = 22/7$)
(A) 2 4/7 cm   (B) 3 9/11 cm
(C) 3 1/3 cm   (D) 4 cm
(E) None of these

QUADRILATERALS

11. If the area of trapezium, whose parallel sides are 5 cm & 7 cm is 48 sq.cm, then the distance between the parallel sides is
(A) 7 cm   (B) 8 cm
(C) 6 cm   (D) 9 cm
(E) None of these

12. A parallelogram has sides 14 cm & 30 cm long. The length of one of the diagonals is 40 cm. The area of the parallelogram is
(A) 320 cm²   (B) 336 cm²
(C) 332 cm²   (D) 342 cm²
(E) None of these

RHOMBUS

13. The diagonals of a rhombus are 24 cm & 18 cm respectively. The perimeter of the rhombus is:
(A) 75 cm   (B) 60 cm
(C) 50 cm   (D) 80 cm
(E) None of these

14. The perimeter of a rhombus is 60 cm & its height is 10 cm. Its area is
(A) 150 m²   (B) 180 m²
(C) 120 m²   (D) 140 m²
(E) None of these

COMBINED 2D FIGURES

15. The perimeter of rectangular field is 140 m & the difference between its two adjacent sides is 14 m. The side of a square field, having the same area as that of the rectangle is: (approx.)
(A) 42 cm   (B) 39 cm
(C) 27 cm   (D) 34 cm
(E) None of these

16. Four equally sized circular shapes of maximum size are cut off from a square sheet of paper of area 3136 cm². The circumference of each circular shape is (Use $\pi = 22/7$)
(A) 84 cm   (B) 88 cm
(C) 76 cm   (D) 77 cm
(E) None of these

17. The area of the greatest circle inscribed inside a square of side 28 cm is (use $\pi = 22/7$)
(A) 624 cm²   (B) 616 cm²
(C) 586 cm²   (D) 592 cm²
(E) None of these

18. A copper wire is bent in the form of an equilateral triangle & has area of $484\sqrt{3}$ cm². If the same wire is bent into the form of a circle, the area enclosed by the wire is (Use $\pi = 22/7$)
(A) 1398 cm²   (B) 1328 cm²
(C) 1456 cm²   (D) 1386 cm²
(E) None of these

CUBE

19. The length of a diagonal of a cube with volume 512 cm³ is:
(A) $7\sqrt{3}$ cm   (B) $6\sqrt{3}$ cm
(C) $8\sqrt{3}$ cm   (D) $9\sqrt{3}$ cm
(E) None of these

20. If each edge of a cube is increased by 30%. The percentage increase in surface area is:
(A) 72%   (B) 69%
(C) 63%   (D) 57%
(E) None of these

21. A cube of edge 9 cm is cut into cubes each of edge 3 cm. The ratio of the total surface area of large cube to that of one of the small cubes is equal to:
(A) 9:1   (B) 7:1
(C) 8:3   (D) 8:1
(E) None of these

CUBOID

22. The edges of the cuboid are in the ratio 2:3:4 and its surface area is 208 cm². The volume of the cuboid is:
(A) 190 cm³   (B) 192 cm³
(C) 196 cm³   (D) 186 cm³
(E) None of these

CYLINDER:

23. A circular pit is dug to a depth of 7 m with a diameter of 4 m. What is the volume of the mud dug out? (Use $\pi = 22/7$)
(A) 66 m³   (B) 77 m²
(C) 88 m³   (D) 80 m³
(E) None of these

24. The base radii of two cylinders are in the ratio 3:2 and their heights are in the ratio 2:5. The ratio of their volumes is:
(A) 9:10   (B) 10:9
(C) 4:5   (D) 5:4
(E) None of these

CONE

25. The height and diameter of a cone are 12 cm & 32 cm respectively. Find the curved surface area of the cone (approx.)
(A) 1006 cm²   (B) 982 cm²
(C) 1250 cm²   (D) 1128 cm²
(E) None of these

26. The ratio of the volumes of two cones is 1:3 and the ratio of radii of their bases is 1:2. The ratio of their heights is:
(A) 3:4   (B) 4:3
(C) 1:2   (D) 2:3
(E) None of these

27. The circumference of the base of a right circular cone is 88 cm & its height is 15 cm. The volume of the cone is:
(A) 3548 cm³   (B) 2646 cm³
(C) 3080 cm³   (D) 4628 cm³
(E) None of these

SPHERE

28. A solid hemisphere is of radius 21 cm. The curved surface area in sq.cm is
(A) 2627 cm²   (B) 2772 cm²
(C) 2736 cm²   (D) 2668 cm²
(E) None of these

29. The volume of a solid hemisphere is numerically equal to its total surface area. It radius is
(A) 3 units   (B) 4.5 units
(C) 6.5 units   (D) 5 units
(E) None of these

30. Three solid metallic spheres of diameter 8 cm, 12 cm & 16 cm are melted & recast into a new solid sphere. The diameter of the new sphere is (approx.)
(A) 21 cm   (B) 17 cm
(C) 18.5 cm   (D) 19.25 cm
(E) None of these

COMBINED 3D FIGURES

31. The radii of the base of a cylinder and a cone are in the ratio of 3:4 & their heights are in the ratio 2:3. Their volumes are in the ratio of
(A) 9:8   (B) 8:9
(C) 7:8   (D) 9:7
(E) None of these

32. A cone of height 40 cm & base diameter 40 cm is carved out of a wooden sphere of radius 20 cm. The percentage of left out wooden part is
(A) 80%   (B) 50%
(C) 25%   (D) 75%
(E) None of these

33. The volume of a cuboid is twice the volume of a cube. If the dimensions of the cuboid are 7 cm, 14 cm & 7 cm respectively. The total surface area of the cube is
(A) 294 cm²   (B) 216 cm²
(C) 324 cm²   (D) 286 cm²
(E) None of these

SOLUTION:

1. (B) Acc. To the qn.,
$(\text{Side})^2 = 4 \times \text{Side}$
$\text{Side} = 4 \text{ cm}$

2. (D) Change in area $= (a + b + \frac{ab}{100})\%$
(20 percent out of hundred percent)
$= 2 \times (-20) + \frac{(-20)^2}{100}$
$= -40 + \frac{400}{100} = -40 + 4 = -36\%$

3. (B) Let the side of the square field be 'x' m.
$(x + 3)^2 - x^2 = 39$
$x^2 + 6x + 9 - x^2 = 39$
$6x + 9 = 39$
$6x = 30$
$x = 5 \text{ m}$
Area of the field $= 5^2 = 25 \text{ m}^2$

4. (A) Let length & breadth of rectangle be 4x & 3x respectively.
Perimeter $= 2(4x + 3x) = 14x$
Area $= 4x \times 3x = 12x^2$
$\frac{14x}{12x^2} = \frac{7}{6}$
$\frac{7}{6x} = \frac{7}{6}$

x = 1

Length of rectangle = 4(1) = 4 units

5. (B) Area of field that can be grazed by

$$\text{cow} = \frac{1}{4}(\pi r^2) = \frac{1}{4}\left(\frac{22}{7} \times 21 \times 21\right)$$
$$= 346.5 \text{ m}^2$$

Area of field that cannot be grazed by

$$\text{cow} = (50 \times 40) - 346.5$$
$$= 2000 - 346.5$$
$$= 1653.5 \text{ m}^2$$

6. (D) Perimeter = 2(l + b) = 1020

Area of boundary

$$= [(l + 4) \times (b + 4)] - lb$$
$$= lb + 4l + 4b + 16 - lb$$
$$= 4(l + b) + 16$$
$$= 2(1020) + 16$$
$$= 2056 \text{ m}^2$$

Cost of gardening = 2056 × 10
$$= \text{Rs } 20{,}560$$

7. (C)

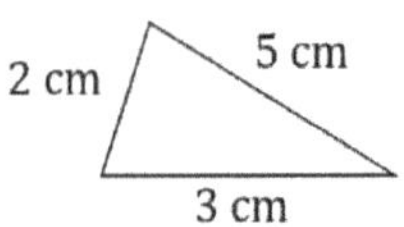

$$\text{Area} = \frac{1}{2} \times 2 \times 3 = 3 \text{ cm}^2$$

Acc. To the qn.,

$$\frac{1}{2} \times 5 \times x = 3$$
$$x = \frac{6}{5} = 1.2 \text{ cm}$$

8. (B)

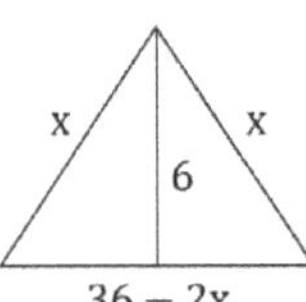

By Pythagoras theorem,

$$x^2 + 6^2 + \left(\frac{36-2x}{2}\right)^2$$
$$x^2 = 36 + 324 + x^2 - 36x$$
$$36x = 360$$
$$x = 10$$
$$\text{Area} = \frac{1}{2} \times bh = \frac{1}{2} \times 6 \times 16 = 48 \text{ cm}^2$$

9. (A) Acc. To the qn.,

$$\frac{270°}{360°}(\text{Total area}) = 462 \text{ cm}^2$$
$$\frac{3}{4}\left(\frac{22}{7} \times r^2\right) = 462$$
$$r^2 = \frac{462 \times 7 \times 4}{3 \times 22} = 196$$
$$r = 14 \text{ cm}$$

10. (B) Distance covered
= No. of rotations ×
Circumference of the wheel

$$\text{Circumference} = \frac{600}{25} = 24$$
$$2\pi r = 24$$
$$r = \frac{24 \times 7}{2 \times 22} = \frac{42}{11} = 3\frac{9}{11}$$

11. (C) Area of the trapezium

$$= \frac{1}{2}(a + b)h = 48$$
$$a = 5, b = 7$$
$$(5 + 7)h = 96$$
$$h = \frac{96}{12} = 8 \text{ cm}$$

12. (B) Area of parallelogram
= 2 × Area of its half − triangles

$$= 2 \times \sqrt{s(s - a)(s - b)(s - c)}$$
$$= 2 \times \sqrt{42(42 - 14)(42 - 30)(42 - 40)}$$
$$= 2 \times \sqrt{42 \times 28 \times 12 \times 2}$$
$$= 2 \times 168$$
$$= 336 \text{ cm}^2$$

13. (B)

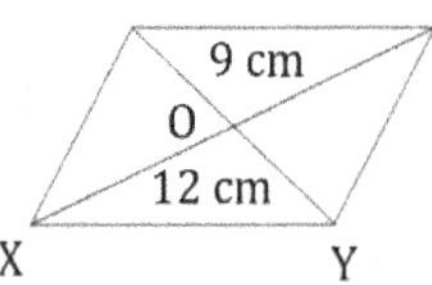

To find the side length of rhombus:

$$OX^2 + OY^2 = XY^2$$
$$12^2 + 9^2 = 225 = 15^2$$
$$XY = 15 \text{ cm}$$

Perimeter = 15 × 4 = 60 cm

14. (A) Perimeter = 4a = 60

$$\text{Side, } a = \frac{60}{4} = 15 \text{ cm}$$

Area = base × height = 15 × 10
$$= 150 \text{ cm}^2$$

15. (D) Perimeter = $2(l + b) = 140$
$l + b = 70$ cm
$l - b = 14$ cm (given)
$l = \frac{70+14}{2} = 42$ cm
$b = \frac{70-14}{2} = 28$ cm
Area of square = 42×28 cm^2
Side = $\sqrt{42 \times 28} = 34$ cm

16. (B)

Side of the square = $\sqrt{3136} = 56$ cm
Radius of each plate = $\frac{56}{4} = 14$ cm
Circumference of each circle
$= 2 \times \frac{22}{7} \times 14$
$= 88$ cm

17. (B)

Diameter of circle = Side of square
Radius of circle = $\frac{28}{2} = 14$ cm
Area of circle = $\pi r^2 = \frac{22}{7} \times 14 \times 14$
$$= 616 \text{ cm}^2$$

18. (D) Area of equilateral triangle
$$= \frac{\sqrt{3}}{4} \times \text{side}^2$$
$484\sqrt{3} = \frac{\sqrt{3}}{4} \times \text{side}^2$
$\text{side}^2 = 484 \times 4$
$\text{side} = \sqrt{484 \times 4} = 44$ cm
Total length of wire = $3 \times 44 = 132$ cm
Perimeter of circle = 132 cm
$2 \times \frac{22}{7} \times r = 132$
$r = \frac{132 \times 7}{2 \times 22} = 21$ cm

Area enclosed by it = $\pi r^2 = \frac{22}{7} \times 21^2$
$$= 1386 \text{ cm}^2$$

19. (C) Side of cube = $\sqrt[3]{512} = 8$ cm
Diagonal = $a\sqrt{3} = 8\sqrt{3}$ cm

20. (B) Percentage increase = $x + y + \frac{xy}{100}$
$= 30 + 30 + \frac{(30 \times 30)}{100} = 69\%$

21. (A) TSA of large cube = $6a^2 = 6(9^2)$
$$= 486 \text{ cm}^2$$
TSA of smaller cube = $6(3^2) = 54$
Required ratio = $\frac{486}{54} = 9:1$

22. (B) Let the sides be 2x, 3x & 4x respectively.
Surface area = $2(lb + bh + lh)$
$= 2(6x^2 + 12x^2 + 8x^2)$
$= 2(26x^2) = 52x^2$
$52x^2 = 208$
$x^2 = 4$
$x = 2$ cm
Sides are 4 cm, 6 cm & 8 cm
Volume of cuboid = $4 \times 6 \times 8$
$$= 192 \text{ cm}^3$$

23. (C) Volume of pit = $\pi r^2 h$
$= \frac{22}{7} \times 2^2 \times 7 = 88$ m^2

24. (A) Required ratio = $\frac{\pi (3^2)2}{\pi (2^2)5} = \frac{9}{10} = 9:10$

25. (A) Radius = $\frac{1}{2}(32) = 16$ cm
Slant height, $l = \sqrt{h^2 + r^2}$
$$= \sqrt{12^2 + 16^2} = 20$$
CSA = $\pi r l = \frac{22}{7} \times 16 \times 20$
$\cong 1006$ cm^2(approx.)

26. (B) Volume of cone = $\frac{1}{3}\pi r^2 h$
Acc. To the qn.,

$$\frac{1}{3} = \frac{\frac{1}{3}\pi(1)^2.h1}{\frac{1}{3}\pi(2)^2.h2}$$

$$\frac{h1}{h2} = \frac{4}{3}$$

27. (C) $2\pi r = 88$

$$r = \frac{88 \times 7}{22 \times 2} = 14 \text{ cm}$$

$$\text{Volume} = \frac{1}{3}\pi r^2 h$$

$$= \frac{1}{3} \times \frac{22}{7} \times 14 \times 14 \times 15$$

$$= 3080 \text{ cm}^3$$

28. (B) Curved surface area $= 2\pi r^2$

$$= 2 \times \frac{22}{7} \times 21 \times 21 = 2772 \text{ cm}^2$$

29. (C) Acc. To the qn.,

$$\frac{2}{3}\pi r^3 = 3\pi r^2$$

$$r = \frac{9}{2} = 4.5 \text{ units}$$

30. (C) Total volume $= \frac{4}{3}\pi(4^3 + 6^3 + 8^3)$

$$= \frac{4}{3} \times \frac{22}{7} \times 792$$

$$r^3 = 792$$

$$r = \sqrt[3]{792} \cong 9.25$$

$$D = 18.5 \text{ cm}$$

31. (A) Volume of cylinder $= \pi r^2 h$

$$\text{Volume of cone} = \frac{1}{3}\pi r^2 h$$

$$\text{Required ratio} = \frac{\pi(3)^2 \times 2}{\frac{1}{3}\pi(4)^2 \times 3} = \frac{9 \times 2}{16} = \frac{9}{8}$$

32. (D) Volume of total wood $= \frac{4}{3}\pi(20)^3$

$$\text{Volume of wasted wood} = \frac{4}{3}\pi r^3 - \frac{1}{3}\pi r^3$$

$$= \pi r^3 = \pi(20)^3$$

$$\text{Required percentage} = \frac{\pi(20)^3}{\frac{4}{3}\pi(20)^3} \times 100$$

$$= \frac{3}{4} \times 100 = 75\%$$

33. (A) Volume of cuboid $= 7 \times 14 \times 7$

$$= 686 \text{ cm}^3$$

$$\text{Volume of cube} = \frac{686}{2} = 343 \text{ cm}^3$$

$$\text{Side of cube} = \sqrt[3]{343} = 7$$

$$\text{TSA of cube} = 6 \times (\text{side})^2 = 6 \times 7^2$$

$$= 294 \text{ cm}^2$$

PRACTICE:

SQUARE

1. The perimeter of two squares are 24cm & 40cm. The perimeter of the third square whose area is the difference of the areas of two squares is:

(A) 34 cm   (B) 28 cm

(C) 32 cm   (D) 24 cm

(E) None of these

2. A person running at the rate of 12 km/hr crosses a square field diagonally in 120 seconds. What is the area of the field?

(A) 80,000 m²   (B) 60,000 m²

(C) 70,000 m²   (D) 40,000 m²

(E) None of these

3. The area of a square is 1764 sq.cm whose side is twice the radius of the circle. The circumference of the circle is equal to the length of a rectangle. If the perimeter of the rectangle is 400 cm. What is the breadth of the rectangle?

(A) 52 cm   (B) 68 cm

(C) 36 cm   (D) 64 cm

(E) None of these

RECTANGLE

4. If the length is increased by 30% and the width is decreased by 20%, then the area of the rectangle is

(A) Decreased by 2%

(B) Increased by 2%

(C) Decreased by 4%

(D) Increased by 4%

(E) None of these

5. A 4 m wide pathway is to be constructed around a rectangular plot. The area of the plot is 184 sq.m. The cost of construction is Rs 100 per sq.m, then find the total cost of construction.
(A) Rs 2800   (B) Rs 4800
(C) Rs 6000   (D)Data inadequate
(E) None of these

TRIANGLE

6. If the area of a triangle is 576 cm² and the ratio between base & corresponding altitude is 8:9, then the altitude of the triangle is
(A) 36 cm   (B) 32 cm
(C) 28 cm   (D) 40 cm
(E) None of these

7. If the length of hypotenuse of a right-angled triangle is 10 cm & its area is 24 cm², then the length of the remaining sides is
(A) (5 cm, 4 cm)   (B) (6 cm, 9 cm)
(C) (5 cm, 8 cm)   (D) (6 cm, 8 cm)
(E) None of these

CIRCLE

8. The area of a circle is 154 sq.cm. Its circumference (in cm) is
(A) 22 cm   (B) 48 cm
(C) 33 cm   (D) 44 cm
(E) None of these

9. If the perimeter of a semi-circular field is 288 m, then the diameter of the field is
(A) 56 m   (B) 79 m
(C) 112 m   (D) 104 m
(E) None of these

10. If the area of a semi-circular plot is 2272 m², then its perimeter is (Use $\pi = 22/7$)
(A) 216 cm   (B) 254 cm
(C) 182 cm   (D) 208 cm
(E) None of these

11. The circumference of two circles are 132 cm and 88 cm respectively. What is the difference between the areas of the larger and smaller circles?
(A) 820 cm²   (B) 770 cm²
(C) 745 cm²   (D) 660 cm²
(E) None of these

QUADRILATERALS

12. One side of a parallelogram is 12 cm and the perpendicular distance between this and the opposite is 16 cm, then the area is
(A) 190 cm²   (B) 184 cm²
(C) 196 cm²   (D) 192 cm²
(E) None of these

13. A field is of the form of a trapezium with height 6 m & parallel sides being 4 m & 5 m. What is the cost of ploughing the field, if the rate of ploughing is Rs 50 per square metre?
(A) Rs 1350   (B) Rs 1250
(C) Rs 1425   (D) Rs 1375
(E) None of these

RHOMBUS

14. The perimeter of a rhombus is 80 cm. If the length of one of its diagonals be 32 cm. The length of the other diagonal is
(A) 26 cm   (B) 22 cm
(C) 24 cm   (D) 25 cm
(E) None of these

COMBINED 2D FIGURES

15. If the areas of a circle & a square are equal, then the ratio of their perimeter is
(A) $2: \sqrt{\pi}$ (B) $4: \sqrt{\pi}$
(C) $\sqrt{\pi}: 2$ (D) $\sqrt{\pi}: 4$
(E) None of these

16. If the diagonal of a square is 4 cm, then the area of an equilateral triangle drawn on a side of the square will be
(A) $2\sqrt{3}$ cm²   (B) $\sqrt{3}/2$ cm²

(C) 2√3/3 cm² (D) 3√3 cm²
(E) None of these

17. A circular wire of diameter 56 cm is folded in the shape of a rectangle whose sides are in the ratio 7:4. Find the area enclosed by the rectangle.
(A) 7168 cm² (B) 6156 cm²
(C) 6972 cm² (D) 7345 cm²
(E) None of these

CUBE

18. If the volume of two cubes are in the ratio 125:64, the ratio of their edges is:
(A) 5:4 (B) 6:5
(C) 5:3 (D) 2:1
(E) None of these

19. What is the volume of a cube (in cm³) whose diagonal measures 5√3 cm?
(A) 54 (B) 64
(C) 150 (D) 125
(E) None of these

CUBOID

20. The volume of air in the room is 240 cm². The height of the room is 8m. What is the floor area of the room?
(A) 32 m² (B) 36 m²
(C) 30 m² (D) 28 m²
(E) None of these

CYLINDER

21. The lateral surface area of a cylinder is 66 cm². If the height of a cylinder is 3 cm, then the diameter of the cylinder is:
(A) 8 cm (B) 3.5 cm
(C) 14 cm (D) 7 cm
(E) None of these

22. If the height of a right circular cylinder is doubled and the radius is halved then the ratio between the previous volume and the new volume of the cylinder is:

(A) 1:2 (B) 2:1
(C) 3:2 (D) 2:3
(E) None of these

CONE

23. If the area of the base of a cone is 154 cm² and the area of the curved surface is 286 cm², then its slant height is:
(A) 12 cm (B) 15 cm
(C) 26 cm (D) 13 cm
(E) None of these

24. The diameter of the base of a right circular cone is 12 cm and its height is 8 cm. The slant height of the cone is
(A) 10 cm (B) 12 cm
(C) 8 cm (D) 13 cm
(E) None of these

SPHERE

25. The sum of radii of two spheres is 10 cm & the sum of their volumes is 440 cm³. What will be the product of their radii?
(A) $31 \frac{1}{3}$ (B) $21 \frac{2}{3}$
(C) $27 \frac{4}{5}$ (D) $29 \frac{5}{6}$
(E) None of these

26. The volumes of two spheres are in the ratio 27:125. The ratio of their surface area is
(A) 9:16 (B) 9:25
(C) 16:25 (D) 25:36
(E) None of these

27. If the surface areas of two spheres are in the ratio 9:16, then the ratio of their volumes will be
(A) 27:64 (B) 64:27
(C) 16:27 (D) 27:81
(E) None of these

COMBINED 3D FIGURES

28. A sphere and a cylinder have equal volume and equal radius. The ratio of the curved surface area of the cylinder to that of the sphere is

(A) 3:2   (B) 2:3

(C) 1:2   (D) 2:1

(E) None of these

29. The radii of a sphere and that of a right circular cylinder are equal and their curved surface areas are also equal. The ratio of their volumes is

(A) 3:2   (B) 1:3

(C) 2:3   (D) 2:5

(E) None of these

SOLUTION:

1. (C) Sides of square $= \left(\dfrac{24}{6}, \dfrac{40}{4}\right)$

$\qquad = (6,10)$cm

Difference in their areas $= 10^2 - 6^2$

$\qquad = 100 - 36 = 64 \text{ cm}^2$

Side of the third square $= \sqrt{64} = 8$ cm

Perimeter of the third square $= 8 \times 4$

$\qquad\qquad = 32$ cm

2. (A) Distance covered in 50 seconds

$= \left(12 \times \dfrac{5}{18}\right) \times 120 = 400$ m

$=$ Diagonal of the field

Area of field $= \dfrac{(\text{Diagonal})^2}{2} = \dfrac{400 \times 400}{2}$

$\qquad = 80{,}000 \text{ m}^2$

3. (C) Sides of square $= \sqrt{1764} = 42$ cm

Radius of circle $= \dfrac{42}{2} = 21$ cm

Circumference of circle $= 2 \times \dfrac{22}{7} \times 21$

Length of rectangle $= 132$ cm

Perimeter of rectangle $= 2(l + b)$

$= 2(132+b) = 400$

$132 + b = 200$

$b = 68$ cm

4. (D) % change in area $= \left(x + y + \dfrac{xy}{100}\right)\%$

$x =$ change in length $= 30\%$

$y =$ change in breadth $= -20\%$

% change in area $= 30 - 20 + \dfrac{(30)(-20)}{100}$

$\qquad = 10 - 6 = 4\%$

5. (C) Since, neither length nor breadth of the rectangular plot is given, the required answer can't be derived.

6. (A) Let base & altitude be 8x & 9x respectively.

Area $= \dfrac{1}{2}$bh $= \dfrac{1}{2}(8x)(9x) = 576$

$36x^2 = 576$

$x^2 = 16$

$x = 4$ cm

Altitude of triangle $= 9x = 9(4)$

$\qquad = 36$ cm

7. (D) Hypotenuse$^2 = b^2 + h^2$

$10^2 = b^2 + h^2 \qquad ....\text{I}$

Area $= \dfrac{1}{2}$bh $= 24$

bh $= 48 \text{ cm}^2$

$b = \dfrac{48}{h}$

Subs in I:

$10^2 = \left(\dfrac{48}{h}\right)^2 + h^2$

$2304 + 10^2 h^2$

Put $h^2 = x$

$x^2 - 100x + 2304$

$x = 36$ or 64

$h = 6$ or 8

8. (D) Area $= 154 \text{ cm}^2$

$\dfrac{22}{7} \times r^2 = 154$

$r^2 = \dfrac{154 \times 7}{22} = 49$

$r = 7$ cm

Circumference $= 2\pi r = 2 \times \dfrac{22}{7} \times 7$

$\qquad = 44$ cm

9. (C) Perimeter of semicircle $= \pi r + 2r$

$r(2 + \pi) = 288$

$r = \dfrac{288}{2+\frac{22}{7}} = \dfrac{288}{36} \times 7 = 56$ m

Diameter $= 2 \times 56 = 112$ m.

10. (A) Area of semi-circular plot $= \dfrac{\pi r^2}{2}$

$$= 2272$$

$r^2 = \dfrac{2 \times 2272 \times 7}{22} = 1764$

$r = 42$ cm

Perimeter $= \pi r + 2r = 42\left(\dfrac{22}{7} + 2\right)$

$$= 42 \times \dfrac{36}{7} = 216 \text{ cm}$$

11. (B) Radius of

- Larger circle $= \dfrac{132}{2\pi} = \dfrac{132 \times 7}{2 \times 22} = 21$ cm
- Smaller circle $= \dfrac{88 \times 7}{2 \times 22} = 14$ cm

Area of

- Larger circle $= \dfrac{22}{7} \times 21 \times 21$

$$= 1386 \text{ cm}^2$$

- Smaller circle $= \dfrac{22}{7} \times 14 \times 14$

$$= 616 \text{ cm}^2$$

Required difference $= 1386 - 616$

$$= 770 \text{ cm}^2$$

12. (D) Area of parallelogram

$= $ height $\times$ breadth $= 12 \times 16$

$= 192 \text{ cm}^2$

13. (A) Area of trapezium $= \dfrac{1}{2}h(a + b)$

$$= \dfrac{1}{2}(6)(4 + 5) = 3 \times 9 = 27 \text{ m}^2$$

Cost of ploughing $= 27 \times 50$

$$= \text{Rs } 1350$$

14. (C) Perimeter $= 4a = 80$ cm

Base, $a = \dfrac{80}{4} = 20$ cm

Side of a rhombus $=$

$\dfrac{1}{2}\sqrt{d1^2 + d2^2}$ (d1 & d2 are diagonals)

$\dfrac{1}{2}\sqrt{32^2 + d2^2} = 20$

$\sqrt{1024 + d2^2} = 40$

$d2^2 = 1600 - 1024 = 576$

$d2 = \sqrt{576} = 24$ cm

15. (C) Let side of square be 'a' and radius of circle be 'r'

$a^2 = \pi r^2$

$a = \sqrt{\pi}r$

Required ratio $= \dfrac{2\pi r}{4a} = \dfrac{2\pi r}{4\sqrt{\pi}r} = \sqrt{\pi}: 2$

16. (A) Side of square $= \dfrac{\text{Diagonal}}{\sqrt{2}} = \dfrac{4}{\sqrt{2}}$

Area of equilateral triangle $= \dfrac{\sqrt{3}}{4}(\text{side})^2$

$$= \dfrac{\sqrt{3}}{4}\left(\dfrac{4}{\sqrt{2}}\right)^2 = \dfrac{\sqrt{3}}{4} \times \dfrac{16}{2} = 2\sqrt{3} \text{ cm}^2$$

17. (A) Radius of circular wire $= \dfrac{56}{2}$

$$= 28 \text{ cm}$$

Perimeter/ Length of wire $= 2 \times \dfrac{22}{7} \times 28$

$$= 176 \text{ cm}$$

Rectangle:

- Length $= \dfrac{7}{11} \times 176 = 112$ cm
- Breadth $= 64$ cm

Area enclosed by it $= 112 \times 64$

$$= 7168 \text{ cm}^2$$

18. (A) Ratio of edges $= \sqrt[3]{125}: \sqrt[3]{64} = 5: 4$

19. (D) Diagonal of cube $=$ side $\times \sqrt{3}$ cm

Side $= \dfrac{5\sqrt{3}}{\sqrt{3}} = 5$ cm

Volume $= (5)^3 = 125 \text{ cm}^3$

20. (C) Volume of room $= 240$

Floor area $\times$ height $= 240$

Floor area $= \dfrac{240}{8} = 30 \text{ m}^2$

21. (D) LSA of cylinder $= 2\pi rh$

$$= 2 \times \dfrac{22}{7} \times r \times 6 = 66$$

$r = \dfrac{66 \times 7}{2 \times 22 \times 3} = 3.5$ cm

Diameter = 7 cm

22. (B) Let height & radius be h & r respectively.

New h & r are '2h' & 'r/2' respectively

Required ratio $= \dfrac{\pi r^2 h}{\pi\left(\frac{r}{2}\right)^2 \times 2h} = \dfrac{r^2 h}{\frac{r^2}{4}\times 2h} = 2:1$

23. (D) Let height & radius of base of cone be h cm & r cm respectively.

$\pi r^2 = 154$

$r^2 = \dfrac{154\times 7}{22} = 49$

$r = 7$ cm

$\pi r l = 286$

$l = \dfrac{286}{\pi r} = \dfrac{286\times 7}{22\times 7} = 13$ cm

24. (A) Slant height, $l = \sqrt{h^2 + r^2}$

$\qquad = \sqrt{8^2 + \left(\dfrac{12}{2}\right)^2} = \sqrt{8^2 + 6^2} = \sqrt{100}$

$\qquad = 10$ cm

25. (D) $r_1 + r_2 = 10$

$\dfrac{4}{3}\pi r_1^{\,3} + \dfrac{4}{3}\pi r_2^{\,3} = 440$

$r_1^{\,3} + r_2^{\,3} = \dfrac{440}{\frac{4}{3}\pi} = 105$

$(r_1 + r_2)^3 = r_1^{\,3} + r_2^{\,3} + 3r_1 r_2 (r_1 + r_2)$

$1000 = 105 + 3r_1 r_2 (10)$

$30 r_1 r_2 = 895$

$r_1 r_2 = \dfrac{895}{30} = 29\dfrac{5}{6}$

26. (B) Ratio of their volumes

$= \sqrt[3]{27} : \sqrt[3]{125} = 3:5$

Ratio of their surface areas $= 3^2 : 5^2$

$\qquad\qquad\qquad = 9:25$

27. (A) Ratio of radii $= \sqrt{9} : \sqrt{16} = 3:4$

Ratio of their volumes $= 3^3 : 4^3$

$\qquad\qquad\qquad = 27:64$

28. (B) Acc. To the Qn.,

$\dfrac{4}{3}\pi r^3 = \pi r^2 h$

$\dfrac{r}{h} = \dfrac{3}{4}$

Required ratio $= \dfrac{2\pi r h}{4\pi r^2} = \dfrac{h}{2r} = \dfrac{4}{2(3)} = 2:3$

29. (C) Acc. To the qn.,

$4\pi r^2 = 2\pi r h$

$h = 2r$

Required ratio $= \dfrac{\frac{4}{3}\pi r^3}{\pi r^2 h} = \dfrac{4r}{3h} = \dfrac{4r}{3(2r)}$

$\qquad\qquad = 2:3$

Unit **18**

DATA INTERPRETATION

Data interpretation is the process of making sense of numerical data that has been collected, analysed & presented.

It also refers to implementation of procedures through which data is reviewed for the purpose of arriving at an inference.

<u>DI graphs/charts can be in formats of</u>

- Pie charts
- Line charts
- Bar charts
- Tabular charts
- Radar charts
- Mixed graphs

<u>Types of questions that are asked under any format of DI:</u>

1. <u>Sum or Difference based:</u>
   - Sum or difference of 2 or more values in the given data
   - How much a value is more/less than other value.
2. <u>Average based:</u>
   - Average or mean of few values in the given data.
3. <u>Ratio based:</u>
   - Ratio between any 2 values that is directly given or the values to be found out.
4. <u>Percentage based:</u>
   - Percentage of a value out of other value.
   - Percentage of a value more/less than another value.

EXERCISE:

BAR GRAPH:

[1-5]
Given bar graph shows the no. of book copies sold in a particular month. Study the graph carefully and answer the questions.

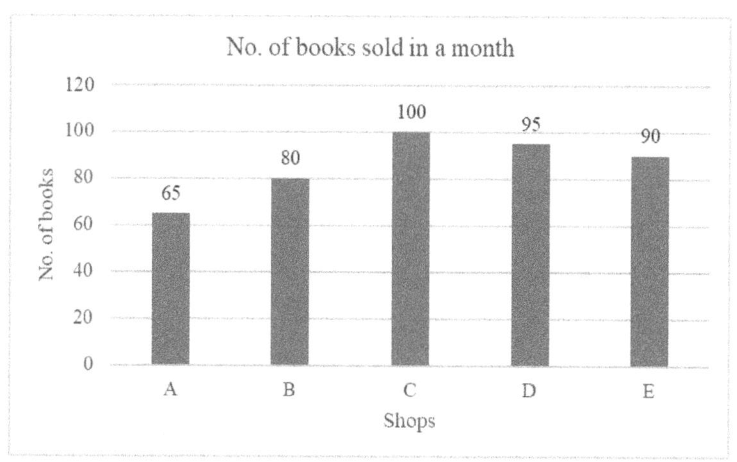

1. No. of copies sold of C & D together are what present more/less than no. of copies of A & B? (approx.)
   (A) 35%   (B) 36%   (C) 33%   (D) 32%   (E) None of these
2. What is the difference between the average no. of copies sold of B, D & A together and average no. of copies sold of E & C together?
   (A) 25   (B) 15   (C) 20   (D) 10   (E) None of these
3. No. of copies sold of A are what percent of that of B?
   (A) 82.15%   (B) 80.5%   (C) 81.75%   (D) 81.25%   (E) None of these
4. How many average no. of copies are sold in the given month?
   (A) 84   (B) 85   (C) 86   (D) 87   (E) None of these
5. How many book copies sold in the month are more than the average no. of copies sold of all books in the given month?
   (A) Two   (B) Three   (C) One   (D) None   (E) None of these

[5-10]

Given bar graph shows the production of cars by Maruti and Hyundai in 2 years. Study the data carefully and answer the questions.

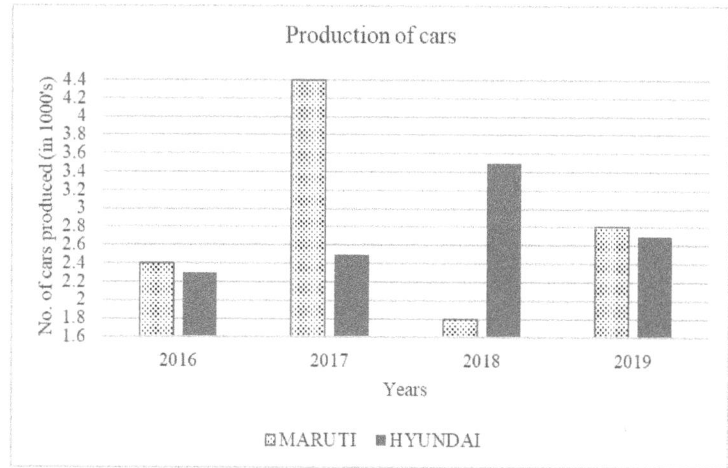

6. How many cars have been produced of Maruti over all the years?
   (A) 12,100   (B) 10,600   (C) 11,400   (D) 11,200   (E) None of these

7. Hyundai cars produced in 2016 & 2017 together are how much more than Maruti cars produced in 2018 & 2019?

    (A) 300   (B) 400   (C) 500   (D) 200   (E) None of these

8. Maruti cars produced in 2018 are what percent of Hyundai cars produced in 2019?

    (A) $66\,\frac{2}{3}\%$ (B) $33\,\frac{1}{3}\%$ (C) 68%   (D) 72%   (E) None of these

9. What is the ratio of Hyundai cars produced in 2018, 2017, 2016 together to Maruti cars produced 2019, 2017 & 2016 together?

    (A) 83:94   (B) 83:96   (C) 96:83   (D) 82:95   (E) None of these

10. In which year, the increase in production was maximum as compared to previous year & for which company?

    (A) Maruti 2019   (B) Hyundai 2018   (C) Hyundai 2017   (D) Maruti 2017   (E) None of these

[11-15]

Given bar graph shows the details of number of students in a particular class of 3 different schools in 5 different years.

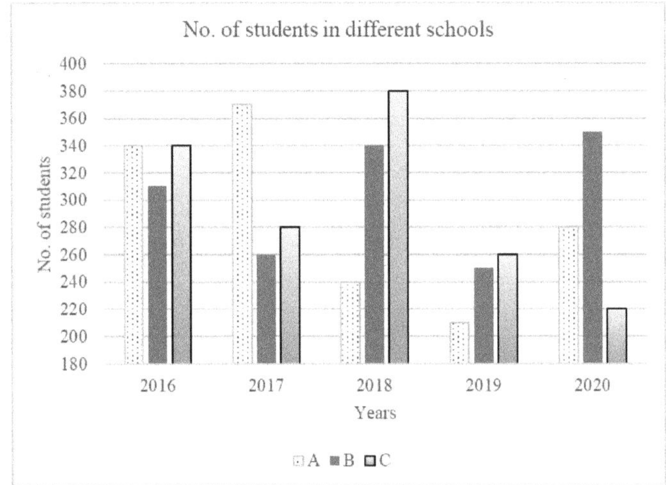

11. What is the difference between average no. of students of school A across all the years and the average number of students of school B across all the years?

    (A) 16   (B) 12   (C) 10   (D) 14   (E) None of these

12. Find the respective ratio of the total number of students in school A in 2016 and 2020 together to the total number of students of school C in 2017 and 2018 together?

    (A) 31:33   (B) 33:31   (C) 31:34   (D) 30:37   (E) None of these

13. If in 2021, the total number of students in School A, School B and School C increases by 10%, 20 % & 15% respectively as compared to 2019, then find the total number of students in 2021 in all the schools together.

    (A) 780   (B) 830   (C) 860   (D) 800   (E) None of these

14. Total students of all the Schools together in 2017 is approximately what percentage more/less than the total students of school B in 2020 and 2019 together? (approx.)

    (A) 50   (B) 54   (C) 52   (D) 49   (E) None of these

15. Find the difference between the number of total students from all the schools in 2020 and 2017 together and the total number of students from all the schools in 2018 and 2019 together?

    (A) 80   (B) 60   (C) 100   (D) 40   (E) None of these

[16-20]

The following bar graph indicates the production of mobile phones (in Lakhs) by three different companion Apple, Samsung, Lenovo, over the years from 2017 to 2020.

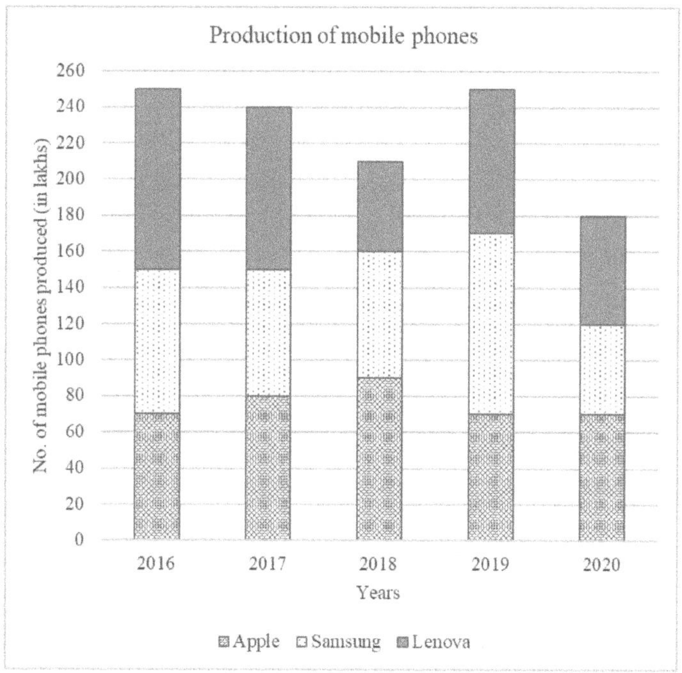

16. The percentage decrease in production of the company, Samsung from the year 2019 to the year 2020?

(A) 50% (B) 80% (C) 60% (D) 90% (E) None of these

17. The average production over the years 2016-2020 was minimum for the company?

(A) Apple (B) Samsung (C) Lenovo (D) Lenovo & Apple (E) None of these

18. The percentage rise or fall in production of company Samsung as compared to the previous year is maximum in the year?

(A) 2017 (B) 2018 (C) 2019 (D) 2020 (E) None of these

19. The percentage of production of company Apple as compared to production of company Samsung is maximum in the year?

(A) 2019 (B) 2016 (C) 2020 (D) 2017 (E) None of these

20. The ratio of the average production of company Lenovo during the year 2016, 2017 & 2018 to the average production of company Samsung for the same period is?

(A) 12:11 (B) 11:12 (C) 12:13 (D) 13:12 (E) None of these

TABLE:

[21-25]

Given below table shows total three type of items (A, B, & C) sold by a store on 5 days of a week. Table also shows total type A items sold by store and percentage of item B and item C sold by store.

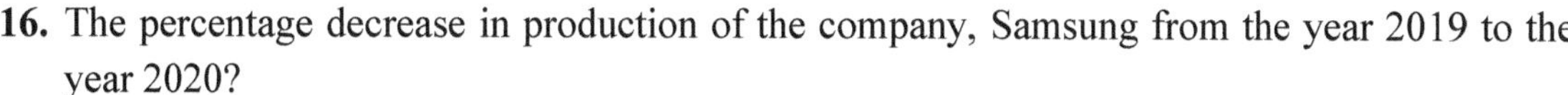

Days	No. of items of A	% of items of B	% of items of C
Monday	320	48%	12%
Tuesday	360	56%	20%
Wednesday	240	32%	20%
Thursday	340	22%	10%
Friday	420	45%	20%

Note: Only three type of items sold by the store

21. Total items of B sold by store on Wednesday & Tuesday together are what percent less than total items of C sold by store on Tuesday and Friday together?
(A) 55%   (B) 60%   (C) 40%   (D) 50%   (E) None of these

22. Find the difference between average number of items of B sold by store on Monday & Tuesday and average number of items A sold by store on Tuesday &Thursday?
(A) 254   (B) 262   (C) 268   (D) 252   (E) None of these

23. If total items of B sold by store on Saturday is 25%. more than that sold on Tuesday and total items of C sold on Saturday is 300% more than that sold on Tuesday than find total number of item B & items C sold by store on Saturday?
(A) 2250   (B) 2300   (C) 2150   (D) 2200   (E) None of these

24. Total items of C sold by store on Friday is what percent more than total items of C sold by store on Monday & Wednesday together (approx.)
(A) 26%   (B) 20%   (C) 23%   (D) 18%   (E) None of these

25. Find the ratio between total items sold by store on Wednesday to total items sold by store on Tuesday?
(A) 3:1   (B) 1:3   (C) 1:4   (D) 4:1   (E) None of these

[26-30]

In the given below table graph, details of candidates from 5 different cities is mentioned. Read carefully all the instruction and answer the following question.

City	No. of candidates who appeared in online exam	No. of candidates who appeared in offline exam	No. of candidates who did not complete exam (online + offline)
P	320	36%	120
Q	440	45%	105
R	460	54%	170
S	525	30%	140
T	500	60%	90

Note: Total candidates = candidates appeared in online exam + Candidates appeared in offline exam.

26. Total number of candidates who completed the exam from city Q is how much more/ less than total number of candidates who completed the exam from city T?
(A) 455   (B) 465   (C) 470   (D) 460   (E) None of these

27. If number of candidates who didn't complete online exam and who didn't complete the offline exam from city T are equal, then no. of candidates who completed offline exam from city T is

approximately what percent more than number of candidates who completed online exam from same city? (approx.)

(A) 45%   (B) 51%   (C) 49%   (D) 55%   (E) None of these

28. What is the difference between the total number of candidates who appeared in online and offline exams from all the cities together?

(A) 180   (B) 170   (C) 190   (D)200   (E) None of these

29. Find the ratio of total number of candidates who appeared for online exam from city R & city T together to the total number of candidates who appeared for offline exams from city Q & city P together?

(A) 16:9   (B) 9:16   (C) 5:3   (D) 3:5   (E) None of these

30. Total candidates who appeared for offline exams from city P & city Q together is what percentage of total candidates who appeared for online exams from city Q?

(A) 170.05%   (B) 156.25%   (C) 168.75%   (D) 163.15%   (E) None of these

[31-35]
The following table shows the total no. of persons with disability in five different cities and ratio of males to females in them.

City	No. of persons with disabilities	Ratio of male to female
Chennai	36,300	2:1
Pune	42,400	3:1
Mumbai	18,600	5:1
Delhi	24,500	3:2
Bangalore	27,000	5:4

31. Total no. of females who are disabled from Chennai is what percent of disabled females from Mumbai (approx.)?

(A) 390 %   (B) 290%   (C) 410 %   (D) 350%   (E) None of these

32. What is the average no. of males who are physically disabled from cities Pune & Delhi?

(A) 19,460   (B) 23,250   (C) 21,750   (D) 42,580   (E) None of these

33. What is the total no. of females who are physically disabled from all the cities together?

(A) 49,300   (B) 47,400   (C) 46,800   (D) 47,600   (E) None of these

34. What is the difference between total no. of males disabled from Chennai and Bangalore together and females disabled from same cities together?

(A) 15,100   (B) 15,700   (C) 15,000   (D) 14,980   (E) None of these

35. Total no. of persons with disabilities in Chennai is what percent more/ less than that in Bangalore?

(A) 42 4/9%   (B) 32 1/9 %   (C) 34 4/9 %   (D) 34 8/9 %   (E) None of these

[36-40]
The following table chart gives the details of 5 student of a particular school in five different subject in the annual exam.

	Maths (150)	**Physics (150)**	**Chemistry (150)**	**English (100)**	**Computer (100)**
P	50	64	78	65	75
Q	70	66	58	54	80
R	76	82	64	72	94
S	80	76	84	75	85
T	48	72	88	70	86

<u>Note:</u> The data provided in the table is percentage of marks out of total marks in that particular subject.

36. Total marks scored by S in Physics, chemistry and maths together is how much more/ less than total marks scored by Q in the same three subjects together?
   (A) 70   (B) 66   (C) 69   (D) 73   (E) None of these
37. Find the overall percentage of marks scored by T in the exam?
   (A) 74%   (B) 72%   (C) 68%   (D) 70%   (E) None of these
38. Find the difference of total marks scored by R in all the given subjects together and total marks scored by P in all the given subjects together?
   (A) 71   (B) 69   (C) 73   (D) 72   (E) None of these
39. Find the average marks scored in physics subject by all the given five students together.
   (A) 112   (B) 102   (C) 109   (D) 108   (E) None of these
40. Total marks scored by P, S and T in English is what percentage of the total marks scored by P, Q and S in maths?
   (A) 72%   (B) 60%   (C) 75%   (D) 70%   (E) None of these

PIE CHART

[41-45]
Given pie graph shows the number of players in various sports. Study the pie chart carefully and answer the questions.

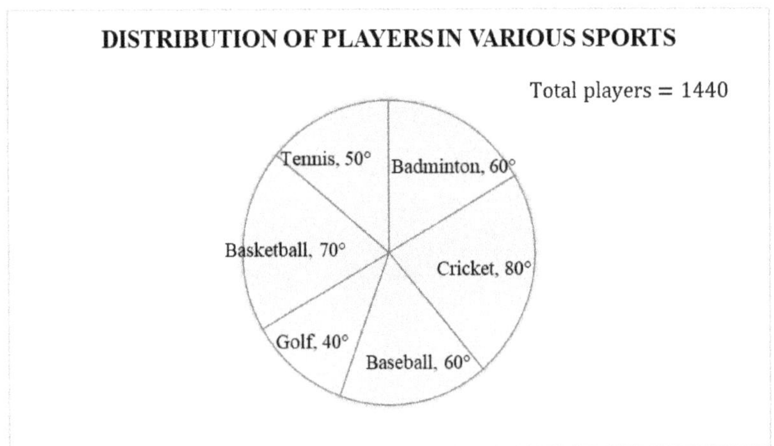

41. How many players play Cricket & Baseball together?
   (A) 620   (B) 560   (C) 600   (D) 580   (E) None of these
42. What is the ratio of players playing Basketball & Badminton together to players playing Tennis & Golf together?
   (A) 13:9   (B) 8:13   (C) 13:8   (D) 9:13   (E) None of these

43. What is the average of players playing Basketball, Tennis & Baseball?

    (A) 300   (B) 280   (C) 260   (D) 240   (E) None of these

44. If 50% Cricket players are female which is same as female Baseball players. Find male Baseball players.

    (A) 75   (B) 70   (C) 80   (D) 90   (E) None of these

45. Badminton, Golf and Basketball players are what percent of Cricket & Baseball players? (approx.)

    (A) 116.8%   (B) 121.43%   (C) 119.2%   (D) 123.12%   (E) None of these

[46-50]

Study the pie charts given below and answer the following questions. Pie chart shows the percentage distribution of total employees of a company in 5 different departments & percentage distribution of total male employees of the company in these 5 departments. There are only five departments in the company.

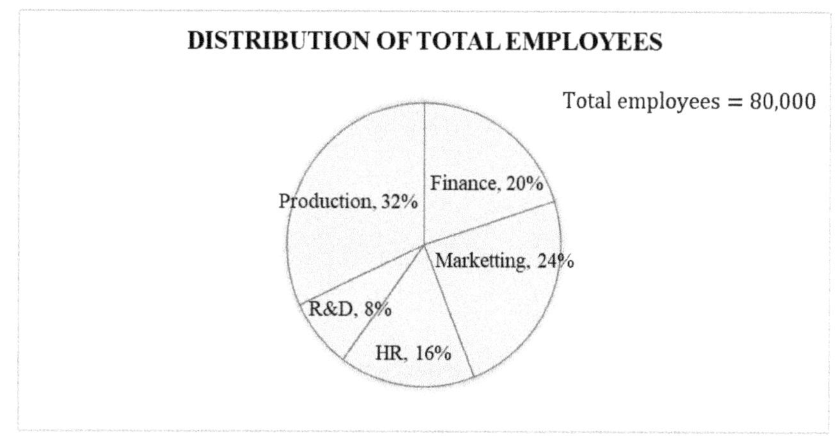

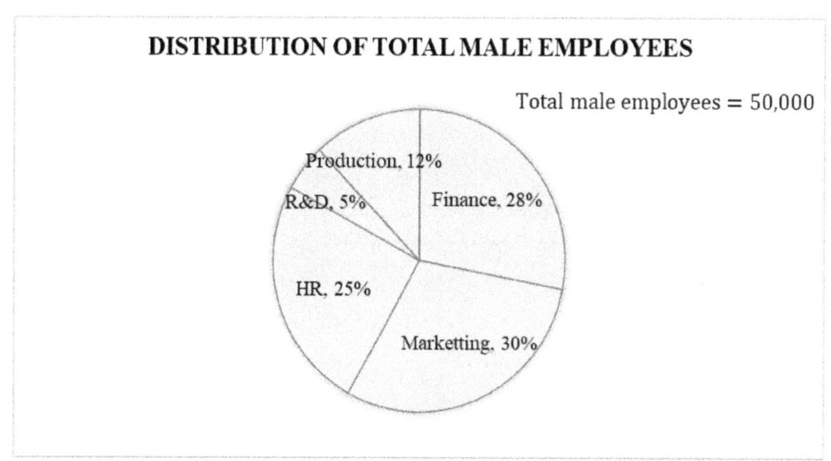

46. Find the total number of female employees in Production, HR and R&D together.

    (A) 24,600   (B) 23,400   (C) 23,800   (D) 23,500   (E) None of these

47. Female employees in Marketing & HR together are what percent of total employees in Production Department? (approx.)

    (A) 19.46%   (B) 17.58%   (C) 16.2%   (D) 14.69%   (E) None of these

48. Find the average number of male employees in HR, R&D & Production Departments.

(A) 9000   (B) 8000   (C) 7000   (D) 6000   (E) None of these

49. Male employees in R&D and Marketing are what percent of total employees in R&D and Marketing departments together? (approx.)

(A) 68%   (B) 65%   (C) 62%   (D) 58%   (E) None of these

50. Find the ratio of male employees in Production and Finance departments together to female employees in Production and Finance departments together.

(A) 27:25   (B) 25:29   (C) 24:29   (D) 25:27   (E) None of these

[51-55]

Given pie chart shows the percentage distribution of total spectators of a particular city loving different sports as shown below:

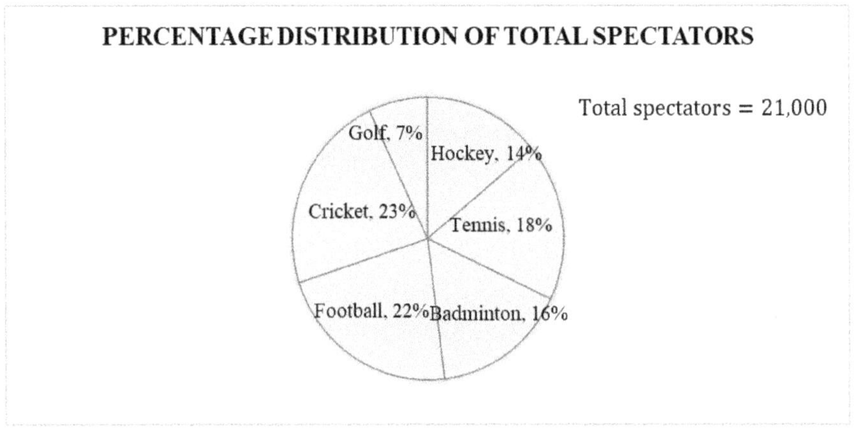

51. Total spectators of Cricket and Golf together is what percentage of total spectators of Tennis and Football together?

(A) 76%   (B) 75%   (C) 72%   (D) 80%   (E) None of these

52. Find the ratio of total spectators of Badminton & Hockey together to the total spectators of Football.

(A) 11:14   (B) 14:11   (C) 11:15   (D) 15:11   (E) None of these

53. Find the central angle of total spectator of Cricket and Hockey together.

(A) 133.2°   (B) 132.8°   (C) 134.6°   (D) 128.2°   (E) None of these

54. Out of total Tennis spectators, male & female are in the ratio 9:6 respectively, then find the difference between male and female spectators of Tennis.

(A) 732   (B) 746   (C) 756   (D) 748   (E) None of these

55. Total spectators of Badminton & Football together are how much more/less than the total spectators of Cricket & Hockey together?

(A) 215   (B) 210   (C) 220   (D) 230   (E) None of these

[56-60]

Pie chart given below shows percentage break up of revenue generated by six different items (A, B, C, D, E and F) of a shop in a month? (Assume that the shop sells only these six items)

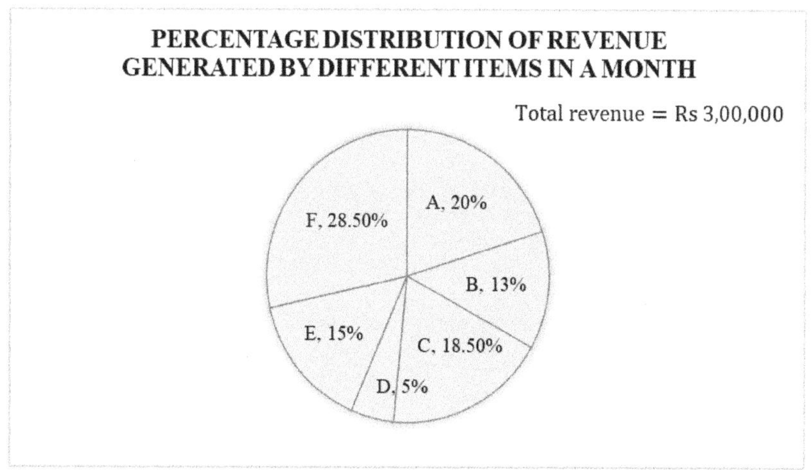

56. Revenue from product F is how much more than the revenue from product B?
(A) Rs 47,000   (B) Rs 47,800   (C) Rs 46,900   (D) Rs 46,500   (E) None of these

57. What is the difference between central angle (in degrees) formed by revenue from products B, C and F together and revenue from product A?
(A) 144°   (B) 168°   (C) 120°   (D) 210°   (E) None of these

58. Revenue from product C is how much percent more than the revenue from product D?
(A) 280%   (B) 270%   (C) 250%   (D) 240%   (E) None of these

59. If total 4 items of product A were sold in that month and selling price of each product B in that month is Rs 7800, find no. of items of products of B sold is how much percent more than no. of items of product A sold in that month?
(A) 28%   (B) 30%   (C) 25%   (D) 35%   (E) None of these

60. What is the total revenue (in Rs.) from product A and product C together?
(A) Rs 1,15,800   (B) Rs 1,15,500   (C) Rs 1,14,600   (D) Rs 1,18,500   (E) None of these

LINE GRAPH:

[61-65]

The following line graph gives the annual percent profit earned by two business-men during the period 2015-2020. Study the graph and answer the questions based on it.

61. What is the average profit percentage earned by A & B throughout the year? (approx.)
(A) 60%   (B) 51%   (C) 65%   (D) 54%   (E) None of these

62. If in 2016, the expenditure maybe by B was Rs 10 lakhs, then what was the income in that year?
(A) Rs 12,45,000   (B) Rs 14,50,000   (C) Rs 10,80,000   (D) Rs 16,25,000
(E) None of these

63. If the income of A in 2020 was Rs 41.6 lakhs & the income of B in 2018 was Rs 37.4 and respectively, the expenditure of A in 2020 was by about what percentage more or less than that of expenditure of B in 2018?

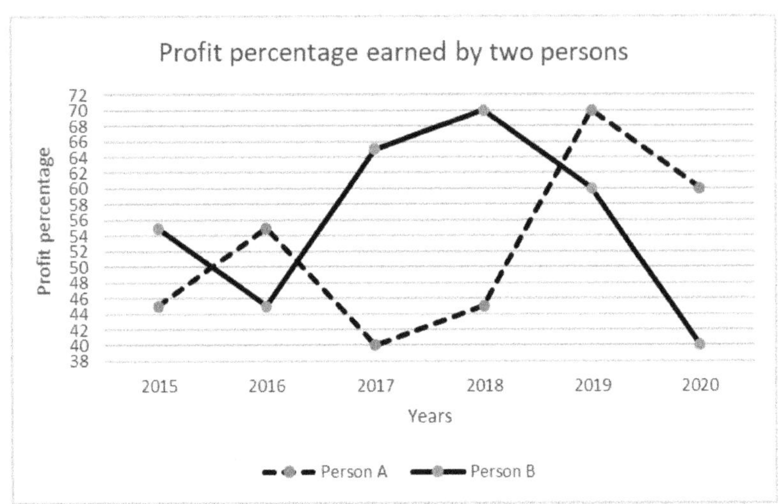

(A) 19.19%   (B) 18.67%   (C) 18.18%   (D) 17.42%   (E) None of these

64. If the income of A remains same throughout the year ie., Rs 6.8 lakhs then in which year his expenditure was minimum and what was the expenditure in that year?
(A) Rs 4,00,000   (B) Rs 5,00,000   (C) Rs 2,50,000   (D) Rs 4,50,000   (E) None of these

65. In which year the ratio of profit percent of A & B has maximum numeric value?
(A) 2016   (B) 2020   (C) 2019   (D) 2018   (E) None of these

[66-70]

Study the given line graph carefully and answer the questions. Line graph shows the percentage of stools sold in six different shops.

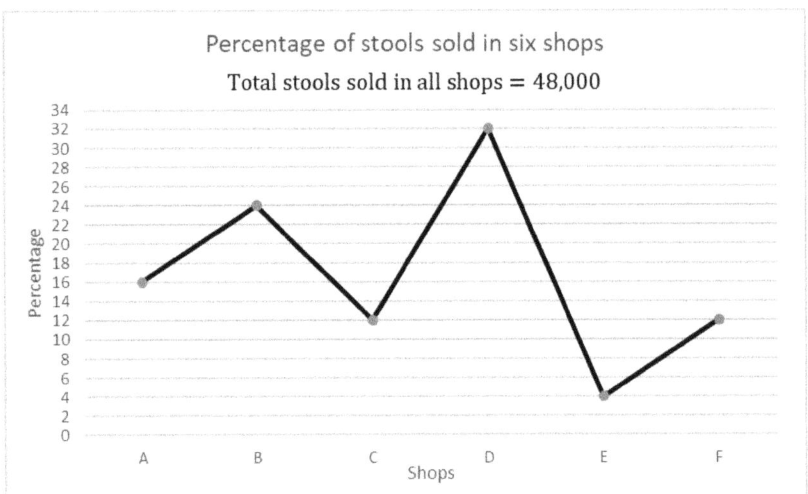

66. Stools sold in shops D & F together is how much percentage more than stools sold in shops A & B together
(A) 10%   (B) 8%   (C) 15%   (D) 14%   (E) None of these

67. E sold only three types of stools ie., X, Y & Z in the ratio 5:4:3. Find the difference of stools sold by E of type Z and Y together & that of type X.
(A) 360   (B) 320   (C) 450   (D) 300   (E) None of these

68. How many shops sold stools more than the average of stools sold in all 6 shops?
(A) None   (B) 3   (C) 1   (D) 2   (E) None of these

69. Stools sold in shops A &C together is how much more than stools sold in shops E & F together?
(A) 5720   (B) 5670   (C) 5760   (D) 5450   (E) None of these

70. What is the ratio of average no. of stools sold in shops A, B & C together to average no. of stools sold in shops D and F together?
(A) 37:25   (B) 33:26   (C) 26:33   (D) 33:27   (E) None of these

[71-75]

Line graph shows the quantity of different products produced in different years.

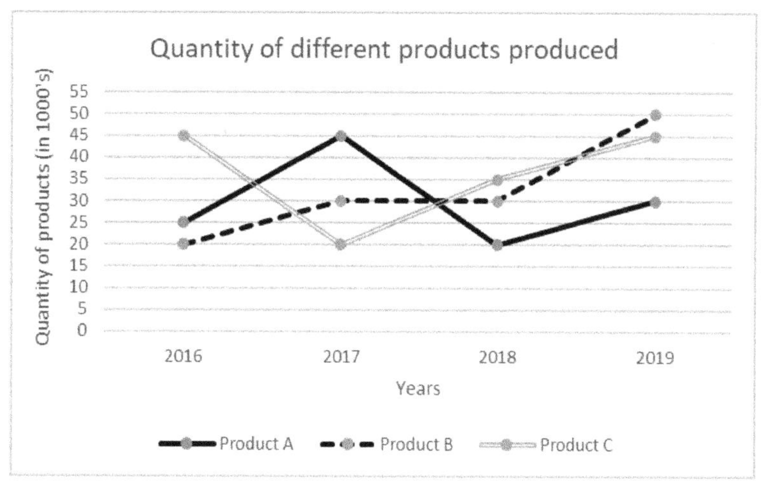

71. Find the difference between the average of product C produced in 2016 and 2018 and average of product A in 2017 and 2019?
(A) 2500   (B) 2000   (C) 2520   (D) 2250   (E) None of these

72. The product B produced in 2016 and 2019 together is approximately what percent of product A produced in 2017 & 2018 together? (approx.)
(A) 110   (B) 108   (C) 106   (D) 104   (E) None of these

73. In 2020, if production of product A & C shows an increment of 25% and 20% respectively in their production while production of product B decreased by 10% with respect to previous year then find the ratio of product A & C produced together in 2020 to that of product B produced in 2020.
(A) 60:29   (B) 30:61   (C) 61:30   (D) 29:60   (E) None of these

74. The product A and C produced in 2016, 2017 & 2018 together is what percent more/less than product B produced in 2018 & 2019 together?
(A) 141.25%   (B) 144.5%   (C) 143.75%   (D) 137.5%   (E) None of these

75. If the product A produced in 2017 remains 15% unsold and 95% sold in 2018 as well as in 2019, then find the ratio of product A sold in 2017 & 2018 together to that of sold in 2019?
[Total production = Sold + Unsold products]
(A) 229:114   (B) 113:230   (C) 114:229   (D) 230:113   (E) None of these

[76-80]

Study the line graph carefully and answer the following questions. The line graph shows the runs scored by two different teams in a series of five cricket matches.

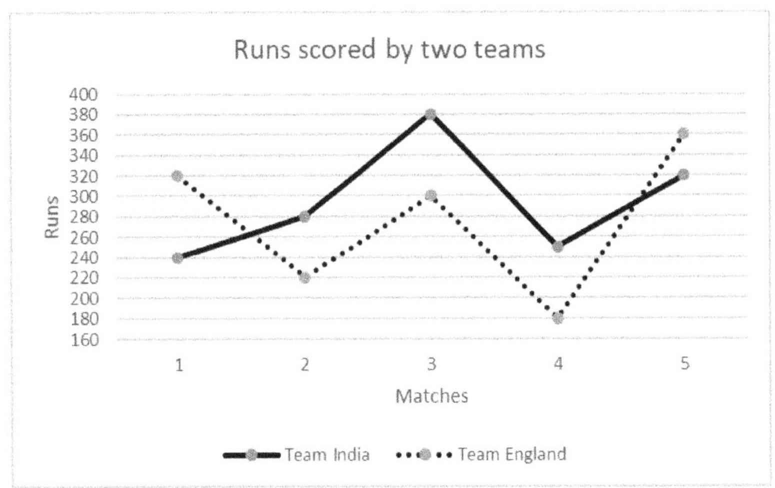

76. Runs scored by India in second & fifth matches together is what percent of runs scored by England in first and fourth matches together?
(A) 110%   (B) 120%   (C) 130%   (D) 140%   (E) None of these

77. Find the difference between maximum runs scored by England and minimum runs scored by India.
(A) 120   (B) 115   (C) 130   (D) 110   (E) None of these

78. What is the ratio between total runs scored by India to that of England in all matches?
(A) 47:49   (B) 49:47   (C) 46:49   (D) 49:46   (E) None of these

79. Runs scored by India in first match is what percent more/less than runs scored by England in third match?
(A) 28%   (B) 25%   (C) 20%   (D) 30%   (E) None of these

80. India won how many matches out of all the five matches?
(A) Three   (B) Two   (C) One   (D) None   (E) None of these

RADAR CHART:

[81-85]

Study the radar chart given below and answer the following questions. Radar chart shows the number of employees (in hundreds) in five different departments (A, B, C, D and E) in 2018, 2019 & 2020.

81. Average number of employees in C, D and E in 2020 is what percent of employees in D & E together in 2019?
(A) 60%   (B) 40%   (C) 50%   (D) 58%   (E) None of these

82. Find the ratio of employees in D in 2018, 2019 & 2020 together to employees in E in 2019 & 2020 together.
(A) 26:15   (B) 16:27   (C) 27:16   (D) 15:26   (E) None of these

83. Employees in company in 2020 are approximately what percent more or less than employees in company in 2019? (approx.)
(A) 4%   (B) 9%   (C) 12%   (D) 7%   (E) None of these

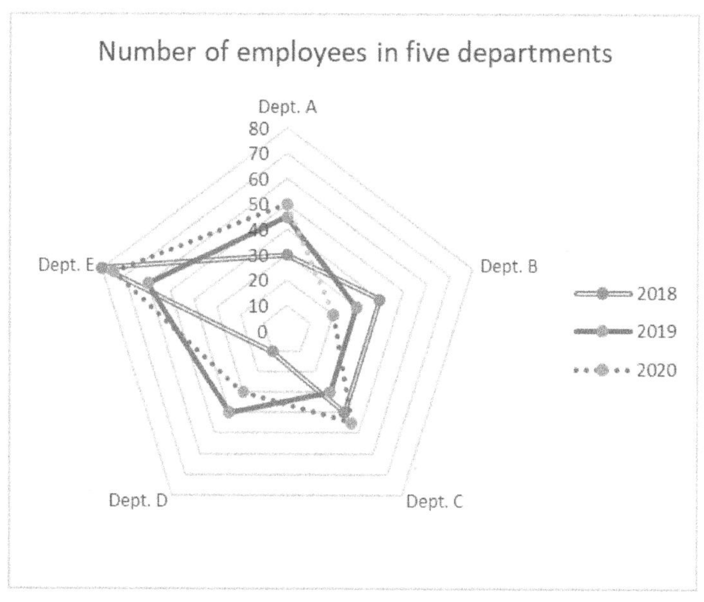

84. If in 2021, total employees in company are increased by 5% as compared to total employees in company in 2018 and ratio of employees (A: B: C: D: E) in 2021 is 14:5:10:4:9, then find the total employees in B & C together in 2021 are how much more/less than total employees in A in 2018 and 2020 together?

(A) 700   (B) 500   (C) 800   (D) 600   (E) None of these

85. Employees in A & E together in 2019 are what percent more /less than the employees in B, C & D together in 2018? (approx.)

(A) 17%   (B) 14%   (C) 20%   (D) 23%   (E) None of these

[86-90]

Given radar graph shows the number of products A, B, C & D manufactured in years 2019 & 2020. Study the graph carefully and answer the questions carefully.

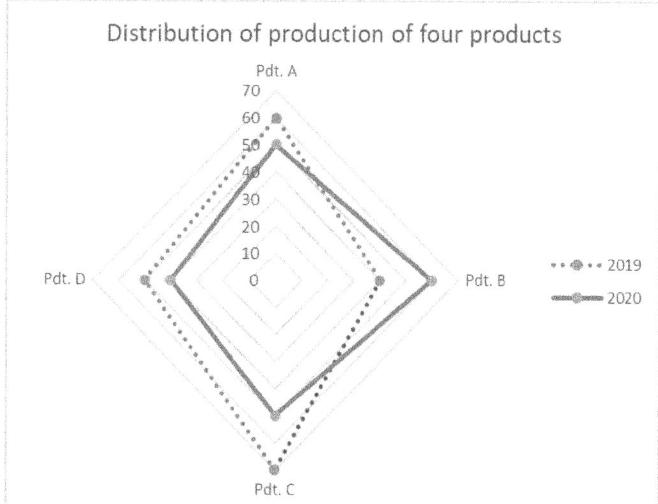

86. Product D manufactured in both years is what percent of product B manufactured in both years?

(A) 85%   (B) 80%   (C) 90%   (D) 95%   (E) None of these

87. What is the average production of products B & C together in 2020?
    (A) 50   (B) 60   (C) 65   (D) 55   (E) None of these

88. What is the ratio of products B & D manufactured in 2019 together to products A & C manufactured in 2020?
    (A) 9:10   (B) 10:9   (C) 9:8   (D) 8:9   (E) None of these

89. Average production of how many products in both the years together is more than average production of all products in 2019?
    (A) 1   (B) 2   (C) 3   (D) 4   (E) None of these

90. Product B manufactured in 2020 is what percent more/less than product C manufactured in 2019?
    (A) 14 2/7% less   (B) 14 4/7% more   (C) 14 4/7% less   (D) 14 2/7% more   (E) None of these

[91-95]

The given radar graph shows the number of students studying in five different sections in each of the two different classes.

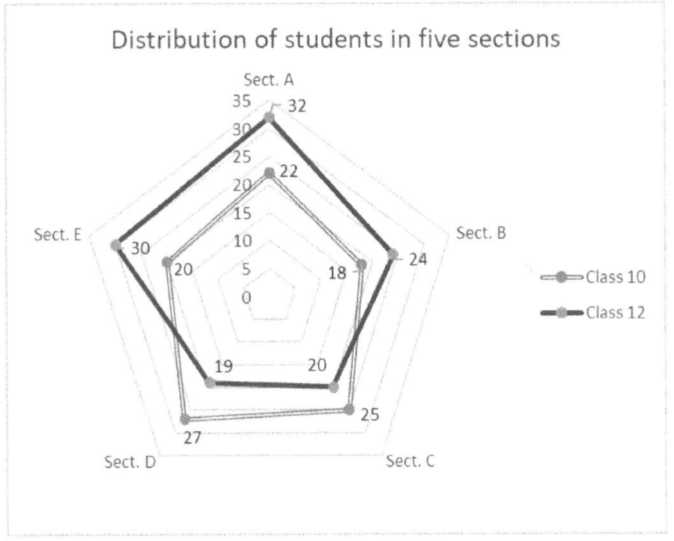

91. Number of students in section B &D together in class 10 is what percentage of students in section E of both the class together?
    (A) 70%   (B) 90%   (C) 85%   (D) 80%   (E) None of these

92. Find difference between the average number of students in section A, B and E of class 10 and average of students in section B, C and D of class 12
    (A) 2   (B) 3   (C) 1   (D) 5   (E) None of these

93. In a test, 50% of the students of section A, B and E of class 10 are passed and 18 students from each of the remaining two sections are passed in this test. Find the total number of students who failed in the test in class 10.
    (A) 50   (B) 42   (C) 48   (D) 46   (E) None of these

94. In class 10, ratio of number of girls to boys is 7:9 while in class 12 ratio of girls to boys is 2:3, then find the total number of girls in these two classes is what percent of total students in these classes? (approx.)
    (A) 42%   (B) 46%   (C) 38%   (D) 36%   (E) None of these

95. Find the ratio of number of students in section A, B and E in class 10 and students in section D in class 12 together to the total number of students in these two classes together.

    (A) 1:4   (B) 3:1   (C) 1:3   (D) 4:1   (E) None of these

SOLUTION:

[1-5]

A	65
B	80
C	100
D	95
E	90

1. (A) No. of copies of A & D sold $= 100 + 95 = 195$

No. of copies of A & B sold $= 65 + 80 = 145$

Required percentage $= \frac{195-145}{145} \times 100 = 34.48\% = 35\%$

2. (B) Required difference $= \left(\frac{65+80+95}{3}\right) \sim \left(\frac{100+90}{2}\right) = 80 - 95 = 15$

3. (D) Required percentage $= \frac{65}{80} \times 100 = 81.25\%$

4. (C) Required average $= \frac{65+80+100+95+90}{5} = \frac{430}{5} = 86$

5. (B) Average $= 86$

C, D, E are sold more than the average

[6-10]

COMPANIES	2016	2017	2018	2019
MARUTI	2400	4400	1800	2800
HYUNDAI	2300	2500	3500	2700

6. (C) Total Maruti cars $= 2400 + 4400 + 1800 + 2800 = 11,400$

7. (D) Difference $= (2300 + 2500) - (1800 + 2800) = 200$

8. (A) Required % $= \frac{1800}{2700} \times 100 = \frac{2}{3} \times 100 = 66\frac{2}{3}\%$

9. (B) Required ratio $= \frac{2300+2500+3500}{2400+4400+2800} = \frac{8300}{9600} = 83:96$

10. (D) Clearly, Maruti in 2017 shows maximum increase in production

Maruti (2017) $= \frac{4400-2400}{2400} \times 100 = 83.33\%$

[11-15]

SCHOOLS	2016	2017	2018	2019	2020
A	340	370	240	210	280
B	310	260	340	250	350
C	340	280	380	260	220

11. (D) Average number of students in

(i) School A across all the years $= \dfrac{340+370+340+210+280}{5} = 288$

(ii) School B across all the years $= \dfrac{260+340+250+350+310}{5} = 302$

Required difference $= 302 \sim 288 = 14$

12. (A) Required ratio $= \dfrac{340+280}{280+380} = \dfrac{620}{660} = \dfrac{31}{33}$

13. (B) Total number of students in 2021 in all the schools together

$$= \left(210 \times \frac{110}{100}\right) + \left(250 \times \frac{110}{100}\right) + \left(260 \times \frac{110}{100}\right)$$

$$= 231 + 300 + 299 = 830$$

14. (C) Required percentage $= \dfrac{(370+260+280)-(350+250)}{(350+250)} \times 100$

$$= \dfrac{910-600}{600} \times 100 = \dfrac{310}{600} \times 100 = 51.667\% \;\; = 52\%$$

15. (A) Total no. of students from all the schools 2017 & 2020 together

$= (370 + 260 + 280) + (280 + 350 + 220) = 1760$

Total no. of students from all the schools in 2018 & 2019 together

$= (240 + 340 + 380) + (210 + 250 + 260) = 1680$

Required difference $= 1760 - 1680 = 80$

[16-20]

Production of mobile phone

	2016	2017	2018	2019	2020
Apple	70	80	90	70	70
Samsung	80	70	70	100	50
Lenova	100	90	50	80	60

16. (A) Required % $= \dfrac{100 \sim 50}{100} \times 100 = 50\%$

17. (D) Average production over the years for

(i) Lenovo: $= \dfrac{100+90+50+80+60}{5} = \dfrac{380}{5} = 76$ lakhs

(ii) Samsung: $\dfrac{80+70+70+100+50}{5} = \dfrac{370}{5} = 74$ lakhs

(iii) Apple : $\dfrac{70+80+90+70+70}{5} = \dfrac{380}{5} = 76$ lakhs

18. (D) Percentage rise /fall in the production of Samsung in different years.

(i) $2017 = \dfrac{80\sim70}{80} \times 100 = 12.5\,\%$ fall

(ii) $2018 = \dfrac{70\sim70}{70} \times 100 = 0\,\%$

(iii) $2019 = \dfrac{100\sim70}{70} \times 100 = 42.8\%$ rise

(iv) $2020 = \dfrac{100\sim50}{100} \times 100 = 50\%$ fall

2020 has the highest numeric value.

19. (C) Percentage of production of company Apple as compared to Samsung for the year,

(i) $2016 = \dfrac{70}{80} \times 100 = 87.5\,\%$

(ii) $2017 = \dfrac{80}{70} \times 100 = 114.3\%$

(iii) $2018 = \dfrac{90}{70} \times 100 = 128.6\%$

(iv) $2019 = \dfrac{70}{100} \times 100 = 70\,\%$

(v) $2020 = \dfrac{70}{50} \times 100 = 140\%$

It is clear, 2020 has the highest value.

20. (A) Required ratio $= \dfrac{\frac{100+90+50}{3}}{\frac{80+70+70}{3}} = \dfrac{240}{220} = \dfrac{12}{11}$

[21-25]

Days	No. of items of A	% of items of B	% of items of C
Monday	320	48%	12%
Tuesday	360	56%	20%
Wednesday	240	32%	20%
Thursday	340	22%	10%
Friday	420	45%	20%

21. (D) Total items of B sold by store on Wednesday & Thursday

$= \dfrac{240}{(100-(32+20))} \times 32 + \dfrac{340}{(100-(22+10))} \times 22$

$= \dfrac{240}{48} \times 22 + \dfrac{340}{68} \times 22 = 160 + 110 = 270$

Total items C sold by store on Tuesday & Friday $= \dfrac{420}{35} \times 20 + \dfrac{360}{24} \times 20$

$$= 240 + 300 = 540$$

Required % $= \dfrac{540-270}{540} \times 100 = \dfrac{270}{540} \times 100 = 50\%$

22. (B) Average no. of item B sold by store on Monday & Tuesday

$$= \frac{\left(\frac{320}{40}\times 48\right) + \left(\frac{360}{24}\times 56\right)}{2} = \frac{384+840}{2} = 612$$

Average no. of item A sold by store on Tuesday & Thursday $= \frac{360+340}{2} = \frac{700}{2} = 350$

Required difference = 612 - 350 = 262

23. (A) Total items B sold by store on Saturday $= \frac{360}{4} \times 56 \times \frac{125}{100} = 1050$

Total items C sold by store on Saturday $= \frac{340}{68} \times 10 \times \frac{400}{100} = 1200$

Total items B & C sold by store on Saturday $= 1050 + 1200 = 2250$

24. (C) Total items C sold by store on Friday $= \frac{420}{35} \times 20 = 240$

Total item C sold on Monday & Tuesday together $= \left(\frac{240}{48} \times 20\right) + \left(\frac{320}{40} \times 12\right)$

$$= 100 + 96 = 196$$

Required $= \frac{240-196}{196} \times 100 = \frac{44}{196} \times 100 = 22.45\%$

25. (B) Required ratio $= \frac{\frac{240}{48}\times 100}{\frac{360}{24}\times 100} = \frac{500}{1500} = 1:3$

[26-30]

Days	No. of items of A	% of items of B	% of items of C
Monday	320	48%	12%
Tuesday	360	56%	20%
Wednesday	240	32%	20%
Thursday	340	22%	10%
Friday	420	45%	20%

26. (B) Total candidates from city Q $= 440 \times \frac{100}{55} = 800$

Total candidates who completed exam from Q $= 800 - 105 = 695$

Total candidates from city T $= 500 \times \frac{100}{40} = 1250$

Total candidates who completed exam from T $= 1250 - 90 = 1160$

Required difference $= 1160 - 695 = 465$

27. (D) Candidates who did not complete online & offline exam from city T $= \frac{90}{2} = 45$

Candidates from city T who completed

(i) Online exams $= 500 - 45 = 455$

(ii) Offline exams $= 750 - 45 = 705$

Required % = $\frac{705-455}{455} \times 100$

28. (C) Total candidates who appeared in online exam in all cities

= 320 + 440 + 460 + 525 + 500 = 2245

Total candidates who appeared in offline exam in all cities

= $\left(320 \times \frac{36}{100}\right) + \left(440 \times \frac{45}{100}\right) + \left(460 \times \frac{54}{100}\right) + \left(525 \times \frac{30}{100}\right) + (500 \times \frac{60}{100})$

= 360 + 180 + 540 + 750 + 225 = 2055

Required difference = 2245 – 2055 = 190

29. (A) Total candidates who appeared in online exam in cities R & T together

= 460 + 500 = 960

Total candidates who appeared in offline exam in cities Q & R together

= $\left(320 \times \frac{36}{64}\right) + \left(\frac{440}{55} \times 45\right)$

= 360 + 180 = 540

Required ratio = $\frac{960}{540} = \frac{16}{9}$

30. (E) Total candidates who appeared in offline exam in cities P & Q together

= $\left(\frac{440}{55} \times 45\right) + \left(\frac{320}{64} \times 36\right)$ = 360 + 180 = 540

Total candidates who appeared in online exams in city Q = 440

Required % = $\frac{540}{440} \times 100 = 122.72\,\%$

[31-35]

City	No. of persons with disabilities	Ratio of male to female
Chennai	36,300	2:1
Pune	42,400	3:1
Mumbai	18,600	5:1
Delhi	24,500	3:2
Bangalore	27,000	5:4

31. (A) Required % = $\frac{\frac{1}{3}\times36,300}{\frac{1}{6}\times18,600} \times 100 = \frac{12,100}{31} = 390\%$

32. (B) Required average = $\frac{1}{2}\left(\left(\frac{3}{4} \times 42,400\right) + \left(\frac{3}{5} \times 24,500\right)\right)$

= $\frac{1}{2}(31,800 + 14,700) = \frac{1}{2} \times 46,500 = 23,250$

33. (A) Total No. of females

$$= \frac{1}{3}(36,300) + \frac{1}{4}(42,400) + \frac{1}{6}(18,600) + \frac{2}{5}(24,500) + \frac{4}{9}(27,000)$$

$$= 49,300$$

34. (A) Required difference $= \left[\frac{2}{3}(36,300) + \frac{5}{9}(27,000)\right] - \left[\frac{1}{3}(36,300) + \frac{4}{9}(27,000)\right]$

$$= 24,200 + 15,000 - 12,100 - 12,000 = 15,100$$

35. (C) Required $= \frac{36,300 - 27,000}{27,000} \times 100 = \frac{310}{9}\,\% = 34\,\frac{4}{9}\,\%$

[36-40]

	Maths (150)	Physics (150)	Chemistry (150)	English (100)	Computer (100)
P	50	64	78	65	75
Q	70	66	58	54	80
R	76	82	64	72	94
S	80	76	84	75	85
T	48	72	88	70	86

36. (C) Total marks scored by

(i) S in given three subjects $= \left(\frac{80}{100} \times 150\right) + \left(\frac{76}{100} \times 150\right) + \left(\frac{84}{100} + 150\right)$

$$= 120 + 114 + 126 = 360$$

(ii) Q in given three subjects $= \left(\frac{70}{100} \times 150\right) + \left(\frac{66}{100} \times 150\right) + \left(\frac{58}{100} \times 150\right)$

$$= 105 + 99 + 87 = 291$$

Required difference $= 360 - 291 = 69$

37. (B) Total marks scored by T in all subject

$$= \left(\frac{48}{100} \times 150\right) + \left(\frac{72}{100} \times 150\right) + \left(\frac{88}{100} \times 150\right) + \left(\frac{70}{100} \times 100\right) + \left(\frac{86}{100} \times 100\right)$$

$$= 72 + 108 + 132 + 70 + 86 = 468$$

Overall personage $= \frac{468}{650} \times 100 = 72\%$

38. (A) Total Marks scored in all subject

(i) By R $= \left(\frac{76}{100} \times 150\right) + \left(\frac{82}{100} \times 150\right) + \left(\frac{64}{100} \times 150\right) + \left(\frac{72}{100} \times 100\right) + \left(\frac{94}{100} \times 100\right)$

$$= 114 + 123 + 96 + 72 + 94 = 499$$

(ii) By P $= \left(\frac{50}{100} \times 150\right) + \left(\frac{64}{100} \times 150\right) + \left(\frac{78}{100} \times 150\right) + \left(\frac{65}{100} \times 100\right) + \left(\frac{75}{100} \times 100\right)$

$$= 75 + 96 + 117 + 65 + 75 = 428$$

Required difference $= 499 - 428 = 71$

39. (D) Marks scored in physics by all 5 students

$$= \left(150 \times \frac{64}{100}\right) + \left(150 \times \frac{66}{100}\right) + \left(150 \times \frac{82}{100}\right) + \left(150 \times \frac{76}{100}\right) + \left(150 \times \frac{72}{100}\right)$$

$$= 99 + 96 + 108 + 114 + 123 = 540$$

$$\text{Average} = \frac{540}{5} = 108$$

40. (D) Total marks scored by P, S & T in English

$$= \left(\frac{65}{100} \times 100\right) + \left(\frac{70}{100} \times 100\right) + \left(\frac{75}{100} \times 100\right) + \left(\frac{75}{100} \times 100\right)$$

$$= 65 + 70 + 75 = 210$$

Total marks scored by P, Q & S in months $= \left(\frac{70}{100} \times 150\right) + \left(\frac{50}{100} \times 150\right) + \left(\frac{80}{100} \times 150\right)$

$$= 105 + 75 + 120 = 300$$

Required % $= \frac{210}{300} \times 100 = 70\%$

[41-45]

Sports	Distribution	No. of players
Badminton	60°	240
Cricket	80°	320
Baseball	60°	240
Golf	40°	160
Basketball	70°	280
Tennis	50°	200

41. (B) No. of players playing Cricket & Baseball $= \frac{80+60}{360} \times 1440 = \frac{140}{360} \times 1440 = 560$

42. (A) Required ratio $= \dfrac{\frac{60+70}{360} \times 1440}{\frac{50+40}{360} \times 1440} = \frac{130}{90} = 13:9$

43. (D) Required average $= \dfrac{\frac{(70+50+60)}{360} \times 1440}{3} = \frac{180}{360} \times \frac{1440}{3} = 240$

44. (C) Female cricket players $= \frac{80}{360} \times 1440 \times \frac{50}{100} = 160$

Female baseball players $= 160$

Total baseball players $= \frac{60}{360} \times 1440 = 240$

Male baseball players $= 240 - 160 = 80$

45. (B) Required percentage $= \dfrac{\frac{(60+40+70)}{360} \times 1440}{\frac{(80+60)}{360} \times 1440} \times 100 = \frac{170}{140} \times 100 = 121.43\%$

[46-50]

Depts.	Total employees		Male employees		Female
Finance	20%	16000	28%	14000	2000
Marketing	24%	19200	30%	15000	4200
HR	16%	12800	25%	12500	300
R&D	8%	6400	5%	2500	3900
Production	32%	25600	12%	6000	19600

46. (C) Required no. of female employees

$$= \left(80{,}000 \times \tfrac{32}{100} - 50{,}000 \times \tfrac{12}{100}\right) + \left(80{,}000 \times \tfrac{16}{100} - 50{,}000 \times \tfrac{25}{100}\right) + \left(80{,}000 \times \tfrac{8}{100} - 50{,}000 \times \tfrac{5}{100}\right)$$

$$= (25{,}600 - 6000) + (12800 - 12{,}500) + (6400 - 2500)$$

$$= 19{,}600 + 300 + 3{,}900 = 23{,}800$$

47. (B) Female employees in Marketing & HR

$$= \left(80{,}000 \times \tfrac{24}{100} - 50{,}000 \times \tfrac{30}{100}\right) + (80{,}000 \times \tfrac{16}{100} - 50{,}000 \times \tfrac{25}{100})$$

$$= (19{,}200 - 15{,}000) + (12{,}800 - 12{,}500) = 4200 + 300 = 4500$$

Total employees in production department $= \dfrac{32}{100} \times 80{,}000 = 25{,}600$

Required percentage $= \dfrac{4500}{25{,}600} \times 100 \approx 17.58\%$

48. (C) Required percentage $= \dfrac{\left(\frac{25+5+12}{100} \times 50{,}000\right)}{3} = \dfrac{42}{300} \times 50{,}000 = 7000$

49. (A) Required percentage $= \dfrac{\frac{(30+5)}{100} \times 50{,}000}{\frac{(24+8)}{100} \times 80{,}000} \times 100 = \dfrac{35 \times 5}{32 \times 8} \times 100 \approx 68.36\% \approx 68\%$

50. (D) Male employees in Production & Finance departments $= \dfrac{28+12}{100} \times 50{,}000 = 20{,}000$

Female employees in production & finance departments

$$= \left[\left(\tfrac{32}{100} \times 80{,}000\right) - \left(\tfrac{12}{100} \times 50{,}000\right) + \left(\tfrac{20}{100} \times 80{,}000\right) - \left(\tfrac{28}{100} \times 50{,}000\right)\right]$$

$$= (25{,}600 - 6000) + (16{,}000 - 14{,}000) = 19{,}600 + 2000 = 21{,}600$$

Ratio $= \dfrac{20{,}000}{21{,}600} = \dfrac{25}{27}$

[51-55]

Sports	Spectators	No.
Hockey	14%	2940
Tennis	18%	3780
Badminton	16%	3360

Football	22%	4620
Cricket	23%	4830
Golf	7%	1470

51. (B) Total spectators of

(i) Cricket & Golf $= 21,000 \times \frac{(23+7)}{100} = 6300$

(ii) Tennis & Football $= 21,000 \times \frac{(18+22)}{100} = 8400$

Required % $= \frac{6300}{8400} \times 100 = 75\%$

52. (D) Ratio $= \frac{\frac{16+14}{100} \times 21,000}{\frac{22}{100} \times 21,000} = \frac{30}{22} = 15:11$

53. (A) Required central angle $= \frac{23+14}{100} \times 360 = \frac{37}{100} \times 360 = 133.2°$

54. (C) Total tennis spectators $= \frac{18}{100} \times 21,000 = 3780$

Required difference $= \frac{3}{15} \times 3780 = 756$

55. (B) Total spectators of

- Badminton & Football $= \frac{16+22}{100} \times 21,000 = 7980$

- Cricket & Hockey $= \frac{23+14}{100} \times 21,000 = 7770$

Required difference $= 7980 - 7770 = 210$

[56-60]

Product	Revenue	
A	20%	60,000
B	13%	39,000
C	18.50%	55,500
D	5%	15,000
E	15%	45,000
F	28.50%	85,000

56. (D) Required difference $= \frac{28.5-13}{100} \times 3,00,000 = Rs\ 46,500$

57. (A) Required central angle $= \frac{(13.5+18.5+28.5)\sim20}{100} \times 360 = \frac{60\sim20}{100} \times 360 = 144°$

58. (B) Required % $= \frac{\frac{(18.5-5)}{100} \times 3,00,000}{\frac{5}{100} \times 3,00,000} \times 100 = \frac{13.5}{5} \times 100 = 270\%$

59. (C) Total no. of items of product B sold $= 3,00,000 \times \frac{13}{100} \times \frac{1}{7800} = \frac{39,00,000}{7,80,000} = 5$

Required % $= \frac{5-4}{4} \times 100 = \frac{1}{4} \times 100 = 25\%$

60. (B) Required revenue $= 3,00,000 \times \frac{(20+18.5)}{100} = 3,00,000 \times \frac{38.5}{100} = $ Rs 1,15,500

[61-65]

	2015	2016	2017	2018	2019	2020
Person A	45	55	40	45	70	60
Person B	55	45	65	70	60	40

61. (D) Overall profit percentage of

- A $= 45 + 55 + 40 + 45 + 70 + 60 = 315$

- B $= 55 + 45 + 65 + 70 + 60 + 40 = 335$

Average profit percentage $= \frac{335+315}{12} = \frac{650}{12} = 54.167\% \approx 54\%$

62. (B) Required income = Profit + Expenditure

$= \frac{45}{100} \times 10,00,000 + 10,00,000 = 4,50,000 + 10,00,000 = $ Rs 14,50,000

63. (C) Expenditure of

- A $= \frac{41,60,000}{1.6} = 26,00,000$

- B $= \frac{37,40,000}{1.7} = 22,00,000$

Required % $= \frac{26,00,000-22,00,000}{22,00,000} \times 100 = \frac{4,00,000}{22,00,000} \times 100 = 18.18\%$

64. (A) Clearly, since the profit percentage is maximum in 2019, Expenditure is minimum in 2019.

Expenditure in 2019 $= \frac{6,80,000}{1.7} = $ Rs 4,00,000

65. (B) Required ratio in

- 2015 $= \frac{45}{55} \cong 0.82$

- 2016 $= \frac{55}{45} \cong 1.22$

- 2017 $= \frac{40}{65} \cong 0.62$

- 2018 $= \frac{45}{70} \cong 0.64$

- 2019 $= \frac{70}{60} \cong 1.17$

- 2020 $= \frac{60}{40} \cong 1.5$

2020 has the highest numerical value.

[66-70]

Shops	Percentage
A	16
B	24
C	12
D	32
E	4
F	12

66. (A) Required % $= \frac{(32+12)-(16+24)}{(16+24)} \times 100 = \frac{44-40}{40} \times 100 = 10\%$

67. (B) Total stools sold in shop E $= \frac{4}{100} \times 48{,}000 = 1920$

Required difference $= \frac{(4+3)-5}{12} \times 1920 = \frac{2}{12} \times 1920 = 320$

68. (D) Average % of stools sold $= \frac{16+24+12+32+4+12}{6} = \frac{100}{6} = 16.67\%$

2 shops sold stools more than the average.

69. (C) Required difference $= \left[\frac{(16+12)}{100} - \frac{(4+12)}{100}\right] \times 48{,}000 = \frac{28-16}{100} \times 48{,}000 = 5760$

70. (C) Required ratio $= \frac{\frac{16+24+12}{3}}{\frac{32+12}{2}} = \frac{52 \times 2}{44 \times 3} = \frac{26}{33}$

[71-75]

	2016	2017	2018	2019
Product A	25,000	45,000	20,000	30,000
Product B	20,000	30,000	30,000	50,000
Product C	45,000	20,000	35,000	45,000

71. (A) Required difference $= \frac{45{,}000+35{,}000}{2} \sim \frac{45{,}000+30{,}000}{2} = 40{,}000 - 37{,}500 = 2500$

72. (B) Required % $= \frac{20{,}000+50{,}000}{45{,}000+20{,}000} \times 100 = \frac{70{,}000}{65{,}000} \times 100 \cong 108\%$

73. (C) For 2020, production of

- Product A $= 30{,}000 \times \frac{125}{100} = 37{,}500$

- Product B $= 50{,}000 \times \frac{90}{100} = 45{,}000$

- Product C $= 45{,}000 \times \frac{120}{100} = 54{,}000$

Required ratio $= \frac{37{,}500+54{,}000}{45{,}000} = \frac{91{,}500}{45{,}000} = \frac{61}{30}$

74. (D)

- Product A & C produced in 2016, 2017 & 2018

$$= 25{,}000 + 45{,}000 + 20{,}000 + 45{,}000 + 20{,}000 + 35{,}000 = 1{,}90{,}000$$

- Product B produced in 2018 & 2019 $= 30{,}000 + 50{,}000 = 80{,}000$

Required % $= \dfrac{1{,}90{,}000 - 80{,}000}{80{,}000} \times 100 = 137.5\%$

75. (A) Product A sold in

- $2017 = 45{,}000 \times \dfrac{85}{100} = 38{,}250$

- $2018 = 20{,}000 \times \dfrac{95}{100} = 19{,}000$

- $2019 = 30{,}000 \times \dfrac{95}{100} = 28{,}500$

Required ratio $= \dfrac{38{,}250 + 19{,}000}{28{,}500} = \dfrac{57{,}250}{28{,}500} = \dfrac{229}{114}$

[76-80]

	1	2	3	4	5
Team India	240	280	380	250	320
Team England	320	220	300	180	360

76. (B) Required % $= \dfrac{280 + 320}{320 + 180} \times 100 = \dfrac{600}{500} \times 100 = 120\%$

77. (A) Difference $= 360 - 240 = 120$ runs

78. (D) Required ratio $= \dfrac{240 + 280 + 380 + 250 + 320}{320 + 220 + 300 + 180 + 360} = \dfrac{1470}{1380} = \dfrac{49}{46}$

79. (C) Required % $= \dfrac{300 - 240}{300} \times 100 = \dfrac{60}{300} \times 100 = 20\%$

80. (A) It is clear that India won 3 matches (2nd, 3rd & 4th)

[81-85]

	2018	2019	2020
Dept. A	30	45	50
Dept. B	40	30	20
Dept. C	40	30	45
Dept. D	10	40	30
Dept. E	80	60	75

81. (C) Average no. of employees in C, D, E in 2020 $= \dfrac{4500 + 3000 + 7500}{3} = 5000$

Employees in D & E in 2019 $= 4000 + 6000 = 10{,}000$

Required % $= \dfrac{5000}{10{,}000} \times 100 = 50\%$

82. (B) Employees in D in 2018, 2019 & 2020 $= 1000 + 4000 + 3000 = 8000$

Employees in E in 2019 & 2020 $= 6000 + 7500 = 13{,}500$

Required ratio $= \dfrac{8000}{13,500} = \dfrac{16}{27}$

83. (D) Employees in the company 2020 $= 5000 + 2000 + 4500 + 3000 + 7500 = 22,000$

Employees in the company 2019 $= 4500 + 3000 + 3000 + 4000 + 6000 = 20,500$

Required % $= \dfrac{22,000 - 20,500}{20,500} \times 100 = 7.31\% \cong 7\%$

84. (B) Total employees in company in 2021 $= \dfrac{105}{100} \times (3000 + 4000 + 4000 + 1000 + 8000)$

$= \dfrac{105}{100} \times 20,000 = 21,000$

Total employees in B & C together in 2021 $= 21,000 \times \dfrac{5+10}{(14+5+10+4+9)} = 21,000 \times \dfrac{15}{42} =$

7500

Total employees in A in 2018 & 2020 together $= 3000 + 5000 = 8000$

Required difference $= 8000 - 7500 = 500$

85. (A) Employees in A & E together in 2019 $= 4500 + 6000 = 10,500$

Employees in B, C & D together in 2018 $= 4000 + 4000 + 1000 = 9000$

Required % $= \dfrac{10,500 - 9000}{9000} \times 100 = \dfrac{1500}{9000} \times 100 = 16.67\% \cong 17\%$

[86-90]

	2019	2020
Pdt. A	60	50
Pdt. B	40	60
Pdt. C	70	50
Pdt. D	50	40

86. (C) Required % $= \dfrac{50+40}{40+60} \times 100 = \dfrac{90}{100} \times 100 = 90\%$

87. (D) Required average $= \dfrac{60+70}{2} = \dfrac{130}{2} = 55$

88. (A) Required ratio $= \dfrac{40+50}{50+60} = 9:10$

89. (B) Average production in 2019 $= \dfrac{60+40+70+50}{4} = \dfrac{220}{4} = 55$

Average production of

- A $= \dfrac{60+50}{2} = \dfrac{110}{2} = 55$

- B $= \dfrac{40+60}{2} = \dfrac{100}{2} = 50$

- C $= \dfrac{70+50}{2} = \dfrac{120}{2} = 60$

- D $= \dfrac{50+40}{2} = \dfrac{90}{2} = 45$

Product C alone is more than average.

90. (A) Required % $= \frac{70-60}{70} \times 100 = \frac{1000}{70} = 14\,^2/_7\,\%$ less

[91-95]

	Class 10	Class 12
Sect. A	22	32
Sect. B	18	24
Sect. C	25	20
Sect. D	27	19
Sect. E	20	30

91. (B) Required % $= \frac{(18+27)}{(20+30)} \times 100 = \frac{45}{50} \times 100 = 90\%$

92. (C) Required difference $= (\frac{22+18+20}{3}) \sim (\frac{24+20+19}{3}) = \frac{60}{3} \sim \frac{63}{3} = \frac{3}{3} = 1$

93. (D) Total number of students who failed in the test

$$= (22 + 18 + 20) \times \frac{50}{100} + (25 - 18) + (27 - 18)$$

$$= 60 \times \frac{50}{100} + 7 + 9 = 30 + 16 = 46$$

94. (A) Total students in class $10 = 22 + 18 + 25 + 27 + 20 = 112$

No. of girls in class $10 = 112 \times \frac{7}{(7+9)} = 49$

Total students in class $12 = 32 + 24 + 20 + 19 + 30 = 125$

No. of girls in class $12 = 125 \times \frac{2}{(2+3)} = 50$

Required percentage $= \frac{(49+50)}{(112+125)} \times 100 = \frac{99}{237} \times 100 = 41.77\% \cong 42\%$

95. (C) Required ratio $= \frac{(22+18+20+19)}{112+125} = \frac{79}{237} = 1:3$

PRACTICE:

BAR GRAPH

Study the charts given below and answer the following questions:

[1-5]
The bar group given below show the production of wheat (in tonnes) in a village in 5 different years.
1. Wheat production in 2020 is what percent of that in 2017?
    (A) 54.2%　　　　(B) 55.55%　　(C) 52%　　　　(D) 58%　　　　(E) None of these
2. Find the average production of wheat in given period.
    (A) 389 tonnes　　(B) 394 tonnes　(C) 372 tonnes　(D) 386 tonnes　(E) None of these

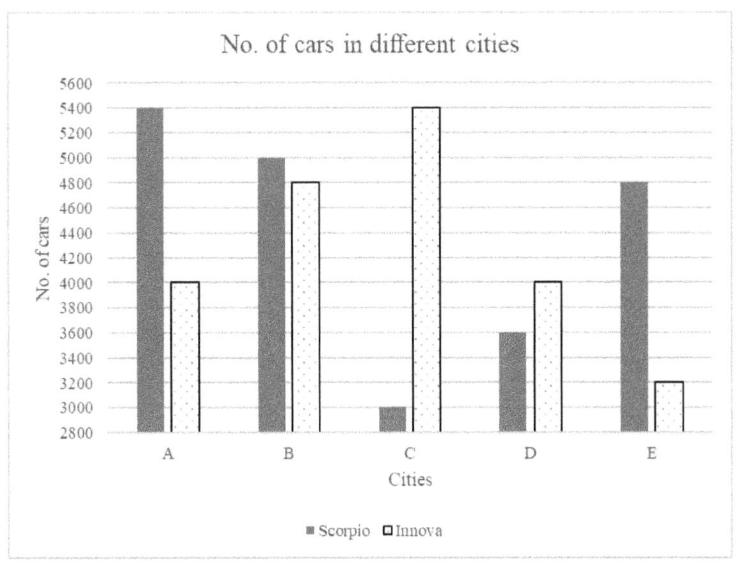

3. What is percentage rise or fall in production of wheat in 2017 from 2016?
   (A) 15%   (B) 40%   (C) 20%   (D) 35%   (E) None of these
4. What is the ratio of wheat produced in 2019 and 2020 together to that in 2017 & 2018 together?
   (A) 29:45   (B) 45:29   (C) 29:46   (D) 28:47   (E) None of these
5. Wheat produced in 2020 is what percentage more (or) less than that in 2018?
   (A) 15%   (B) 16.67%   (C) 18%   (D) 15.45%   (E) None of these

[6-10]

Bar chart shown the total number of scored and Innova cars in 5 different circus A, B, C, D and E in 2019.

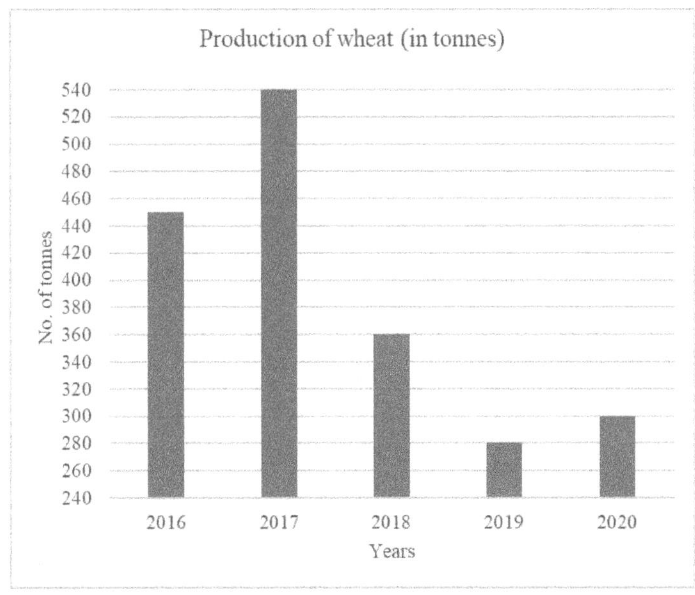

6. Total number of Scorpio cars in A & B together is what percent more /less than total number Innova cars in A & C together? (approx.)
   (A) 7%   (B) 9%   (C) 13%   (D) 11%   (E) None of these

7. Find ratio of total Scorpio cars in D & E together to total Innova cars in B & E together
   (A) 22:19   (B) 21:20   (C) 20:21   (D) 21:19   (E) None of these
8. Total number of Innova cars in D & E together is how much more or less than total number of Scorpio cars in C & A together (approx.)
   (A) 14.3 %   (B) 12.8%   (C) 13.6%   (D) 15.5 %   (E) None of these
9. If total number of Baleno cars in E are 20% less than total number of Scorpio are in B, then find total number of Baleno cars in E are how much more or less than total number of Scorpio cars in E?
   (A) 750   (B) 800   (C) 600   (D) 850   (E) None of these
10. Find difference between the total number of Scorpio cars in all five cities together and total number of Innova cars in five cities together.
   (A) 200   (B) 300   (C) 500   (D) 450   (E) None of these

[11-15]
Preference of people in playing different games over the years.

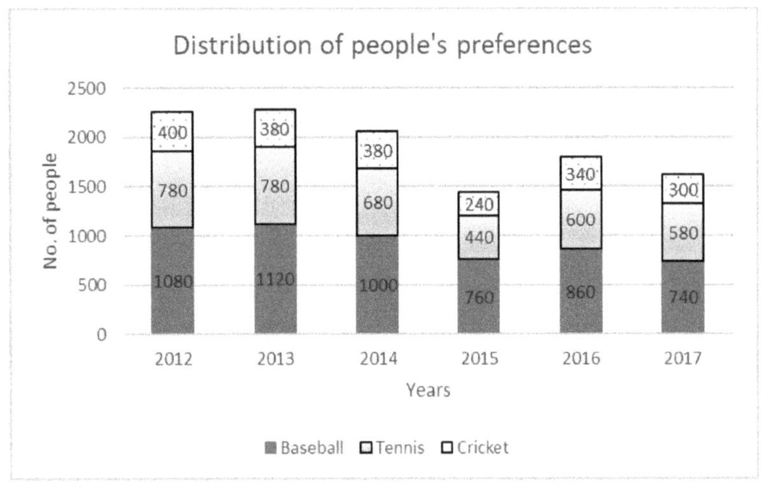

11. In the year 2017, the people preferring to play Baseball is what percent of the people preferring to play Baseball, Tennis & Cricket together in that year?
    (A) 23 4/7 %   (B)19 14/17 %   (C) 21 33/37 %   (D) 21 21/26 %   (E) None of these
12. From 2012 to 2017, the total number of people who preferred to play Tennis was how much? (in millions)
    (A) 1760   (B) 1840   (C) 1880   (D) 1920   (E) None of these
13. The number of people preferring to play Baseball in 2017 is how many million fewer than the number of people preferring to play Baseball in 2016?
    (A) 200   (B) 150   (C) 100   (D) 50   (E) None of these
14. What is the respective ratio of the number of people preferring to play cricket to the number of people preferring to play baseball in the year 2014?
    (A) 19:16   (B) 16:19   (C) 18:17   (D) 19:21   (E)None of these
15. How many people (in millions) have preferred to play cricket in all the years together?
    (A) 2050   (B) 2030   (C) 2020   (D) 2040   (E) None of these

TABLE:

[16-20]

Given table shows the data of students of a class related to results of semester 1 and semester 2 examination.

Students who have	Department 1	Department 2	Department 3
• Failed in both semesters	10	15	20
• Passed in semester I	40	25	30
• Passed in semester I	30	30	35
• Passed in both semesters	20	20	25

16. How many students are there in Department 2 of class?
(A) 50   (B) 100   (C) 60   (D) 40   (E) None of these

17. Students passed in both exams in all sections are what percent more/less than students failed in both exams in all sections?
(A) 47.23%   (B) 41%   (C) 44.44%   (D) 49%   (E) None of these

18. What is the average of students who passed in only one examination in all sections together? (approx.)
(A) 38.6   (B) 41.7   (C) 40.3   (D) 43.2   (E) None of these

19. Students failed in both exams in department 2 are what percent of total students in Department 2?
(A) 38%   (B) 25%   (C) 20%   (D) 30%   (E) None of these

20. Which Departments have equal number of students?
(A) Dept A & B   (B) Dept B & C   (C) Dept A & C   (D) All three depts   (E) None of these

[21-25]

Following table gives the details of items sold by two different stores ie., Store A and Store B and among them percentage of number of items purchased by females are given.

Days	Store A		Store B	
	Total items	% of items purchased by females	Total items	% of items purchased by females
Monday	280	45%	440	65%
Tuesday	230	30%	320	30%
Wednesday	335	40%	270	80%
Thursday	420	65%	275	40%
Friday	360	60%	380	25%

21. Items purchased by females from store A on Wednesday & Friday together is how much percent more/less than the total items purchased by males from store B on Friday and Thursday together? (approx.)
(A) 22.22%   (B) 44.44%   (C) 33.33%   (D) 11.11%   (E) None of these

22. Find the respective ratio between total number of items purchased by males from store A on Monday and Wednesday together to the total number of items purchased by females from store B on Friday & Thursday together?
(A) 41:73   (B) 41:71   (C) 43:71   (D) 71:41   (E) None of these

23. Find the total number of items purchased by males from store B on all the given days together?
(A) 879   (B) 885   (C) 874   (D) 882   (E) None of these

24. Total items purchased on Thursday & Friday together of store A is what percentage of total items purchased on Wednesday & Friday together of store B?
(A) 140%   (B) 120%   (C) 100%   (D) 110%   (E) None of these

25. If total items purchased from store A and store B on Saturday are 20% more and 30% more respectively than the total items sold by store A and store B on Wednesday, then find the total number of items purchased from store A and store B together on Saturday?
(A) 743   (B) 757   (C) 753   (D) 750   (E) None of these

[26-30]

Table given below shows the percentage of football players in five different colleges in two different years and the difference between football and basketball players in five different colleges in the given years. Note: In all the five given colleges only two games are being played (Football and Basketball).

College	2018		2019	
	% of football players	Difference in no. of players	% of football players	Difference in no. of players
A	25%	150	45%	80
B	40%	80	80%	120
C	55%	100	75%	250
D	70%	320	60%	140
E	20%	180	48%	160

26. Basketball players in colleges B and E together in year 2018 is how much more/less than Football players in same colleges together in the year 2019?
(A) 1500   (B) 1600   (C) 1800   (D) 1900   (E) None of these

27. Football players in colleges C and D together in year 2018 is what percent of Basketball Players in college A in year 2019? (approx.)
(A) 270%   (B) 247%   (C) 253%   (D) 223%   (E) None of these

28. Find the average of Football players in college A in year 2018, college E in the year 2018 and college E in the year 2019?
(A) 685   (B) 675   (C) 692   (D) 650   (E) None of these

29. What is the ratio of Basketball players in college A in the year 2019 to the Football players in college C in the year 2018?
(A) 5:4   (B) 5:3   (C) 3:5   (D) 4:5   (E) None of these

30. Basketball players in college D in year 2019 is what percent more/less than Football players in same college in the year 2018?
(A) 42%   (B) 50%   (C) 56%   (D) 60%   (E) None of these

PIE CHART

[31-35]

Given below pie chart shows percentage distribution of total students in five different schools.

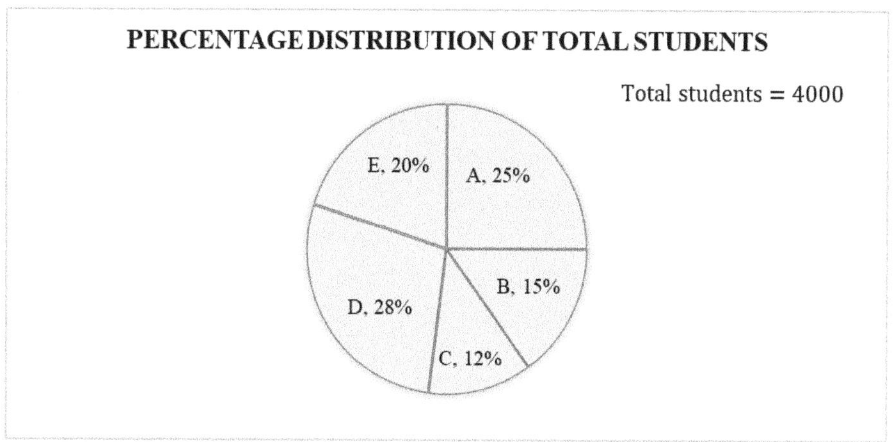

31. If the ratio of girls to boys in the schools E & B are 3:5 and 5:7 respectively, then find the difference between no. of girls in schools E & B.

(A) 50   (B) 60   (C) 40   (D) 80   (E) None of these

32. Find the central angle for total number of students in schools D and E together.

(A) 170.6°   (B) 172.8°   (C) 168.4°   (D) 174.5°   (E) None of these

33. Total students in school D is what percent more than the total students in school A?

(A) 15%   (B) 10%   (C) 14%   (D) 12%   (E) None of these

34. Find the average number of students in C, D and E.

(A) 500   (B) 600   (C) 800   (D) 700   (E) None of these

35. If the total students in school F is 25% more than that of in school C and ratio of girls to boys in school F is 3:5, find the difference between boys and girls in school F.

(A) 75   (B) 150   (C) 100   (D) 125   (E) None of these

[36-40]

Pie chart given below shows percentage breakup of marks obtained by Edward in five different exams of 100 marks each.

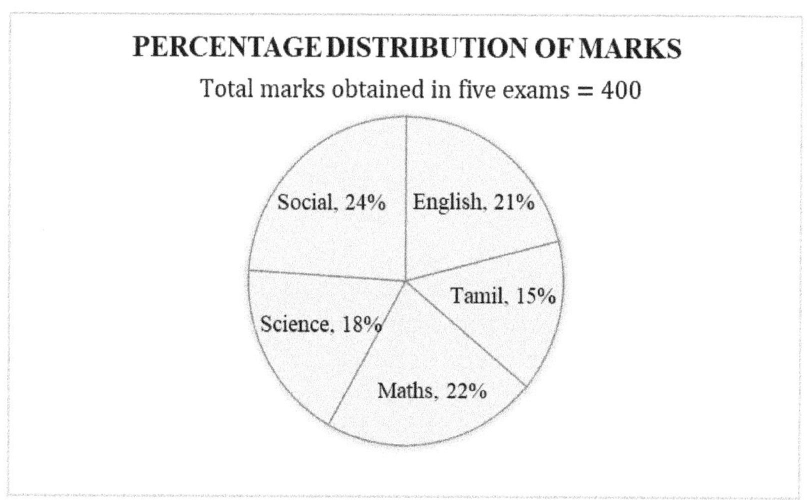

36. How much marks is scored by Edward in Tamil, Maths & Science together?
    (A) 180   (B) 220   (C) 240   (D) 200   (E) None of these

37. How much percentage of marks scored by Edward in English, Science & Social together?
    (A) 84%   (B) 82%   (C) 81%   (D) 85%   (E) None of these

38. Marks scored by Edward in science is what percent less than marks scored by Edward in English? (approx.)
    (A) 12.8%   (B) 13.6%   (C) 14.3%   (D) 15.8%   (E) None of these

39. Marks scored by Edward in English, Tamil, Maths together is how much more than marks scored by him in Science & Social together?
    (A) 48   (B) 56   (C) 52   (D) 64   (E) None of these

40. Find the ratio of marks scored by Edward in Maths & Science together to marks scored by Edward in English & Tamil together?
    (A) 11:8   (B) 8:11   (C) 10:9   (D) 9:10   (E) None of these

[41-45]

The given pie chart shows the distribution (in degree) of total monthly income of a person into 6 different categories.

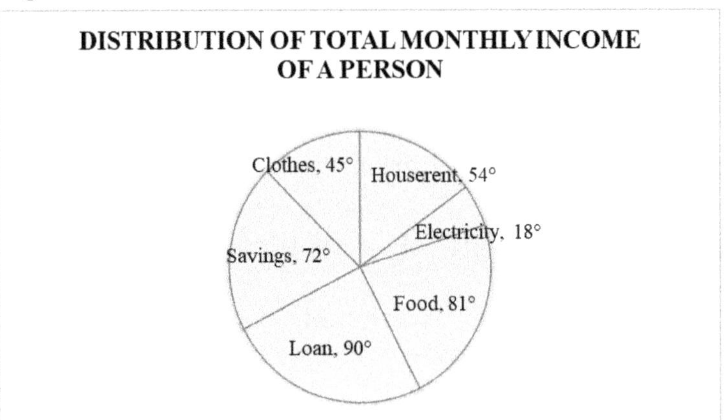

Note: Consider all categories except savings as monthly expenditure of the person.

41. If monthly salary is Rs 36,000 find monthly expenditure on Loan.
    (A) Rs 12,000   (B) Rs 10,000 (C) Rs 8,500 (D) Rs 9,000 (E) None of these

42. If difference between monthly expenditure on savings and house rent is Rs 5600, then find monthly income of person.
    (A) Rs 1,12,000   (B) Rs 1,24,000   (C) Rs 1,06,000   (D) Rs 96,000   (E) None of these

43. Find the average of monthly expenditure on house rent, loan, savings, if monthly expenditure on clothes is Rs 7200.
    (A) Rs 11,520   (B) Rs 11,660 (C) Rs 12,540 (D) Rs 11,840 (E) None of these

44. What is the total monthly expenditure if monthly income of the person is Rs 48,000?
    (A) Rs 37,600   (B) Rs 39,200 (C) Rs 38,400 (D) Rs 40,100 (E) None of these

45. Monthly expenditure on house rent is what percent of monthly expenditure on savings?
    (A) 76%   (B) 75%   (C) 70%   (D) 72%   (E) None of these

LINE GRAPH

[46-50]

The line graph shows the no. of regular consumers of rice and wheat in a city in 5 different years.

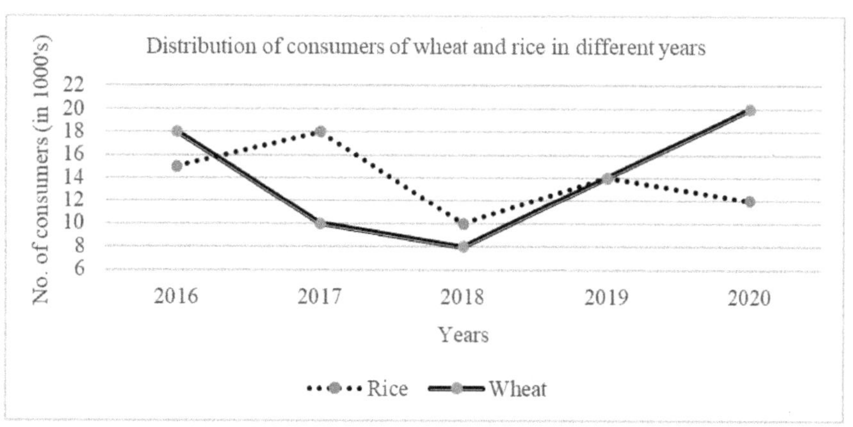

46. Find the ratio between rice consumers in 2017 & 2020 together to the wheat consumers in 2017 & 2018 together.

(A) 3:4   (B) 5:3   (C) 3:5   (D) 4:3   (E) None of these

47. Find the no. of rice consumers increased/decreased in 2019 over 2020.

(A) 2000   (B) 4000   (C) 5000   (D) 1000   (E) None of these

48. What is the average no. of wheat consumers over all the years?

(A) 14,500   (B) 13,000   (C) 14,000   (D) 13,500   (E) None of these

49. Wheat consumers is what percent of rice consumers in 2016?

(A) 100%   (B) 140%   (C) 110%   (D) 120%   (E) None of these

50. Rice consumers in 2016 & 2018 together is what percent more/less than wheat consumers in 2017 & 2020 together?

(A) 15 1/3%   (B) 16 1/3%   (C) 16 2/3%   (D) 18 2/5%   (E) None of these

[51-55]

The line graph shows the no. of passengers that travels by train in a given week.

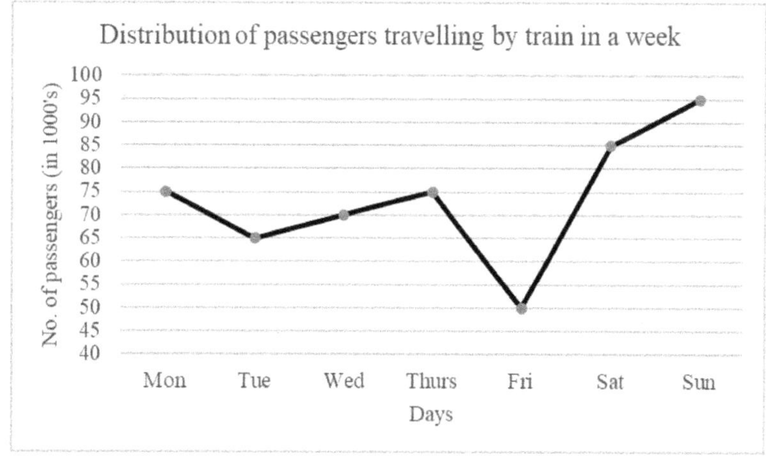

51. Find the ratio of no. of passenger travels on Wednesday & Sunday together to Monday & Saturday together.
(A) 33:32   (B) 32:33   (C) 31:34   (D) 32:34   (E) None of these

52. What is the average no. of passengers travel from Monday to Friday?
(A) 64,000   (B) 68,000   (C) 67,000   (D) 66,000   (E) None of these

53. Passengers who travel on Wednesday are what percentage of passengers who travel on Friday?
(A) 130%   (B) 140%   (C) 150%   (D) 160%   (E) None of these

54. Passengers travelling on Monday are what percentage more/less than that on Tuesday? (approx.)
(A) 16.2%   (B) 15.9%   (C) 14.8%   (D) 15.4%   (E) None of these

55. Passengers travelling on Tuesday & Thursday are how much more or less than that on Saturday & Sunday together?
(A) 45,000   (B) 50,000   (C) 40,000   (D) 58,000   (E) None of these

[56-60]

The line graph shows the time taken by five persons to complete the same work alone.

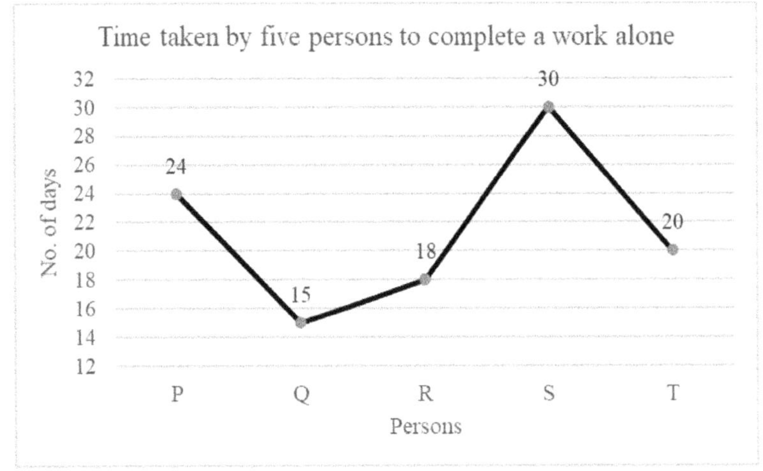

56. Find the time taken by S and T to complete the work, when they work together.
(A) 6 days   (B) 12 days   (C) 8 days   (D) 14 days   (E) None of these

57. What is the ratio of efficiencies of P, Q and R?
(A) 24:15:20   (B) 20:15:24   (C) 15:24:20   (D) 16:24:20   (E) None of these

58. P and R starts working together on alternate days. Find the time taken by them to complete the work if R starts the work.
(A) 20.5 days   (B) 20 days   (C) 21 days   (D) 19.5 days   (E) None of these

59. If efficiency of S increase by 20%, then find the time taken by S to complete the work.
(A) 26 days   (B) 24 days   (C) 23 days   (D) 25 days   (E) None of these

60. What is the difference between efficiencies of Q and R?
(A) 2   (B) 1   (C) 3   (D) 4   (E) None of these

RADAR

[61-65]

Radar chart shows the number of students (in hundreds) in five different schools (A, B, C, D & E) in 2019 & 2020.

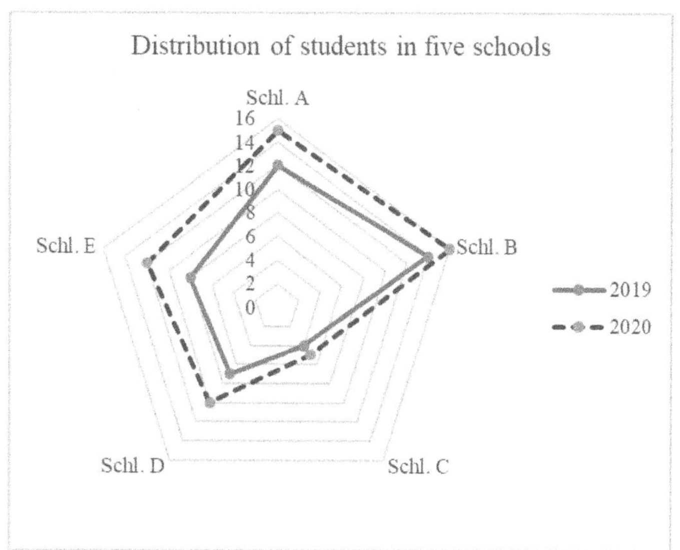

61. Students in E in 2019 & 2020 together are what percent more/less than students in A & D together in 2020?
(A) 10%   (B) 25%   (C) 30%   (D) 20%   (E) None of these

62. If the ratio of girls to boys in B in 2019 & 2020 is 2:3 and 3:5 respectively, then find ratio of number of boys in B in 2019 & 2020 together to total students in A in 2019.
(A) 23:26   (B) 25:23   (C) 23:25   (D) 24:23   (E) None of these

63. Students in B and D together in 2019 are what percent of students in C in 2019 & 2020 together? (approx.)
(A) 233.33%   (B) 223.34%   (C) 236.45%   (D) 231.67%   (E) None of these

64. If total students in F in 2019 are 900 more than total students in D in 2019 & ratio of girls to boys in A & F in 2019 is 9:11 and 7:3 respectively, then find the number of girls in A & F together in 2019.
(A) 1560   (B) 1660   (C) 1650   (D) 1670   (E) None of these

65. Average number of students in A, B & C in 2020 are how much more/less than the students in D & E together in 2019?
(A) 310   (B) 320   (C) 300   (D) 350   (E) None of these

[66-70]

Given radar graph shows the number of male & female employees in four different companies in a particular year.

Note: [Employees = Male + Female employees]

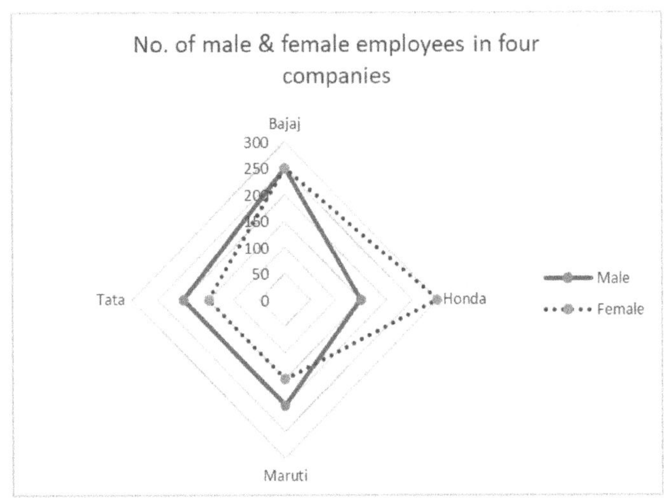

66. Total employees in Tata are what percent of total female employees in all companies? (approx.)

(A) 45%   (B) 39%   (C) 43%   (D) 41%   (E) None of these

67. Which company has maximum percentage of female employees?

(A) Maruti   (B) Tata   (C) Bajaj   (D) Honda   (E) None of these

68. What is the ratio of male employees in Bajaj & Honda together to that of total employees in Maruti?

(A) 7:6   (B) 8:7   (C) 7:8   (D) 6:7   (E) None of these

69. If in next year, the male population increases by 10% in both Tata & Bajaj while female population remains same. Find the ratio of male employees to female employees in both the offices together.

(A) 99:80   (B) 89:90   (C) 79:99   (D) 80:99   (E) None of these

70. Find the total no. of employees in all the companies.

(A) 1560   (B) 1640   (C) 1650   (D) 1570   (E) None of these

[71-75]

Given radar graph shows the data of users (male & females) registered for a Science Expo in five different slots.

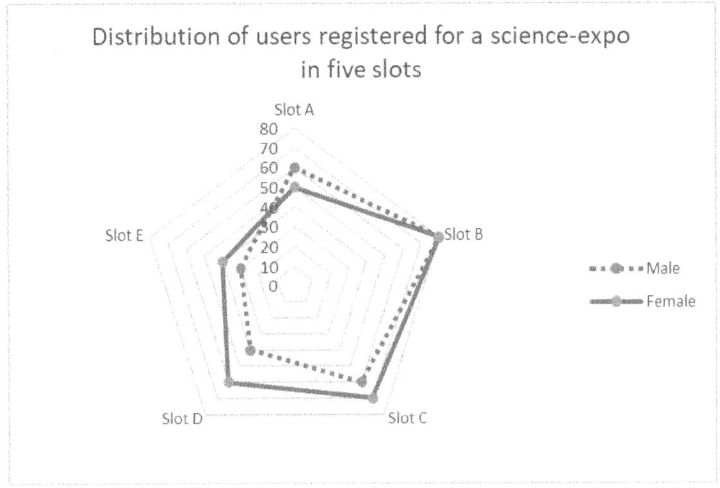

71. Females registered for Science Expo in slots B & E together are what percent more/less than males registered for Science Expo in slots A & C together?

(A) 0% (B) 10% (C) 20% (D) 5% (E) None of these

72. What is the average number of female users registered for Expo in all the slots?

(A) 80 (B) 100 (C) 60 (D) 40 (E) None of these

73. In which slot, does the maximum no. of users registered for the Expo?

(A) Slot A (B) Slot B (C) Slot C (D) Slot D (E) None of these

74. What is the average number of users in all the slots?

(A) 118 (B) 110 (C) 116 (D) 114 (E) None of these

75. In how many slots, does the percentage of males registered in a slot over all users in same slot is more than 50%?

(A) One slot (B) Two slots (C) Three slots (D) Four slots (E) None of these

SOLUTION:

[1-5]

Years	2016	2017	2018	2019	2020
Production of wheat (in tonnes)	450	540	360	280	300

1. (B) Required % $= \frac{300}{540} \times 100 = 55.55\%$

2. (D) Required average $= \frac{450+540+360+280+300}{5} = \frac{1930}{5} = 386$ tonnes

3. (C) Required % $= \frac{540-450}{450} \times 100 = \frac{90}{450} \times 100 = 20\%$

4. (A) Required ratio $= \frac{280+300}{540+360} = \frac{580}{900} = 29:45$

5. (B) Required % $= \frac{360-300}{360} \times 100 = \frac{60}{360} \times 100 = \frac{1}{6} \times 100 = 16.67\%$

[6-10]:

	A	B	C	D	E
Scorpio	5400	5000	3000	3600	4800
Innova	4000	4800	5400	4000	3200

6. (D) Required % $= \frac{(5400+5000)\sim(4000+5400)}{4000+5400} \times 1000 = \frac{10400\sim9400}{9400} \times 100 = \frac{1000}{9400}$

$= 10.64\% \cong 11\%$

7. (B) Required ratio $= \frac{3600+4800}{4800+3200} = \frac{8400}{8000} = 21:20$

8. (A) Required % $= \frac{(4000+3200)-(5400+3000)}{5400+3000} \times 100 = \frac{7200-8400}{8400} \times 100 = \frac{1200}{8400} \times 100$

$= 14.28\% \cong 14.3\%$

9. (B) Total no. of Baleno cars in E $= \frac{80}{100} \times 5000 = 4000$

Required difference $= 4800 - 4000 = 800$

10. (E) Total no. of

(i) Scorpio cars in all cities = 5400 + 5000 + 3000 + 3600 + 4800 = 21,800

(ii) Innova cars in all cities = 4000 + 4800 + 5400 + 4000 + 3200 = 21,400

Required difference = 21800 − 21400 = 400

[11-15]:

	2012	2013	2014	2015	2016	2017
Baseball	1080	1120	1000	760	860	740
Tennis	780	780	680	440	600	580
Cricket	400	380	380	240	340	300

11. (C) Required % $= \dfrac{160}{160+280+300} \times 100 = \dfrac{160}{740} \times 100 = 21\dfrac{23}{37}$ %

12. (B) Total no. of people = 400 + 300 + 200 + 260 + 280 = 1840

13. (C) Required difference = 160 ~ 260 = 100

14. (A) Required ratio = 380: 320 = 19: 16

15. (D) Required no. of people = 400 + 380 + 380 + 240 + 340 + 300 = 2040

[16-20]:

16. (A) Total students in a Dept. = Students failed in both semesters +

Students passed in Semester 1 + Students passed in Semester 2 −

Students passed in both semesters.

Total students in Dept 2 = 15 + 25 + 30 − 20 = 50

17. (C) Students failed in both semesters in all Depts. = 10 + 15 + 20 = 45

Students passed in both semesters in all Depts. = 20 + 20 + 25 = 65

Required % $= \dfrac{65-45}{45} \times 100 = 44.44\%$

18. (B) Students passed in only one semester in all depts

$= (40 + 30 − 20) + (25 + 30 − 20) + (30 + 35 − 25) = 50 + 35 + 40 = 125$

Average $= \dfrac{125}{3} = 41.67$

19. (D) Required % $= \dfrac{15}{(15+25+30-20)} \times 100 = \dfrac{15}{50} \times 100 = 30\%$

20. (C) Total no. of students in

- Dept. A = 10 + 40 + 30 − 20 = 60

- Dept. B = 15 + 25 + 30 − 20 = 50

- Dept. C = 20 + 30 + 35 − 25 = 60

[21-25]:

21. (A) Items purchased by

- Females from store A on Wednesday & Friday $= \left(335 \times \frac{40}{100}\right) + \left(360 \times \frac{60}{100}\right) =$

  $134 + 216 = 350$

- Males from store B on Thursday & Friday $= \left(275 \times \frac{60}{100}\right) + \left(382 \times \frac{75}{100}\right) = 165 +$

  $285 = 450$

Required $\% = \frac{450-350}{450} \times 100 = \frac{100}{450} \times 100 = 22.22\%$

22. (D) Required ratio $= \frac{\left(280 \times \frac{55}{100}\right) + \left(335 \times \frac{60}{100}\right)}{\left(275 \times \frac{40}{100}\right) + \left(380 \times \frac{25}{100}\right)} = \frac{154+201}{110+95} = \frac{355}{205} = \frac{71}{41}$

23. (D) Total no. of items purchased by males from store B on all days together

$= \left(440 \times \frac{35}{100}\right) + \left(320 \times \frac{70}{100}\right) + \left(270 \times \frac{20}{100}\right) + \left(275 \times \frac{60}{100}\right) + \left(380 \times \frac{75}{100}\right)$

$= 154 + 224 + 54 + 165 + 285 = 882$

24. (B) Required $\% = \frac{420+360}{270+380} = \frac{780}{650} \times 100 = 120\%$

25. (C) Total items purchased from store A & B on Saturday $= \left(335 \times \frac{120}{100}\right) + \left(270 \times \frac{130}{100}\right)$

$= 402 + 350 = 753$

[26-30]:

26. (B) Basketball players in 2018 in

- College B: $60\%x - 40\%x = 80$

  20% of $x = 80$

  $x = 400$

  Basketball players $= 60\%$ of $400 = 240$

- College E $= \frac{180}{80-20} \times 80 = \frac{180}{60} \times 80 = 240$

  Football players in 2019 in

- College B $= \frac{120}{80-20} \times 80 = 160$

- College E $= \frac{160}{52-48} \times 48 = 1920$

Required difference $= (240 + 240) \sim (160 + 1920) = 480 \sim 2080 = 1600$

27. (C) Football players in school C & D together in 2018 $= \left(\frac{100}{55-45} \times 55\right) + \left(\frac{320}{70-30} \times 70\right)$

$= 560 + 550 = 1110$

Basketball players in school A in 2019 $= \frac{80}{(55-45)} \times 55 = 440$

Required % $= \frac{1110}{440} \times 100 = 252.27\% \cong 253\%$

28. (A) Required average $= \frac{1}{3}\left(\frac{150}{(75-25)} \times 25 + \frac{180}{(80-20)} \times 20 + \frac{160}{(52-48)} \times 48\right)$

$= \frac{1}{3}(75 + 60 + 1920) = \frac{2055}{3} = 685$

29. (D) Required ratio $= \frac{\frac{80}{(55-45)} \times 55}{\frac{100}{(55-45)} \times 55} = \frac{80}{100} = 4:5$

30. (B) Required percentage $= \frac{\frac{140}{(60-40)} \times 40 \sim \frac{320}{(70-30)} \times 70}{\frac{320}{(70-30)} \times 70} \times 100 = \frac{280 \sim 560}{560} \times 100 = 50\%$

[31-35]:

Schools	Percentage of students
A	25
B	15
C	12
D	28
E	20

31. (A) No. of girls in E $= 4000 \times \frac{20}{100} \times \frac{3}{8} = 300$

No. of girls in B $= 4000 \times \frac{15}{100} \times \frac{5}{12} = 250$

Required difference $= 300 - 250 = 50$

32. (B) Required central angle $= \frac{28+20}{100} \times 360° = \frac{48}{100} \times 360° = 172.8°$

33. (D) Required % $= \frac{28-25}{25} \times 100 = \frac{3}{25} \times 100 = 12\%$

34. (C) Required average $= \frac{12+28+20}{3} \times \frac{1}{100} \times 4000 = \frac{20}{100} \times 4000 = 800$

35. (B) Total students in F $= 4000 \times \frac{12}{100} \times \frac{125}{100} = 600$

Required difference $= 600 \times \frac{5-3}{8} = 150$

[36-40]:

Subjects	Percentage
English	21
Tamil	15
Maths	22
Science	18
Social	24

36. (B) Total marks $= \frac{(15+22+18)}{100} \times 400 = \frac{55}{100} \times 400 = 220$

37. (A) Total marks $= \frac{(21+18+24)}{100} \times 400 = \frac{63}{100} \times 400 = 252$

Required % $= \frac{252}{300} \times 100 = 84\%$

38. (C) Required % $= \frac{21-18}{21} \times 100 = \frac{100}{7}\% = 14.285 \cong 14.3\%$

39. (D) Required value $= \frac{(21+15+22-18-24)}{100} \times 400 = (58-42) \times 4 = 16 \times 4 = 64$

40. (C) Required ratio $= \frac{\frac{(22+18)}{100} \times 400}{\frac{(15+21)}{100} \times 400} = \frac{10}{9}$

[41-45]:

Expenditure	Distribution
Houserent	54°
Electricity	18°
Food	81°
Loan	90°
Savings	72°
Clothes	45°

41. (D) Expenditure of loan $= \frac{90°}{360°} \times 36{,}000 = \frac{1}{4} \times 36{,}000 = $ Rs 9000

42. (A) Monthly income: $\frac{72-54}{360} \times$ Income $= 5600$

Income $= \frac{5600 \times 360}{72-54} = \frac{5600 \times 360}{18} = $ Rs 1,12,000

43. (A) $\frac{45}{360} \times$ Income $= 7200$

Income $= \frac{7200 \times 360}{45} = 57{,}600$

Required average $= \frac{\frac{54+90+72}{360} \times 57600}{3} = \frac{216}{360} \times 19{,}200 = $ Rs 11,520

44. (C) Expenditure = Income - Savings

Monthly expenditure $= 48{,}000 - \frac{72}{360} \times 48{,}000 = 48{,}000 - 9600 = $ Rs 38,400

45. (B) Required % $= \frac{54}{72} \times 100 = 75\%$

[46-50]:

	2016	2017	2018	2019	2020
Rice	15	18	10	14	12
Wheat	18	10	8	14	20

46. (B) Required ratio $= \frac{18{,}000+12{,}000}{10{,}000+8{,}000} = \frac{30{,}000}{18{,}000} = 5:3$

47. (A) Required difference $= 14{,}000 \sim 12{,}000 = 2000$

48. (C) Required average $= \dfrac{(18+10+8+14+20)1000}{5} = \dfrac{70 \times 1000}{5} = 14{,}000$

49. (D) Required percentage $= \dfrac{18{,}000}{15{,}000} \times 100 = \dfrac{18}{15} \times 100 = \dfrac{600}{5} = 120\%$

50. (C) Required percentage $= \dfrac{(15{,}000+10{,}000) \sim (10{,}000+20{,}000)}{(10{,}000+20{,}000)} \times 100 = \dfrac{25{,}000 \sim 30{,}000}{30{,}000} \times 100 =$

$\dfrac{100}{6} = 16\dfrac{2}{3}\%$

[51-55]:

	Mon	Tue	Wed	Thurs	Fri	Sat	Sun
No. of passengers	75	65	70	75	50	85	95

51. (A) Required ratio $= \dfrac{(70+95)1000}{(70+85)1000} = \dfrac{165}{160} = \dfrac{33}{32}$

52. (C) Required average $= \dfrac{(75+65+70+75+50)1000}{5} = \dfrac{335 \times 1000}{5} = 67{,}000$

53. (B) Required percentage $= \dfrac{(70)1000}{(50)1000} \times 100 = \dfrac{700}{5} = 140\%$

54. (D) Required percentage $= \dfrac{75{,}000 \sim 65{,}000}{65{,}000} \times 100 = \dfrac{10}{65} \times 100 = \dfrac{1000}{65} = 15.38\% \cong 15.4\%$

55. (C) Required difference $= [(65+75) \sim (85 + 95))] \times 1000 = (140 \sim 180) \times 1000 = 40{,}000$

[56-60]:

	P	Q	R	S	T
Days	24	15	18	30	20

56. (B) Let time taken by them be X days.

$\therefore \ X\left[\dfrac{1}{30} + \dfrac{1}{20}\right] = 1$

$X\left[\dfrac{50}{600}\right] = 1$

$X = \dfrac{600}{50} = 12$ days

57. (C) Efficiency $\propto \dfrac{1}{\text{time taken}}$

$\therefore$ Ratio of efficiency $= \dfrac{1}{24} : \dfrac{1}{15} : \dfrac{1}{18} = 15{:}24{:}20$ (LCM = 360)

58. (A) No. of days taken by P & R to complete work = 24, 18 days respectively

Let total work = 72 units (LCM of 24 & 18)

Efficiency = 3 & 4 units /days respectively

2-day work of P & R $= 3 + 4 = 7\ units$

20-day work $= 7 \times 10 = 70$ units

Remaining work $= 72 - 70 = 2$ units

21st day work will be done by R.

Required time $= 20 + \dfrac{2}{4} = 20.5$ days

59. (D) Time taken by S $= 30 \times \dfrac{100}{120} = 25$ days

60. (B) Days of work:

Q = 15 days

R = 18 days

Let total work be 90 units (LCM)

Efficiency of

$Q = \dfrac{90}{15} = 6$ units /day; $\qquad R = \dfrac{90}{18} = 5$ units /day

Required difference = 6 - 5 = 1 unit/day.

[61-65]:

(in 100's)	2019	2020
Schl. A	12	15
Schl. B	14	16
Schl. C	4	5
Schl. D	7	10
Schl. E	8	12

61. (D) Required % $= \dfrac{(800+1200)\sim(1500+1000)}{(1500+1000)} \times 100 = \dfrac{2000\sim2500}{2500} \times 100 = \dfrac{500}{2500} \times 100 = 20\%$

62. (C) No. of boys in B in 2019 & 2020 $= 1400 \times \dfrac{3}{5} + 1600 \times \dfrac{5}{8} = 840 + 1000 = 1840$

Total students in A in 2019 = 1200

Required ratio $= \dfrac{1840}{1200} = \dfrac{23}{25}$

63. (A) Required % $= \dfrac{1400+700}{400+500} \times 100 = \dfrac{2100}{900} \times 100 = 233.33\%$

64. (B) Total students in F $= 700 + 900 = 1600$

Number of girls in A $= 1200 \times \dfrac{9}{20} = 540$

Number of girls in F $= 1600 \times \dfrac{7}{10} = 1120$

Required no. of girls $= 1120 + 540 = 1660$

65. (C) Average no. of students in A, B & C in 2020 $= \dfrac{1500+1600+500}{3} = \dfrac{3600}{3} = 1200$

Students in D & E together in 2019 $= 700 + 800 = 1500$

Required difference = 1500~1200 = 300

[66-70]:

	Male	Female
Bajaj	250	250
Honda	150	300
Maruti	200	150
Tata	200	150

66. (D) Required % $= \frac{200+150}{(250+300+150+150)} \times 100 = \frac{350}{850} \times 100 = 41.17\% \cong 41\%$

67. (D) Percentage of females in

- Bajaj $= \frac{250}{500} \times 100 = 50\%$

- Honda $= \frac{300}{450} \times 100 = 66.67\%$

- Maruti $= \frac{150}{350} \times 100 = 42.86\%$

- Tata $= \frac{150}{350} \times 100 = 42.86\%$

Honda has maximum percentage of females.

68. (B) Required ratio $= \frac{250+150}{200+150} = \frac{400}{350} = 8:7$

69. (A) No. of male employees in Tata & Bajaj in next year $= (250 + 200) \times \frac{110}{100} =$

$450 \times \frac{110}{100} = 495$

Required ratio $= \frac{495}{(150+250)} = \frac{495}{400} = \frac{99}{80}$

70. (C) Total employees in all companies

$= (250 + 250) + (150 + 300) + (200 + 150) + (200 + 150)$

$= 500 + 450 + 350 + 350$

$= 1650$

[71-75]:

	Male	Female
Slot A	60	50
Slot B	80	80
Slot C	60	70
Slot D	40	60
Slot E	30	40

71. (A) Required % $= \frac{(80-40)\sim(60+60)}{(60+60)} \times 100 = \frac{120\sim120}{120} \times 100 = 0\%$

72. (C) Required average $= \frac{50+80+70+60+40}{5} = \frac{300}{5} = 60$

73. (B) No. of users registered in

- Slot A: $60 + 50 = 110$
- Slot B: $80 + 80 = 160$
- Slot C: $60 + 70 = 130$
- Slot D: $40 + 60 = 100$
- Slot E: $30 + 40 = 70$

Slot B has maximum no. of users.

74. (D) Required average $= \frac{110+160+130+100+70}{5} = \frac{570}{5} = 114$

75. (A) For the given condition, no. of males registered must be higher than the no. of females to exceed 50% mark.

In this case, only slot 1 has more males.

ADVANCED DI

Advanced DI involves more than one type of graph/chart ie., data will be provided in more than one graphical form.

EXERCISE:

Study the charts given below and answer the following questions.

[1-5]

Given pie chart shows the percentage distribution of production of cars by 5 different companies while the table shows the data shows the data of ratio of Sedans to SUVs produced by these 5 companies.

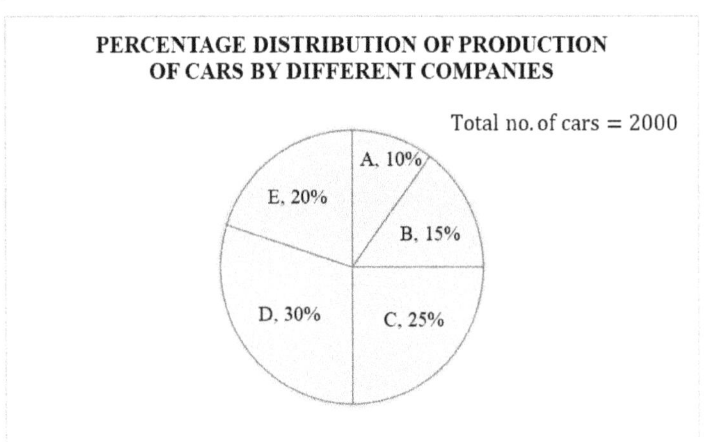

Companies	Sedan : SUVs
A	3:2
B	8:7
C	12:13
D	13:17
E	1:1

1. How many Sedan cars were produced by companies A & B together?
   (A) 260   (B) 280   (C) 290   (D) 270   (E) None of these
2. What is the ratio of SUV cars produced by company C & E together to Sedan cars produced by company D?
   (A) 13:23   (B) 12:23   (C) 23:13   (D) 23:12   (E) None of these

3. Sedan cars produced by company A are what percent of SUVs produced by company C? (approx.)
   (A) 44%　　　　(B) 48%　　　　(C) 46%　　　　(D) 50%　　　　(E) None of these
4. What is the average of SUVs produced by company B & C together?
   (A) 250　　　　(B) 300　　　　(C) 100　　　　(D) 200　　　　(E) None of these
5. What is the ratio of Sedan cars produced by company A to the SUV cars produced by company B?
   (A) 6:7　　　　(B) 7:6　　　　(C) 5:6　　　　(D) 6:5　　　　(E) None of these

[6-10]

Bar charts shows the total number of Pleasure and Maestro bikes in 5 different cities (A, B, C, D & E) in 2019 & 2020 and line chart shows percentage of Maestro in these cities in 2019 & 2020.

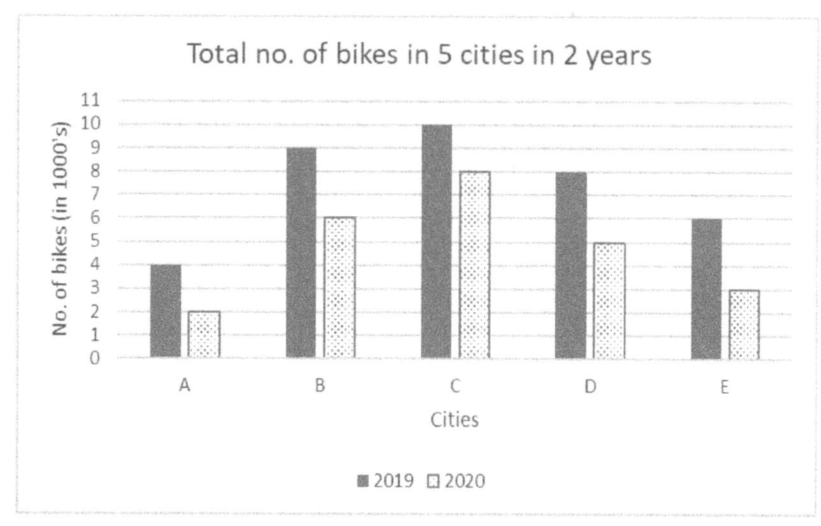

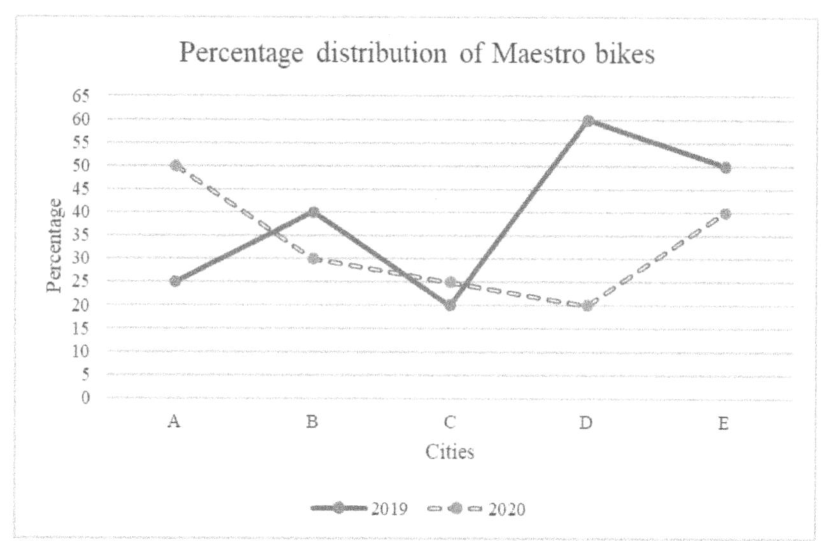

6. Number of Pleasure in cities A & E together in 2019 is what percent of number of Pleasure in cities C & D together in 2020?
   (A) 80%　　　　(B) 60%　　　　(C) 50%　　　　(D) 40%　　　　(E) None of these

7. Find the average number of Maestro in cities B, C & D in 2020 is how much more/less than average number of Maestro in cities C & E in 2019.
   (A) 900   (B) 1100   (C) 800   (D) 1000   (E) None of these

8. Find the number of Pleasure in cities A, B & E together in 2020.
   (A) 7500   (B) 6500   (C) 6000   (D) 7000   (E) None of these

9. Number of Maestro in B & D together in 2019 is what percent more/less than number of Pleasure in cities C & D together in 2019?
   (A) 30%   (B) 35%   (C) 25%   (D) 20%   (E) None of these

10. Find the number of Maestro in cities A & E together in 2020.
    (A) 2100   (B) 2300   (C) 2200   (D) 2250   (E) None of these

[11-15]

Bar graph given below shows quantity of five different products (wheat, rice, pulse, salt & sugar) sold (in kg) by a shopkeeper & table shows total revenue (in Rs.) generated by selling these individual products.

Name of the product	Total revenue (in Rs.)
Wheat	2200
Rice	3750
Pulse	900
Salt	1200
Sugar	600

11. Cost price of per kg of wheat is how much more/less than per kg selling price of salt when wheat is sold at 60% profit?
    (A) Rs 5   (B) Rs 10   (C) Rs 15   (D) Rs 12   (E) None of these

12. If 2 kg of sugar and 3 kg of pulse is mixed, then what will be the selling price per kg of such mixture?
    (A) Rs 15   (B) Rs 18   (C) Rs 16   (D) Rs 20   (E) None of these

13. Total revenue generated from pulse is what percent of difference between total revenue generated from wheat & sugar?

(A) 57.65%   (B) 56.25%   (C) 58%   (D) 55.3%   (E) None of these

14. If cost price of per kg rice is Rs 60, find profit earned on selling 40 kg of rice (in Rs.)
    (A) Rs 650   (B) Rs 700   (C) Rs 800   (D) Rs 600   (E) None of these

15. What is the average quantity of wheat, rice and pulse sold by shopkeeper?
    (A) 60 kg   (B) 40 kg   (C) 50 kg   (D) 70 kg   (E) None of these

[16-20]

Study the line chart and table given below and answer the following question.

Line chart shows the number of chairs manufactured by four different chair manufacturers (P, Q, R & S) in 2018 & 2019.

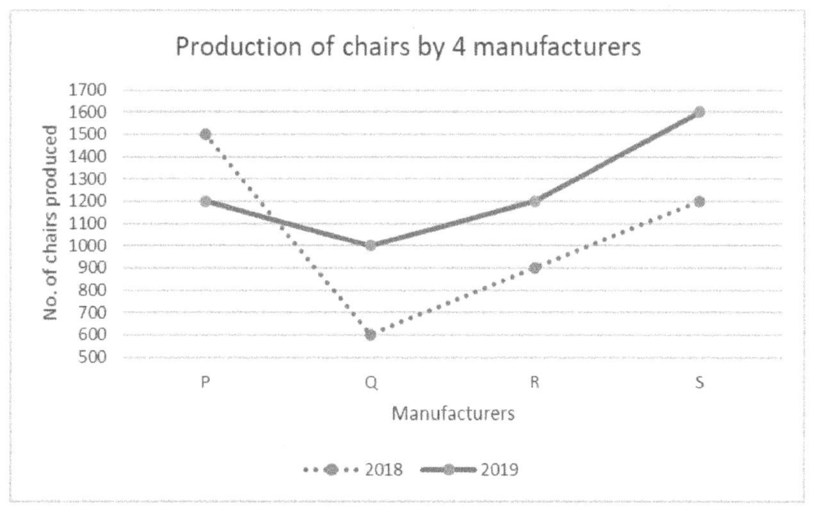

Manufacturer	Chairs sold	
	2018	2019
P	900	1080
Q	570	900
R	810	720
S	840	1440

Note: Total chairs manufactured by any manufacturer in any year = Total chairs (no. of sold+ unsold chairs) of that manufacturer in that year.

16. Unsold chairs of R & S together in 2018 are what percent of sold chairs of P & R together in 2019?
    (A) 26%   (B) 28%   (C) 20%   (D) 25%   (E) None of these

17. If manufacturing cost of a chair for R in 2018 & 2019 is Rs 400 and selling price of a chair for R in 2018 & 2019 is Rs 500 & Rs 800 respectively, then find profit % is maximum in which year among 2018 & 2019 for R. (R does not resell any of the remaining chairs in the next year)

(A) Max. in 2018 (B) Equal in both years (C) Max. in 2019
(D) Can't be determined (E) None of these

18. Find the ratio of chairs manufactured by Q & S together in 2018 to chairs sold by Q & R together in 2019.
(A) 9:8 (B) 8:9 (C) 9:10 (D) 10:9 (E) None of these

19. If chairs manufactured by S in 2020 are 50% more than chairs sold by P in 2018 and ratio of sold to unsold chairs of S in 2020 is 2:1, then find the average of chairs sold by S in 2018, 2019 & 2020.
(A) 1060 (B) 1080 (C) 1050 (D) 1100 (E) None of these

20. Find the average number of chairs sold by P, Q, R & S in 2018 is how much more/less than total unsold chairs of P, Q, R & S together in 2019.
(A) 100 (B) 80 (C) 70 (D) 110 (E) None of these

[21-25]

The pie chart given below shows the percentage distribution of population of 6 different cities in 2019 & bar graph shows the female percentage in each city in the same year.

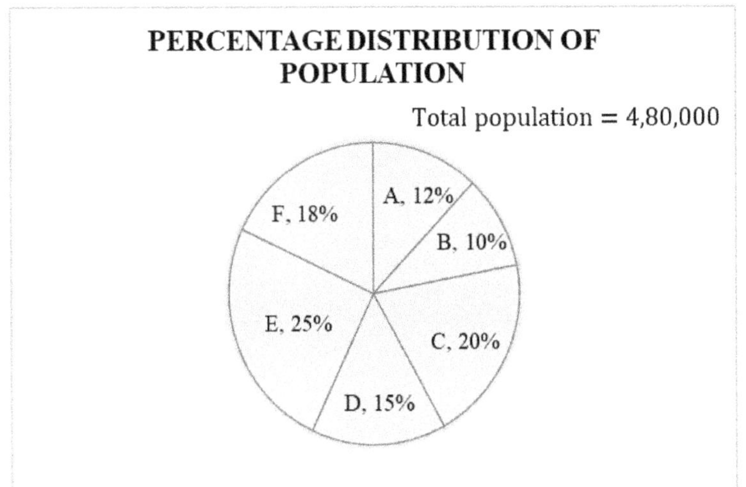

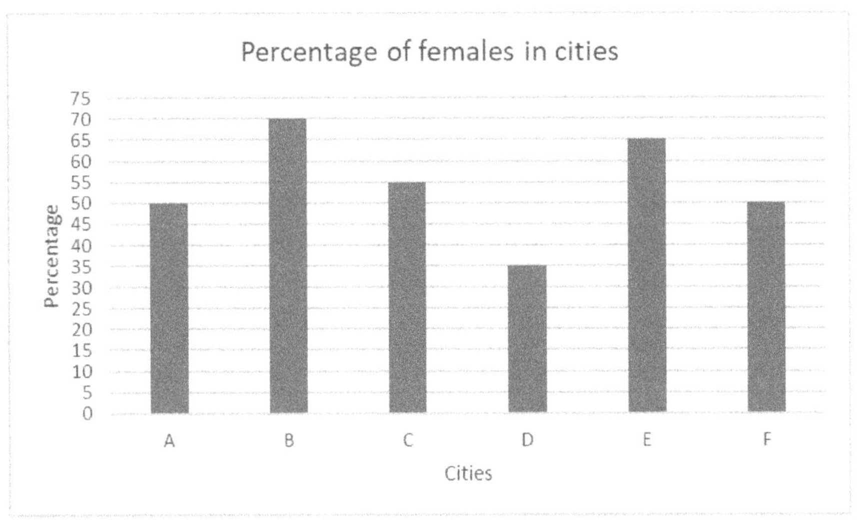

21. What is the average no. of males in cities D & E?
    (A) 44,600   (B) 44,400   (C) 42,400   (D) 44,200   (E) None of these
22. Males in city F are what percent of males in city A?
    (A) 160%   (B) 120%   (C) 100%   (D) 150%   (E) None of these
23. What is the ratio between female population of city E to male population of city A & C together?
    (A) 13:14   (B) 12:13   (C) 13:12   (D) 14:13   (E) None of these
24. What is the sum of female population in city B & male population in city D?
    (A) 80,400   (B) 80,200   (C) 80,500   (D) 80,300   (E) None of these
25. Female population in city A is what percentage more/less than male population in city B?
    (A) 98%   (B) 105%   (C) 102%   (D) 100%   (E) None of these

[26-30]

Study the following table & bar graph to answer the questions given below it. Percentage of appeared & qualified candidates in a competitive examination from different institutes.

Appeared candidates: 72,000

Qualified candidates: 16,000

Institute	% of appeared candidates
A	20%
B	15%
C	10%
D	25%
E	12%
F	18%

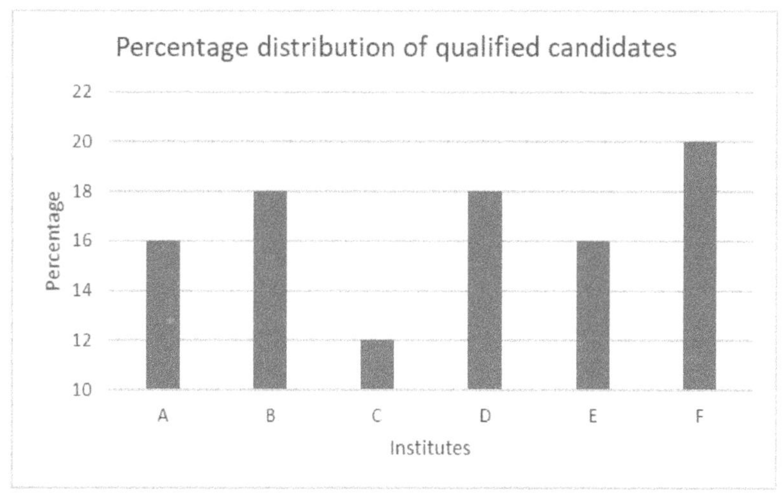

26. what is the ratio of the qualified candidates from the institutes A, E & F together to the appeared candidates from the institutes B, C & D?
    (A) 220:51   (B) 52:225   (C) 225:52   (D) 53:225   (E) None of these
27. What percent of the candidates from the institute C has been declared qualified out of the total candidates appeared from this institute? (approx.)
    (A) 27%   (B) 24%   (C) 30%   (D) 29%   (E) None of these

28. What is the approximate percentage of students qualified with respect to those appeared from the institutes A & F together? (approx.)
   (A) 19%   (B) 32%   (C) 24%   (D) 21%   (E) None of these
29. Which institute has the highest percentage of candidates qualified with respect to those appeared?
   (A) A   (B) E   (C) C   (D) B   (E) None of these
30. What is the average number of appeared candidates from the institutes B, C & D together?
   (A) 14,000   (B) 8,000   (C) 12,000   (D) 10,000   (E) None of these

SOLUTION:

[1-5]:

Company	Percentage of cars
A	10%
B	15%
C	25%
D	30%
E	20%

1. (B) No. of Sedan cars $= \left(\frac{10}{100} \times \frac{3}{5} + \frac{15}{100} \times \frac{8}{15}\right) \times 2000 = \left(\frac{6}{100} + \frac{8}{100}\right) \times 2000$

$$= \frac{14}{100} \times 2000 = 280$$

2. (C) Required ratio $= \dfrac{[\left(\frac{25}{100}\times\frac{13}{25}\right)+\left(\frac{20}{100}\times\frac{1}{2}\right)]\times 2000}{\frac{30}{100}\times\frac{13}{30}\times 2000} = \dfrac{\left(\frac{13}{100}+\frac{10}{100}\right)}{\frac{13}{100}} = 23:13$

3. (C) Required % $= \dfrac{\frac{10}{100}\times\frac{3}{5}\times 2000}{\frac{250}{100}\times\frac{13}{25}\times 2000} \times 100 = \dfrac{10\times 3\times 5}{25\times 13} \times 100 = \dfrac{6}{13} \times 100 = 46.15\% \cong 46\%$

4. (D) Required average $= \dfrac{[\left(\frac{15}{100}\times\frac{7}{15}\right)+\left(\frac{25}{100}\times\frac{13}{25}\right)]\times 2000}{2} = \left(\frac{7}{100} + \frac{13}{100}\right) \times \dfrac{2000}{2} = \dfrac{1}{5} \times 1000 = 200$

5. (A) Required ratio $= \dfrac{\frac{10}{100}\times\frac{3}{5}\times 2000}{\frac{15}{100}\times\frac{7}{15}\times 2000} = \dfrac{6}{7}$

[6-10]:

Bikes in city	2019	2020
A	4,000	2,000
B	9,000	6,000
C	10,000	8,000
D	8,000	5,000
E	6,000	3,000

Percentage of Maestro	2019	2020
A	25	50
B	40	30
C	20	25
D	60	20
E	50	40

6. (B) No. of pleasure in A & E in 2019 $= \left(4000 \times \frac{75}{100}\right) + \left(6000 \times \frac{50}{100}\right)$

$$= 3000 + 3000 = 6000$$

No. of pleasure in C & D in 2020 $= \left(8000 \times \frac{75}{100}\right) + \left(5000 \times \frac{80}{100}\right)$

$$= 6000 + 4000 = 10{,}000$$

Required % $= \frac{6000}{10{,}000} \times 100 = 60\%$

7. (A) Average no. of Maestro in B, C, D in 2020

$$= \frac{1}{3}\left[\left(6000 \times \frac{30}{100}\right) + \left(8000 \times \frac{25}{100}\right) + \left(5000 \times \frac{20}{100}\right)\right]$$

$$= \frac{1}{3}(1800 + 2000 + 1000) = \frac{1}{3} \times 4800 = 1600$$

Average no. of Maestro in C & E in 2019 $= \frac{1}{2}\left[\left(10{,}000 \times \frac{20}{100}\right) + \left(6000 \times \frac{50}{100}\right)\right]$

$$= \frac{1}{2}(2000 + 3000)$$

$$= \frac{1}{2} \times 5000 = 2500$$

Required difference $= 1600 \sim 2500 = 900$

8. (D) No. of pleasure in A, B & E in 2020 $= \left[\left(2000 \times \frac{50}{100}\right) + \left(6000 \times \frac{70}{100}\right) + \left(3000 + \frac{60}{100}\right)\right]$

$$= 1000 + 4200 + 1800 = 7000$$

9. (C) No. of Maestro in B & D in 2019 $= \left(9000 \times \frac{40}{100}\right) + \left(8000 \times \frac{60}{100}\right)$

$$= 3600 + 4800 = 8400$$

No. of Pleasure in C & D in 2019 $= \left(10{,}000 \times \frac{80}{100}\right) + \left(8000 \times \frac{40}{100}\right)$

$$= 8000 + 3200 = 11{,}200$$

Required % $= \frac{11200 \sim 8400}{11200} \times 100 = \frac{2800}{11200} \times 100 = 25\%$

10. (C) No. of Maestro in A & E in 2020 $= \left(2000 \times \frac{50}{100}\right) + \left(3000 \times \frac{40}{100}\right) = 1000 + 1200 =$

2200

[11-15]:

Products	No. of Kg
Wheat	55
Rice	50
Pulses	45
Salt	40
Sugar	60

11. (A) Cost price of per kg of wheat $= \dfrac{2200}{55} \times \dfrac{100}{160} = $ Rs 25

Selling price of salt $= \dfrac{1200}{40} = $ Rs 30

Required difference = Rs $30 - 25 = $ Rs 5

12. (C) Selling price of 1 kg of sugar $= \dfrac{600}{60} = $ Rs 10

Selling price of 1 kg of pulse $= \dfrac{900}{45} = $ Rs 20

Selling price of mixture $= \dfrac{(10 \times 2)+(20 \times 3)}{(2+3)} = \dfrac{20+60}{5} = \dfrac{80}{5} = $ Rs 16

13. (B) Required % $= \dfrac{900}{2200-600} = \dfrac{900}{1600} \times 100 = 56.25\%$

14. (D) Selling price of 1 kg of rice $= \dfrac{3750}{50} = $ Rs 75

Profit earned on selling 1 kg of rice = Rs $75 - $ Rs $60 = $ Rs 15

Total profit = Rs $15 \times 40 = $ Rs 600

15. (C) Required average $= \dfrac{1}{3}(55 + 50 + 45) = \dfrac{150}{3} = 50$ kg

[16-20]:

	2018	2019
P	1500	1200
Q	600	1000
R	900	1200
S	1200	1600

16. (D) Unsold chairs R & S in 2018 $= (900 - 810) + (1200 - 840) = 90 + 360 = 450$

Sold chairs of P & R in 2019 $= 1080 + 720 = 1800$

Required % $= \dfrac{450}{1800} \times 100 = 25\%$

17. (C) Total manufacturing cost of chairs for R in

- 2018 $= 400 \times 900 = $ Rs 3,60,000

- 2019 $= 400 \times 1200 = $ Rs 4,80,000

Total revenue from chairs for R in

- $2018 = 500 \times 810 = \text{Rs } 4,05,000$
- $2019 = 800 \times 720 = \text{Rs } 5,76,000$

Profit % of R in

- $2018 = \dfrac{4,05,000 - 3,60,000}{3,60,000} \times 100 = \dfrac{45,000}{3,36,000} \times 100 = 12.5\%$
- $2019 = \dfrac{5,76,000 - 4,80,000}{4,80,000} \times 100 = \dfrac{96,000}{4,80,000} \times 100 = 20\%$

Profit % is maximum in 2019 for R.

18. (D) Required ratio $= \dfrac{600 + 1200}{900 + 720} = \dfrac{1800}{1620} = \dfrac{10}{9}$

19. (A) Chairs manufactured by S in 2020 $= 900 \times \dfrac{150}{100} = 1350$

Chairs sold by S in 2020 $= 1350 \times \dfrac{2}{3} = 900$

Required average $= \dfrac{840 + 1440 + 900}{3} = \dfrac{3180}{3} = 1060$

20. (B) Average of chairs sold by P, Q, R & S in 2018 $= \dfrac{(900 + 570 + 810 + 840)}{4} = \dfrac{3120}{4} = 780$

Total unsold chairs of P, Q, R & S in 2019

$= (1200 - 1080) + (1000 - 900) + (1200 - 720) + (1600 - 1440)$

$= 120 + 100 + 480 + 160 = 860$

Required difference $= 860 \sim 780 = 80$

[21-25]:

Cities	Percentage of total population
A	12
B	10
C	20
D	15
E	25
F	18

Cities	Percentage of female
A	50
B	70
C	55
D	35
E	65
F	50

21. (B) Required average $= \frac{1}{2}\left[\left(4,80,000 \times \frac{15}{100} \times \frac{100-35}{100}\right) + \left(4,80,000 \times \frac{25}{100} \times \frac{100-65}{100}\right)\right]$

$= \frac{1}{2}(46,800 + 42,000) = \frac{1}{2}(88,800) = 44,400$

22. (D) Required % $= \dfrac{4,80,000 \times \frac{18}{100} \times \frac{50}{100}}{4,80,000 \times \frac{12}{100} \times \frac{50}{100}} \times 100 = \frac{18}{12} \times 100 = 150\%$

23. (C) Required ratio $= \dfrac{4,80,000 \times \frac{25}{100} \times \frac{65}{100}}{4,80,000\left[\left(\frac{12}{100} \times \frac{50}{100}\right) + \left(\frac{20}{100} \times \frac{45}{100}\right)\right]}$

$= \dfrac{(25 \times 65)}{(12 \times 50) + (20 \times 45)} = \dfrac{1625}{600 + 900} = \dfrac{1625}{1500} = 13:12$

24. (A) Required sum $= 4,80,000 \times \left[\left(\frac{10}{100} \times \frac{70}{100}\right) + \left(\frac{15}{100} \times \frac{65}{100}\right)\right] = 48(700 + 975)$

$= 48(1675) = 80,400$

25. (D) Required percentage $= \dfrac{4,80,000\left[\left(\frac{12}{100} \times \frac{50}{100}\right) \sim \left(\frac{10}{100} \times \frac{30}{100}\right)\right]}{4,80,000 \times \frac{10}{100} \times \frac{30}{100}} \times 100 = \dfrac{600 \sim 300}{300} \times 100 = 100\%$

[26-30]:

Institute	Percentage of qualified candidates
A	16%
B	18%
C	12%
D	18%
E	16%
F	20%

26. (B) Required ratio $= \dfrac{\frac{(16+16+20)}{100} \times 16,000}{\frac{(15+10+25)}{100} \times 72,000} = \dfrac{52 \times 2}{50 \times 9} = \dfrac{52}{225}$

27. (A) Required % $= \dfrac{\frac{12}{100} \times 16,000}{\frac{10}{100} \times 72,000} \times 100 = \dfrac{12}{45} \times 100 = 26.67\%$

28. (D) Required % $= \dfrac{\frac{(16+20)}{100} \times 16,000}{\frac{(20+18)}{100} \times 72,000} \times 100 = \dfrac{36 \times 16}{38 \times 72} \times 100 = 21.05\% \cong 21\%$

29. (B) Percentage of candidates qualified from institute

- $A = \dfrac{16\%(16,000)}{20\%(72,000)} = 17.78\%$

- $B = \dfrac{18\%(16,000)}{15\%(72,000)} = 26.67\%$

- $C = \dfrac{12\%(16,000)}{10\%(72,000)} = 26.67\%$

- $D = \dfrac{18\%(16,000)}{25\%(72,000)} = 16\%$

- $E = \dfrac{16\%(16,000)}{12\%(72,000)} = 29.63\%$

- $F = \dfrac{20\%(16,000)}{18\%(72,000)} = 24.69\%$

Institute E has highest numerical value.

30. (C) Required average $= \dfrac{1}{3}\left[\dfrac{(15+10+25)}{100} \times 72,000\right] = \dfrac{1}{3} \times \dfrac{50}{100} \times 72,000 = 12,000$

PRACTICE:

[1-5]

Bar graph given below shows number of people visited a zoo on four different days & table shows no. of females visited zoo on these days.

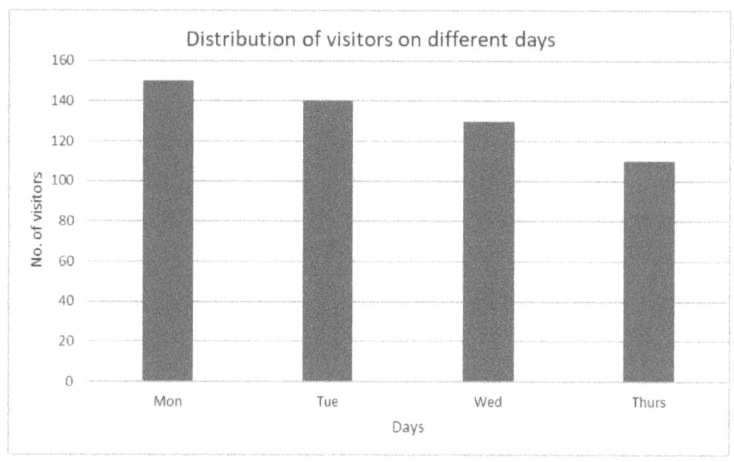

Days	No. of females
Monday	66
Tuesday	64
Wednesday	46
Thursday	52

1. Find the ratio of total males visited zoo on Monday & Tuesday together and total females visited zoo on Tuesday & Wednesday together?
   (A) 16:11　　(B) 11:16　　(C) 11:15　　(D) 15:11　　(E) None of these
2. Total males visited on Sunday in zoo are 42 more than that of on Thursday & total no. of males visited the zoo on Sunday are 66 2/3% of total people visited zoo on that day. Find total males visited zoo on Wednesday is what percent less than total people visited zoo on Sunday?
   (A) 42%　　(B) 48%　　(C) 44%　　(D) 52%　　(E) None of these
3. Find difference between average number of males visited zoo on Wednesday & Thursday and average number of females visited zoo on Monday & Tuesday?
   (A) 7　　　　(B) 4　　　　(C) 5　　　　(D) 6　　　　(E) None of these

4. Total males visited on Tuesday is what percent less than total male visited on Monday (approx.)
   (A) 10.2%   (B) 9.5%   (C) 9.9%   (D) 8.6%   (E) None of these

5. Total people visited on Friday are 9 1/11% more than that of on Thursday, then find total people visited on Monday is what percent more than that of on Friday?
   (A) 30%   (B) 28%   (C) 25%   (D) 32%   (E) None of these

[6-10]

The pie chart given below shows the percentage distribution of total employees of five different companies and bar graph shows the no. of male companies of given companies. Study the graphs carefully and answer the following questions.

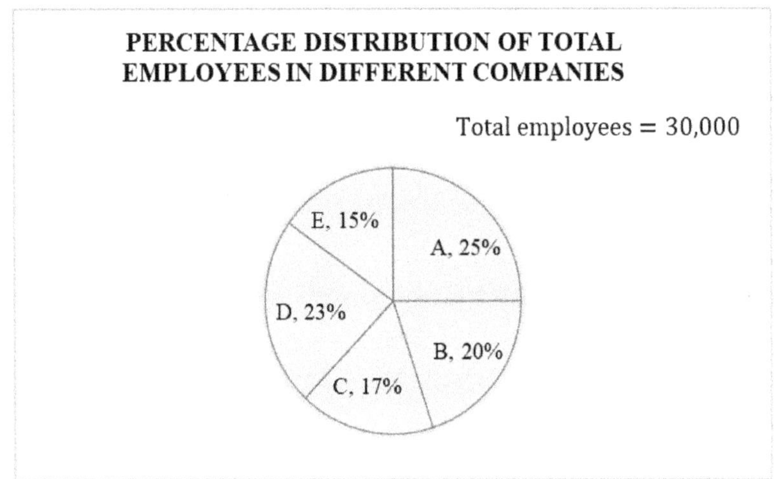

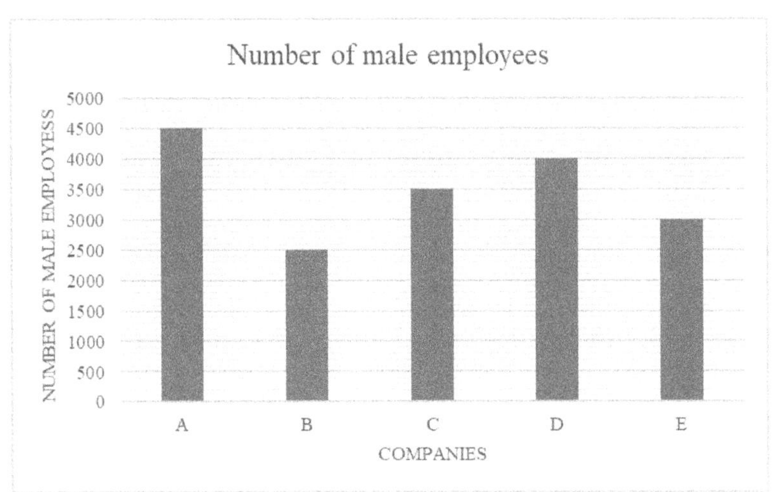

6. What is the ratio between no. of male and female employees in Company A?
   (A) 4:3   (B) 2:3   (C) 3:2   (D) 2:5   (E) None of these

7. What is the total no. of female employees in B & D together?
   (A) 5600   (B) 3600   (C) 6200   (D) 6400   (E) None of these

8. What is the central angle corresponding to male employees in company E out of total employees of five companies?

(A) 36°   (B) 72°   (C) 18°   (D) 32°   (E) None of these

9. Female employees of company C is what percent more/less than that of in company A? (approx.)
   (A) 46.67%   (B) 50%   (C) 42.5%   (D) 55%   (E) None of these

10. Male employees in company E are how much more/less than female employees of company A?
   (A) 1000   (B) 0   (C) 500   (D) 1500   (E) None of these

[11-15]

Line graph given below shows number of total visitors in a park on five different days & table shows number of male visitors on these five days.

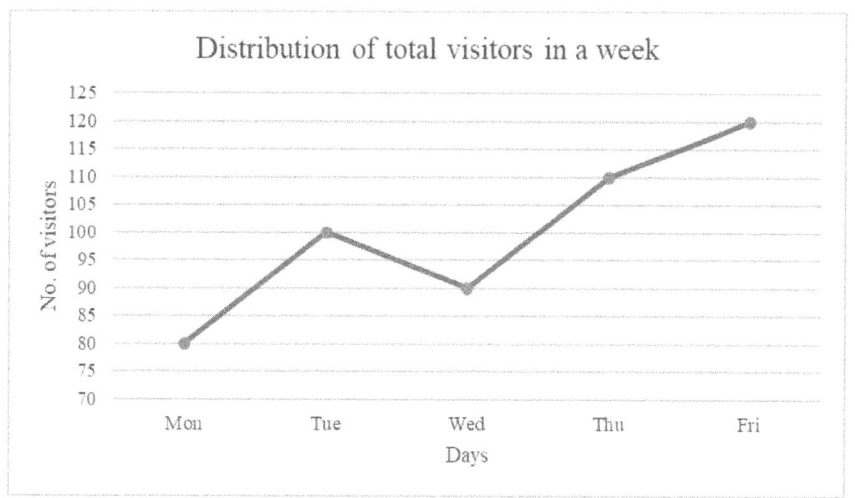

Days	Male visitors
Mon	30
Tue	35
Wed	50
Thurs	25
Fri	40

11. Total females visited on Thursday is what percent more than total females visited on Monday?
   (A) 90%   (B) 70%   (C) 60%   (D) 80%   (E) None of these

12. Find the ratio of total females visited on Friday to total females visited on Tuesday.
   (A) 13:15   (B) 15:13   (C) 13:16   (D) 16:13   (E) None of these

13. Find the average number of females visited on Wednesday & Friday?
   (A) 80   (B) 40   (C) 60   (D) 50   (E) None of these

14. Total females visited on Wednesday is what percent less than total females visited on Friday?
   (A) 50%   (B) 60%   (C) 45%   (D) 56%   (E) None of these

15. If total visitors in that park on Sunday is 20% more than that of on Wednesday and total female visitors on Sunday are 20% more than that of on Tuesday, then find total male visitors on Sunday?
   (A) 30   (B) 20   (C) 25   (D) 40   (E) None of these

[16-20]

The bar graph given below provides the information of students who appeared for Banking & TNPSC exams from given cities & line graph provides details of percentage of qualified students of these two exams from given cities.

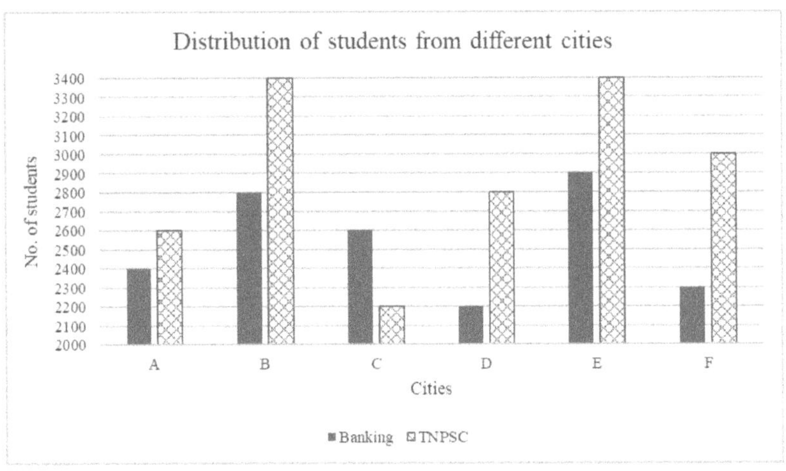

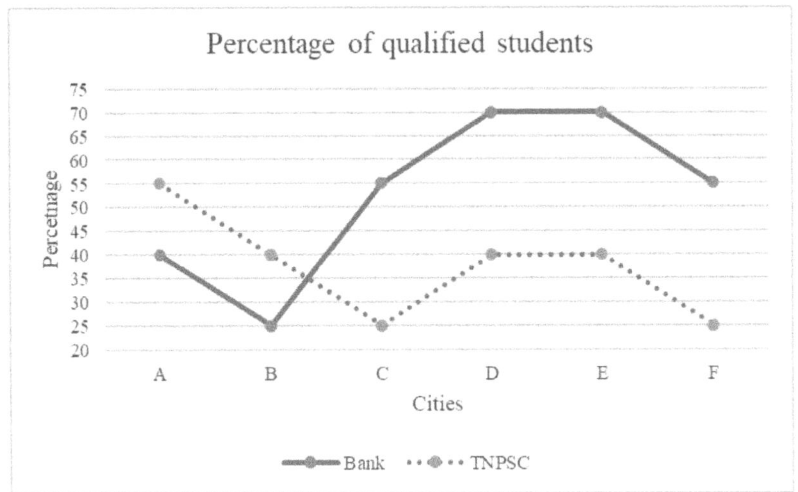

16. What is the ratio of number of TNPSC qualified students from the cities A & E together and TNPSC students from cities B & D together?

    (A) 279:248   (B) 248:279   (C) 277:243   (D) 243:277   (E) None of these

17. What is the average number of students qualified in Banking exams from cities A, B & C together?

    (A) 1080   (B) 1050   (C) 1030   (D) 1020   (E) None of these

18. Find the difference between qualified students of Banking to Tnpsc students in cities C, E & F together?

    (A) 2065   (B) 2060   (C) 2055   (D) 2062   (E) None of these

19. Number of Banking students who qualified from cities A & B together is how much more/less than number of TNPSC students who are qualified from cities D & F together?

    (A) 10   (B) 15   (C) 25   (D) 20   (E) None of these

20. Find the total number of qualified students of TNPSC exams from all the given cities together?

    (A) 6560   (B) 6570   (C) 6650   (D) 6750   (E) None of these

[21-25]

Study the following table carefully to answer these questions. Percentage of students studying various languages as their second languages in a school is given.

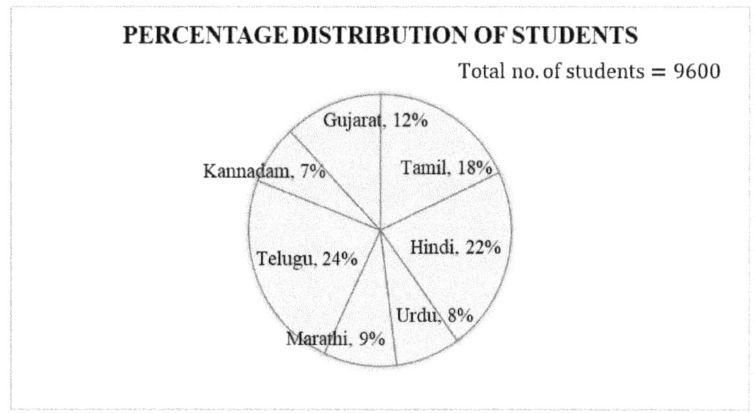

Ratio of male & female candidates in each category:

Category	F:M
Tamil	3:5
Hindi	7:5
Urdu	2:1
Marathi	4:5
Telugu	5:3
Kannadam	4:3
Gujarati	3:6

21. How many male students are studying Hindi & Telugu together?

(A) 1756   (B) 1644   (C) 1748   (D) 1744   (E) None of these

22. What is the ratio between the number of female students studying Gujarati & Tamil respectively?

(A) 16:27   (B) 29:13   (C) 13:29   (D) 27:16   (E) None of these

23. What is the total no. of female students studying Hindi, Marathi & kannadam together?

(A) 1500   (B) 1600   (C) 2000   (D) 2500   (E) None of these

24. What is the difference between the male students studying Telugu & female students studying Urdu?

(A) 156   (B) 176   (C) 167   (D) 172   (E) None of these

25. Number of female students for which of the following categories are exactly the same?

(A) Marathi & Hindi

(B) Telugu & Marathi

(C) Tamil & Urdu

(D) Marathi, Kannadam & Gujarati

(E) None of these

SOLUTION:

[1-5]:

Days	No. of visitors
Mon	150
Tue	140
Wed	130
Thurs	110

1. (A) Required ratio $= \frac{(150-66)+(140-64)}{64+46} = \frac{84+76}{110} = \frac{160}{110} = 16:11$

2. (C) Total males visited on Sunday $= (110 - 52) + 42 = 58 + 42 = 100$

   Total people visited on Sunday $= 100 \times \frac{3}{2} = 150$

   Total male visited zoo on Wednesday $= 130 - 46 = 84$

   Required % $= \frac{150-84}{150} \times 100 = \frac{66}{150} \times 100 = 44\%$

3. (D) Required difference $= \left[\frac{(130-46)+(110-52)}{2} \sim \frac{(66+64)}{2}\right] = \frac{84+58}{2} \sim \frac{130}{2} = 71 \sim 65 = 6$

4. (B) Required % $= \frac{(140-64) \sim (150-66)}{150-66} \times 100 = \frac{76 \sim 84}{84} \times 100 = \frac{8}{84} \times 100 \cong 9.52\%$

5. (C) Total people visited on Friday $= \frac{110 \times \frac{100}{11}}{100} + 110 = 110 + 10 = 120$

   Required % $= \frac{150-120}{120} \times 100 = \frac{30}{120} \times 100 = 25\%$

[6-10]:

Company	Percentage of total employees
A	25
B	20
C	17
D	23
E	15

Company	No. of male employees
A	4500
B	2500
C	3500
D	4000
E	3000

6. (C) Required ratio $= \dfrac{4500}{\left(30{,}000 \times \frac{25}{100}\right) - 4500} = \dfrac{4500}{7500 - 4500} = \dfrac{4500}{3000} = 3:2$

7. (D) Required sum $= \left[\left(30{,}000 \times \dfrac{20}{100}\right) - 2500\right] + \left[\left(30{,}000 \times \dfrac{23}{100}\right) - 4000\right]$

$= (6000 - 2500) + (6900 - 4000) = 3500 + 2900 = 6400$

8. (A) Central angle $= \dfrac{3000}{30{,}000} \times 360° = 36°$

9. (A) Female employee of company C $= \left(30{,}000 \times \dfrac{17}{100}\right) - 3500 = 5100 - 3500 = 1600$

Female employee in company A $= \left(30{,}000 \times \dfrac{25}{100}\right) - 4500 = 7500 - 4500 = 3000$

Required % $= \dfrac{3000 - 1600}{3000} \times 100 = \dfrac{1400}{3000} \times 100 = 46.67\%$

10. (B) Required difference $= 3000 \sim \left[\left(30{,}000 \times \dfrac{25}{100}\right) - 4500\right] = 3000 \sim (7500 - 4500)$

$= 3000 \sim 3000 = 0$

[11-15]:

Days	Total visitors
Mon	80
Tue	100
Wed	90
Thu	110
Fri	120

11. (B) Required % $= \dfrac{(110-25) \sim (80-30)}{80-40} \times 100 = \dfrac{85 \sim 50}{50} \times 100 = \dfrac{35}{50} \times 100 = 70\%$

12. (D) Required ratio $= \dfrac{120-40}{100-35} = \dfrac{80}{65} = \dfrac{16}{13}$

13. (C) Required average $= \dfrac{1}{2}[(90 - 50) + (120 - 40)] = \dfrac{1}{2}(40 + 80) = 60$

14. (A) Required percentage $= \dfrac{(90-50) \sim (120-40)}{(120-40)} \times 100 = \dfrac{40 \sim 80}{80} \times 100 = \dfrac{40}{80} \times 100 = 50\%$

15. (A) Total visitors on Sunday $= 90 \times \dfrac{120}{100} = 108$

Total female visitors on Sunday $= (100 - 35) \times \dfrac{120}{100} = 65 \times \dfrac{120}{100} = 78$

Total male visitors on Sunday $= 108 - 78 = 30$

[16-20]:

No. of students appeared for exams:

Cities	Banking	TNPSC
A	2400	2600
B	2800	3400

C	2600	2200
D	2200	2800
E	2900	3400
F	2300	3000

No. of qualified students:

Cities	Banking	TNPSC
A	40	55
B	25	40
C	55	25
D	70	40
E	70	40
F	55	25

16. (A) Number of TNPSC students qualified from A & E cities $= \left(2600 \times \frac{55}{100}\right) + \left(3400 \times \frac{40}{100}\right)$

$= 1430 + 1360 = 2790$

Number of TNPSC students qualified from B & D cities $= \left(3400 \times \frac{40}{100}\right) + \left(2800 \times \frac{40}{100}\right)$

$= 1360 + 1120 = 2480$

Required ratio $= \frac{2790}{2480} = \frac{279}{248}$

17. (C) Required average $= \frac{1}{3}\left[\left(2400 \times \frac{40}{100}\right) + \left(2800 \times \frac{25}{100}\right) + \left(2600 \times \frac{55}{100}\right)\right]$

$$= \frac{1}{3}(960 + 700 + 1430)$$

$$= \frac{1}{3}(3090) = 1030$$

18. (A) Total qualified students from C, E & F cities in

- Banking $= \left(2600 \times \frac{55}{100}\right) + \left(2900 \times \frac{70}{100}\right) + \left(2300 \times \frac{55}{100}\right)$

$= 1430 + 2030 + 1265 = 4725$

- TNPSC $= \left(2200 \times \frac{25}{100}\right) + \left(3400 \times \frac{40}{100}\right) + \left(3000 \times \frac{25}{100}\right)$

$= 550 + 1360 + 750 = 2660$

Required difference $= 4725 - 2660 = 2065$

19. (D) Required difference $= \left[\left(2400 \times \frac{40}{100}\right) + \left(2800 \times \frac{25}{100}\right)\right] \sim \left[\left(2800 \times \frac{40}{100}\right) + \left(3000 \times \frac{25}{100}\right)\right]$

$= [(960 + 700) \sim (1120 + 750)] = 1660 \sim 1870 = 20$

20. (B) Required total no. students

$$= \left[\left(2600 \times \tfrac{55}{100}\right) + \left(3400 \times \tfrac{40}{100}\right) + \left(2200 \times \tfrac{25}{100}\right) + \left(2800 \times \tfrac{40}{100}\right) + \left(3400 \times \tfrac{40}{100}\right) + \right.$$

$$\left.\left(3000 \times \tfrac{25}{100}\right)\right]$$

$$= 1430 + 1360 + 550 + 1120 + 1360 + 750 = 6570$$

[21-25]:

Language	Percentage of students
Tamil	18%
Hindi	22%
Urdu	8%
Marathi	9%
Telugu	24%
Kannadam	7%
Gujarat	12%

21. (D) Required no. of male students $= 9600 \left[\left(\tfrac{22}{100} \times \tfrac{5}{12}\right) + \left(\tfrac{24}{100} \times \tfrac{3}{8}\right)\right]$

$$= 9600 \left(\frac{55}{600} + \frac{9}{100}\right) = 9600 \times \frac{109}{600}$$

$$= 16 \times 109 = 1744$$

22. (A) Required ratio $= \dfrac{9600 \times \tfrac{12}{100} \times \tfrac{3}{9}}{9600 \times \tfrac{18}{100} \times \tfrac{3}{8}} = \dfrac{12 \times 8}{18 \times 9} = \dfrac{16}{27}$

23. (C) Required no. of female students $= 9600 \left[\left(\tfrac{22}{100} \times \tfrac{7}{12}\right) + \left(\tfrac{9}{100} \times \tfrac{4}{9}\right) + \left(\tfrac{7}{100} \times \tfrac{4}{7}\right)\right]$

$$= 9600 \left(\frac{77}{600} + \frac{8}{100}\right)$$

$$= 9600 \times \frac{125}{600} = 2000$$

24. (B) Required difference $= \left(9600 \times \tfrac{24}{100} \times \tfrac{3}{8}\right) - \left(9600 \times \tfrac{8}{100} \times \tfrac{2}{3}\right) = 432 - 256 = 176$

25. (D) Female students in various categories:

- Tamil $= 9600 \times \dfrac{18}{100} \times \dfrac{3}{8} = 648$

- Hindi $= 9600 \times \dfrac{22}{100} \times \dfrac{7}{12} = 1232$

- Urdu $= 9600 \times \dfrac{8}{100} \times \dfrac{2}{3} = 512$

- Marathi $= 9600 \times \dfrac{9}{100} \times \dfrac{4}{9} = 384$

- Telugu $= 9600 \times \dfrac{24}{100} \times \dfrac{5}{8} = 1440$

- Kannadam $= 9600 \times \dfrac{7}{100} \times \dfrac{4}{7} = 384$

- Gujarati $= 9600 \times \dfrac{12}{100} \times \dfrac{3}{9} = 384$

Unit **20**

CASELETS

Caselet is a type of DI in which information provided will be in the form of paragraph. We need to comprehend the data & solve the given question. In order to do that, we must understand the given data & know how the data is linked.

EXERCISE:

Study the given passages carefully and answer the questions.

[1-5]

Three shops P, Q and R sells pen and scale. The ratio of number of scales to pens sold by shop R was 7:5 and that sold by shop P was 3:2 respectively. The number of scales and pens sold by shop Q was 128 and ratio of number of scales to pens sold by shop Q was 5:3. The total number of scales sold by shop R was 10% more than the scale sold by shop P. The total number of scales and pens sold by all the shops was 874.

1. If cost of each scale and each pen sold by shop R is Rs 20 & Rs 10 respectively, then find total amount earned by shop R.
   (A) Rs 6270　　(B) Rs 6370　　(C) Rs 6240　　(D) Rs 6290　　(E) None of these

2. What is the ratio of scales sold by shop P & R together to pens sold by P & Q together?
   (A) 441:188　　(B) 188:441　　(C) 443:187　　(D) 443:181　　(E) None of these

3. Find average number of scales sold by all the three shops (approx.)
   (A) 171.45　　(B) 173.67　　(C) 172.32　　(D) 175.15　　(E) None of these

4. If no. of scales sold by shop P is increased by 20% and number of pens sold by shop Q is increased by 25%, then what is the sum of total scales sold by shop P and pens sold by shop Q?
   (A) 306　　(B) 308　　(C) 312　　(D) 315　　(E) None of these

5. What is the difference between total number of scales sold by all the three shops together and total number of pens sold by all the 3 shops together?
   (A) 178　　(B) 148　　(C) 150　　(D) 168　　(E) None of these

[6-10]

In an office, there are 400 employees who consume Tea, Coffee & Black coffee. 50 employees consume Tea and Black coffee both. While 30 consume Tea & Coffee both. 70 consume only Black Coffee. 190 employees consume Tea. 60 employees consume all three drinks. 200 employees consume exactly one drink.

6. How many employees do drink exactly 2 drinks?
   (A) 120　　(B) 130　　(C) 140　　(D) 150　　(E) None of these

7. Employees consuming coffee are approximately what percent of employees consuming Black coffee? (approx.)
   (A) 95.83%   (B) 94.63%   (C) 98.25%   (D) 92.15%   (E) None of these
8. What is the ratio of employees consuming only Tea to employees consuming Coffee & Black coffee both?
   (A) 6:5   (B) 5:6   (C) 2:5   (D) 3:5   (E) None of these
9. What is the total no. of employees that consume more than one drink?
   (A) 180   (B) 150   (C) 220   (D) 200   (E) None of these
10. Average no. of employees consuming only Tea & only Black coffee are how much more/less than average no. of employees consuming Coffee & Black coffee both and all three drink?
    (A) 20   (B) 10   (C) 5   (D) 0   (E) None of these

[11-15]

There are 420 persons in a ceremony, and all of them eat different flavoured ice-creams. 80 people eat only chocolate, 60 people eat all the three flavoured ice-creams, there are totally 260 people who eat chocolate and 200 people who eat strawberry. 80 people eat chocolate and strawberry only, 20 people eat vanilla and strawberry only.

11. How many persons eat only vanilla flavoured ice-cream?
    (A) 90   (B) 100   (C) 120   (D) 150   (E) None of these
12. People eating vanilla and chocolate only are what percent of people eating only chocolate?
    (A) 45%   (B) 40%   (C) 50%   (D) 30%   (E) None of these
13. Number of people eating only strawberry ice-creams is how much less than the people eating all three types of ice-creams?
    (A) 20   (B) 15   (C) 18   (D) 30   (E) None of these
14. People eating Vanilla are what percent of people eating strawberry ice-creams?
    (A) 100%   (B) 90%   (C) 120%   (D) 110%   (E) None of these
15. What is the ratio of people eating only vanilla and only chocolate together to the persons eating only strawberry ice-creams?
    (A) 9:2   (B) 2:9   (C) 2:7   (D) 7:2   (E) None of these

[16-20]

There are total 900 tickets which are used either to watch Football or to watch Cricket match on the same day. The ratio of females and males who use their tickets in watching cricket match is 7:13 respectively. The number of males who use their tickets in Football is 144 more than the number of females who use their tickets in Cricket. Total number of males who use their tickets in Football and Cricket together is 348 more than the total number of females who use their tickets in Football & Cricket together.

16. Find the ratio of total number of persons who use their tickets in Football to the total number of persons who use their tickets in Cricket.
    (A) 6:7   (B) 7:6   (C) 7:8   (D) 8:7   (E) None of these
17. Total number of females who uses their ticket in Football & Cricket together is how much more/less than the total number of males who uses their tickets for watching Cricket?
    (A) 34   (B) 36   (C) 38   (D) 40   (E) None of these

18. Out of total males who use their tickets in watching Football match, 25% are special guest, then find the total number of males who use their tickets in watching Football excluding the special guests?
    (A) 234   (B) 232   (C) 230   (D) 228   (E) None of these
19. Find the difference between total no. of male & female visitors.
    (A) 349   (B) 351   (C) 350   (D) 348   (E) None of these
20. What is the average number of male & female persons who use their tickets to watch Cricket?
    (A) 235   (B) 240   (C) 245   (D) 230   (E) None of these

[21-25]

There are 3600 students in an Engineering college. The ratio of girls to boys is 5:7 respectively. All the students are enrolled in three different specialization ie. BE(CS), BE(IT) & BE(ECE). 30% of girls are enrolled in BE(IT) and out of the remaining girls are enrolled in BE(CS) & BE(ECE) in the ratio 3:2. 50% of boys are enrolled in BE(ECE). The ratio of boys enrolled in BE(CS) and BE(IT) is 4:3.

21. What is the total number of girls enrolled in the college?
    (A) 1540   (B) 1500   (C) 1450   (D) 1400   (E) None of these
22. What is the total number of girls enrolled in BE(ECE)?
    (A) 415   (B) 400   (C) 420   (D) 380   (E) None of these
23. What is the total no. of boys enrolled in the college?
    (A) 2100   (B) 1400   (C) 2400   (D) 1800   (E) None of these
24. Number of girls enrolled in BE(CS) form what percentage of total number of girls in the college?
    (A) 38   (B) 36   (C) 40   (D) 42   (E) None of these
25. What is the average no. of boys enrolled in BE(IT) & BE(CS)?
    (A) 535   (B) 520   (C) 525   (D) 530   (E) None of these

SOLUTION:

[1-5]

Let no. of scale to pen sold by R be 7x & 5x respectively & that of by P be 3y & 2y respectively.

Total no. of scale & pen sold by P & Q = 7x + 5x + 3y + 2y = 12x + 5y

$12x + 5y = 874 - 128 = 746$

$7x = 3y \times \dfrac{110}{100}$

$x = \dfrac{33y}{70}$

$12x + 5y = 746$

Subs. x, $\left(12 \times \dfrac{33y}{70}\right) + 5y = 746$

$396y + 350y = 746 \times 70$

$y = \dfrac{746 \times 70}{746} = 70$

$$x = \frac{33y}{70} = \frac{33 \times 70}{70} = 33$$

	P	Q	R
Scale	$3y = 3 \times 70 = 210$	$5z = \dfrac{128}{8} \times 5 = 80$	$7x = 7 \times 33 = 231$
Pen	$2y = 2 \times 70 = 140$	$3z = \dfrac{128}{8} \times 3 = 48$	$5x = 5 \times 33 = 165$

1. (A) Total amount earned by R = $(231 \times 20) + (165 \times 10) = 4620 + 1650 =$ Rs 6270

2. (A) Required ratio $= \dfrac{210+231}{140+48} = \dfrac{441}{188}$

3. (B) Required average $= \dfrac{210+80+231}{3} = \dfrac{521}{3} = 173.67$

4. (C) Required sum $= \left(210 \times \dfrac{120}{100}\right) + \left(48 \times \dfrac{125}{100}\right) = 252 + 60 = 312$

5. (D) Required difference $= (210 + 80 + 231) \sim (140 + 48 + 165) = 521 \sim 353 = 168$

[6-10]

Employees who consume only tea $= 190 - (30 + 60 + 50) = 190 - 140 = 50$

Employees who consume only coffee $= 200 - (50 + 70) = 200 - 120 = 80$

Employees who consume coffee & Black coffee both $= 400 - (50 + 30 + 80 + 50 + 60 + 70) = 60$

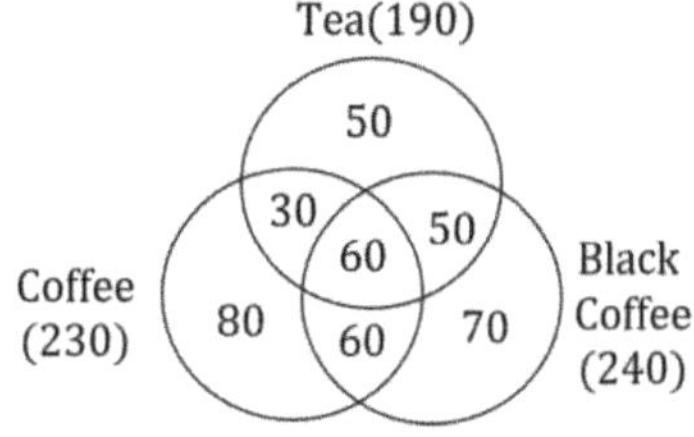

6. (C) Employees who drink exactly 2 drinks $= 30 + 50 + 60 = 140$

7. (A) Required percentage $= \dfrac{230}{240} \times 100 = 95.83\%$

8. (B) Required ratio $= \dfrac{50}{60} = 5:6$

9. (D) Required no. of employees $= 30 + 50 + 60 + 60 = 200$

10. (D) Required difference $= \dfrac{50+70}{2} \sim \dfrac{60+60}{2} = \dfrac{120}{2} \sim \dfrac{120}{2} = 0$

[11-15]

No. of persons who eat only strawberry $= 200 - (80 + 20 + 60) = 40$

No. of persons who eat chocolate & vanilla only $= 260 - (80 + 80 + 60) = 40$

No. of persons who eat only vanilla $= 420 - (80 + 80 + 60 + 20 + 40 + 40) = 100$

No. of persons who eat vanilla $= 100 + 40 + 60 + 20 = 220$

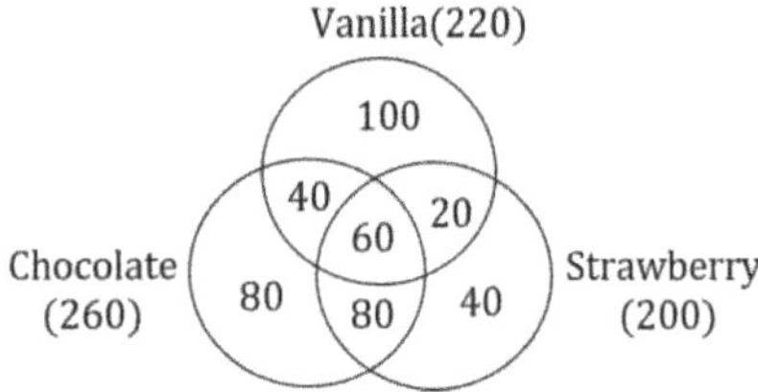

11. (B) No. of people who eat only vanilla $= 100$

12. (C) Required % $= \dfrac{40}{80} \times 100 = 50\%$

13. (A) Required difference $= 40 \sim 60 = 20$

14. (D) Required % $= \dfrac{220}{200} \times 100 = 110\%$

15. (A) Required ratio $= \dfrac{100+80}{40} = \dfrac{180}{40} = 9:2$

[16-20]

Let number of males & females who use their tickets to watch Cricket be 13x & 7x respectively.

No. of males who use their ticket in watching football $= 144 + 7x$

Let no. of females who use their ticket in watching Hockey be y.

Total no. of tickets $= 900$

$7x + 144 + 13x = 7x + y + 348$

$13x - y = 204$

$7x + 144 + 13x + y + 7x = 900$

$27x + y = 756$

Solving: $x = 24$

$y = 13x - 204 = 312 - 204 = 108$

	Male	Female
Football	$7x + 144 = 312$	$y = 108$
Cricket	$13x = 312$	$7x = 168$

16. (C) Required ratio $= \dfrac{312+108}{312+168} = \dfrac{420}{480} = 7:8$

17. (B) Required difference $= (108 + 168) \sim 312 = 276 \sim 312 = 36$

18. (A) No. of special guest in football match $= \dfrac{25}{100} \times 312 = 78$

Required difference = $312 \sim 78 = 234$

19. (D) Required difference = $(312 + 312) \sim (108 + 168) = 624 \sim 276 = 348$

20. (B) Required average $= \frac{312+168}{2} = \frac{480}{2} = 240$

[21-25]

21. (B) Total no. of girls $= 3600 \times \frac{5}{12} = 1500$

22. (C) 30% of girls enrolled in BE(IT) $= \frac{30}{100} \times 1500 = 450$

Remaining girls $= 1500 - 450 = 1050$

Girls enrolled in BE(CS) & BE(ECE) in the ratio 3:2

Girls enrolled in BE(ECE) $= \frac{2}{5} \times 1050 = 420$

23. (A) Total no. of boys $= \frac{7}{12} \times 3600 = 2100$

24. (D) Required % $= \frac{\frac{3}{5} \times 1050}{1500} \times 100 = \frac{630}{1500} \times 100 = 42$

25. (C) Required average $= \frac{2100-1050}{2} = \frac{1050}{2} = 525$

PRACTICE:

Study the given passages carefully and answer the questions.

[1-5]

In an IT company, there are three different company laptops are available for usag e ie. Apple, Dell and HP. There are 2000 employees in total. Some employees use single laptop while some use more than one. 40 users use all 3 company laptops. 300 employees use more than one company's laptop. 400 employees use only HP's laptop while 560 use only Dell's laptop. 40% of total employees use Dell's laptop & same no. of employees use Apple & Dell both and Dell & HP both.

1. How many employees are using only Apple & HP together?
(A) 62　　(B) 55　　(C) 50　　(D) 60　　(E) None of these

2. Employees using only Apple's laptop are what percent of employees using only HP's laptop?
(A) 142%　　(B) 185%　　(C) 176%　　(D) 182%　　(E) None of these

3. What is the ratio of employees using both Apple & HP laptops together to employees using all 3 company laptops?
(A) 5:2　　(B) 2:5　　(C) 3:2　　(D) 2:3　　(E) None of these

4. Employees using Apple laptop are what percent more than the employees using HP's laptop? (approx.)
(A) 56.67%　　(B) 54.45%　　(C) 59.32%　　(D) 55.25%　　(E) None of these

5. How many employees use only one company laptop?
(A) 1500　　(B) 1600　　(C) 1800　　(D) 1700　　(E) None of these

[6-10]

Six students A, B, C, D, E and F participated in a test of 400 marks. C scored 50% marks which are 25% higher than that of E. Ratio of marks obtained by A, B and F is 9:12:8 respectively. D scored 62.5% more marks than E who scored same marks as by B.

6. Who scored highest marks among the 6 students?
   (A) D   (B) B   (C) A   (D) C   (E) None of these

7. If passing marks is 40% of maximum marks, then marks scores by D is what percent more than the passing marks?
   (A) 62%   (B) 61.75%   (C) 63%   (D) 62.5%   (E) None of these

8. What is the ratio of marks obtained by F, B and D?
   (A) 8:7:13   (B) 9:5:13   (C) 9:8:13   (D) 9:6:13   (E) None of these

9. What is the average marks obtained by all 6 students?
   (A) 210   (B) 200   (C) 180   (D) 150   (E) None of these

10. The marks obtained by C is what percentage more/less than the marks obtained by D? (approx.)
    (A) 25%   (B) 21%   (C) 24%   (D) 23%   (E) None of these

[11-15]

In a family there are four members ie. P, Q, R & S. Ratio of income of Q, S & R is 3:4:6 respectively and income of P is equal to average of the income of R & S. Expenditure of P and S is same whereas the expenditure of Q & R is same. Savings of R is equal to income of S. Saving of S is Rs 3000 more than the savings of Q. Savings & expenditure of P is same.

11. Find the average of savings of P, Q & R.
    (A) Rs 15,000   (B) Rs 16,000   (C) Rs 15,500   (D) Rs 14,500   (E) None of these

12. Find the difference between total income of R & S together and total income of P & Q together?
    (A) Rs 13,500   (B) Rs 12,000   (C) Rs 14,000   (D) Rs 13,000   (E) None of these

13. Savings of S is what percent of the expenditure of Q?
    (A) 80%   (B) 72%   (C) 76%   (D) 75%   (E) None of these

14. 40% & 30% of the total expenditure of S & P respectively are on clothes then find the total expenditure on clothes by these two.
    (A) Rs 10,500   (B) Rs 11,500   (C) Rs 10,000   (D) Rs 9,800   (E) None of these

15. Total savings of P & R together is what percent more than the income of S?
    (A) 62.5%   (B) 61.25%   (C) 62%   (D) 63%   (E) None of these

[16-20]

In a showroom there were cars from three companies ie, Maruti, Suzuki, Tata. 300 customers have bought cars from the showroom. 50% customers purchased Maruti, 55% customers purchased Tata, 45% customers purchased Suzuki. 20% of customers who purchased Maruti also purchased other two brands. Customers who purchased any of two brands are 95. Customers of only Maruti are 20 more than that of only Suzuki. Customers who purchased only Maruti and Suzuki are 40.

16. How many of them did not purchase any of the three cars?
    (A) 10   (B) 5   (C) 15   (D) 2   (E) None of these

17. How many of them purchased only one company car?

(A) 175   (B) 165   (C) 168   (D) 170   (E) None of these

18. How many of them purchased at least two companies' cars?

(A) 125   (B) 120   (C) 130   (D) 115   (E) None of these

19. How many of them didn't purchase only Suzuki car?

(A) 260   (B) 255   (C) 265   (D) 250   (E) None of these

20. What is the total number of cars which have been sold?

(A) 400   (B) 450   (C) 420   (D) 460   (E) None of these

SOLUTION:

[1-5]

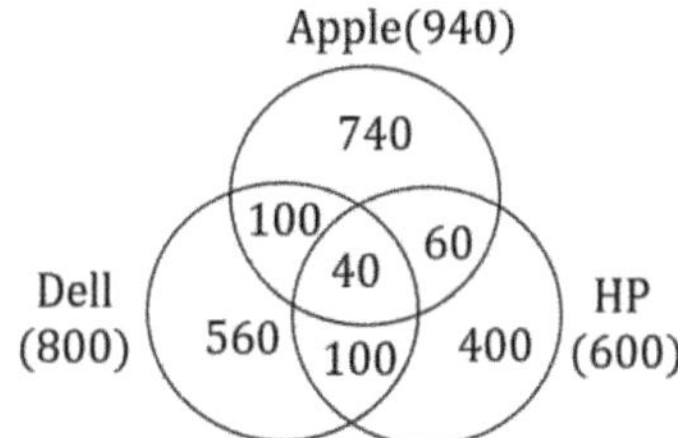

1. (D) Employees using only Apple & HP = 60

2. (B) Required % $= \frac{740}{400} \times 100 = 185\%$

3. (C) Required ratio $= \frac{60}{40} = 3:2$

4. (A) Required % $= \frac{940-600}{600} \times 100 = \frac{340}{6} = 56.67\%$

5. (D) Required no. of employees $= 740 + 400 + 560 = 1700$

[6-10]

Marks of

- C $= \frac{50}{100} \times 400 = 200$

- E $= \frac{100}{125} \times 200 = 160$

- B $=$ E $= 160$

- D $= \frac{162.5}{100} \times 160 = 260$

- A $= \frac{12}{8} \times 160 = 240$

- F $= \frac{9}{8} \times 160 = 180$

6. (A) D scored the highest marks.

7. (D) Passing marks $= \frac{40}{100} \times 400 = 160$

Required % $= \frac{260-160}{160} \times 100 = \frac{100}{160} \times 100 = 62.5\%$

8. (C) Required ratio $= 180:160:260 = 9:8:13$

9. (B) Required average $= \dfrac{200+160+160+260+240+180}{6} = 200$

10. (D) Required % $= \dfrac{200\sim260}{260} \times 100 = \dfrac{60}{260} \times 100 = 23.077\% = 23\%$

[11-15]

	Income	Expenditure	Savings
P	30,000	15,000	15,000
Q	18,000	12,000	6,000
R	36,000	12,000	24,000
S	24,000	15,000	9,000

11. (A) Required average $= \dfrac{15,000+6,000+2,4000}{3} = \dfrac{45,000}{3} = $ Rs 15,000

12. (B) Required difference $= (36,000 + 24,000)\sim(30,000 + 18,000) = 60,000 \sim 48,000 =$ Rs 12,000

13. (D) Required % $= \dfrac{9,000}{12,000} \times 100 = 75\%$

14. (C) Required amount $= \left(\dfrac{40}{100} \times 15,000\right) + \left(\dfrac{30}{100} \times 15,000\right) = 6000 + 4500 = $ Rs 10,500

15. (A) Required % $= \dfrac{(15,000+24,000)\sim 24,000}{24,000} \times 100 = \dfrac{39,000\sim24,000}{240} = \dfrac{15,000}{240} = 62.5\%$

[16-20]

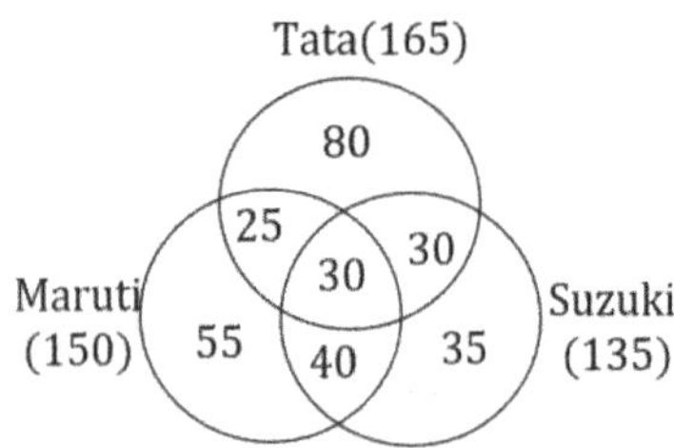

16. (B) Required no. of customers $= 300 - (80 + 55 + 35 + 25 + 40 + 30 + 30)$

$$= 300 - 295 = 5$$

17. (D) Required value $= 80 + 55 + 35 = 170$

18. (A) Required value $= 25 + 30 + 40 + 30 = 125$

19. (C) Required value $= 300 - 35 = 265$

20. (B) Total cars sold $= 165 + 135 + 150 = 450$

QUANTITY BASED INEQUALITY

Two statements of separate questions are given. We need to solve them & find out the value of two quantities asked in the statements. We need to establish a comparative relation between the two quantities, we found out.

The conclusions that can be made are

(A) $x < y$

(B) $x > y$

(C) $x \leq y$

(D) $x \geq y$

(E) $x = y$

(F)   No relation can be established (in some cases of comparison between more than 2 roots)

EXERCISE:

In the following questions, two quantities Q1 and Q2 are given. By solving both the quantities determine the relation between their values and choose the appropriate answer.

(A) If Q1 < Q2

(B) If Q1 > Q2

(C) If Q1 ≥ Q2

(D) If Q1 ≤ Q2

(E) If Q1 = Q2 or no relation can be established

1. What is the number?
    Q1: 35% of a number is 42.
    Q2: 20% of a number is 36.

2. Find the distance covered.
    Q1: The speed of a bike is 40 kmph throughout the journey of 4 hours.
    Q2: It takes 5 hours to cover a distance at uniform speed of 15 kmph.

3. Find the population of town in the previous year.
    Q1: The population increases by 12% every year and it is 12,000 at present.
    Q2: In previous year, female population was 45% more than the male population which was 4000.

4. **Q1:** 94.
    Q2: Average marks in Maths & Physics is 82 while that in Chemistry, Maths & Physics is 86. Find marks in chemistry.

5. **Q1:** Arun's present monthly salary is Rs 20,000 of which he spends 70% on food, clothes & rent. If he saves Rs 3000. What can be his other expenditures?
    Q2: Ravi spends 30% of his income on travel and 40% of remaining on other expenses and saves the remaining Rs 1260. Find his income.

6. 6x men can complete a piece of work in x days while 5y men can complete the same work in 5y/6 days.
    Q1: Value of $y + 2$.
    Q2: Value of $\frac{4}{5}x$

7. **Q1:** A can do a piece of work in 22 days & B can do the same piece of work in 15 days. On working together, find the no.

of days required by A and B to complete the work.

Q2: P can do a piece of work in 6 days; Q can do the same piece of work in 4 days. R is 20% more efficient than P, find the no. of days required to complete the work when all work together?

8. **Q1:** A can complete a work in 30 days and A & B together can complete the same work in 18 days. In how many days B alone will complete the same work?
   Q2: A train crosses a pole in 10 seconds and a 250 m long platform in 35 seconds. What is the speed of the train? (km/hr)

9. **Q1:** $y^2 - 31y - 66 = 0$
   Q2: Area of a rectangle is 270 cm² & differences between length & breadth is 3 cm. Find the sum of length & breadth.

10. **Q1:** Find a.
    70% of a = 7000
    Q2: Anu invested Rs X at 15% pa at SI for 1 year and Rs (X-2000) at 10% pa at SI for 2 years. If Anu received total interest of Rs 2400, then find X.

11. A boat takes total 15 hours, to cover 200 km each in upstream & in downstream. Ratio of speed of boat in still water to speed of stream is 3:1.
    Q1: Find the time taken by same boat to cover 180 km in still water.
    Q2: Find the time taken by the same boat to cover 150 km in upstream.

12. **Q1:** Pipe A and Pipe B alone can fill the tank in 25 hours and 18 hours respectively. Efficiency of pipe C is 20% more than that of pipe B. Find the time taken by pipe C alone to fill the tank.
    Q2: 15 hours.

13. **Q1:** Find X if 65% of X = 26.
    Q2: There are 2 numbers A & B. A is 25% more than B and product of A & B = 5120. Find A.

14. **Q1:** A shopkeeper marked up the price of the bottle by 50% and gave a discount of 16 2/3%. The cost price of the bottle is Rs 320. Find the selling price of the bottle.
    Q2: If the book is sold at a profit of 5% instead of 5% loss, the shopkeeper gets Rs 36 more. Find the cost price of the book.

15. **Q1:** x: $9x^2 - 18x + 8 = 0$
    Q2: y: $35y^2 - 41y + 12 = 0$

16. **Q1:** x: $x^2 + 13x + 40 = 0$
    Q2: y: $y^2 + 7y + 10 = 0$

17. **Q1:** Pipe A alone & Pipe B alone can fill a tank in 30 mins & 20 mins respectively. But it is found that there is leakage in a tank, due to which pipes take 3 minutes extra to fill the tank when both pipes are opened together. Find the time taken by leakage alone to empty the filled tank alone (in hours).
    Q2: 1 hour.

18. **Q1:** x: $15x^2 - 44x + 21 = 0$
    Q2: y: $20y^2 - 51y + 28 = 0$

19. **Q1:** Length of platform (in metres): A train moving with a speed of 72 kmph crosses a man who is moving in opposite direction of train at a speed of 3 kmph in 18 seconds and crosses a platform in 36 seconds.
    Q2: Length of the train (in metres): A train crosses a tree in 20 seconds & crosses a bridge of 600 metre in 45 seconds.

20. Q1: $x: 25/x^2 = 64$
Q2: $y: 63y^2 - 71y + 20 = 0$

SOLUTION:

1. (A) Let the required no. be x.
Q1: $\frac{35}{100} \times x = 42; \quad x = 120$
Q2: $\frac{20}{100} \times x = 36; \quad x = 180$
Q1 < Q2

2. (B) **Q1:** Distance covered
$= 40 \times 4 = 160 \text{ kms}$
Q2: Distance covered
$= 15 \times 5 = 75 \text{ kms}$
Q1 > Q2

3. (B) **Q1:** Previous year population
$= 12{,}000 \times \frac{100}{120} = 10{,}000$
Q2: Female population $= \frac{145}{100} \times 4000$
$= 5800$
Total population $= 5800 + 4000$
$= 9800$
Q1 > Q2

4. (E) **Q1:** 94
Q2: Marks in chemistry
$= (86 \times 3) - (82 \times 2) = 94$
Q1 = Q2

5. (E) **Q1:** Spent amount $= 20{,}000 \times \frac{70}{100}$
$= \text{Rs } 14{,}000$
Other expenditure
$= 20{,}000 - (1{,}40{,}000 + 3000)$
$= \text{Rs } 3000$
Q2: Let the income be x.
- Amount of spent on travel $= 0.3x$
- Other expenses $= (0.7 \times 0.4)x = 0.28x$
Remaining $= x - (0.3x + 0.28x)$
$= x - 0.58x = 0.42x$
$0.42x = 1260$

$x = 3000$
Q1 > Q2

6. (B) $6x \times x = 5y \times \frac{5y}{6}$
$36x^2 = 25y^2$
$\frac{x^2}{y^2} = \frac{25}{36}$
$\frac{x}{y} = \frac{5}{6}$
$x = 5a, y = 6a$
Q1: $6a + 2$
Q2: $\frac{4}{5}(5a) = 4a$
Q1 > Q2

7. (B) **Q1:** Let total work be 330 units (LCM)
Efficiency of
- $A = \frac{330}{22} = 15 \frac{\text{units}}{\text{day}}$
- $B = \frac{330}{15} = 22 \frac{\text{hours}}{\text{day}}$
- $A + B = \frac{330}{15+22} = 8\frac{34}{37}$ days

Q2: Let total work be 60 units.
- $P = \frac{60}{6} = 10$ units/day
- $Q = \frac{60}{4} = 15$ units/day
- $R = \frac{60}{\left(6 \times \frac{100}{120}\right)} = \frac{60}{5}$
$= 12$ units/ days
- $P+Q+R = \frac{60}{15+10+12} = \frac{60}{37}$
$= 1\frac{23}{37}$ days

Q1 > Q2

8. (B) **Q1:** Work done by Q alone
$= \frac{1}{18} - \frac{1}{30} = \frac{1}{45}$
No. of days $= 45$ days
Q2: Speed of train $= \frac{250}{(35-10)} \times \frac{18}{5}$
$= \frac{250}{25} \times \frac{18}{5}$
$= 36 \text{ km/hr}$
Q1 > Q2

9. (D) **Q1:** $y^2 - 31y - 66 = 0$
$y - 33y + 2y - 66 = 0$

$$(y - 33)(y + 2)$$
$$y = 33, -2$$

Q2: $lb = 270$

$$b = \frac{270}{l}$$
$$b = l - 3$$
$$\frac{270}{l} = l - 3$$
$$l^2 - 3l - 270 = 0$$
$$l = 18, b = 15 \text{ cm}$$
$$l + b = 33 \text{ cm}$$
$$\textbf{Q1} \leq \textbf{Q2}$$

10. (B) Q1: $a = \frac{7000 \times 100}{70} = 10{,}000$

Q2: $X \times \frac{15}{100} + (X - 2000) \times \frac{10}{100} \times 2$
$$= 2400$$
$$0.35x = 2800$$
$$x = 8000$$
$$\textbf{Q1} > \textbf{Q2}$$

11. (A) $\frac{200}{3x+x} + \frac{200}{3x-x} = 15$

$$\frac{200}{4x} + \frac{200}{2x} = 15$$
$$x = 10$$

Speed of boat in still water $= 10 \times 3$
$$= 30 \text{ kmph}$$

Speed of stream $= 10 \times 1 = 10$ kmph

Q1: Required time $= \frac{180}{30} = 6$ hours

Q2: Required time $= \frac{150}{30 - 10} = 7.5$ hours

$$\textbf{Q1} < \textbf{Q2}$$

12. (E) Q1: Let total capacity be 450 litres.
Efficiency of

- $A = \frac{450}{25} = 18$ litres/hours
- $B = \frac{450}{18} = 25$ litres/hour
- $C = \frac{120}{100} \times 25 = 30$ litres/hours

Required time $= \frac{450}{30} = 15$ hours

Q2: 15 hours
$$\textbf{Q1} = \textbf{Q2}$$

13. (A) Q1: $X = \frac{26 \times 100}{65} = 40$

Q2: $A = 1.25 B$
$$AB = 2560$$
$$B(1.25B) = 2560$$
$$B^2 = \frac{5120}{1.25} = 4096$$
$$B = \sqrt{4096} = 64$$
$$\textbf{Q1} < \textbf{Q2}$$

14. (B) Q1: SP of the bottle

$$= 320 \times \frac{150}{100} \times \frac{\left(1 - {}^{50}/_3\right)}{100}$$
$$= 320 \times \frac{150}{100} \times \frac{5}{6} = \text{Rs } 400$$

Q2: Let cost price of the book be Rs 100x.

$$105x - 95x = 36$$
$$10x = 36$$
$$x = 3.6$$

CP of book $= 3.6 \times 100 = $ Rs 360
$$\textbf{Q1} > \textbf{Q2}$$

15. (B) Q1: $9x^2 - 18x + 8 = 0$
$$9x^2 - 12x - 6x + 8 = 0$$
$$(3x - 4)(3x - 2) = 0$$
$$x = \frac{4}{3}, \frac{2}{3}$$

Q2: $35y^2 - 41y + 12 = 0$
$$35y^2 - 20y - 21y + 12 = 0$$
$$5y(7y - 4) - 3(7y - 4) = 0$$
$$(5y - 3)(7y - 4) = 0$$
$$y = \frac{3}{5}, \frac{4}{7}$$

$$\textbf{Q1} > \textbf{Q2}$$

16. (D) Q1: $x^2 + 13x + 40 = 0$
$$x^2 + 8x + 5x + 40 = 0$$
$$x(x + 8) + 5(x + 8) = 0$$
$$(x + 5)(x + 8) = 0$$
$$x = -5, -8$$

Q2: $y^2 + 7y + 10 = 0$
$$y^2 + 5y + 2y + 10 = 0$$
$$y(y + 5) + 2(y + 5) = 0$$
$$(y + 2)(y + 5) = 0$$
$$y = -2, -5$$

$$\textbf{Q1} \leq \textbf{Q2}$$

17. (E) Q1: Let leakage take T minutes to empty the tank.

A & B take $= \dfrac{1}{\left(\frac{1}{20}+\frac{1}{30}\right)} = \dfrac{600}{50}$

$= 12$ minutes to fill the tank.

$\dfrac{1}{20} + \dfrac{1}{30} - \dfrac{1}{T} = \dfrac{1}{12+3}$

$\dfrac{1}{12} - \dfrac{1}{T} = \dfrac{1}{15}$

$\dfrac{1}{T} = \dfrac{1}{60}$

$T = 60$ minutes $= 1$ hour

Q2: 1 hour

Q1 < Q2

18. (E) Q1: $15x^2 - 44x + 21 = 0$

$\qquad 15x^2 - 35x - 9x + 21 = 0$

$\qquad 5x(3x - 7) - 3(3x - 7) = 0$

$\qquad (5x - 3)(3x - 7) = 0$

$\qquad x = \dfrac{3}{5}, \dfrac{7}{3}$

Q2: $20y^2 - 51y + 28 = 0$

$\qquad 20y^2 - 35y - 16y + 28 = 0$

$\qquad 5y(4y - 7) - 4(4y - 7) = 0$

$\qquad (5y - 4)(4y - 7) = 0$

$\qquad y = \dfrac{4}{5}, \dfrac{7}{4}$

No relation can be established.

19. (A) Q1: $18 \times (72 + 3) \times \dfrac{5}{18} = l$

$\qquad l = 375$ meter

$\qquad 375 + P = 36 \times 72 \left(\dfrac{5}{18}\right)$

$\qquad 375 + P = 720$

$\qquad P = 720 - 375 = 345$ metres

Q2: Let speed of the train $= x$ m/s

$\qquad l = 20 \times x$

$\qquad 45x = 600 + l = 600 + 20x$

$\qquad 25x = 600; x = 24$

$\qquad l = 20 \times 24 = 480$ metres

Q1 < Q2

20. (E) Q1: $x^2 = \dfrac{25}{64}$

$\qquad x = \pm \dfrac{5}{8}$

Q2: $63y^2 - 71y + 20 = 0$

$63y^2 - 35y - 36y + 20 = 0$

$7y(9y - 5) - 4(9y - 5) = 0$

$(7y - 4)(9y - 5) = 0$

$y = \dfrac{4}{7}, \dfrac{5}{9}$

No relation can be established.

PRACTICE:

In the following questions, two quantities Q1 and Q2 are given. By solving both the quantities determine the relation between their values and choose the appropriate answer.

(A) If Q1 < Q2

(B) If Q1 > Q2

(C) If Q1 $\geq$ Q2

(D) If Q1 $\leq$ Q2

(E) If Q1 = Q2 or no relation can be established

1. **Q1:** $x: 4x^2 - 12x + 9 = 0$
    Q2: $y: 8y^2 - 22y + 15 = 0$

2. **Q1:** Distance (in km): A person covers one-third of distance by train with an average speed of 60 kmph, another one-third of a distance by bus with an average speed of 45 kmph & the remaining distance by car with an average speed of 30 kmph. In the whole journey, he takes 13 hours.
    Q2: Distance travelled in 7.2 hours at a rate of 75 kmph.

3. **Q1:** CP of book: Shopkeeper earns a profit of 25% when he sold the book Rs 120 above cost price.
    Q2: Difference between SI & CI after 2 years: A person invests Rs 10,000 each on SI & CI for two years at 20% per annum.

4. A, B & C start a business by investing Rs 5000, Rs 8000 & Rs 10,000 respectively. After 4 months, B invests Rs 4000 more, after another 4 months. A invests Rs 3000 more & C withdraws Rs 2000.
Q1: Average profit of A, B & C after 1 year.
Q2: Profit of C at the end of the year.

5. **Q1:** t (in months): A starts a business with an investment of Rs 30,000 after 't' months. B joins him with an investment of Rs 40,000. At the end of the year the profit share of A & B are Rs 45,000 and Rs 35,000 respectively.
Q2: T (in years): A person invests Rs 36,000 at simple interest at the rate of 40% per annum for T years. After T years, he got the interest of Rs 36,000.

6. P, Q & R started a business with investment of Rs 4000, Rs 6000 and Rs 10,000. After 6 months, A invests Rs 4000 more & B invests Rs 2000 more. In the end of the year, total profit earned by them was Rs 92,000.
Q1: Total profit of A & B together.
Q2: Total profit of B & C together.

7. **Q1:** Time (in months): A borrows Rs 24,000 from a bank at SI at the rate of 15% per annum. He settled up the amount by Rs 34,800 to the bank after some time.
Q2: Time (in months): B invests Rs 23,600 at CI at the rate of 20% per annum and after some time he got Rs 10,384 as interest.

8. **Q1:** A train can cross a pole in 12 seconds and a tunnel in 55.2 seconds. If the length of the tunnel is 2100 m. Find the length of the train.

Q2: A train can cross a tree in 30 seconds with a speed of 72 km/hr. Find the length of the train.

9. **Q1:** x: $x^2 - 29x + 204 = 0$
Q2: x: $(x + 3)^2 - (x - 3)^2 = x^2$

10. **Q1:** Time taken (in mins) by Sara to cover a distance of 480 km (without stoppage) by car through which he covers a distance of 200 km in 2 hours when he stops to get fuel for 20 minutes.
Q2: Time taken (in mins) by Clare to travel 40 km downstream, if speed of the boat and speed of stream be 7 kmph & 3 kmph respectively.

11. **Q1:** The length & breadth of a rectangle of perimeter 96 cm are in the ratio 3:1. Find area.
Q2: $23^2 - (10^2 - 3)$

12. $(a + b)/ab = ?$
Q1: $x^2 + x - 6 = 0$; a, b are roots of the equation
Q2: $a^2 + b^2 = 20, ab = 8$

13. What is the number?
Q1: 45% of number is 36.
Q2: 5/9 of number is 55.

14. Find the time taken to cover 60 km (in hours)
Q1: The speed of bicycle is 20 kmph.
Q2: A car covers 30 km in 45 minutes.

15. Three numbers A, B & C are in the ratio 4:7:6 respectively and their average is $192\,{}^{2}/_{3}$
Q1: Sum of A & C.
Q2: Sum of 75% of B and 20% of sum of A & C.

16. Average of present ages of A, B & C is 35 years. 1 year ago, B is twice old as C

while 5 years hence, A is two-third as old as B.

Q1: Find the age of A, when C was born.

Q2: 6 years.

17. **Q1:** A cylinder of height 14 metres radius of base is 50 centimetres. The curved surface area of cylinder is

Q2: A square of side 7 m is bent into the form of a circle. Find the area of the circle.

18. A boat covers 10 km distance in 60 minutes in still water. Speed of stream is half of the speed of boat in still water.

Q1: If boat takes 4 hours to row to a place & back, then how far is the place?

Q2: Thrice the speed of stream.

19. There are 5 green and 3 blue balls in the box.

Q1: The probability of drawing 2 green balls and 1 blue ball.

Q2: The probability of drawing 1 green ball and 2 blue balls.

20. In how many ways can 5 boys or 4 girls be selected?

Q1: The group comprises 10 boys and 10 girls.

Q2: There are 20 persons in which 8 are boys.

SOLUTION:

1. (C) **Q1:** $4x^2 - 12x + 9 = 0$

$$4x^2 - 6x - 6x + 9 = 0$$
$$2x(2x - 3) - 3(2x - 3) = 0$$
$$(2x - 3)(2x - 3) = 0$$
$$x = \frac{3}{2}, \frac{3}{2}$$

Q2: $8y^2 - 22y + 15 = 0$

$$8y^2 - 12y - 10y + 15 = 0$$
$$4y(2y - 3) - 5(2y - 3) = 0$$
$$(4y - 5)(2y - 3) = 0$$

$$y = \frac{5}{4}, \frac{3}{2}$$

Q1 ≥ Q2

2. (E) Let total distance be x km.

Q1: $\dfrac{\frac{x}{3}}{60} + \dfrac{\frac{x}{3}}{45} + \dfrac{\frac{x}{3}}{30} = 13$

$$\frac{x}{180} + \frac{x}{135} + \frac{x}{90} = 13$$
$$\frac{3x + 4x + 6x}{540} = 13$$
$$\frac{13x}{540} = 13$$
$$x = 540 \text{ km}$$

Q2: Distance $= 75 \times 7.2 = 540$ km

Q1 = Q2

3. (B) **Q1:** $25\% = 120$

$$100\% = \text{Rs } 480$$
$$CP = \text{Rs } 480$$

Q2: $SI = 40\%$ of P

$$CI = 20 + 20 + \frac{(20)^2}{100}$$
$$= 44\% \text{ of } P$$

Required difference $= 4\%$ of P

$$= \frac{4}{100} \times 10,000$$
$$= \text{Rs } 400$$

Q1 > Q2

4. (A) Ratio of the profits of A, B & C.

$$(5k \times 8) + (8k \times 4):$$
$$(8k \times 4) + (12k \times 8):$$
$$(10k \times 8) + (8k \times 4)$$
$$= 9 : 16 : 14$$

Q1: Required average $= \dfrac{39}{3} = 13x$

Q2: $14x$

Q1 < Q2

5. (B) **Q1:** Profit share: $\dfrac{30,000 \times 12}{40,000 \times (12 - t)}$

$$= \frac{45,000}{35,000} = \frac{9}{7}$$
$$\frac{9}{12 - t} = \frac{9}{7}$$
$$108 - 9t = 63$$
$$9t = 45$$
$$t = 5 \text{ months}$$

Q2: $36,000 \times \frac{40}{100} \times T = 36,000$

$$T = \frac{100}{40} = 2.5 \text{ years}$$

Q1 > Q2

6. (A) Profit ratio of A, B & C:

$(4000 \times 6) + (8000 \times 6)$:

$(6000 \times 6) + (8000 \times 6)$:

$10,000 \times 12$

$= 6 : 7 : 10$

Q1: $\frac{13}{23} \times 92,000 = \text{Rs } 52,000$

Q2: $\frac{17}{23} \times 92,000 = \text{Rs } 68,000$

Q1 < Q2

7. (B) **Q1:** Let time be 'T' years.

SI: $34,800 - 24,000 = \text{Rs } 10,800$

$24,000 \times \frac{15}{100} \times T = 10,800$

$$T = \frac{10,800 \times 100}{24,000 \times 15} = 3 \text{ years}$$

$= 36$ months

Q2: Let time be 't' years.

$$23,600\left(\left(1 + \frac{20}{100}\right)^T - 1\right) = 10,384$$

$T = 2$ years $= 24$ months

Q1 > Q2

8. (E) **Q1:** Let length of train be 'D' meters respectively.

Since, speed of the train is constant,

$$\frac{D}{12} = \frac{D+2100}{54}$$

$54D = 12D + 25,200$

$42D = 25,200$

$D = 600$ m

Q2: Length of the train $= 30 \times 72 \times \frac{5}{18}$

$$= 600 \text{ m}$$

Q1 = Q2

9. (C) **Q1:** $x^2 - 29x + 204 = 0$

$x^2 - 12x - 17x + 204 = 0$

$x(x - 12) - 17(x - 12) = 0$

$(x - 17)(x - 12) = 0$

$x = 17, 12$

Q2: $(x + 3)^2 - (x - 3)^2 = x^2$

$x^2 + 6x + 9 - (x^2 - 6x + 9) = x^2$

$12x = x^2$

$x = 0, 12$

Q1 $\geq$ Q2

10. (B) **Q1:** Actual time

$= 120 - 20 = 100 \; mins$

$$\text{Speed of car} = \frac{200}{100/60}$$

$= 120$ kmph

$$\text{Required time} = \frac{480}{120} \times 100$$

$= 400$ mins

Q2: Required time $= \frac{40}{7+3} = 4$ hours

$= 240$ mins

Q1 > Q2

11. (E) **Q1:** Perimeter $= 2(l + b) = 96$

$2(3x + x) = 96$

$8x = 96$

$x = 12$

$l = 36$ cm, $b = 12$ cm

Area $= 36 \times 12 = 432 \text{ cm}^2$

Q2: $23^2 - (10^2 - 3)$

$= 529 - (100 - 3)$

$= 529 - 97 = 432$

Q1 = Q2

12. (E) **Q1:** $x^2 + x - 6 = 0$

$x^2 + 3x - 2x - 6 = 0$

$x(x + 3) - 2(x + 3) = 0$

$(x - 2)(x + 3) = 0$

$x = 2, -3$

$a = 2, b = -3$

$$\frac{a+b}{ab} = \frac{2-3}{2(-3)} = \frac{-1}{-6} = \frac{1}{6}$$

Q2: $(a + b)^2 = a^2 + b^2 + 2ab$

$$= 20 + 2(8)$$

$(a + b)^2 = 36$

$a + b = \pm 6$

Case 1: $a + b = +6$

$$\frac{a+b}{ab} = \frac{6}{8} = \frac{3}{4}$$

Case 2: $a + b = -6$

$$\frac{a+b}{ab} = \frac{-6}{8} = \frac{-3}{4}$$

No relation can be established.

13. (A) **Q1:** Number $= \frac{36}{45} \times 100 = 80$

Q2: Number $= 55 \times \frac{9}{5} = 99$

Q1 < Q2

14. (B) **Q1:** Time taken $= \frac{60}{20} = 3$ hours

Q2: Speed of car $= \frac{30}{\frac{45}{60}} = 40$ kmph

Time taken $= \frac{60}{40} = 1.5$ hours

Q1 > Q2

15. (A) $\frac{4x+7x+6x}{3} = 192\,{}^{2}/_{3}$

$\frac{17x}{3} = \frac{578}{3}$

$17x = 578;\ x = 34$

$A = 4 \times 34 = 136$

$B = 7 \times 34 = 238$

$C = 6 \times 34 = 204$

Q1: $A + C = 136 + 204 = 340$

Q2: $\frac{75}{100}(234) + \frac{20}{100}(136 + 204)$

$= 175.5 + 68 = 243.5$

Q1< Q2

16. (E) $\frac{A+B+C}{3} = 35$

$A + B + C = 105$

$(B - 1) = 2(C - 1) = 2C - 2$

$C = \frac{B+1}{2}$

$A + 5 = \frac{2}{3}(B + 5)$

$3A + 15 = 2B + 10$

$3A = 2B - 5$

$A = \frac{2B-5}{3}$

On solving, $A = 31; B = 49; C = 25$

Q1: When C was born, A was 6 years old.

Q2: 6 years

Q1 = Q2

17. (A) **Q1:** CSA $= 2\pi rh$

$= 2 \times \frac{22}{7} \times \frac{50}{100} \times 14 = 44$ m^2

Q2: Perimeter of square

$=$ Circumference of circle

$= 4 \times 7 = 28$ cm

Radius of circle $= \frac{28}{2\times\frac{22}{7}} = \frac{28\times7}{2\times22}$

$= \frac{49}{11}$ m

Area $= \frac{22}{7} \times \frac{49}{11} \times \frac{49}{11} = 62.36$ m

Q1 < Q2

18. (E) Speed of boat in still water $= 10$ kmph

Speed of stream $= 5$ kmph

Q1: Let the distance be D km.

$\frac{D}{10+5} + \frac{D}{10-5} = 4$

$\frac{D}{15} + \frac{D}{5} = 4$

$\frac{D+3D}{15} = 4$

$4D = 4 \times 15 = 15$ km

Q2: $3 \times 5 = 15$ km

Q1 = Q2

19. (B) **Q1:** Required probability $= \frac{5C2\times3C1}{8C3}$

$= \frac{10\times3}{56} = \frac{15}{28}$

Q2: Required probability $= \frac{5C1\times3C2}{8C3}$

$= \frac{5 \times 3}{56} = \frac{15}{56}$

Q1 > Q2

20. (A) **Q1:** Boys $= 10$, Girls $= 10$

No. of ways $= 10C5 + 10C4$

$= 462$

Q2: Boys $= 8$, Girls $= 12$

No. of ways $= 8C5 + 12C4 = 551$

Q1 < Q2

DATA SUFFICIENCY

A question followed by two or three statements is given. We need to determine whether any of the statements individually or together is required to find the solution.

Questions can be asked in any topics of quantitative aptitude

Note: There is no need to completely solve the given problem. We need to find out whether the given statements are sufficient to solve the problem.

EXERCISE:

Given below in each question there are two statements (I) and (II). You have to read both the statements and determine which statement(s) is enough to give the answer for the question. There are five alternatives given, choose one alternative as your answer.

(A) Only statement I alone is sufficient, whereas statement II alone is not sufficient

(B) Only statement II alone is sufficient, whereas statement I alone is not sufficient

(C) Either statement I or statement II is sufficient

(D) Neither statement I nor statement II is sufficient

(E) Both statements I and II together are necessary to answer the question

1. What is the volume of the conical building?
   I. The height & radius of the building are in the ratio 5:4, when the sum of radius & height is 18 m.
   II. The slant height is $2\sqrt{41}$ m while the radius is 8 m.

2. Find the value of a & b.
   I. $a^3 + b^3 = 91$
   II. $a:b = 3:4$

3. Find half of the fraction.
   I. Numerator of the fraction is 80% less than the denominator.
   II. Difference between denominator & numerator of the fraction is 4 and numerator of fraction is lesser than denominator.

4. What is the time period for which Varun invested his capital?
   I. Varun and Rana invest in a partnership with total capital of Rs 10 lakhs.
   II. Ratio of time period of investment of Varun & Rana is 4:3 and their profit ratio is 8:9.

5. What is the area of the rectangle?
   I. Length is 50% more than the breadth.
   II. Perimeter of square is 24 cm and breadth of the rectangle is equal to the side of the square.

6. What is the age of James after 2 years?
I. Average age of Anu and Sasi is 24 years and the ratio of age of James to Anu is 2:3.
II. Sasi is 4 years older than Vinoth and ratio of age of Vinoth to James is 1:2.

7. What is the speed of boat in still water when the upstream speed of boat is equal to the speed of the stream?
I. Time required to cover certain distance downstream is 4 hours.
II. Time required to cover same distance upstream is 12 hours.

8. What is the time taken by Sasi to cover a distance of 200 km by car?
I. Sasi covers a distance of 200 km in 5 hours using bike.
II. Speed of bike and that of car is in the ratio 4:5.

9. In how much time can Shoba do the work?
I. Karthiga & Shoba can complete a piece of work in 12 days.
II. Sara & Karthiga can complete the work in 6 days working together.

10. In how many ways can 3 boys & 4 girls be selected?
I. There are 25 persons (boys & girls) in the group out of which 10 are boys.
II. The ratio of boys to girls in the group is 2:3.

11. What is the speed of boat in still water?
I. The speed of boat in upstream is 16 kmph.
II. The speed of boat in downstream is 8 kmph.

12. How many black balls are in the bag?
I. There are 30 balls in a bag of which 14 are yellow.
II. The probability of drawing a black ball from the bag having 30 balls is 0.4

13. What is the speed of bus?
I. The bus can cover a certain distance in 2 hours without stoppage.
II. The bus can cover the same distance in 1 hour if speed increases by 10 kmph.

14. What is the cost price of the mobile?
I. The product is marked up at Rs 12,000.
II. The mobile is sold at a profit of 8%.

15. How many flags are there in the box?
I. There are 8 blue flags in the box.
II. The probability of drawing 2 green flags from 5 green flags from that box is 2/9.

16. In how many days 8 men can finish the work?
I. 5 women can complete the work in 4 days and a man is 2 times as efficient as a woman.
II. 3 men & 6 women take 2 days to complete the same work.

17. What is the speed of the car?
I. The car can cover 80 km in 2 hours if it stops 20 mins after every hour.
II. The car takes 6 hours to cover 240 km.

18. What is the two-digit number?
I. The difference between the actual two-digit no. and the no. after interchanging the digits is 27.
II. The unit digit is 3 more than the digit at ten's place.

19. What will be the age of Tarun after 5 years?
I. Ratio of present ages of Ragu and Tarun is 2:3. Ganesh is 8 years older than Ragu.

II. Present ages of Tarun and Ganesh are in the ratio 9:8.

20. What is the radius of the cylinder?
I. The ratio between the curved surface area and volume of the cylinder is 2:7.
II. The total surface area of the cylinder is 7392 cm². The radius of the base of the cylinder and the height are in the ratio of 3:5.

21. What is the area of the right-angled triangle?
I. Perimeter of the triangle is 'x' cm.
II. Length of the hypotenuse is 'a' cm.
III. Perpendicular sides of the triangle are in the ratio 4:3.
(A) Only statements I & II alone are necessary
(B) Only statements II & III alone are necessary
(C) Only statements I & III alone are necessary
(D) Either (B) or (C)
(E) All the three statements are necessary

22. What is the speed of the train?
I. Length of the train is 240 metres.
II. The train crosses a platform of equal length in 24 seconds,
III. The train crosses a signal pole in 12 seconds.
(A) Only statements I & II alone are necessary
(B) Only statements II & III alone are necessary
(C) I and Either II or III only
(D) II and Either I or III only
(E) All the three statements together are not sufficient

SOLUTION:

1. (C) I. $\dfrac{h}{r} = \dfrac{5}{4}$
$h + r = 18$

$h = 10$ m, $r = 9$ m
Volume of cone can be found.
II. $l = 2\sqrt{41}$ m
$r = 8$ m
$l = \sqrt{r^2 + h^2}$
'h' can be determined & then volume can be found.
Either statement I or statement II is sufficient

2. (E) I. $a^3 + b^3 = 91$
II. $\dfrac{a}{b} = \dfrac{3}{4}$
I + II: Let $a = 3x, b = 4x$
$a^3 + b^3 = (a + b)(a^2 + b^2 - ab)$
$(3x + 4x)[(3x)^2 + (4x)^2 - (3x)(4x)]$
$7x(9x^2 + 16x - 12x)$
$7x(25x^2 - 12x) = 91$
$175x^3 - 84x^2 = 91$
$x^2(175x - 84) = 91$
Thus, $x = 1$
$\therefore a = 3, b = 4$
Both statements I and II together are necessary

3. (A) I. Let denominator of the fraction be a.
Fraction $= \dfrac{a \times \frac{20}{100}}{a} = \dfrac{20}{100} = \dfrac{1}{5}$
Required value $= \dfrac{1}{5} \times \dfrac{1}{2} = \dfrac{1}{10}$
II. $D - N = 4$
Required value can't be determined.
Statement I alone is sufficient

4. (D) I. Let capital of
- Varun be 'P' lakhs
- Rana be '10 − P' lakhs
II. Let time period of investment be '4t' & '3t' respectively.
$\dfrac{P \times 4t}{(10-P) \times 3t} = \dfrac{8}{9}$
$36P = 240 - 24P$
$60P = 204$
$P = 4$ lakhs

Since, total time period of investment is not given, the required value can't be found.

Neither statement I nor statement II is sufficient

5. (E) I. l = 1.5b.
II. Perimeter of square = 24 cm
Side of square = Breadth of rectangle
$= \frac{24}{4} = 6$ cm
l = 6 × 1.5 = 9 cm
Area = 9 × 6 = 54 cm²

Both statements I and II together are necessary

6. (E) I. Total age of Anu & Sasi = 48 years
II. Let age of Vinoth be x years.
Sasi = (x + 4) years
Age of James = 2x years
Age of Anu = 3x years
$\frac{3x+(x+4)}{2} = 24$
4x + 4 = 48
4x = 44
x = 11 years
Age of James after 2 years = 22 + 2
$\qquad\qquad\qquad\qquad = 24$ years

Both statements I and II together are necessary

7. (D) Let the speed of the
- Boat in still water be x kmph
- Stream be y kmph
x − y = y
x = 2y
From I & II:
Distance travelled is constant
(x − y) × 12 = (x + y)4
12x − 12y = 4x + 4y
8x = 16y
Required answer cannot be determined from I & II together.

Neither statement I nor statement II is sufficient

8. (E) I. Speed of bike $= \frac{200}{5} = 40$ km/hr
II. Speed ratio of bike to car $= \frac{4}{5}$
Speed of car = 50 km/hr
Time taken $= \frac{200}{50} = 4$ hours

Both statements I and II together are necessary

9. (D) I. $\frac{1}{K} + \frac{1}{SH} = \frac{1}{12}$
II. $\frac{1}{SA} + \frac{1}{K} = \frac{1}{6}$
From both we can't determine the time taken by Shoba alone when working alone.

Neither statement I nor statement II is sufficient

10. (A) I. No. of boys = 10
No. of girls = 15
Required no. of ways = 10C3 × 15C4
II. Ratio of boys to girls = 2:3
Required no. of ways can't be determined.

Statement I alone is sufficient

11. (E) Let speed of boat in still water & speed of stream be x & y kmph respectively.
I. x + y = 16
II. x − y = 8
I+II: 2x = 24
x = 12 kmph, y = 4 kmph

Both statements I and II together are necessary

12. (B) I. We don't know about the other colour balls in the bag.
II. Let no. of black balls be x.
$\frac{x}{30} = 0.4$
x = 12

Statement II alone is sufficient

13. (E) I+II: Let speed of car be x kmph.

$2x = 1(x + 10)$

$2x = x + 10$

$x = 10$ kmph

Both statements I and II together are necessary

14. (D) No data regarding the relation between CP & MP (or) MP & SP is given.

Neither statement I nor statement II is sufficient

15. (B) II. Let total no. of flags be x.

$\dfrac{5C2}{xC2} = \dfrac{2}{9}$

$\dfrac{5 \times 4}{x(x-1)} = \dfrac{2}{9}$

$x(x - 1) = 90$

$x = 10$

Statement II alone is sufficient

16. (A) I. Time taken by each woman $= 5 \times 4 = 20$

Time taken by each man $= \dfrac{20}{2} = 10$ days

Per day work of

- 1 man $= \dfrac{1}{10}$ units
- 6 men $= 8 \times \dfrac{1}{10} = \dfrac{4}{5}$

Required no. of days $= \dfrac{5}{4} = 1.25$ days

Statement I alone is sufficient

17. (C) I. Total time $= (2 \times 60) - 20$

$= 120 - 20 = 80$ mins $= \dfrac{80}{60}$ hrs $= \dfrac{4}{3}$ hrs

Speed $= \dfrac{80}{4/3} = \dfrac{80 \times 3}{4} = 60$ km/hr

II. Speed of car $= \dfrac{240}{6} = 40$ km/hr

Either statement I or statement II is sufficient

18. (D) Let the digit at unit's place & ten's place be x & y respectively.

I. $(10y + x) \sim (10x + y) = 27$

II. $x = y + 3$

$x - y = 3$

$10x + y - (10y + x) = 27$

$9x - 9y = 27$

$x - y = 3$

Neither statement I nor statement II is sufficient

19. (E) I+II: Let present age of

- Ragu be 2x
- Tarun be 3x
- Ganesh = 2x+8

$\dfrac{3x}{2x+8} = \dfrac{9}{8}$

$24x = 18x + 72$

$6x = 72$

$x = 12$ years

Age of Tarun after 5 years $= 3x + 5 = 3(12) + 5 = 41$ years

Both statements I and II together are necessary

20. (C) I. $\dfrac{2\pi rh}{\pi r^2 h} = \dfrac{2}{7}$

$\dfrac{2}{r} = \dfrac{2}{7}$

$r = 7$ cm

II. $2\pi r(r + h) = 2 \times \dfrac{22}{7} \times 3x \times 8x = 7392$

$x^2 = \dfrac{7392 \times 7}{2 \times 22 \times 3 \times 8} = 49$

$x = 7$ cm

Radius $= 3 \times 7 = 21$ cm

Either statement I or statement II is sufficient

21. (E) **All the three statements are necessary.**

22. (C) I+II: Speed $= 2 \times \dfrac{240}{24} = 20$ m/s

I+III: Speed $= \dfrac{240}{12} = 20$ m/s

Statements I and either II or III only.

PRACTICE:

Given below in each question there are two statements (I) and (II). You have to read both the statements and determine which statement(s) is enough to give the answer for the question. There are five alternatives given, choose one alternative as your answer.

(A) Only statement I alone is sufficient, whereas statement II alone is not sufficient

(B) Only statement II alone is sufficient, whereas statement I alone is not sufficient

(C) Either statement I or statement II is sufficient

(D) Neither statement I nor statement II is sufficient

(E) Both statements I and II together are necessary to answer the question

1. Total no. of male in a block is how much more than total female in year 2020?
   I. Total no. of people in block is 500 in 2019 and no. of male & female are increased by 25% and 25% respectively in 2020 as compared to 2019.
   II. Total male in 2020 in village is 76 more than total female in village in 2019.

2. Workers A & B start working together and every second day (alternate) day B works alone, then find the time taken to complete the work.
   I. Efficiency of B is 20% more than efficiency of A and working together they can complete the work in 34 days.
   II. A & B started the work and A left 22 days and remaining work was completed by B. Total time taken in this process to complete the work is 22 days.

3. What is the rate of simple interest?
   I. Simple interest is Rs 280.
   II. Duration is 2 years.

4. What is the present salary of Yokesh?
   I. Yokesh saves Rs 2500 which is 5% of his salary.
   II. Yokesh spends Rs 15000 more than he spends.

5. What is the present population?
   I. The population last year was 9500.
   II. The population increases 12% every year.

6. What tis the ratio of x to y?
   I. 25% of x is 80% of y.
   II. 32% of x is 64% of y.

7. How many people (male + female) are there in the bus?
   I. There are 12 females in the bus.
   II. 40% of total passengers are females.

8. What is the age of A?
   I. A is younger than B.
   II. Average age of A & B is 14 years.

9. Find the breadth of the rectangle, if the length of the rectangle is 32 cm.
   I. Perimeter of the rectangle is equal to the perimeter of the square whose area is 484 cm².
   II. The perimeter of square is 96 cm. The area of the square is equal to the area of the rectangle.

10. A bag contains 'a' red balls, 'b' green balls and 9 white balls. Find the difference between red & green balls.
    I. If one ball is taken out randomly from bag, the probability of it being red is 3/16.

II. If one ball is taken out randomly from bag, the probability of it being green is 1/4.

11. What is the total strength of the office?
I. Ratio of male to female employees is 2:3.
II. Total female employees are 180 and males are 80% of females.

12. What is the ratio of boys to girls in the class?
I. Total no. of students in the class is 70.
II. Boys are 40% more than girls.

13. How many bicycles are there in the parking lot?
I. If 7 bicycles are removed and 17 more are parked, no. of bicycles become 1 more than 5 times the no. of bicycles removed.
II. 28% of parking lot is available for parking.

14. What is the average type of A, B & C.
I. B is 4 years younger to A.
II. Average age of A & C is 16 years.

15. Find the area of the floor.
I. Painting cost of the floor is Rs 18/sq.m
II. Flooring of the hall at the rate of Rs 80/sq.m is Rs 9600.

16. What is the area of the isosceles triangle?
I. Height of the triangle is 10 metres.
II. Base of the triangle is 28 metres.
III. Perimeter of the triangle is 28 metres.
(A) Only statements I & II alone are necessary
(B) Only statements II & III alone are necessary

(C) Only statements I & III alone are necessary
(D) All the three statements are necessary
(E) All the three statements together are not sufficient

17. What is the monthly salary of A?
I. A earns Rs 8000 more than B.
II. The ratio of B and C's monthly salary is 2:3.
III. C earns Rs 2000 less than A.
(A) Only statements I & II alone are necessary
(B) Only statements II & III alone are necessary
(C) Only statements I & III alone are necessary
(D) All the three statements are necessary
(E) All the three statements together are not sufficient

18. What is the difference between two nos. A and B?
I. A is 40 percent more than another number C.
II. B is 40 percent less than C.
III. The sum of B and C is 144.
(A) Only statements I & II alone are necessary
(B) Only statements II & III alone are necessary
(C) Only statements I & III alone are necessary
(D) All the three statements are necessary
(E) All the three statements together are not sufficient

SOLUTION:

1. (E) I & II: Let no. of male & female in 2019 be 'x' & 'y' respectively.
$1.25x - y = 76$
$x + y = 500$
Thus, $2.25x = 576$
$x = 256, y = 244$
Required value $= 1.25x - 1.25y$
$= 320 - 305 = 15$
Both statements I and II together are necessary

2. (A) I. Let efficiency of A be 10x units/day
Efficiency of B $= 10x \times \dfrac{120}{100}$
$= 12x$ units/days
Total work $= (10x + 12x) \times 34$
$= 748x$ units
2 days work $= (10x + 12x) + 12x$
$= 34x$
Required no. of days $= \dfrac{748x}{34x} \times 2$
$= 44$ days
Statement I alone is sufficient

3. (D) Since principle is not given, SI can't be determined.
Neither statement I nor statement II is sufficient

4. (A) I. Salary $= \dfrac{2500}{5} \times 100 = 50,000$
II. Expenditure $= 15,000 +$ Savings
Salary can't be determined
Statement I alone is sufficient

5. (E) I+II: Present population
$= \dfrac{112}{100} \times 9500$
$= 10,640$
Both statements I and II together are necessary

6. (C) I. $\dfrac{25}{100}x = \dfrac{80}{100}y$
$25x = 80y$
$\dfrac{x}{y} = \dfrac{80}{25} = \dfrac{16}{5}$
II. $\dfrac{32}{100}x = \dfrac{64}{100}y$
$x = 2y$
$\dfrac{x}{y} = \dfrac{2}{1}$
Either statement I or statement II is sufficient

7. (E) I+II: Total passengers $= \dfrac{12}{40} \times 100 = 30$
Both statements I and II together are necessary

8. (D) I+II: Since, age of neither of them is given, age of A can't be determined
Neither statement I nor statement II is sufficient

9. (C) I. Side of square $= \sqrt{484} = 22$ cm
Perimeter of square $= 22 \times 4 = 88$ cm
Perimeter of rectangle $= 2(l + b) = 88$
$2(32 + b) = 88$
$32 + b = 44$
$b = 12$ cm
II. Side of square $= \dfrac{96}{4} = 24$ cm
Area of square $= 576$ cm²
Area of rectangle $= l \times b = 576$
$b = \dfrac{576}{32} = 18$ cm
Either statement I or statement II is sufficient

10. (E) Total balls in bag $= a + b + 9$
I. $\dfrac{a}{a+b+9} = \dfrac{3}{16}$
$16a = 3a + 3b + 27$
$13a - 3b = 27$
II. $\dfrac{b}{a+b+9} = \dfrac{1}{4}$
$4b = a + b + 9$
$3b - a = 9$
Solving I & II,
$a = 3, b = 4$
Both statements I and II together are necessary

11. (B) II. No. of males $= 180 \times \frac{80}{100} = 144$

Total no. of employees $= 144 + 180 = 324$

Statement II alone is sufficient

12. (B) II. Let no. of girls be x.

No. of boys $= \frac{140}{100} x$

Required ratio $= \frac{\frac{140x}{100}}{x} = \frac{7}{5} = 7:5$

Statement II alone is sufficient

13. (A) I. Let the initial no. of bicycle be x.

$x - 7 + 17 = (5 \times 7) + 1$

$x + 10 = 36$

$x = 26$

II. Total no. of a parking spots is not given.

Statement I alone is sufficient

14. (D) I. $B = A - 4$

II. $\frac{A+C}{2} = 16$

$A + C = 32$

None of their ages can be determined.

Neither statement I nor statement II is sufficient

15. (B) I. Total painting cost is not given.

II. Area of floor $= \frac{9600}{80} = 120 \, \text{sq. m}$

Statement II alone is sufficient

16. (B) Let the sides of the triangle be a, b & c

II & III: $a + b + c = 28$

$28 + b + c = 28$

$b + c = 0$

Impossible case.

Only statements II & III alone are necessary

17. (D) I. $A = B + 8000$

II. $\frac{B}{C} = \frac{2}{3}$

III. $C = A - 2000$

All three statements are required to get the monthly salary of A.

18. (D) I. $A = \frac{140}{100} C$

II. $B = \frac{60}{100} C$

III. $B + C = 144$

To find A-B, all three statements are necessary